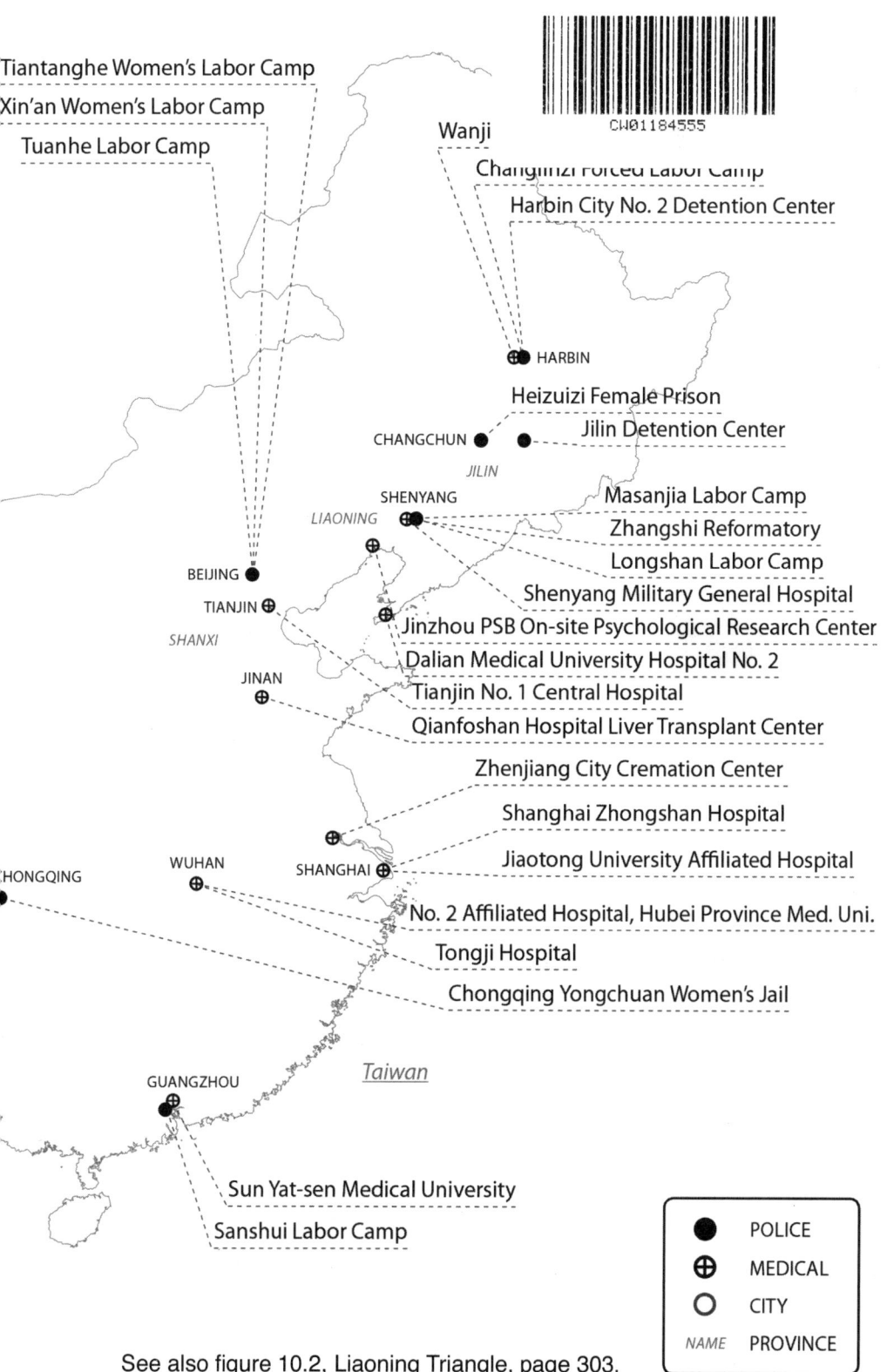

See also figure 10.2, Liaoning Triangle, page 303.

THE
SLAUGHTER

THE SLAUGHTER

MASS KILLINGS, ORGAN HARVESTING, AND CHINA'S SECRET SOLUTION TO ITS DISSIDENT PROBLEM

ETHAN GUTMANN

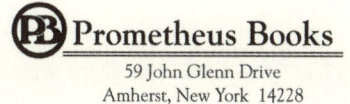

Prometheus Books
59 John Glenn Drive
Amherst, New York 14228

Published 2014 by Prometheus Books

The Slaughter: Mass Killings, Organ Harvesting, and China's Secret Solution to Its Dissident Problem. Copyright © 2014 by Ethan Gutmann. All rights reserved. No part of this publication may be reproduced, stored in a retrieval system, or transmitted in any form or by any means, digital, electronic, mechanical, photocopying, recording, or otherwise, or conveyed via the Internet or a website without prior written permission of the publisher, except in the case of brief quotations embodied in critical articles and reviews.

Every attempt has been made to trace accurate ownership of copyrighted material in this book. Errors and omissions will be corrected in subsequent editions, provided that notification is sent to the publisher.

Prometheus Books recognizes the following trademarks mentioned within the text: Aston Martin®, AstroTurf®, Baidu®, Dayglo®, eBay®, Gatorade®, Google®, Google Earth™, iPhone®, Jell-O®, Members Only®, Monty Python®, Pilates®, Plexiglas®, PowerPoint®, Taobao®, Walmart®.

The Internet addresses listed in the text were accurate at the time of publication. The inclusion of a website does not indicate an endorsement by the author(s) or by Prometheus Books, and Prometheus Books does not guarantee the accuracy of the information presented at these sites.

Cover image © 2014 Shutterstock
Cover design by Nicole Sommer-Lecht

Inquiries should be addressed to
Prometheus Books
59 John Glenn Drive
Amherst, New York 14228
VOICE: 716–691–0133
FAX: 716–691–0137
WWW.PROMETHEUSBOOKS.COM

18 17 16 15 14   5 4 3 2 1

Library of Congress Cataloging-in-Publication Data

Gutmann, Ethan.
    The slaughter : mass killings, organ harvesting, and China's secret solution to its dissident problem / by Ethan Gutmann.
        pages cm.
    Includes bibliographical references and index.
    ISBN 978-1-61614-940-6 (hardback) — ISBN 978-1-61614-941-3 (ebook)
    1. Organ trafficking—China. 2. Transplantation of organs, tissues, etc.—Corrupt practices—China. 3. Political persecution—China. 4. Prisoners—China. 5. Human rights—Government policy—China. 6. Falun Gong (Organization) I. Title.

HV6627.G88 2014
323'.044—dc23

2014006787

Printed in the United States of America

To my son

CONTENTS

Chapter 1: The Xinjiang Procedure — 9

Chapter 2: The Peaceable Kingdom — 31

Chapter 3: An Occurrence on Fuyou Street — 73

Chapter 4: Snow — 109

Chapter 5: The Events on Dragon Mountain — 131

Chapter 6: Alive in the Bitter Sea — 159

Chapter 7: Into Thin Airwaves — 191

Chapter 8: The Nameless — 217

Chapter 9: Organs of the State — 253

Chapter 10: A Night at the Museum — 287

Afterword — 309

Appendix: A Survey-Based Estimate of Falun Gong Harvested from 2000 to 2008 — 317

Acknowledgments — 323

Notes — 329

Index — 357

1
THE XINJIANG PROCEDURE

To figure out what is taking place today in a closed society such as China, sometimes you have to go back a decade, sometimes more.[1]

One clue might be found on a hilltop near southern Guangzhou, on a partly cloudy autumn day in 1991. A small medical team and a young doctor starting a practice in internal medicine had driven up from Sun Yat-sen Medical University in a van modified for surgery. Pulling in on bulldozed earth, they found a small fleet of similar vehicles—clean, white, with smoked glass windows and prominent red crosses on the side. The police had ordered the medical team to stay inside for their safety. Indeed, through the side window of the van, its occupants could see lines of ditches—some filled in, others freshly dug—suggesting that the hilltop had served as a killing ground for years.[2]

Thirty-six scheduled executions would translate into seventy-two kidneys and corneas divided among the regional hospitals. Every van contained surgeons who could work fast: fifteen to thirty minutes to extract. Drive back to the hospital. Transplant within six hours. Nothing fancy or experimental; execution would probably ruin the heart.

Right after the first shots the van door was thrust open and two men with white surgical coats thrown over their uniforms carried a body in, the head and feet still twitching slightly. The young doctor noted that the wound was on the right side of the chest, as he had expected. When a third body was laid down, he went to work.

Male, forty-ish, Han Chinese. While the other retail organs in the van were slated for the profitable foreigner market, the doctor had seen the paperwork indicating this kidney was tissue-matched for transplant into a fifty-year-old Chinese man. Without the transplant, that man would

9

die. With it, the same man would rise miraculously from his hospital bed and go on to have a normal life for twenty-five years or so. By 2016, given all the immunosuppressive drug advances in China, they could theoretically replace the liver, lungs, or heart—maybe buy that man yet another ten to fifteen years.

The third body had no special characteristics save an angry purple line on the neck. The doctor recognized the forensics. Sometimes the police would twist a wire around a prisoner's throat to prevent him from speaking up in court. The doctor thought it through methodically. Maybe the police didn't want this prisoner to talk because he had been a deranged killer, a thug, or mentally unstable. After all, the Chinese penal system was a daily sausage grinder, executing hardcore criminals on a massive scale. Yes, the young doctor knew the harvesting was wrong. Whatever crime had been committed, it would be nice if the prisoner's body were allowed to rest forever. Yet was his surgical task that different from an obstetrician's? Harvesting was rebirth; harvesting was life, as revolutionary an advance as antibiotics or steroids—*or maybe they didn't want this man to talk because he was a political prisoner.*

Nineteen years later, in a secure location, the doctor laid out the puzzle. He asked that I keep his identity a secret.

The first experimental organ transplants were carried out in China during the 1960s. Organ harvesting of criminals condemned for capital offenses began on a small scale in the late 1970s.[3] Beginning in the mid-1980s, Chinese medical transplant expertise accelerated with the help of new immunosuppressive agents that could effectively tamp down the new host's tendency to reject foreign tissue.[4] Suddenly organs once considered scraps no longer went to waste. It wasn't public knowledge exactly, but Chinese medical schools taught that many otherwise wicked criminals volunteered their organs as a final penance.

Chinese medical authorities admit that the lion's share of transplant organs originate with executions, but no mainland Chinese doctors, even in exile, will normally speak of performing such surgery.[5] To do so would remind international medical authorities—the World Health Organization, the Transplantation Society—of an issue they would rather avoid—

not China's horrendous execution rate or the exploitation of criminal organs, but rather the systematic elimination of China's religious and political prisoners. Yet even if this doctor feared consequences to his family and his career, he did not fear embarrassing China, for he was born into an indigenous minority group, the Uyghurs.[6]

A typical execution ground in China. The weapon appears to be a Type-81-1 assault rifle, suggesting that the photo was taken after 1986; because the weapon is aimed at the woman's head, it is likely that the execution took place before the advent of live organ harvesting.

Behind closed doors, the doctor (and practically every other Uyghur witness I spoke with) calls this vast region in China's northwest corner (bordering India, Pakistan, Afghanistan, Tajikistan, Kyrgyzstan, Kazakhstan, and Mongolia) "East Turkestan." The Uyghurs are ethnically Turkic, not East Asian. They are Muslims with a smattering of Christians, and their language is more readily understood in Tashkent than in Beijing. The importance of "East Turkestan" is that the name references a future independent nation. Uyghurs have had different ideas about the composition of such a state over the years, with the possibilities ranging from an Islamic republic (following the Cultural Revolution when the Red Guards literally turned mosques into pigpens) to a Soviet protectorate (until the Soviet Union collapsed) or, most promising, a "Uyghurstan" that would take its place among the new Central Asian nations. At the top leadership level, Rebiya Kadeer speaks about a Western-style democracy.

By contrast, Beijing's name for the so-called Autonomous Region, Xinjiang, literally translates as "new frontier." The Chinese conflict with the Uyghurs over that land is China's longest running territorial war. When Mao invaded in 1949, Han Chinese constituted only 7 percent of the regional population. Following the flood of Communist Party administrators, soldiers, shopkeepers, and construction corps, Han Chinese now constitute the majority, the mass migration creating a rationale for suppressing Uyghur language and culture, most vividly seen in the bulldozing of vast historic centers of ancient Silk Road cities such as Ghulja, Karamay, and Kashgar. Originally driven by cotton, Maoist modernization principles, and countering the Soviets, the Chinese expansion is now fueled by the party's calculation that Xinjiang will be its top oil and natural gas production center by the end of this century.[7]

To protect this investment, Beijing traditionally depicted all Uyghur nationalists—violent rebels and nonviolent activists alike—as proxies for the US Central Intelligence Agency.[8] Shortly after 9/11, that conspiracy theory was tossed down the memory hole. Suddenly China was, and always has been, at war with al Qaeda–led Uyghur terrorists. No matter how transparently opportunistic the switch, the American intelligence community saw an opening for Chinese cooperation in the war on terror, and they signaled their acquiescence by allowing Chinese state security personnel into Guantánamo to interrogate Uyghur detainees.[9]

While it is difficult to know the strength of the claim that detainees were connected to al Qaeda, the basic facts are these: During the 1990s, when the Chinese drove the Uyghur rebel training camps from neighboring countries such as Kazakhstan and Pakistan, some Uyghurs fled to Afghanistan, where a portion became Taliban soldiers.[10] Nor is there

"The mother of all Uyghurs": Rebiya Kadeer, president of the World Uyghur Congress. Photo by Alim Seytoff.

little question that the level of violence within Xinjiang, and indeed within China, has increased in recent years. Both Uyghur separatists and the Chinese internal military apparatus play a part, yet because the party bureaucracy controls the Web (the Internet in Xinjiang was shut down for six months following the Urumqi riots of July 2009) as well as Western reporters' physical access to Xinjiang, the Chinese narrative is dominated by lurid—and unverifiable—stories such as that of the 2014 Kunming train-station massacre, while hundreds of enforced disappearances of young Uyghur males—verifiable but relatively dull from a Western editor's perspective—rarely penetrate the Western consciousness.

The party intends to frame the Uyghurs as international terrorists. And yet, even as the Chinese government claims that Uyghurs constitute an Islamic fundamentalist threat, the fact is that I've never met a Uyghur woman who won't shake hands or a man who won't have a drink with me. Nor does my Jewish-sounding name appear to make anyone flinch. In one of those *vino veritas* sessions, I asked a local Uyghur leader if he was able to get any sort of assistance from groups such as the Islamic Human Rights Commission (where, as I found during a brief visit to their London offices, veiled women flinch from an extended male hand, drinks are forbidden, and my Jewish surname is a very big deal indeed). "Useless!" he snorted, returning to the vodka bottle. So if Washington's goal is to promote a reformed China, then taking Beijing's word for who is a terrorist is to play into the party's hands.

Xinjiang has long served as the party's illicit laboratory. In the mid-sixties, the Chinese military conducted atmospheric nuclear testing in Lop Nur that resulted in a significant rise in cancers in Urumqi, Xinjiang's capital.[11] In several tests, live prisoners were apparently placed at varying distances from ground zero to measure the effects of the blasts and fallout.[12] At some point during the last decade, the Communist Party authorized the creation in the Tarim Desert of another grand experiment—the world's largest labor camp, roughly estimated to hold fifty thousand Uyghurs, religious prisoners, and hardcore criminals.[13] In between these two ventures, the first organ harvesting of political prisoners was implemented. And again, Xinjiang was ground zero.

THE XINJIANG PROCEDURE   15

The fifty-yard stare: "Little brother" Nijat Abdureyimu played the good cop in Chinese Public Security Bureau interrogation of Uyghur dissidents. Photo by Jaya Gibson, 2009.

Every Uyghur witness I approached over the course of two years—police, medical, and security personnel scattered across two continents—related compartmentalized fragments of information to me, often through halting translation. With the exception of the surgeon who opened this chapter, who is still an active medical professional in China, those who asked me to conceal their identities by using a pseudonym in my writing ultimately agreed to my request that they openly testify if the United States Congress called upon them to do so—and they did this even while they acknowledged risks to their careers, their families, and, in several cases, their lives. Their testimony reveals not just a procedure evolving to meet the lucrative medical demand for living organs, but the genesis of a wider atrocity.

In 1989, not long after Nijat Abdureyimu turned twenty, he graduated from Xinjiang Police School and was assigned to a special police force, Regiment No. 1 of the Urumqi Public Security Bureau. As one of the first Uyghurs in a Chinese unit that specialized in "social security"—essentially squelching threats to the Communist Party—Nijat was employed as the good cop in Uyghur interrogations, particularly the high-profile cases. I first met Nijat—thin, depressed, and watchful—in a crowded refugee camp on the outskirts of Rome.[14]

Nijat explained to me that he was well aware that his Chinese colleagues kept him under constant surveillance. But Nijat presented the image they liked: the little brother with the guileless smile. By 1994 he had penetrated all of the government's secret bastions: the detention center, its interrogation rooms, and the killing grounds. Along the way, he had witnessed his fair share of torture, executions, even a rape. So his curiosity was in the nature of professional interest when he questioned one of the Chinese cops who had come back from an execution shaking his head. According to his colleague, it had been a normal procedure—the unwanted bodies kicked into a trench, the useful corpses hoisted into the harvesting vans, but then he heard something coming from a van, like a man screaming.

"Like someone was still alive?" Nijat remembers asking. "What kind of screams?"

"Like from hell."

Nijat shrugged. The regiment had more than enough sloppiness to go around.

A few months later, three death row prisoners were being transported from detention to execution. Nijat had become friendly with one in particular, a very young man. As Nijat walked alongside, the young man turned to Nijat with eyes like saucers: "Why did you inject me?"

Nijat hadn't injected him; the medical director had. But the director and some legal officials were watching the exchange, so Nijat lied smoothly: "It's so you won't feel much pain when they shoot you."

The young man smiled faintly, and Nijat, sensing that he would never quite forget that look, waited until the execution was over to ask the medical director: "Why did you inject him?"

"Nijat, if you can transfer to some other section, then go as soon as possible."

"What do you mean? Doctor, exactly what kind of medicine did you inject him with?"

"Nijat, do you have any beliefs?"

"Yes. Do you?"

"It was an anticoagulant, Nijat. And maybe we are all going to hell."

* * *

I first met Enver Tohti—a soft-spoken, husky, Buddha of a man—through the informal Uyghur network of London. I confess that my first impression was that he was just another émigré living in public housing. But Enver had a secret.[15]

His story began on a Tuesday in June 1995, when he was a general surgeon at Urumqi Central Railway Hospital. Enver recalled an unusual conversation with his immediate superior, the chief surgeon: "Enver, we are going to do something exciting. Have you ever done an operation in the field?"

"Not really. What do you want me to do?"

"Get a mobile team together and request an ambulance. Have everyone out front at nine tomorrow."

On a cloudless Wednesday morning, Enver led two assistants and an anesthesiologist into an ambulance and followed the chief surgeon's car out of Urumqi going west. The ambulance had a picnic atmosphere until they realized they were entering the Western Mountain Execution Grounds, which specialized in killing political dissidents. On a dirt road by a steep hill the chief surgeon pulled off and came back to talk to Enver: "When you hear a gunshot, drive around the hill."

"Can you tell us why we are here?"

"Enver, if you don't want to know, don't ask."

"I want to know."

"No. You don't want to know."

The chief surgeon gave him a quick, hard look as he returned to the car. Enver saw that beyond the hill there appeared to be some sort of armed police facility. People were milling about—civilians. Enver sarcastically commented that perhaps they were family members waiting to collect the bodies and pay for the bullets and the team responded with increasingly sick jokes to break the tension. Then they heard a gunshot, possibly a volley, and drove around to the execution field.

Focusing on not making any sudden moves as he followed the chief surgeon's car, Enver never really did get a good look. He briefly registered that there were ten, maybe twenty bodies lying at the base of the hill, but the armed police saw the ambulance and waved him over.

"This one. It's this one."

Sprawled on the blood-soaked ground was a man, around thirty, dressed in navy blue overalls. All convicts were shaved, but this one had long hair.

"That's him. We'll operate on him."

"Why are we operating?" Enver protested, feeling for the artery in the man's neck. "Come on. This man is dead."

Enver stiffened and corrected himself. "No. He's not dead."

"Operate then. Remove the liver and the kidneys. Now! Quick! Be quick!"

Following the chief surgeon's directive, the team loaded the body into the ambulance. Enver felt himself going numb: Just cut the clothes off. Just strap the limbs to the table. Just open the body. He kept making attempts to follow normal procedure—sterilize, minimal exposure, sketch the cut. Enver glanced questioningly at the chief surgeon. "No anesthesia," said the chief surgeon. "No life support."

The anesthesiologist just stood there, arms folded—like some sort of ignorant peasant, Enver thought. Enver barked at him. "Why don't you do something?"

"What exactly should I do, Enver? He's already unconscious. If you cut, he's not going to respond."

But there was a response. As Enver's scalpel went in, the man's chest heaved spasmodically and then curled back again. Enver, a little frantic now, turned to the chief surgeon. "How far in should I cut?"

"You cut as wide and deep as possible. We are working against time."

Enver worked fast, not bothering with clamps, cutting with his right hand, moving muscle and soft tissue aside with his left, slowing down only to make sure he excised the kidneys and liver cleanly. Even as

Enver stitched the man back up—not internally, there was no point to that anymore; all he could do was make the body look presentable—he noticed the blood was still pulsing.[16] He was sure the man was still alive. I am a killer, Enver screamed inwardly. He did not dare to look at the face again, just as he imagined a killer would avoid looking at his victim.

First confession: Dr. Enver Tohti extracted the liver and kidneys from a living human being on a Xinjiang execution ground. Photo by Simon Gross and Jaya Gibson.

The team drove back to Urumqi in silence.

On Thursday, the chief surgeon confronted Enver: "So. Yesterday. Did anything happen? Yesterday was a usual, normal day. Yes?"

Enver said yes, and it took years for him to understand that live organs have lower rejection rates in the new host and that the bullet to the chest had—other than that first sickening lurch—acted like some sort of magical anesthesia. He had done what he could; he had stitched the body back neatly for the family. And fifteen years would elapse before Enver revealed what had happened that Wednesday.

* * *

As for Nijat, it was 1996 when he put it all together.

It happened just about midnight, well after the cell block's lights were turned off. Nijat found himself hanging out in the detention compound's administrative office with the medical director. Following a pause in the conversation, the director, in an odd voice, asked Nijat if he thought the place was haunted.

"Maybe it feels a little weird at night," Nijat answered. "Why do you think that?"

"Because too many people have been killed here. And for all the wrong reasons."

Nijat finally understood. The anticoagulant. The expensive "execution meals" for the regiment following a trip to the killing ground. The plainclothes agents in the cells who persuaded the prisoners to sign statements donating their organs to the state. And now the medical director was confirming it all: Those statements were real. They just didn't take account of the fact that the prisoners would still be alive when they were cut up.

"Nijat, we really are going to hell."

Nijat nodded, pulled on his beer, and didn't bother to smile.

* * *

On February 2, 1997, Bahtiyar Shemshidin began wondering whether he was a policeman in name only. Two years before, the Chinese Public Security Bureau of the Western city of Ghulja recruited Bahtiyar for the drug enforcement division. It was a natural fit because Bahtiyar was tall, good-looking, and exuded effortless Uyghur authority. Bahtiyar would ultimately make his way to Canada and freedom, but he had no trouble recalling his initial idealism; back then, Bahtiyar did not see himself as a Chinese collaborator but as an emergency responder.[17]

For several years, heroin addiction had been creeping through the neighborhoods of Ghulja, striking down young Uyghurs like a medieval

THE XINJIANG PROCEDURE   21

Working for the Public Security Bureau after the Ghulja massacre, Bahtiyar Shemshidin was aware of wide-scale atrocities and the presence of medical vans at executions. Photo courtesy of Bahtiyar Shemshidin.

plague. Yet inside the force, Bahtiyar quickly grasped that the Chinese heroin cartel was quietly protected, if not encouraged, by the authorities cartel—typified by a Chinese dealer who got caught with six hundred grams yet received only a two-month sentence. Even Bahtiyar's recruitment was a bait-and-switch. Instead of sending him after drug dealers, his Chinese superiors ordered him to investigate the *Meshrep*—a traditional Muslim get-together promoting clean living, sports, and Uyghur music and dance. If the Meshrep had flowered like a traditional herbal remedy against the opiate invader, the Chinese authorities read it as a disguised attack on the Chinese state.

In early January 1997, on the eve of Ramadan, the entire Ghulja police force—Uyghurs and Chinese alike—were suddenly ordered to surrender their guns "for inspection." Now, almost a month later, the weapons were being released. But Bahtiyar's gun was held back. Bahtiyar went to the Chinese bureaucrat who controlled supplies and asked after it. "Your gun has a problem," Bahtiyar was told.

"When will you fix the problem?"

The bureaucrat shrugged, glanced at his list, and looked up at Bahtiyar with an unblinking stare that said: It is time for you to go. By the end of the day, Bahtiyar got it: Every Chinese officer had a gun. Every Uyghur officer's gun had a problem.

Three days later, Bahtiyar understood why. On February 5, approximately one thousand Uyghurs gathered in the center of Ghulja. The day before, the Chinese authorities arrested (and, it was claimed, severely abused) six women, all Muslim teachers, all participants in the Meshrep. The young men came without their winter coats to show they were unarmed, but, planned or unplanned, the Chinese police fired on the demonstrators.

Casualty counts of what is known as the *Ghulja Incident* remain shaky. Bahtiyar recalls internal police estimates of four hundred dead, but he didn't see it; all Uyghur policemen had been sent to the local jail "to interrogate prisoners" and were locked in the compound throughout the crisis. However, Bahtiyar witnessed Uyghurs herded into the compound and thrown naked onto the snow—some bleeding, others clearly suffering from internal injuries. Ghulja's main Uyghur clinic was overwhelmed with casualties; then it was effectively shut down when a squad of Chinese special police arrested ten of the doctors and gratuitously destroyed the ambulance. As the arrests mounted by late April, the jail became hopelessly overcrowded, and Uyghur political prisoners were selected for daily executions. On April 24, Bahtiyar's colleagues witnessed the killing of eight political prisoners, accompanied by doctors in "special vans for harvesting organs." The bodies were then encased in cement and buried in secrecy.

* * *

On the continent of Europe, I went to the home of a nurse who worked in a major Ghulja Hospital following the incident. Nervously requesting that I provide no personal details, she told me that the hospitals were forbidden to treat Uyghur protesters. A doctor who bandaged an arm received a fifteen-year sentence, while another got twenty years, and hospital staff were told, "If you treat someone, you will get the same result." Silence between the Uyghur and Chinese medical personnel deepened and then became a chasm.[18]

In that separation, little things started to happen: If it was a long weekend, the Chinese doctors would stockpile prescriptions for three days rather than allow a Uyghur doctor to have a key to the pharmacy. On her daily rounds, the nurse picked up that Uyghur patients were only receiving 50 percent of their usual doses—out of Chinese meticulous habit, it was even showing up in their charts. The forced abortion and sterilization policy had been in full swing since 1986, but Uyghurs had always been given a partial dispensation. No longer. If it was a Uyghur couple's second child, Chinese maternity doctors administered an injection (described as an antibiotic) to Uyghur babies; the nurse could not recall a single instance of the same injection given to a Chinese baby. She observed a pattern—within three days the infant would turn a grotesque shade of blue and die shortly thereafter. She witnessed Chinese staffers offering the same explanation over and over to Uyghur mothers: Your baby was too weak; your baby could not handle the drug. At the end of March, the nurse resigned. The hospital had been split in two, the doctors too passive, the crimes too great, the guilt too intense. There was nothing left to heal.

24 THE SLAUGHTER

The eternal face of execution. The man on the left, an enlisted People's Armed policeman, takes pains to look "official." His comrade to the right (the mustache hints that he is Uyghur) seems to suggest it's all a big joke. Wearing a white glove to protect against the inevitable back splatter of blood, the man in the foreground appears to be a Supreme Procuratorate officer. He meets our gaze defiantly. This photo was taken in the last fifteen years, yet if we blur the racial features and uniforms we can recognize the same uneasy postures we've seen for well over a century in most authoritarian states; over time, the psychological toll on the executioners becomes obvious. In the last ten years, the Chinese state has transferred its traditional dependence on armed policemen to military surgeons.

Shortly after the Ghulja incident, a young Uyghur protester's body returned home from a military hospital. Perhaps the fact that the abdomen was stitched up was just evidence of an autopsy, but it nearly sparked another round of riots. After that, the corpses were wrapped, buried at gunpoint, and Chinese soldiers patrolled the cemeteries (one is not far from the current Urumqi airport). By June, the nurse was pulled into a new case: A young Uyghur protester had been arrested and beaten severely. His family paid for his release, only to discover that their son had kidney damage. The family was told to visit a Chinese military hospital in Urumqi, where the hospital staff laid it out: One kidney, 30,000 RMB (roughly $4,700). The kidney will be healthy, they were assured, because the transplant was to come from a twenty-one-year-old Uyghur male—the same profile as their son. The family paid, the operation failed, and the nurse was briefly brought into the family's attempt to obtain some sort of justice. There was a problem though. Although the source of the kidney was indeed a twenty-one-year-old male, it turned out he was not a murderer or a rapist but a young man who had protested for the rights of Uyghurs. Compensation was impossible. The donor, indeed the transplant, didn't exist in any official record.[19]

* * *

In the early autumn of 1997, fresh out of a blood-work tour in rural Xinjiang, a young Uyghur doctor—let's call him Murat—was pursuing a promising medical career in a large Urumqi Hospital. Two years later he was planning his escape to Europe, where I met him some years after.[20]

One day Murat's instructor quietly informed him that five Chinese government officials—big guys, party members—had checked into the hospital with organ problems. Now he had a job for Murat: "Go to the Urumqi prison. The political wing, not the criminal side. Take blood samples. Small ones. Just to map out the different blood types. That's all you have to do."

"What about tissue matching?"

"Don't worry about any of that. We'll handle that later. Just map out the blood types."

Clutching the authorization, and accompanied by an assistant from the hospital, Murat, slight and bookish, found himself facing approximately fifteen prisoners, mostly tough-guy Uyghurs in their late twenties. As the first prisoner sat down and saw the needle, the pleading began.

"You are a Uyghur like me. Why are you going to hurt me?"

"I'm not going to hurt you. I'm just taking blood."

At the word *blood*, everything collapsed. The men howled and stampeded, the guards screaming and shoving them back into line. The prisoner shrieked that he was innocent. The Chinese guards grabbed his neck and squeezed it hard.

"It's just for your health," Murat said evenly, suddenly aware that the hospital functionary was probably watching to make sure that Murat wasn't too sympathetic. "It's just for your health."

Murat said it again and again as he drew blood.

When Murat returned to the hospital, he asked the instructor, "Were all those prisoners sentenced to death?"

"That's right, that's right. Yes. Just don't ask any more questions. They are bad people—enemies of the country."

But Murat kept asking questions, and over time, he learned the drill. Once they found a matching blood type, they would move to tissue matching. Then the political prisoner would get a bullet to the right side of the chest. Murat's instructor would visit the execution site to match blood types. The officials would get their organs, rise from their beds, and check out.

Six months later, around the first anniversary of Ghulja, five new officials checked in and the instructor told Murat to go back to the political wing for fresh blood. This time there was far less pretense about it. Murat was told that harvesting political prisoners was normal. A growing export. High volume. The military hospitals are leading the way.

By early 1999, the officials stopped coming and Murat no longer heard about the harvesting of political prisoners. Perhaps it was over, he thought. Perhaps the Xinjiang Procedure had been an experiment, like those inexplicable blood tests of rural Uyghur schoolchildren that he had been ordered to do just before he started in the Urumqi Hospital. Or perhaps, *Tian gao, huangdi yuan*—Heaven high, emperor far—and what happens in Xinjiang, stays in Xinjiang. It was all just a local official's idea of revenge for the Ghulja uprising. The procedure wouldn't go national. Murat knew from first-hand experience that the party believed in a racial firewall, a genetic border between Uyghurs and Han Chinese. Perhaps they wouldn't cross it.

A few months later, the Uyghur crackdown would be eclipsed by Chinese security's largest-scale action since Mao: the elimination of a Chinese religious movement named Falun Gong.

* * *

This book is not intended to be a textbook on Chinese organ harvesting. In fact, none of us who have investigated this topic has the capability to write such a book until the party allows a comprehensive, transparent, on-the-ground investigation into the harvesting of political and religious prisoners—Uyghurs, Falun Gong, Tibetans, and House Christians—from 1997 to the present. That will never occur until many voices join us in that demand. Yet, quite understandably, few will do so until they begin to grapple with the scale of the crime. The twist is that the first step toward achieving that support is to admit how provisional our findings are and to explain the severity of the limitations under which we operate. Back in 2008, before I began interviewing the Uyghurs, I put it this way:

> Indeed, the entire investigation must be understood to be still at an early, even primitive, stage. We do not really know the scale of what is happening yet. Think of 1820, when a handful of doctors, scientists, and amateur fossil hunters were trying to make sense of scattered suggestive evidence and a disjointed pile of bones. Twenty-two years would pass before an English paleontologist so much as coined the term "dinosaur"—"terrible lizard"—and the modern study of these extinct creatures got seriously underway. Those of us researching the harvesting of organs from involuntary donors in China are like the early dinosaur hunters. We don't work in close consultation with each other. We are still waiting for even one doctor who has harvested organs from

living prisoners of conscience to emerge from the mainland. Until that happens, it is true, we don't even have dinosaur bones.[21]

The main point is still relevant—trying to see into the unmarked compounds of China is like examining a star. Any light we can see may have already occurred years ago. Our assumptions about the present hinge on faint radio signals over time. Yet I am also repeating my statement to suggest how far we have come. As we shall see in subsequent chapters, we now have bones, and as new defectors emerge from the Tibetan and Uyghur communities, we have a broader landscape for excavation. The problem for this investigation actually lies elsewhere.

Let me explain exactly why I say that. Although the BBC investigative team periodically rediscovers the fact that British women apply the collagen of executed prisoners to their faces every night, the Chinese medical establishment admitted seven years ago that they routinely strip executed prisoners of organs that are subsequently transplanted into wealthy Chinese and foreigners.[22] Aside from the ethical considerations, the only real distinction between the organ harvesting of common prisoners—murderers, rapists, and so on—and the organ harvesting of prisoners of conscience is that the Chinese authorities still deny the latter has ever taken place at all. The first charges of harvesting the organs of Falun Gong practitioners emerged in the *Epoch Times* and was followed by the seminal *Bloody Harvest* report of 2006.[23] The evidence has built considerably since then, in the recently published *State Organs* and on the website of the World Organization to Investigate the Persecution of Falun Gong.[24]

Collectively, we are at the midpoint of our investigation, and yet there are still many worldwide who prefer not to think about the issue. If forced to comment, the allegation might even be dismissed as a sort of urban legend, a kidney in the bathtub story, a conspiracy theory gone mainstream. While I don't care for intellectual laziness—one ought to read some of the actual material before dismissing it—I don't begrudge anyone their right to initial skepticism. These are serious allegations, toxic allegations. The reader should start from a safe intellectual base before exploring further.

In 2006, when the first allegations of organ harvesting of Falun Gong emerged, there was no question in my mind that the conflict between the Chinese state and Falun Gong was the number one issue in China, and that a comprehensive account was long overdue. So I was open-minded about harvesting—I had to be, knowing what I already knew about the atrocities committed in labor camps—but I confess that I, too, wore a heavy coat of skepticism on one of my first moon walks in 2007.

It was an interview with an elderly woman fresh out of forced-labor camp.[25] She wasn't particularly articulate, but she had an appealing salt-of-the-earth quality. At one point she mentioned a "funny" physical exam in passing. I asked her to explain. She did not consider the matter important and continued on with her story. I dragged her back. Had she been hunger-striking? No. Was anyone else examined? Yes, some other Falun Gong. What were the tests?

What she described was terrifying and inexplicable—rather than the doctor administering a normal physical examination, it was more like he was already picking over a fresh corpse. She had no idea of these implications. In fact, she was growing increasingly irritated by the entire interview, by my Western inability to see the woods for the trees—the woods, in this case, being her spiritual battle. While I don't believe that she had been seriously considered as a candidate for organ harvesting—too old, really—she did mention that some of the younger women had disappeared following the examination, and I remember feeling an unfamiliar chill as my safe, hedging cloak of skepticism fell away for a moment.

As you may have gathered, I like evidence like that, evidence I can put my arms around. Whenever possible I anchor my work in witness testimony. And the witnesses will add—quite significantly, I hope—to the growing pile of evidence surrounding harvesting. But another key contribution is what I have just shown you in this chapter: That the organ harvesting of prisoners of conscience did not begin with Falun Gong but evolved organically from the practice of criminal executions and organ harvesting in China. In fact, one could say that the central decision to start exploiting prisoners of conscience on a mass scale was little more than a sort of legal blurring around the edges, a technical triviality.

Yet the implications were far from trivial; tens of thousands of people by my estimate, people who had committed no capital crimes under Chinese law, would be slaughtered on the operating table. And why would the Chinese Communist Party, so rich in resources and power, so eager for international acclaim, take such a wild risk? Thus the investigative problem starts to become one of motive, of plausibility. It is not just the *how*, but the *why*.

As we move into organ harvesting of scale, and indisputably that means Falun Gong, the *why* question becomes the central task of the next six chapters. Evidence can actually be relatively simple. Human motivation—assuming one rejects cartoon figures of pure good and evil and accepts that, even in China, the God of Mammon only rules conditionally—can be an exceedingly complex matter. And that is why I interviewed well over one hundred witnesses in depth across four continents. The witnesses trusted me, sometimes with their own safety, and even more important to most of them, with the safety and welfare of their families. They worried that I was getting it all wrong at times—I was clearly not the shiny Western knight they had prayed for—but they went ahead and filled in the critical pieces anyway. And, like the Uyghurs, no individual possessed the entire Rosetta Stone. If a witness had claimed that he or she could supply the entire organ-harvesting story from arrest to the grim disposal of what remained of the corpse—well, as the Zen saying goes: If you meet the Buddha on the road, kill him. Spies know everything; humans miss stuff. Credibility is a human attribute; it can't be created in a lab so easily because it comes with limitations and prejudices and failings that are hard to reproduce. And of all the humans I have met, refugees from Chinese labor camps in particular carry a great deal of pain and expectation and need.

As I sit here alone in my flat in north London, on a late night in early December, I feel them when they breathe. My account—so long in coming yet so trivial an effort compared to the struggle that has been waged, so inadequate for the families across China that have lost loved ones—cannot fully answer everything about this terrible chapter in modern Chinese history. But I pray that, after seven years of trying, I have finally come up with the right questions.

2
THE PEACEABLE KINGDOM

Changchun lies in the center of northeast China. And in the center of the city, just south of Victory Park and north of Liberation Road, lies the concrete-tiled expanse of Changchun City Cultural Square. Below a soaring ersatz arch, a cast iron socialist-realist muscleman throws up his arms in triumph, or perhaps despair. Few Westerners see him; foreigners seldom sightsee or invest in this city of seven million. Yet just as there is a certain gritty security in Changchun's role as a "pillar industry" town—the cradle of the state-owned Chinese automotive industry—there's a certain native freedom in not having to perform for outsiders either. For Cultural Square, in all other respects a monument to the ascendancy of the New China, also served as the birthplace of Falun Gong.[1]

It was there in 1992 that one Li Hongzhi, who lived a few blocks away in a rundown apartment block, chose a neglected leafy corner and began teaching very slow, meditative exercises to anyone who was interested. In the wake of the 1980s qigong exercise craze, there were still vast numbers of people performing mind-body cultivation quite publicly, and there was nothing about this to catch the eye of the authorities, particularly as money didn't seem to be changing hands. But something about Li inspired unshakable loyalty among his first students, and underneath the baby-faced appearance of the forty-one-year-old man and the apparent simplicity of the movements lay a deep coding: a hardcore Buddhist morality system of compassion, truthfulness, and forbearance. The novel twist was that these moral precepts were to be carried out in Changchun rather than a monastery. And Li didn't attract a narrow market segment like most qigong spiritual masters. He attracted individuals from all walks of life: old ladies and young soldiers, wealthy industrialists and illiterate unemployed wanderers from rural villages.[2] As their numbers grew, they moved out from the leafy corner.

THE SLAUGHTER

Framed by the weak light of the northeast rising sun, a soldier from the People's Liberation Army performs Falun Gong exercises in Changchun Cultural Square. Courtesy of New Tang Dynasty Television.

That year, 1992, was also the first year of Youfu's spiritual crisis. If qigong became a sort of spiritual superhighway during the 1980s, Li Youfu (no relation to Li Hongzhi), was a sort of professional mystic, and he never strayed much from the fast lane. Actually he found himself enjoying all the traffic—over one hundred million people were involved in one form or another by 1989—and new movements and disciplines would merge into the highway, pick up followers, and exit just as quickly, all in a row, like a funeral procession. There were so many distractions along the way—charismatic healing, gymnastic technique, divination, trances, UFOs—that most people probably didn't even think about where the highway ultimately ended. But that was all Youfu thought about back then. He wasn't looking for a quick health fix or social bonding or a fleeting transcendental experience; his destination was divine super-normal powers.[3]

An outgoing, warm, and clear-eyed man in his early thirties, Youfu had been fixated on this goal since he could walk. Even as a young boy, Youfu had managed to persuade various martial arts experts, including the reticent ones who had been persecuted during the Cultural Revolution, to personally train him. As an adolescent, he moved into the study of Chinese medicine, and he rounded out his education as a graduate student in the physical education department of Shanxi University with a major in martial arts and intensive study of tai chi under an advanced master. It all worked as a piece. He began to experience the full gamut of powers: double-blind past-lives recognition, reading with the hands, premonition, even teleportation—Youfu could *see* other dimensions. The daily developments in the mass qigong world became almost an amusement, a movie, a way to relax. Youfu sensed that he might not need the highway much longer, but until then, Youfu's instinct was to not get distracted by the politics of qigong.

Back in 1949, a handful of Communist Party cadres had glanced at some obscure spiritual texts and pulled out one word *qigong*—*qi* meaning animating universal energy, life-force, or simply breath; *gong* meaning training, mastery, or discipline. No matter how deeply such Daoist and Buddhist cultivation disciplines were baked into Chinese history, the cadres had no intention of lifting the quarantine on the dreaded poison of religion or breathing new life into China's superstitious feudal culture—they were simply amazed to find that half an hour of controlled breathing with proper focus on the acupuncture points seemed to bring tangible health benefits. At a time when there was less than one doctor available for thousands of people, could a secular, firewalled, scientifically based, spiritual-lite exercise regimen bring robust health to the masses and higher productivity? The party gambled that it could.

As a political creation then, qigong (and its second reanimation, Chinese medicine, particularly acupuncture) would rise and fall with the communist tide. Up during the do-it-yourself ethos of the Great Leap Forward: down during the Cultural Revolution. Qigong was almost singlehandedly kept alive in the 1970s by Guo Lin, a charismatic middle-aged woman who claimed to have cured herself of uterine cancer by

The quest for supernormal power: Li Youfu performs at a traditional martial arts competition. Source: Minghui.

practicing her own special blend of qigong. By moving her classes, initially for cancer patients only, into the parks of Beijing, and organizing "experience-sharing assemblies," she prepared the ground for qigong to move out of medical institutions. Following the death of Mao in 1976, people flooded into parks and squares across China looking for power, health, and a new mass experience. The qigong boom was on. As the 1980s began, the idea that extraordinary powers were attainable quickly lost its transgressive reputation—news broadcasts, even scientific journals, regularly reported to the Chinese public new claims of paranormal incidents: children who could read with their ears (or perhaps even their armpits), and the scientific use of external qi—a sort of laying on of hands—to cure the sick.

The latter practice became part of the standard qigong master rollout, along with a new exercise technique and testimonials from the healed in the rapturous lecture circuit—usually culminating in a bestselling book. Nearly every practice was packaged as ancient but new and improved—and the lecture admission prices and the advanced training packages reflected the increasingly elaborate marketing. Qigong thus became a potent hybrid of the Maoist mass campaigns of recent memory and the new consumer impulse that Deng Xiaoping was liberating with his market reforms.

Li Youfu didn't care for the business side of qigong, and he had no illusions about the ethical problems of many qigong masters. Youfu's main quarrel was with the materialists, the clique of qigong critics who insisted on only dealing with tangible objects that could be measured scientifically under rigorous conditions. So there were questions and suspicions and phrases—*pseudo-science, superstition, the trap of idealism*—that ridiculed the extraordinary powers that Youfu had experienced.

In 1982, when the volume on both sides got too high, the propaganda department of the Party Central Committee stepped into the debate and laid down the Triple No Policy—often referred to as "The Three No's": no publicizing, no criticism, and no controversy in the press in relation to extraordinary powers. Lest this be taken as a rejection of the existence of the supernormal, the state also committed to publishing extraordinary powers research for scientific purposes. Li Youfu believed that Zhao Ziyang, the third premier, and a highly influential politician at the time, was behind the policy shift. Either way, this was as close as the Chinese government would get to a live-and-let-live policy—not a bad thing really—and it was widely interpreted that you could just as easily substitute the word *qigong* for *extraordinary powers*. Perhaps qigong could develop in peace.[4]

Following the Three No's policy, the materialists seemed to be in slow retreat; by the mid-1980s a talented qigong master, Zhang Baosheng, was invited to visit Zhongnanhai, the central leadership compound in the heart of Beijing. Witnesses claimed that Zhang, simply by passing his hands over Marshal Ye Jianying's chest, pulled out a vile organic substance, instantly curing him of his respiratory condition. Eventually it was claimed that the supreme ruler of China, Deng Xiaoping, met with qigong master Zhang in yet another visit to Zhongnanhai. By 1986 the Chinese press declared openly that the existence of extraordinary powers was now a proven fact, and that these powers came from qigong.

Back on the highway, Youfu still noticed the presence of patrol cars, but the state-sanctioned China Qigong Science Research Society, founded in 1986, was now acting as a sort of toll booth—not just to collect a percentage of qigong profits, but also as a bouncer (usually for masters who weren't actually profitable) and as an agent and fixer between qigong masters and the Chinese state.

Around the time of first World Qigong Congress in 1987, a prominent scientist, Qian Xuesen, established an institute in Beijing for the scientific study of the human body, with visions of creating a "phenomenological science of qigong." Under the institute's auspices, Li Youfu established his own research center. Here Youfu was a doctor of Chinese medicine in his own right, and he turned to proving and measuring the new dimensions that he had experienced, conducting research through EEG (electroencephalography) and using advanced technology to map out how energy channels operate in tai chi and qigong. Scientific methods, methods that the materialists had no choice but to accept, were used for verification. Youfu came out with his own book on qigong and health, and his articles, the results of his experiments, and his research notes were now published in major Chinese scientific journals with no opposition.

Then came June 4, 1989. With the Tiananmen massacre and the cultural rollback that followed, popular enthusiasm about seemingly everything, even qigong, seemed to simply deflate. Individual desire for health and power had been the carriage that transported the masses into China's parks and plazas to study qigong. Now the urge for power, and even basic curiosity, was discarded, like a once-precious bicycle crushed on Tiananmen Square. The government made a point of repeating the Three No's policy, yet mass solidarity of practically any type felt suspect, vaguely degenerate. For Youfu, it didn't require a third eye to see that a vast new dimension had been revealed, that of China's entrenched political corruption. Youfu felt depressed, and he felt it keenly: before the Tiananmen massacre he was being seriously tested by several universities as a result of his uncanny ability to identify a person's illness without even seeing the person. Now the research money had magically disappeared, and there was a tangible sense of risk to everything he treasured; even without seeing it, Youfu could identify the illness in Chinese society all too plainly. It disgusted him.

In 1992, Li Youfu saw an exit ramp marked *Los Angeles* and turned the wheel hard.

* * *

It was mid-December 1993 in Beijing, a period of high workload before Chinese New Year. But early on the morning of the eleventh, a mad crush began swarming around the entrance to the 1993 Oriental Health Expo, the premier qigong showcase of China. By the 9 a.m. opening, there were two lines of well over a hundred people, the first for those who wanted to meet Li Hongzhi and get a signed copy of his book *China Falun Gong*, which had just been published in April. The second line was exclusively devoted to those who wanted Li to heal them. Only one health problem was permitted per visitor.[5]

Zhu Jie was a middle-aged woman who had just started to cultivate with Falun Gong. When Zhu heard that Master Li would be attending the expo, she took ten vacation days out of her allotted fifteen and went to work as a volunteer for the Falun Gong expo table. Her depiction of the raw enthusiasm and a kind of frantic excitement for Li Hongzhi—according to Zhu the crowds grew bigger every day—appears to be actually somewhat understated. The China Qigong Science Research Society had officially accepted Falun Gong in September 1992. Now that Li had received a nationwide permit to teach Falun Dafa (the terms *Falun Gong* and *Falun Dafa* are used interchangeably), he had given over thirty lectures and teaching sessions in Changchun and Beijing, but also in major cities such as Wuhan, Guangzhou, and Chongqing.[6] By all accounts, Li's extended lectures were showing a startling, exponential increase in attendance by December 1993, but they were still intimate enough that for many practitioners, the lectures provided a deeply personal experience.

Practitioners said Teacher Li could speak with blinding clarity for hours without consulting notes or using any sort of props or tricks. They said Master Li was able to make an abstract concept—Falun Gong's moral principles as the guiding force of the universe—into something so tangible and so comforting that some practitioners wondered whether life would be worth living if it was not true. They describe Li seamlessly presenting himself as a student, a teacher, and a god. The twist was that everyone had a divine origin. So those who had chosen the path of Falun Gong were gods, too, but fallen ones doomed to repaying karmic debt, condemned to the cycle of reincarnation unless they became true practitioners, freeing themselves of worldly attachments, applying compassion, truth, and forbearance in the crucible of Chinese daily life, and seizing this extraordinary moment in history that Li Hongzhi was providing.

Yet many practitioners also describe feeling an almost parental affection and concern for Teacher Li as well—a sense that he was involved in a great sacrifice on behalf of his disciples. This might sound odd, but the practitioners were tuned to a different frequency than the electricity of the increasingly packed auditoriums, namely that of Li's simplicity, his humility, his quiet in the eye of the storm. A typical example runs like this: Following a lecture in Wuhan, the local qigong society proposed

1993: Li Hongzhi makes the cover of Chinese Qigong—*one of the top medical qigong journals in China. Source: Minghui.*

taking Li out to a fancy lunch—a slightly corrupt long-standing custom for qigong masters. Instead Li made excuses and went wandering on the street. A young practitioner followed him unseen. After a couple of blocks, Li found a vendor selling steamed buns, ubiquitous in China as the cheapest form of street food, and Li purchased a few for his lunch.[7] While we can't know with certainty which buns Li Hongzhi ate from day to day, it is widely reported that a large industrial box of instant noodles followed him and his disciples around China and accounted for at least two meals out of the long day. When Li Hongzhi traveled, instead of private cars or a suite on a train, he often insisted on taking public buses. After a conference, Li would occasionally even walk back to the hotel or wherever he was staying, even if it was miles away. In a qigong culture of veneration and status, it was considered highly unusual to eschew luxuries while speaking under difficult conditions—it was always too hot or too cold, and there were always technical difficulties in the public venues of China in the early 1990s. Nothing seemed to rattle Li's patience. In his followers' eyes then, Teacher Li became a living personification of the Buddhist ideal—life is suffering, and suffering does not matter.

Such were the precious moments of personal bonding, but they did not constitute a mass-marketing strategy. When it came to the qigong marketplace, healing, health miracles, crutches being tossed away—these were the currency of the land. Without health bragging rights, there was nothing to sell (and to this day, if practitioners from the Chinese

Li Hongzhi teaches in Jinan, sometime in 1994. Source: Minghui.

mainland want to convince a Westerner that Falun Gong is good, they won't initially speak about how Master Li eats instant noodles or how an enhanced moral consciousness has changed their lives—not a bad marketing pitch for guilty and overindulged Westerners, come to think of it—but will instead earnestly speak of the miraculous health benefits that they have received, often to alienating effect). Thus the growing personal affection that people seemed to feel toward Teacher Li was often expressed in concrete terms by the claim that Falun Gong, when it came to health, could lick any other qigong practice in the house. And according to Zhu Jie, in the Beijing International Exhibition Center, that's precisely what happened.

Master Li did little healing himself—he had authorized several trusted practitioners to handle the bulk of the complaints. Instead he flitted in and out of the center, but Zhu does remember one specific case of an old man who came in on a wheelchair.

In a perfectly calm voice Li Hongzhi told the old man to stand up.

When the old man hesitated Li told him again, "Just stand up."

The old man stood up. Then Li said, "Now walk."

The old man hesitated at this point and began shaking hard. He hadn't been able to walk for a very long time. Again Li said, "Go ahead and walk. Walk toward me. There's no problem."

The old man walked a few steps—very, very slowly, then with a little more confidence, then with an expression of pure joy. The old man got down on the ground and started bowing to Li Hongzhi.

Over time, Teacher Li made it clear that he was against the practice of bowing to a spiritual master. Instead he consistently encouraged a just-do-it attitude that would come to dominate practitioner culture in the years to come, not only in medicine but in things like journalism, business, literally any skill that practitioners needed. For her part, Zhu describes how precious her time was with Master Li, how inspiring it was to see Master Li with the old man. Yet near the end of the interview Zhu added one more statement: "Falun Gong doesn't do healing, so why did we do this? It was just to make some contribution to this qigong undertaking. Also, through this we could promote Falun Gong."

It worked. From the beginning of the expo it was obvious that this was going to be a sort of smack-down between Falun Gong and all the other qigong practices in China. After a few days all the other tables were practically deserted, even Zhong Gong, Falun Gong's main competitor, which had already claimed to have built a scientology-fee-style structure that thirty million followers had signed on to. In recognition of the obvious, on the last day, the expo awarded two certificates of merit—Falun Gong received a certificate for advancing science, and Master Li received the award for "the most popular qigong teacher."

Li Hongzhi had met the conventions of the expo. He would never do another qigong cattle call.

* * *

Li Youfu had exited the highway to California, where he began driving down real highways in Los Angeles to teach tai chi and Chinese medicine at two universities. His desire for supernormal powers, the urge for truth and to see other dimensions, had followed him to California. But he was increasingly turning that vision on himself.[8]

He started to look into Buddhism. Youfu wanted to cultivate something different, something internal—something that could make him a better teacher to his enigmatic young students. He even considered Christianity, but it had the same sterility issues as Buddhism—so many nuances had been lost over the generations. The teachers had come so long ago. If only a teacher like this could come today.

It was during this period that a friend from Shanxi, his home province, began talking about Master Li. There was no money problem. The exercises, the texts, everything was free. Nor were there any questions about integrity, as the teacher was quite serious about morality. In 1995, his friend arrived in Los Angeles and gave him Li Hongzhi's book *Zhuan Falun*. Youfu read the book and he cried. Just like that.

In the past Li Youfu had encountered so many supernormal abilities, teleportation, seeing into the future. But Youfu realized the people who had these powers didn't understand the Buddha Law—they knew nothing of the real higher level. It was as if he had pulled off the highway, shut off the engine, and could suddenly hear deafening silence. In that quiet, with the vibrations from the road still shaking his body, Youfu wondered—it seemed unthinkable to even ask it at first—were supernormal abilities really that important? Were they worth pursuing? Maybe he had been blind all along. He could remove himself from suffering, remove himself from the cycle of reincarnation. All he had to do was cultivate and listen closely to the patient drumming of his heart. It was over. Youfu was a Falun Gong practitioner.

* * *

Back in 1972, in the city of Changchun, a female automotive engineer gave birth to a boy and named him Ming. He was fortunate by the standards of the time—his parents came from the professional class but were too young to be implicated in the Maoist campaigns before the Cultural Revolution and too old to be pulled into the Red Guards once the Cultural Revolution began. As he grew up, nothing notable appeared in Ming's political history file other than some routine participation in Tiananmen Square activities. Yet Ming's intelligence stood out; his voice was low and expressive, and there was something charismatic in his steady gaze. When it was time for college, he rocketed ahead of his peers and was accepted into Beijing's Tsinghua University—"the MIT of China."[9]

After Ming's mother attended one of Li Hongzhi's early lectures in Changchun, 1993, she became a committed Falun Gong practitioner. In spite of the distance, mother and son had remained very close, and she sent Ming tickets to what would turn out to be one of Li's most famous performances, his lecture series in Dalian in 1994.

Before he left for Dalian, Ming had only a vague perception that a tidal wave far out at sea was building within the qigong world. In eight days in Dalian, Ming experienced Falun Gong up close—an unshakable force that first enveloped Ming, knocked him over, and then carried him along. Ming took a ferry home to Tianjin. While the people around him partied and drank, Ming stared out at the endless horizon, thinking about what Master Li had taught him about the nature of the universe, and about what he would do at Tsinghua when he made land.

Tsinghua University had only a handful of practitioners. Ming sought each of them out, and even though the formal routine of practitioners getting together for "experience-sharing" was a couple of years in the future yet, Ming insisted on their all meeting regularly to talk about the practice. Over the following year, Ming organized the first public Falun Gong exercises on campus. He chose a lawn where Tsinghua students particularly liked to hang out, and that core group seeded eight more Falun Gong practice sites over the next couple of years, flanking the sprawling university's entrances, ensuring that visitors understood that Tsinghua was Falun Gong country.

But something, perhaps a desire for some privacy or just an unconscious mimicry of Li Hongzhi's unpretentious style, led him to wander beyond the university campus. Ming began to explore a decrepit

Saint Ming: The man who brought Falun Gong to Tsinghua University, "the MIT of China." Photo of Zhao Ming at Trinity College, Dublin. Photo by the author.

village that abutted the university's North Gate. It was a forgotten piece of the old China, little more than dirt roads and squalid red brick worker housing probably slated for destruction at some point or another. Ming looked relaxed and pleasant as he strolled, but he drew some stares anyway; it was a place that Tsinghua students had no reason to visit.

Ming noticed a single-story abandoned house in the village, and he asked after it. The rent was seven hundred yuan a month, about a hundred dollars. Ming paid the rent, carried in a few cots, laid linoleum on the uneven cement floor, cleaned the soot off the two windows facing the yard, and tacked up a big poster of Master Li doing the five exercises. There was no real heating system—the house absorbed just enough coal heat from the adjoining house to keep the pipes from freezing—but Ming had a leather jacket and he didn't mind. He went to the Tsinghua practice sites—there were thousands of students and faculty now—and announced that anyone, Falun Gong and outsiders, students, faculty, university staff, or peasants for that matter, were welcome to come to the house at any time. Then he handed out keys.

Ming's house became the Tsinghua nerve center of Falun Gong instruction, group study, publishing—Ming himself created an introductory manual for students called "Falun Dafa at Tsinghua"—along with endless late-night debates over how to carry out the moral principles of Falun Gong in the success-hungry atmosphere of the New China's premier university. Falun Gong practitioners universally reject any sort of star system other than a loyalty to Master Li, but in a very short time, Ming had not only become a coordinator—someone who taught the exercises, kept the practice sites clean, and acted as the Tsinghua contact for the Falun Dafa Research Association—but a minor legend. He was said to be compassionate and patient with those who were just starting on the path, yet there was something in his eyes that signaled firmness, a depth to his moral conviction that went beyond simply following rote principles.

When Chu Tong, a female practitioner friend, asked Ming to moderate a squabble with her husband, he listened carefully and came back with an immediate response: Chu's desire for perfect feelings and a perfect marriage was the problem, not her husband. Chu had been looking forward to a nice, comfortable sit-down session slagging her husband, maybe even a side of harmless flirting, but the stark truth of Ming's words shocked her into silence. After licking her wounds, she realized that Ming, in an uncanny way, personified the teaching of Master Li. Ming is wise, Chu said publicly. Ming is humble.[10]

Chu was not alone in her perception. It was said that Ming lived without artifice or material goods—washing in the cold, even drinking Beijing water straight from the tap (literally everyone—from professor to garbage collector—boiled it first). Ming rejected the praise. When everyone carries the potential to be a god, why should he be considered a saint, as if he could intercede on behalf of other cultivators? It was all laughably primitive, and he would gently mock fellow practitioners for giving too much weight to his words. It was his actions that counted.

Ming had no arrest record. He was a student in good standing. His prominence in Falun Gong was seen as admirable, even enviable, by many in the university. But from the perspective of some of those men who were actually managing the construction of the New China, from the moment that he walked out of the North Gate, Zhao Ming was a problem.

* * *

Retirement did not suit Ding Jing. On the first day she found herself waking up early, as usual, leaving her Western Beijing home at first light, and walking briskly past the government complexes into the sprawling paths and expanses of Yuyuantan, one of the great imperial parks of the ancient capital city. It was a surprisingly quiet, haunting place—the coal smoke of Beijing's old neighborhoods and the early morning mist conspiring to transform the large central lake into a sort of painted stage setting. Only the vast structure of the China Central Television (CCTV) Tower occasionally looming through the yellow smog like an alien tripod from *War of the Worlds* reminded Jing that she was surrounded by the capital city. Ostensibly, Jing was walking to stay healthy, but it was more a question of just finding something to do, and there really wasn't that much going on in Yuyuantan in the mornings back in 1994 other than qigong. Jing had some health complaints, some heart troubles, but she had never been particularly interested in practicing.

After a few days she found herself making a distinct circuit of the park, which would bring her within close view of all the different qigong groups exercising at that hour. Like an amateur social scientist, Jing couldn't help but classify and grade the various practices on her walks—one group catered to young people by employing a commercial-sounding disco beat, another chose ostentatious costumes and dramatic locations and struck self-conscious poses as she walked by, and others just looked like social clubs for the elderly. Jing, the physical embodiment of a friendly little old auntie, found herself subtly interacting with them all even if it was only a smile or a wave.[11]

After a week or two, she noticed one group of about forty people—she didn't actually know what they were called—with a distinctly serious demeanor performing a slow, very simple, almost ethereal form of exercise to metronomic traditional music by the South Gate. They looked a little funny at first because there seemed to be no pattern to the group's composition; alongside the usual old fogies, there were teenagers and young professional couples; a few men, judging by their tailored clothing, were obviously high-ranking officials, too, although there was no sign they were trying to make a big deal about it. She and a coworker went by the practice site every day for a week until she decided that she wanted to try it out.

Jing had stumbled into the epicenter of Falun Gong in Beijing—the "Yuyuantan region," the practitioners called it. The East Gate practice site would ultimately attract seven hundred people every morning—one of thirteen sites enveloping the park. One of Li Hongzhi's first lectures was given at the military museum, just south of Yuyuantan and across the street from China Central Television. It followed that the first Falun Gong exercises in the park were just inside the South Gate, very small at first, but gusting to thirteen hundred people at peak. Yet as Jing became a Falun Gong coordinator—she was a natural, given her dedication, enthusiasm, and sociability—and thus responsible for keeping a series of Falun Gong practice sites tidy, she became aware that there was another practice site close by the South Gate that catered to about fifty people.

This site, almost hidden from view, was for employees of state-controlled media and their families, specifically for China Central Television, the network of the Chinese State. Because CCTV was very protective of its secrets, Jing's responsibility did not go beyond the CCTV "residential zone" site—easy access because it did not require a pass. Behind the CCTV guards she was told there was a CCTV "work zone" Falun Gong exercise site that catered to about twenty high-ranking CCTV officials. After successfully managing the CCTV residential zone site, in early 1995, Jing was asked to take responsibility for yet another practice site with about seventy people. This one was for the Falun Gong practitioners of the Xinhua News Agency, the Communist Party's news outlet.

Naturally Jing was glad to see Falun Gong making such strides in the media, and the sites themselves were relatively trouble free. Yet the secrecy required by government agencies such as the Ministry of State Propaganda demanded a further level of discretion. The propaganda ministry had eighteen practitioners. Jing knew that they hadn't seen Master Li in person, but after meeting with them, she felt they were an extremely steadfast and sincere group. After some discussion everyone agreed that it might be better if they didn't have to leave the state propaganda office at all. Perhaps they could do the exercises in the building and watch Master Li's lectures together on the propaganda ministry's big screens? This ad hoc arrangement would ultimately be put into practice because the head of the Ministry of Propaganda, Ding Guan'gen, was known in practitioner circles as sympathetic to Falun Gong.

This aura of protection and leniency temporarily extended to the Chinese media coverage of Falun Gong in the mid-1990s, a transitional period when Li Hongzhi was remarkably vulnerable.

On December 29, 1994, Li Hongzhi gave his final lecture in China—held in the city of Dalian before an audience of over six thousand people.[12] The Dalian event demarcated the beginning of Li's withdrawal from the mainland (which would ultimately end with Li settling in New York City in 1996). He had prepared for this; in January 1995, *Zhuan Falun*, the complete teachings of Falun Gong, Li's final word on the practice of Falun Dafa, was published by the Radio and Television Broadcasting Press of China. The publishing ceremony was held in the auditorium of the Ministry of Public Security.[13]

Why then did Li withdraw? Perhaps he wanted to encourage practitioners to assume even more responsibility for the direction of Falun Gong as part of their spiritual development. Or perhaps Li sensed a coming storm. Perhaps he reasoned that if the figurehead was not sticking out, lightning would not strike. Or perhaps Li was simply unwilling to take part in the sort of insidious graft and *guanxi*-maintenance with party officials that would have been part of his job had he stayed in the Chinese system. These are theories; none of them are perfectly satisfactory. But from this point on—and from the point of view of this book as well—the story is no longer really about Li Hongzhi. It's about the Falun Gong practitioners themselves.

From a Realpolitik perspective, Teacher Li's abrupt withdrawal from public speaking in the mainland created a vacuum, and practitioners were not initially in a position to fill it. The timing was bad, coming during a renewed China-wide attack on qigong by those who equated extraordinary powers with superstition. Li Hongzhi, still the precocious new kid on the block, with a book rapidly headed toward bestseller status, was an inevitable and tempting target. Perhaps that's why Li also began his move away from the qigong establishment. Tensions with the qigong masters (who felt intensely competitive with Li) were coming due, and inevitably the China Qigong Science Research Society would be drawn into the conflict. Politics aside, it was not at all clear that the society actually constituted an appropriate base for the Falun Gong practice that Li had established. But an institutional safe haven was necessary for legal and political reasons.

Yet it was Falun Gong's internal tensions that created its first serious crisis; Li had made it increasingly clear that in the area of doctrine and spiritual instruction his videotaped lectures and his books were to be studied as scriptures, but in terms of the daily operation he made it equally clear that Falun Gong was essentially an egalitarian organization with little use for hierarchy. As a result, a few practitioners who had

Ten thousand practice in Shenyang, Liaoning Province. Source: Minghui.

been with Li for several years (and had received temporary special honors such as the limited-time-only permission to heal the general public at events like the health expos) felt abandoned, if not cheated, by the more rigorous spiritual direction Falun Gong was taking. Changchun had a number of practitioners who had been running a Falun Gong training facility. As 1994 came to a close they attempted to open up a Falun Gong clinic as well. Li stepped in, denounced the clinic, and roundly criticized the individuals involved. Thus a small splinter group—perhaps the only real example of mutiny in Falun Gong history—briefly flared up.

The dissenters wrote a report attacking Teacher Li and mailed it to several government ministries. From a government perspective, the most damaging charge was that Li Hongzhi had paid no income taxes and was essentially hoarding any profits from lectures, books, and videos. Less interesting to the government but potentially useful to competitive qigong masters was the charge that Li could not heal anyone, had no extraordinary powers, and had forged a new birth date to match that of the Sakyamuni Buddha.[14]

All these charges were debatable: Falun Gong profits were actually rather unimpressive. The practice was free. The Chinese tax system in 1995 was opaque at best.[15] Whatever claims and expectations about healing had been previously bandied about, there was no question that Li was rapidly moving Falun Gong out of the qigong carnival where the expectation was that physical health would be showered on the public like candy from a piñata at a children's birthday party. Li was staking out an explicit position of individual responsibility whereby one's personal moral state (and one's tally of karmic restitution) dictated one's physical well-being. Finally, Li claimed that his original birth date was incorrect to begin with and that he had corrected a bureaucratic error. Falun Gong representatives prepared a detailed rebuttal of each point, which was distributed to the government ministries that had received the original poison-pen report.[16]

The splinter group's charges would be used almost word for word against Falun Gong later on, yet if there was one time in history when Falun Gong's *guanxi*, its political connections inside the Chinese Communist Party, came to the rescue, it was during this period when Falun Gong could well have been quietly strangled in its crib. Mutineers spread charges and rumors, qigong masters laid plots, but from the perspective of the state-controlled media at the time, Li didn't have to publicly confront any conspiracies. The Three No's policy forbids any promotion of qigong, and yet, more than once when Falun Gong held public demonstrations of the exercises in a provincial capital, local party officials would stride in—television cameramen running alongside—and make approving noises while dutifully patting little boys on the head in appreciation of the discipline of their Falun Standing Stance and the fluidity of their Strengthening Divine Powers. In one news segment, a member of the People's Liberation Army in full uniform was interviewed on camera following meditation and exercises in Changchun's Victory Square. He declared that Falun Gong was not only good for China but "for the whole world."[17] To be sure, these sorts of positive television reports tended to air exclusively on local news stations where they were less likely to cause controversy in Beijing. Likewise any complimentary press tended to appear in obscure cultural periodicals. Yet Beijing still wielded power over local media; Jing's practice sites, in particular the Falun Gong practitioners at CCTV, Xinhua News Agency, and the Ministry of Propaganda could easily have pulled the strings to ensure that these signals of party approval occurred on a regular basis, however distant and measured.

As for Teacher Li's decision not to speak in the mainland anymore, his next invitation to give a lecture series came directly from the Chinese ambassador to France. Li Hongzhi agreed to teach in Paris, and according to the vivid account of a well-connected woman in the embassy at the time, "[Li Hongzhi] appeared very clean cut, emanating a very young, vibrant, confident air—serious, solemn, focused, and sincere in what he was doing. [He was] radiant—glowing with health, tall, came across as a good person and very different from other qigong masters.... There were no fees and nothing was sold."[18] Li Hongzhi had previously taught in Thailand, Taiwan, and Australia, but if Paris was a quantum leap for the prospects of Falun Gong going international, the reported success of the French event was even more important for the reputation of Falun Gong in the mainland.

Falun Gong's burgeoning support within the party was not just confined to the media. Jing witnessed that expansion with her own eyes. Not only had the Military Museum workers finally created their own site, so had the China Academy of Sciences and the Academy of Social Sciences—and all these exercise sites were well attended. But Jing paid far more attention in 1995 to a special site that catered exclusively to high-ranking officials and their families—the real China celebrities: the wife of the former general secretary of the Chinese Communist Party, Zhao Ziyang (said to be qigong's most important defender), the head of a CCTV broadcasting station, and then there were the ministers, the vice-ministers, and the department heads who had formed their own Falun Gong study group. Finally, Jing also helped out by making sure there was no garbage on a site that catered exclusively to thirty or forty old cadres, including (let's call him) "General Wu" from the General Staff Headquarters, along with some navy and air force officials.

Jing would ultimately destroy the list of names from these two very sensitive sites (and I have respected her decision throughout this account).

Master Li goes international. His first US lecture in Sunnyvale, California, 1996. Source: Minghui.

Yet there was also one more man showing up to practice Falun Gong on a regular basis; let's call him "Lu." Lu was from the Ministry of State Security, China's secret police. And from a critical party perspective, Lu's presence was a red line.

Western China experts have occasionally compared Chinese society to a pyramid, invoking permanence and stability. While that may be a historically accurate metaphor for Imperial China, the structure of post-Tiananmen China in the mid-1990s more closely resembled a Mercury rocket from the early days of the American space program: ambitious, jerry-rigged, and explosive. The bulk of the rocket was anchored by a vast booster filled with incredible masses of peasants and impoverished workers. The second stage was the intellectual class, the military, the entrepreneurs, and the nouveau riche. Balanced on the top was a tiny, sealed capsule containing the Chinese Communist Party. The Marxist blueprint for seizing power is all about crossing societal lines—urban, rural, lines of class, status, identification—and ultimately forming a mass union between workers, peasants and enlightened members of the bourgeoisie and the intelligentsia, with fellow travelers distributed throughout the military, governmental, and intelligence apparatus. From the party's perspective, Falun Gong had followed that model effortlessly, insidiously spreading through the walls of their rocket like an electrical fire. Now smoke was beginning to permeate the capsule.

This was the vulnerable side of the party psyche—embodied by party operatives who feared Jing's tidy little meditation sites. Although Falun Gong practitioners numbered only in the low millions by 1995, a back-of-the-envelope calculation based on Falun Gong's exponential rate of expansion would yield the result that Falun Gong practitioners could surpass 65 million (the approximate number of Chinese Communist Party membership) by the end of the decade—and the question among some party operatives was whether the party should act now or just plan on waking up in a cold sweat in five years.

The party's sense of vulnerability was one critical reason why the party viewed the regular attendance of Mr. Lu from state security at a Falun Gong practice site with some alarm, and why ultimately the party would turn on Falun Gong. But there was another reason, and it's a bit harder to see at first, largely because there is a marked tendency among Western China analysts—and I include myself in this critique—to focus on the party's fears rather than the full scope of the party's collective ambitions. In fact the party's vision of the future makes Westerners—me too, actually—somewhat uncomfortable. Yet these ambitions, the party's invulnerable aspect, if you will, actually has more explanatory power, particularly because Falun Gong had the misfortune of being born during a key shift in the party's collective belief in its own destiny.

Deng Xiaoping had always advocated a certain external caution while the New China was under construction—downplay your assets, don't attract too much attention, and don't take on the West, particularly America. Above all, be patient. This sort of holding pattern made sense for Deng's particular challenge: To preserve the Party's legitimacy, Deng preached (while he furiously tried to move the country away from Maoism) that there was no contradiction between socialist control and capitalist means. During the Tiananmen days of rage, Deng's formula was revealed as a fake elixir. As the citizens of Beijing lynched soldiers and hung them from telephone poles, it was obvious to all that there were wrenching contradictions in Chinese society. Capitalist production was not just a pure road to wealth; it had a nasty byproduct, namely the desire for political freedom. Therefore China needed not just the sort of harsh discipline and control that had just been meted out in response to the Tiananmen demonstrations; the New China needed faith. Without it Chinese society would split asunder.

Younger cadres—richer than in the past, tough, confident, often English-speaking—aligned with some of the older hard-liners such as Li Peng and Jiang Zemin in the common idea that the worship of Chinese power itself could become China's de facto state religion. But this wasn't meant to be garden-variety nationalism, the sort that every nation promotes; if nineteenth-century nationalists had dreamed of a strong China with a big army, the new Chinese patriots dreamed of China seizing its rightful position as the undisputed dominant global power of the next century.

Western China analysts tend to identify this goal in neutral terms such as Chinese nationalism or patriotism. Yet given China's command economy, and the quasi-spiritual ritualistic displays of a belief in a special fate for the Han Chinese race, the term *fascism*—no matter how loaded the historical connotations, no matter how imprecise the comparison—is clearly a more ball-park description. Yet labels are not critical here; whether one wants to view the new nationalism as patriotic or fascist or even Marxist in nature, there is no question that a large portion of the spiritual oxygen in China was suddenly being allocated for state use.

Thus, to a small but influential group of hard-liners with significant clusters within the People's Liberation Army, the Ministry of State Security, and the politburo, the continued existence of qigong was viewed as nothing more than an outdated bread-and-circus arrangement of the old guard. Yes, it was distinctly Han; yes, it attracted the hippie foreigners; but qigong was also a waste of valuable energy that ought to be phased out in favor of getting rich, building the New China, and loving the motherland. Religion, too, was a necessary evil, but a sleeping one. As long as all religions were state controlled—safe, legal, and rare—religious faith could be tolerated for now with one condition: the firewall between qigong and religion had to be pristine.

If Falun Gong had concentrated on presenting itself as a qigong practice exclusively and had made a deal with the Chinese Health Ministry and the National Sports Commission to establish Falun Gong as a sort of state exercise (this proposition was actually brought to Teacher Li Hongzhi in February 1995, and Li turned it down), in theory, it could have been tolerated.[19] If Falun Gong had just used qigong as a starting point to promote the ancient elixir of religion, particularly Buddhism, in a flashy new bottle, they might even have gotten away with that, too, as long as there were sustained financial kickbacks (this was essentially the proposed course of action by the China Qigong Science Research Society; it was also turned down by Li). But clearly Teacher Li had gone beyond all that, promoting not just rules or rituals or laws, but a coherent system of individual, internalized morality that could be transported everywhere—apparently, as in the case of Ming, while wearing rags and a leather jacket—quite independent of the state, or the presence of Master Li himself.

No. Li Hongzhi had promoted a virus in a bottle, and every symptom of that virus would make China weaker. "Truthfulness" was really just a form of unilateral disarmament—to negotiate, one must lie, and to forbid lying meant a China that could not make favorable deals. "Compassion" boiled down to a China too soft to pull the trigger. "Forbearance" was the worst—instead of getting rich and powerful, Han Chinese were expected to quietly suffer the blows of those who were already rich and powerful; in the international context it meant a China that was good at taking crap, not dishing it out. In short, Falun Gong was weak, feminine, inviting of domination. Well, they would get dominated then. The hard-line cadres were creating a New China that would never get raped by the West again. This time, China would do the raping, and it would begin at home.

Jing noticed the first plainclothes guys walking by her practice sites in early 1996. The first signs of surveillance, like flashes of lightning in the summer night sky, indicated that someone in the party was trying something out. Jing saw them out of the corner of her eye, but she kept her gaze on the cosmos.

* * *

"Minister X"—I won't go beyond that pseudonym—doesn't remember the date or the time of year, he just knows that he received the document sometime in 1996: "This one was a government confidential circular, a 'red-headed document'—the letterhead is red. It's from the central government. The document comes down—we cadres would have to sit down and study it. And then after you study it the document is taken away and you can never find it again."[20]

"Some [red-headed] documents are pretty strange," said Minister X, but their function is clear enough: The central party leadership can implement extraordinary measures at the regional level without launching a public campaign. The masses, even much of the party, can be bypassed, ensuring deniability. While Minister X doesn't remember the exact phrases, this particular red-headed document spoke of "an illegal organization whose activities needed to be controlled," and it spoke of a book: "We were told this book was banned, this was an order from above.... We were told to investigate who is publishing, printing, selling this banned book. Whoever is involved in any stage of the process will get in trouble."

The organization was called Falun Gong or Falun Dafa. The book was Li Hongzhi's *Zhuan Falun*, one of China's top ten bestsellers during the winter and spring of 1996. Minister X doesn't remember if Falun Gong was identified as a "crooked-path religion" (usually translated as "evil cult" in English) in that particular red-headed document—probably that came later. But he's pretty sure he saw the phrase used confidentially long before it became official policy in October 1999. Either way, the Public Security Bureau, the Bureau of Industry and Commerce, and the Taxation Department were expected to work together to control the activities of Falun Gong. It would be a "three-pronged attack."

Back in 1996, Minister X could see the outlines of the party's offensive—he could see the outcome, too, but he didn't really know what to make of this Falun Gong business. As an amateur qigong enthusiast, he had sympathy for these people—what he knew of them anyway, he didn't get out of the office that much. But it didn't matter what he thought.

To drag one's feet on this task was unthinkable—career suicide, implications for his family, or maybe something that would be made to look like suicide. And if he didn't go along would it make any difference? As Minister X said to me sardonically: "If they've already specifically singled out your book, this organization of yours doesn't have a long life expectancy in any case."

But what was the core purpose? From Minister X's qigong experience he knew that Falun Gong, as the most popular qigong practice in China, faced competitive pressures. Minister X knew that the head of the Public Security Bureau (PSB), Luo Gan, was an ambitious man. Everyone knew that Jiang Zemin was desperately trying to establish his legitimacy by rewarding and promoting tough apparatchiks of all stripes. Yet if there was a political imperative it was never about a single individual these days; the attack only made sense if Minister X followed the sometimes crooked path of party logic itself; after Jiang Zemin came to power in late 1989, he created a pithy internal party slogan: "Make June 4th go away." As the date of the Tiananmen Square Massacre, "6-4" was regularly used as a dissident code word, and that date was like scar tissue on the eyes of China. Every time the party told the masses to open their eyes to look at something—the phenomenal GDP growth, the amazing new cities under construction—their eyes smarted and watered over. It was time to change the subject, to focus the mind: *Tiananmen is gone. The hand of cards is over, played out. No apologies, no compensation, no amnesty. New cards are on the table.*

A new hand required a new campaign, and nothing focused the collective Chinese mind like a scapegoat.

In June 1996, an article about Falun Gong appeared in the influential newspaper *Guangming Ribao* [roughly translated as Enlightenment Daily], featuring a laundry list of long-standing materialist gripes against qigong as pseudoscientific, feudal, superstitious nonsense. This time, it was aimed exclusively at Falun Gong. The author was a longstanding critic of qigong, the Marxist theorist He Zuoxiu, and indeed, the brother-in-law of Luo Gan, the head of the PSB. Although thousands of practitioners wrote in to the *Guangming Ribao*, protesting the article's depiction of Falun Gong and claiming the newspaper had violated the Three No's policy, approximately twenty newspapers followed suit with some form of the same critique.[21]

Although Minister X is not sure about the date, he thinks he probably received his marching orders in July 1996: "I was assigned to investigate and confiscate these [Falun Gong] books, put them in storage where only we could have access to them. It was an action coordinated with the Public Security Bureau . . . to hand all of them upwards—to the city level's Industry of Commerce Bureau." It was all done openly, and Minister X says it was legally sanctioned by the Chinese News Publishing Bureau (under the auspices of the propaganda ministry—suggesting that Propaganda Minister Ding Guan'gen's sympathy for Falun Gong apparently had its limits). People who had a copy of *Zhuan Falun* could keep their private copy and, Minister X supposed, copy it for others. Anyway that wasn't his business. He didn't intend to go beyond his professional and legal obligations.

Thus a year that had begun auspiciously for Falun Gong, with a bestselling book and increasing international visibility for Li Hongzhi, ended in apparent disarray: surveillance at the practice sites, a banned book, and a final divorce from the China Qigong Science Research Society. Falun Gong was now the largest civil society—that is, an organization with no formal affiliation with the state—in China.

By the end of the summer Li Hongzhi made it clear to practitioners that he expected them to resist and push back against lies in the media. But, perhaps as a result of his move to the New York City area, Li was late to the party this time. Following the initial flurry of negative press, there was no major follow-up to the *Guangming Ribao* article. By the end of the year, the long knives of the Public Security Bureau appeared to disappear, too, and Jing did not notice a significant drop off in Chinese Communist Party supporters in her practice sites. Instead, Luo Gan launched a quiet PSB investigation into Falun Gong's "illegal religious activities" in January 1997 and a second investigation six months later. Regional PSB representatives came back with the same message: No problem had been found with Falun Gong. Some even referred to the National Sports Commission survey; in an effort to counter the PSB, the commission had put together its own Falun Gong study. Apparently, 97 percent of practitioners claimed that their health had improved.[22] It's hard to imagine that Luo Gan took any particular comfort from the National Sports Commission's results, particularly because the real finding of both investigations was that Falun Gong support ran deep—so deep that Luo did not have the full support of his own agency's rank and file.[23]

Some practitioners have claimed to me that the PSB study led to the cessation of PSB activities—the "false peace" period from January 1997 to April 1998. That strikes me as a Falun Gong parable; it seems more likely that aggressive action against Falun Gong came to a close because Luo Gan thought he had made his point. Ultimately party culture is highly cloistered, unimaginative, and prone to mirror imaging. Why shouldn't the PSB interpret Falun Gong—much as many Chinese scholars still do—as a hierarchical organization requiring simple decapitation? Remove the master. Let him go to America. Ban the book. The movement will wither and die.

Yet the opposite occurred. Jiang Xinxia, a student at the Shanghai Jiaotong University, described a typical practitioner drive that began at the end of 1996 this way: "For about a week, we posted banners on campus and taught many newcomers.... Within one week, a dozen students and teachers became diligent practitioners. Our site grew quickly, and very soon there were twenty to thirty practitioners who came regularly. Then we went to other locations.... There were more sites, emerging like mushrooms, with hundreds of people.... It was like a snowball." The revealing aspect of Xinxia's account is that central control or formal permission simply didn't exist. Practitioners were expected to spread Falun Gong, but there was no master plan, no central Falun Gong office with a huge map of China with pins on it. There were databases, yes, but any hierarchy it described was nominal and highly fluid because there was no money involved—even less now that *Zhuan Falun* was being copied on regular printers and given away or sold at cost (Chinese corruption cuts both ways; by 1998, several government printing houses would be churning out copies of *Zhuan Falun* again).[24] Falun Gong had not only survived Li's withdrawal to America, it was thriving.

Into the heartland. Peasants in their Sunday best performing Falun Gong exercises, probably in the late 1990s. Source: Minghui.

And this was the primary story going into 1998: uncontrolled, unchecked growth. Yet there were exceptions. For example, as 1998 began, Amy Lee, a well-connected practitioner (who was actually married to a PSB agent at the time) returned to her parents' home in Shandong for a visit. Her parents, both active practitioners, had removed every Falun Gong poster and portrait of Master Li from the walls, and all the books were gone. Employing a sixth sense developed over decades of party rule, like animals before a storm, her parents were burrowing in.[25]

By April there were occasional press attacks on Falun Gong, but the practitioners soon developed a method that exploited their ever-expanding numbers: show up en masse (it's easy to arrest a single religious leader, harder with thousands of believers), stay silent, and simply stand around until someone talks to you. However you might choose to see this method—it seems reasonably sincere and nonviolent to me, but several authors imply that it is all rather passive-aggressive and annoying—it reversed negative media coverage repeatedly and definitively. For example, Beijing TV ran a segment in May 1998 that, along with an explanation of Falun Gong health benefits, quoted Falun Gong's old nemesis He Zuoxiu, who publicly referred to Falun Gong as an "evil cult."[26]

In China, when you see such a signal and you know that you are the target, there are two options. You can keep quiet—and probably get crushed. Or you can stand up—and still probably get crushed.[27] Jing was of the opinion that practitioners should go to Beijing TV—the footage of Falun Gong had been shot at *her practice site* by the East Gate of Yuyuantan when she was disabled in a bike accident—but about half the practitioners were worried that physically visiting Beijing TV would be perceived as disruptive, aggressive, or too political—it would be called "a demonstration" and thus a distraction from their spiritual purpose. The other side argued that refuting lies, or more positively phrased as "truth clarification," was essential. Both sides tried to prove the purity of their motivation, rather than a calculus of results. No resolution was reached.

The party would retroactively charge Li Hongzhi with masterminding this and every other Falun Gong demonstration (there were approximately sixteen demonstrations of scale between April 1998 and January 1999) by deploying faxes, phone calls, and e-mails to trusted lieutenants. Undoubtedly there were plenty of communications sent back and forth—but rather than relying on the PSB's inference of what was in those e-mails, consider Jing's account of the practitioner meeting on Beijing TV:

> Now, at the time of the meeting, I didn't know how Master thought or what Master said about it. It's not like we waited for Master to give out an order and then we followed it; that's how everyday people think. What we said is, "The way Master wants us to do things is the way the Fa [truthfulness, compassion, and forbearance—the moral principles that guide the universe] teaches us. When we run into specific issues, we use the Fa to enlighten to things. Am I understanding things in accordance with the Fa? If I am, then I should do things according to that understanding."

About a thousand practitioners, some from CCTV and the Ministry of Propaganda, went to the Beijing TV compound. Several meetings—one very free-floating with plenty of give and take, the others a bit more like formal negotiations—were held between Beijing TV managers and Falun Gong practitioners. Ultimately, Beijing TV fired the producer of the offending segment and ran a new segment praising Falun Gong. Simultaneously, practitioners in Xinhua and the Ministry of Propaganda were still quietly influencing the media environment, although I estimate that ad hoc attack coverage in 1998 outweighed saccharine coverage of Falun Gong by approximately two to one.

For the party, the "false peace" was wrapping up. With the failure of the wither-away strategy, the PSB ordered a new investigation in the summer of 1998. Instead of attempting to establish the character of Falun Gong (already termed a heretical cult in the internal documents), it would probe its strengths and weaknesses. At Tsinghua University, Ming's practice sites were curtailed from employing banners and the like.[28] A central database that covered all the prominent practitioners in the country was in the works.[29] The surveillance at Jing's practice sites became blatantly obvious, and where no Falun Gong hierarchy existed, the Public Security Bureau, seizing on small clues such as Jing's phone calls, would map one.

A second campaign was aimed at well-off Falun Gong practitioners. Suddenly Minister X found himself being called into meetings with the PSB and the tax bureau. Some of these were "study sessions" where they would simply mouth anti–Falun Gong propaganda. Other meetings were with the neighborhood committees—the low-level agents of state surveillance who could actually provide lists of individual practitioners. If the suspected Falun Gong practitioner was self-employed or an unemployed worker, the police or PSB could keep watch. But if they had a private business, Minister X was expected to take the lead: "In my district there were some practitioners who had shops. Once I was supplied with their name lists I had to cancel their license.... Canceling their license would then give the PSB the ability to go shut down the business. [Yet] I couldn't find an excuse to revoke their license. If they sold fake merchandise, or they owed some tax or something like that, I could cancel their license. But they wanted me to just make something up ... any false charge I could come up with."

This outraged Minister X. It was his job to implement the law, not to play games: "It's like what the PSB does—if you exercise in the park they will charge you with 'disturbing social order.' But I couldn't just find a crime to pin on them." Not only did Minister X feel that he could not invent crimes, he had another pressing problem; like so many other offices in China at the time, he had a young subordinate who practiced Falun Gong.

Sometimes the most interesting stories in China cannot be told.

* * *

My story is less interesting than Minister X's, but no one will get hurt if I tell it. As I wrote back in the early 2000s, I first ran into Falun Gong on an extremely cold day in January 1999:

> I had only briefly seen them before—in the dead of winter, as my wife and I clambered around the frigid, wooded hills of Peking University, looking for some obscure museum. I was freezing and in an effort to get her to pick up her irritatingly slow pace, I had been shouting like an Army Sergeant—one, two, three, march!!—when I ran into a group of fifty Chinese students and faculty, eyes closed, arms frozen above their heads in a classic Eastern meditative posture, wearing nothing but shirts, sneakers, and trousers as if they were standing in a warm living room. I stopped shouting, and instantly felt a little foolish. The mysteries of the East, I concluded, and hurried on.[30]

I now recognize the Falun Standing Stance when I see it, but when it comes to the spiritual practice of Falun Gong, I've never made it much beyond "the mysteries of the East."

I try to write about things that I actually have the capacity to understand. Li Hongzhi's book *Zhuan Falun* is readily available on Amazon. com or on FalunDafa.org for free. Anyway, many practitioners would be happy to give you a copy. It's a religious text. Like any other religious text in the world it can be cherry picked to look sublime or ridiculous. I don't believe that Li Hongzhi's writing dictated the conflict between the Chinese state and Falun Gong—a key subject in this book—so I see little point in my creating a wiki-version of *Zhuan Falun* or in pulling out quotes according to my prejudices.[31]

Unavoidably, I have prejudices. I have never found much use for martial arts, or for asking questions about the meaning of life, or harnessing the power of some sort of life force. I drink and I smoke, and given the number of dinners I've had with practitioners, I'm glad they eat meat. I think about health pretty much in Western automotive terms: maintenance, repair, run the engine on full occasionally. In short, I'm a genuine agnostic, too unsure of the working order of my spiritual antenna to even declare myself as an atheist. I have no special feelings either way for Li Hongzhi, although he has never struck me as a hypocrite; I turned down even the dangled possibility of a potential interview with Li Hongzhi because I believed that it could corrupt my interviews with practitioners—I need practitioners to relax, look me in the eye, and tell me what happened to them. I don't need inhibited responses and carefully worded answers because practitioners see me as some sort of appointed arbitrator of their religion (the chosen author of *Falun Gong: The Authorized Biography*, if you will). In any case, an interview with Li might well have been wasted on me. I have to admit that the slogan *Falun Dafa Hao!* (Falun Gong is good!) leaves me as cold as *Just do it!*—but then, immunity to slogans is simply part of my Western birthright, the coat I wore in, for better or worse, and the one I'll probably walk out with.

To a practitioner what I have written above might seem appalling; after all practitioners have been killed shouting *Falun Dafa Hao!* Thus, I would be a cranky, rather self-defeating scribe of the Falun Gong experience, save for one trait: I am deeply moved by commitment—if only I *could* believe, I sometimes say. So I am a baked-in skeptic, but I am also deeply skeptical of Richard Dawkins and his ilk, as well as the even more reductionist faith that religion is somehow the root of all evil in the modern world. By this point in the book you will have noticed that China isn't that simple; evil comes in many guises and has many parents.

I'm not a perfect fit with this subject. It took me years to reach a normal comfort level with practitioners talking about how Falun Gong saved their health, or just expressing simple joy in their experience. And it took me years to come up with a nice, sloppy definition: Falun Gong, simply put, is a Buddhist revival movement: moral passion, occasional talk of miracles, are-you-running-with-me-Master-Li individualism, and a reflexive mistrust of establishments and outsider agendas.[32]

By this point in the book I hope that definition makes some intuitive sense to you, and I hope that I made the right decision to forego the definition game until now; long enough perhaps for you to come up with your own sloppy definition. I'm asking for you to exercise a fair amount of critical thought here because I am trying to reproduce something of my own process of discovery. On July 22, 1999, when the crackdown began, like the vast majority of Westerners in Beijing, I had no ability to define Falun Gong either.[33] It took me years to gain some purchase, and—after years of Western reporters parachuting in to make a quick hit piece that would buy some points with the party—to earn some grudging trust from practitioners. It took me several more years to be relaxed enough to make a comparison that directly speaks to some shared fragments of Western experience, that of great tents being thrown up across the American Midwest like the dust clouds of the buffalo. Why should we make a comparison that relies on traces of our Western ancestral memory? Because it is the same dynamic in China; the Buddhist aspect of Falun Gong may seem antique and exotic not just to Westerners, but to many Chinese as well.

I began practically every interview with practitioners by asking them if there was a grandparent, an uncle, or an auntie who had been religious and had somehow influenced them. I received blank stares from 95 percent of my subjects. Okay, but without invoking five thousand years of Chinese civilization and all that, let's just say that maybe it runs deeper. China can be a crude, deceitful, grasping place at times, and yet I saw glimpses of something that looked like truth, compassion, and forbearance playing out in my Chinese neighborhood every day. And anyone who has studied the group must admit that there *is* something deeply indigenous about Falun Gong. As Dr. Arthur Waldron, noted historian, puts it: "Anyone who knows Asian religion will instantly see that Falun Gong fits into a tradition that extends back before the beginning of recorded history."[34] It is indisputable that what made Falun Gong stand out from all the other qigong exercises and meditation practices in the early 1990s was its moral system of compassion, truthfulness, and forbearance. The idea of a moral code that actually drives the universe itself is unmistakably Buddhist in origin.

Definitions and words alone—there's that style thing again, but consider how deeply debased words can be in a mainland Chinese context—are simply not the full story. I suggest you judge Falun Gong, and indeed, the Chinese Communist Party, by its actions. For that reason, you will find no extended, formal discussion of whether Falun Gong can be defined as a "cult" in this book. You will undoubtedly make up your own mind. Yet you should also be aware of the origin of the claim; the Chinese government defined Falun Gong as a "twisted path" (we usually translate that in turn as "evil cult") in October 1999, months after it had sent thousands off to jail for practicing. The timing strongly suggests that the word "cult" was employed because the party feared that it was losing the public relations battle in the West; certain loaded terms—*racist*, *cult*, and more recently *homophobic*—short-circuit practically any Western mainstream debate, making it seemingly too risky to continue lest one be caught defending bigots or nuts or both. (In the Falun Gong case, the party had the foresight to throw in all three labels—cult, racist, and homophobic, even though Li Hongzhi's observations about homosexuality didn't differ much from standard Catholic, Jewish, Islamic, and Tibetan Buddhist doctrine, and interracial marriage would ultimately become practically routine in Falun Gong circles).

Yet debate, lively, unfettered debate, is precisely what goes on in Falun Gong circles all the time (and, along with the meat, it's why I enjoy dinners with practitioners). Moral interpretation, well-argued, the gospel according to each practitioner: this is what sways the outcome, and this is the spark that makes Falun Gong feel more like a vision of the early Christians rather than a modern-day cult made to order.

Ultimately my perception of cults is culled from a briefly embedded experience with Divine Light Mission—my first girlfriend was a *premie*, a committed devotee—in the late 1970s. That period left a surprisingly bad taste in my mouth, like a flashback from a bad drug experience. I was embedded in Falun Gong for far longer, and with no romantic carrot or stick in play. While I have had good days and bad days, I never felt that anyone was struggling against intellectualism itself—neither mine nor the formidable and diverse intelligence that was evidenced by my friends in the practitioner community. Perhaps that's why my palate feels clean, and my jaw feels relaxed enough to offer a few observations on what it feels like on the inside.

Let's clear a few items out of the way: The Falun Gong structure isn't terribly hierarchical, any break up of families tends to be enforced by the Chinese state rather than any element of Falun Gong doctrine, and there are no substantive money issues—other than not enough of it—and no financial corruption that I ever came across. Nor is the leadership making a killing; after Li Hongzhi settled in the boroughs of New York City, he was asked if he liked his new home and he helpfully replied that he liked America because he could purchase Chinese sauces.

Now let's move to the personal impressions. The majority of practitioners have faith that Li Hongzhi, as a spiritual master, is essentially infallible. I have no opinion on the spiritual side, but I would often point out that he's not particularly astute at politics. Most practitioners would laughingly reply that he doesn't claim to be anything of the sort. Falun Gong is not meant to be a political movement. Li Hongzhi has consistently and repeatedly told practitioners to figure that stuff out—politics, public relations, advocacy, or, in practitioner speak, "truth clarification"—for themselves. Although it is in my nature to recoil from all claims of infallibility, I have to concede the doing-it-for-themselves point appears to be reasonably accurate.

Much has been said, and will be said, about Falun Gong's complex attitudes about health. Some practitioners tend to see sickness as a sign of practice failure or even a chance to pay off karma. In the beginning, I viewed this attitude with concern or even alarm. Over time, I began to see it more as an eccentricity, a sort of spiritual machismo that plays out in practitioners delaying their visit to the doctor over a bladder infection, for example, rather than a formal anti-medical edict. I've yet to meet a practitioner who after a couple of sleepless nights with a tooth abscess won't break down and get a root canal, although I am told they exist. Ultimately, the Chinese state had a very hard time making the medical case against Falun Gong, probably because any neglect of early medical detection is countered by a positive attitude and the practitioner edict to avoid tobacco and alcohol.[35]

From a public-relations perspective the most damaging tendency in mainland practitioner culture (Western and Taiwan practitioners simply don't fit here) is the tendency to reach instinctively for spin control rather than the internal teleprompter of the heart when faced with an outsider. In other words, you will get a straight answer—many of my interviews revolved around having to achieve exactly that—but occasionally it can be a drawn-out Rumpelstiltskin process of coming up with exactly the right question. My Jewish background informs me that mistrust of outsiders is a tragic, inevitable side effect of persecution, and my American journalist background tells me that reporters—and I include myself—can be clueless jerks. Ultimately I suspect this evasive tendency has less to do with collective deceptiveness and more to do with the pervasive mainland Chinese tendency to tell a rapid series of wearisome half-truths when a straightforward answer would have done just fine, thank you. I encountered this during my Beijing years on a daily basis, and I suspect anyone who has lived in China has come across this irritating and ultimately destructive habit. Sadly, Falun Gong's moral edict of truthfulness has not fully overcome mainland culture in this respect.

But my perceptions can only go so far, and you need to make your own judgment: Does Falun Gong meet the cult-like qualities of say, Scientology, the Unification Church (often called *the Moonies* while Rev. Moon was still alive), Divine Light Mission (Prem Rawat, a.k.a. Guru Maharaji's operation), or the Children of God (now called the Family)? Ultimately, formal academic attempts to define what exactly constitutes a cult are absurd, contradictory, and arbitrary exercises. They could just as easily be applied to the Chinese Communist Party, but that too quickly degenerates into a sort of name calling. Yet there is a litmus test, and you can apply it yourself: *listen to those who have actually fled from cults.*

If you search the Internet, other than Chinese-state-proxy anti–Falun

Gong propaganda sites, you'll be very hard pressed to find a website with former practitioners bashing Master Li and Falun Gong.[36] However, within seconds, you will find grassroots websites, featuring constantly updated, bursting-at-the-seams discussion boards for former members of Divine Light Mission, Scientology, and the Unification Church. It is here that they spill their guts, tears, and bile over all the years of mind control, wasted money, and pointless commitment.[37] In the case of those who were sexually abused as children in the Children of God cult, the hauntingly flat testimony—even their ability to be angry has been somehow stripped from them, too—is almost physically painful to read.

* * *

The observation that Falun Gong doesn't fit into the cult paradigm didn't make Falun Gong any less controversial in the New China. Revival movements threaten institutions. Yet this same revivalist aspect—the idea of obeying one's experience rather than obeying rules—helps explain why Falun Gong practitioners insist on being called "practitioners" rather than "followers." Actually, they don't follow well. Ask ten Falun Gong practitioners for a definition of Falun Gong, and you will get ten different answers and ten days of heated discussions. One of the things I learned early on about practitioners is that many don't like to be told what to do. In fact, if you tell some of them what to do, often they will do just the opposite. Yet it was that same do-it-yourself mentality that brought us to this point in the story: Falun Gong had attracted fully seventy million practitioners by January 1999.[38]

That's an internal PSB estimate directly taken from my interview with a former PSB agent, but there was nothing secret about that number; the Chinese media reported it widely, sometimes even suggesting it was as high as a hundred million. Falun Gong was integrated into every walk of life, even at the highest levels of the party. To suggest that anything like the Xinjiang Procedure would be revived for use on Falun Gong would have sounded insane to practitioners and PSB alike in 1999. *Particularly* for the PSB; the decision to take out Falun Gong had already been made,

Ding Jing, coordinator of the Falun Gong Chinese Communist Party wing, Yuyuantan Region, Beijing. Photo taken in 2013 by Ma Yan.

the decision had been disseminated to the high-ranking cadres, yet any planning for the operation probably envisioned something resembling the campaign against Zhong Gong in 1996. A ban on the practice, a brief media expose of Zhong Gong's spiritual master? The entire movement simply melted away in less than two months.

Falun Gong, it was estimated, might take three.

In all those years since 1996 Jing had never really minded the plainclothes PSB agents walking by her practice sites. Some practitioners whispered to her about it. Jing laughed and told them that she had walked by a Falun Gong site a few times herself back in the day. She looked forward to the morning when the agents' curiosity would get the better of them, and they would stop, break the ice, ask some questions, and end up learning the exercises. Now, in the early spring of 1999, two young men with knock-off Members Only jackets muscled into her practice site, flashing their fixed smiles, casually asking where people lived and the characters of their names, performing deep-breathing exercises while taking quick drags off their cigarettes.

The morning had finally come, just not like Jing had hoped. But she was no fool. The Yuyuantan Region had been an oasis where officials and peasants could drink from the same source, yet even when the romantic mist rose off the lake she had always known the CCTV tower was still there. If the peaceable kingdom had to fall, let it fall hard. For Jing, there would be no second retirement.

3

AN OCCURRENCE ON FUYOU STREET

On April 24, 1999, as the last trains and buses pulled in for the night, the first Falun Gong practitioners from the countryside—some carrying light luggage, some carrying only a meditation mat—made their way to the center of Beijing.[1] Their goal was to appeal to the central government at the only location where a Chinese citizen can legally do so: the Letters and Petitions Office, sometimes called the National Appeals Office.[2] The office was said to be somewhere just a bit west of the Forbidden City, near a place called Fuyou Street.

Arriving on that street for the first time, there would be little to grab your attention except for one quality—it's unusually quiet at night. Think about it. You are a shotgun blast from Tiananmen Square, the epicenter of perhaps sixteen million people. And you are standing on a north-south avenue of scale. The southern entrance to Fuyou is Chang'an Avenue, the teeming east-west thoroughfare—Westerners recognize Chang'an because the anonymous "Tank Man" was photographed there during the Tiananmen Square protests of June 1989. Yet whatever is going on in Chang'an, or whatever else is creating ambient noise in the great city of Beijing, is swallowed up by the graceful spreading trees that line Fuyou, and whatever traffic makes it through the carefully designed maze of one-way streets and no-turn intersections is but a trickle.

Actually, there is no reason for you to be standing on Fuyou either. There are no shops or hotels. Tourist attractions are a block away. On the west side of the avenue a continuous gray wall breaks only for a *hutong* or alleyway entrance leading to drab, unmarked government buildings and dorms. The bus barely stops here because there are few real addresses; the east side of Fuyou, nothing but a vast red wall, contains only one. Armed guards in the uniform of the People's Liberation Army (PLA) patrol the

74   THE SLAUGHTER

dual entrances to Zhongnanhai, China's sprawling central leadership compound.

One of the charms of central Beijing is that ancient streets sometimes reassert themselves like a ghost haunting an old house that has changed its layout. So straight lines in the center of Beijing are not always truly straight. Fuyou follows that rule; if you look down it, it bulges out curiously, as if the street itself was straining to contain all of China's political power.

The first meditation-mat practitioners stepped into the shadows of Fuyou Street at about 9 p.m. while a brisk but pleasantly warm spring wind chased away Beijing's stagnant, industrial mist—a good omen. Yet these weren't technically the first practitioners on Fuyou. A Falun Gong witness, possibly an insider at Zhongnanhai, claimed that several employees of the Public Security Bureau—Falun Gong practitioners—had discreetly walked to the gates of Zhongnanhai that afternoon and dropped off their name cards with the armed guards, politely requesting an audience with government officials. It was a plea to quietly resolve a developing crisis.[3]

Fuyou Street with glimpses of the New Forbidden City, Zhongnanhai, beyond the red wall. Photo by Jian Shuo Wang.

Two weeks earlier, on April 11, He Zuoxiu, China's now-permanent house critic of Falun Gong, struck again, this time in a youth magazine published by Tianjin Normal University. If He's title was uninspired—"I Do Not Agree with Adolescents Practicing Qigong"—the charges were lively: Falun Gong was nothing less than a new Boxer Rebellion, now gathering fresh recruits from the schoolyards of China to be trained in the black arts of superstition. Unchecked, Falun Gong would lead to China's ruin.[4]

From a practitioner perspective, the comparison was absurd. Falun Gong was indisputably nonviolent, and the demographics of Falun Gong leaned firmly toward elderly women, not children or adolescents. But the attack was made in a nationwide publication aimed at primary and high school students and sold on a coercive subscription basis. So practitioners spontaneously began yet another silent demonstration at Tianjin University.[5]

Several practitioners who participated recalled for me their sense of initial confidence; as long as they maintained discipline and received an audience with the university authorities, they could invoke the Three No's policy, and, déjà vu, the article would be recalled and a new one placed. Two thoughts never came up: that this attack was somehow different, and that the outcome might be different, too.

Initially everything went according to script. Tianjin administrators duly promised to publish a correction. Then, for unknown reasons, the administrators suddenly reversed themselves. In response, more practitioners flooded in, and by the afternoon of April 23, six thousand practitioners were hanging out on the university square.[6] I've examined police surveillance footage taken that day; as usual, there were no signs or banners, no chants or slogans, just a lot of people standing around, some sitting, reading, or doing meditation.[7] So something that is not present in that video prompted the university administrators to call in the police.

Or so the story goes; some practitioners, including a serious young woman named Jiang Xinxia, were making their way to Tianjin by bus but were turned back by the police in the city of Siping in Jilin Province on the twenty-third. This incident—with the police prematurely telling the practitioners that "the situation in Tianjin was resolved"—hints that the university administrators were no longer driving events.[8]

76   THE SLAUGHTER

Screen shot from the vigil at Tianjin, April 1999. Source: Minghui.

One of the three hundred riot police called into Tianjin that day was a man named Hao Fengjun. Gifted with strong regular features, high intelligence, and an appreciation of strategic discretion, Hao loved his job. He once told me in a slightly drunken moment that he wanted to be the best, most professional policeman in the world. Hao did not know it yet, but his path of law enforcement promotion in the coming years would be symbiotically linked with the group he was about to meet.

In the beginning of April, Hao's Public Security Bureau unit had received a notice from higher authorities: Be secretly cautious of the scheme of Falun Gong.⁹ So something was up, and the order to deploy at Tianjin Education College was not fully unexpected. Yet Hao's initial reaction to the "Falun Gong incident" was bewilderment.

At 4 that afternoon "our entire police force was suddenly maneuvered to the college, even though we all had other tasks to do—such as drug and criminal cases." The police were given no background on the actual issue at hand: "We all knew nothing about Falun Gong. Yet we were called in to enforce martial law and close off the area. When we arrived at the scene, we all realized that it was nothing like what had been described to us—Falun Gong looking for a fight, disturbing public order, and so on."

Hao Fengjun, Tianjin cop: "We were called in to enforce martial law. . . ." By 2000, Hao would be recruited into an officer's position in one of China's most feared secret agencies, The 6-10 Office. Photo by Epoch Times, December 2005.

The police told the Falun Gong to leave campus. The practitioners did not respond. An officer commandeered the campus speaker system. As an angry warning echoed through the square, according to a practitioner, the atmosphere "became very intense." Suddenly a few practitioners saw purple *faluns*, intelligent beings made of high energy that existed in another dimension, spinning near the sun—a sign that something holy was transpiring.

A couple of policemen approached a middle-aged man who was wearing cream-colored clothing. In unison, practitioners began reciting from *Zhuan Falun*[10]:

> *The Buddha Fa is most profound; among all the theories in the world, it is the most intricate and extraordinary science....*

The police punched the man in the face and he began spurting blood.

> *In order to explore this domain, humankind must fundamentally change its conventional thinking....*

A policeman grabbed an old lady under the arms and hoisted her toward the police vans.

> *Otherwise, the truth of the universe will forever remain a mystery to humankind...*

The policemen began shoving, kicking, and dragging away the practitioners around the entrance.

> *and everyday people will forever crawl...*

Hao could see no signs of physical resistance anywhere—no verbal abuse, no anger. Everyone was simply playing their part.

> *within the boundary delimited by their own ignorance.*[11]

And Hao knew he would not argue with the police captains either. No point. He waded in. By 6 p.m. they had arrested forty-five practitioners, the square was clear, and according to Hao, "very clean."

The practitioners asked Tianjin officials and any policemen who would speak with them: What about the arrests? How could they get those practitioners released? Over and over they were told the same thing: *We are powerless. This is a no longer a local matter. These are orders from the Ministry of Public Security. You must go to Beijing. Go to the appeals office.*[12]

In the two days following the Tianjin arrests, that word *appeal* spread widely among Chinese practitioners. Some made out their wills the night before, but on the twenty-fourth of April, thousands of practitioners set off for Beijing. They were blatantly followed. One group was intercepted in Shenyang by a policeman who had carefully memorized phrases from *Zhuan Falun*. One group of twenty Falun Gong took an overnight train from Harbin. Stepping onto a Beijing platform swarming with practitioners, a phalanx of policemen firmly directed them back on the train. Yet I estimate that approximately one in ten Beijingers practiced Falun Gong. If the PSB wanted to maintain a low profile—and it appears from these stories that they did not want a repeat of the arrests and violence that had occurred in Tianjin—agents were only moderating turnout, not extinguishing it.

There was one technical oversight that Li Hongzhi, the coordinators, and the rank-and-file practitioners hadn't considered, and it would have a lasting influence on how their gathering in Beijing was perceived. The National Appeals Office was created in the post-Mao era as a sort of prop to show that the party was doing its bit to get rid of corrupt officials—a fig leaf of party legitimacy, not a center for high-volume truth clarification. Mimicking the party's own ambiguous motives about anything to do with petitioning, the office's location wasn't well publicized. In fact, not a single practitioner that I have interviewed could place it precisely on a map. Some practitioners thought the appeals office was near the Wenjin Street intersection, on Xi'anmen Street.[13] Others thought it was closer to Chang'an to the south. But most believed that it was in the hutongs, the labyrinth of narrow alleyways right off Fuyou Street to the west. And the entrance to those hutongs stands across from the guarded western entrance to Zhongnanhai.

80 THE SLAUGHTER

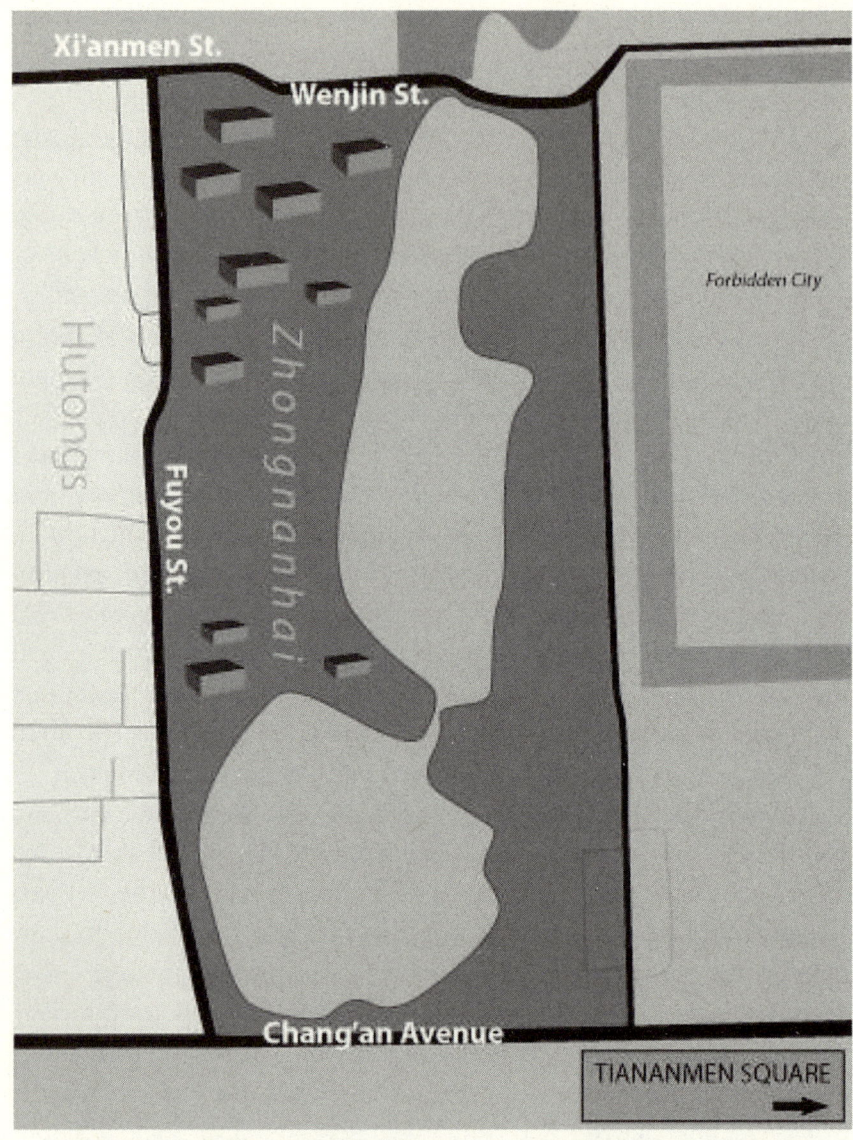

On April 25, 1999, most practitioners believed the National Appeals Office was somewhere in the middle of Fuyou Street near the west gate of Zhongnanhai. Chinese security arranged the Falun Gong practitioners along the west side of Fuyou Street and the north side of Wenjin Street (spillover was allocated to Xi'anmen Street), creating the appearance that Falun Gong "surrounded" or "besieged" Zhongnanhai. Map by Luba Pishchik and Jared Pearman.

AN OCCURRENCE ON FUYOU STREET   81

So as April 25 dawned, a lovely, crisp spring morning, a thirty-three-year old consultant Zeng Zheng—better known by her foreign name Jennifer Zeng—pulled her bike into Fuyou Street and instantly noticed that something was a little off. Jennifer had briefly worked in the Zhongnanhai compound and knew the security intimately. Normally there were so many guards that it was difficult to enter the street without being questioned. Now, just before 7 a.m., practitioners were strolling down Fuyou street chatting and looking around for the appeals office, as if they were in a shopping mall. But a line of police stood on the southern end. The police told the practitioners to go back up the block and stand at the entrance to the hutong, across from Zhongnanhai's western gate. At the same time, up at the north entrance to Fuyou, policemen were carefully leading practitioners to the west side of the street and directing them to walk south. Both groups merged right outside the main entrance of Zhongnanhai. The National Appeals Office would open at 8:00 a.m., they were told. Jennifer understood: "They were very well prepared, they were expecting us."[14]

Jennifer Zeng, Beijing consultant and Falun Gong practitioner in 1998. Jennifer would ultimately write Witnessing History: One Chinese Woman's Fight for Freedom and Falun Gong, *a strikingly vivid account of the Falun Gong repression. Courtesy of Jennifer Zeng.*

82   THE SLAUGHTER

At 7:30, a young couple on their way to the appeals office walked by the moat on the eastern side of the Forbidden City. Incongruous against the ancient setting, they witnessed a large unit of Red Army soldiers sitting in jeeps, bayonets fixed, facing Fuyou.[15]

By 8:00, Luo Hongwei, a young newlywed, had just taken her place close to Zhongnanhai's west gate. Perhaps everything would be okay, she thought, exulting in the practitioner's discipline; it was not like Tiananmen. They couldn't accuse us of shutting down the city: "There were a lot of people, a lot of people.... It's hard to avoid things becoming chaotic.... But the cars driving past were going swish-swish."[16]

Fuyou Street, looking south from a city bus, April 25, 1999. Source: Minghui.

By 8:30, an elderly practitioner—let's call her Auntie Dee—made her way into the intersection of Chang'an and Fuyou. The street was now packed with practitioners, mainly country folk, plainly dressed, with cheap cloth shoes. Watching them mill about carrying their rations of dried food, or squatting and obliviously chewing away, the anxiety Auntie

Dee had been so carefully tamping down suddenly exploded in a vivid sense of déjà vu. Ten years ago, she had felt the tanks thunder down Fuxing street. Ten years ago, students had squatted and eaten and protested peacefully. But they shot them anyway. Now the ground seemed to be shaking beneath her again as she made her way up Fuyou Street, searching for a good place to stand.

People were still smashed together in front of the western gate of Zhongnanhai. Yet it was becoming obvious from the huge police presence moving in from the hutongs that the appeals office, wherever it was, wouldn't be opening. Not today. Auntie Dee pushed through the bodies as quickly as she could, not daring to stand in front of Zhongnanhai, straining to keep her eyes from even glancing at it. Eventually she reached Fuyou's northern intersection with Wenjin. People were flooding in from the northeast now, and she could see policemen carefully herding practitioners along Wenjin directly opposite the northern exposure of Zhongnanhai. *As if they were here to surround Zhongnanhai.* A friend of Auntie Dee's was there, too—let's call her Auntie Sha—and she remembers it well: "They just told us—go *this* way, go *this* way, and we followed."

While buses and police cars cruised around the intersection, Auntie Dee suddenly realized that video cameras had been set up at regular intervals. Sick with fear now, she tried to move back from the front row: "I thought if they caught me on film, they would come for me later."[17] (Auntie Dee and her friend Auntie Sha would ultimately be sentenced to labor camp for three years).

It was now nearly 9:00 a.m., and the Kabuki show began.

Jennifer Zeng was locked in the crowd, fifty yards from the west gate. She was struck by the variety of the faces: scarred from age, young and unmarked, those with professional airs, and those with the hardscrabble resolution of the unemployed, all projecting a sense of purpose, of complete sincerity. She could feel the hush, as if everyone was holding their breath. She began to tremble faintly. She couldn't explain what moved her. Just that nobody had told them to come. And nobody had come just for themselves. Yet there they were, so close that she could feel the warmth of their cheeks, risking their lives for this one precious thing. Squeezed up against the bodies, Jennifer began to cry silently. Then Zhu Rongji, the premier of China's State Council, suddenly emerged from the gate: "Everyone wanted to push forward to see if it was him. But then someone reminded them not to move, because there was a lot of tension, and they didn't want the police to react. Practitioners pulled back quietly and then clapped to welcome him."

Zhu Rongji, tall and stately, was talking with the practitioners. *Oh, it's He Zuoxiu again.* The smile in the eyes, the dismissive nod of the head. *After the Beijing TV incident last year, I wrote a memo. Didn't you see it? No?* The glance around, as if a government circular on Falun Gong policy had been carelessly dropped on Fuyou Street. Then the smoldering turn. The harsh, narrow-eyed look at his aides, which wordlessly invoked the vast, incompetent bureaucracy of all of China, and the duplicitous apparatchiks who stood a respectful pace behind him in particular.[18]

For those practitioners who were party insiders, the meaning of that look was crystal-spanking clear; whatever circular Zhu had written had been suppressed by Luo Gan, the head of the PSB. But it would be okay now. The "Tianjin 45" would be released, the Three No's would be reaffirmed, and maybe *Zhuan Falun* could even be legally published again.

Zhu Rongji went back into Zhongnanhai, followed by a few practitioners. One was carrying a copy of *Zhuan Falun* in his hand. Jennifer kept running that image of the book going into Zhongnanhai over in her mind, and her trembling departed. All they had to do was wait.

When a practitioner suggested that they take turns to go eat or drink, the other practitioners said no, definitely not—if we drink, we'll have to go to the bathroom. That could disturb those living or working in the area.[19] When spectators came by, the practitioners would politely ignore their questions; chatting could slow down pedestrian traffic. When the Western reporters showed up, they were given the silent treatment, too— the practitioners weren't there to be provocative. There were now ten to twenty thousand practitioners on Fuyou Street with the spillover allocated to the north.

At 2:00 p.m., I was attending a high-profile wedding in Beijing when I heard that there was a vast number of people gathered at Zhongnanhai. I called my buddy Jasper Becker, the Beijing bureau chief for the *South China Morning Post*, to find out what was going on. It was apparently a group named "Falun Gong." He didn't know anything beyond that. He admitted to me that he, and the other Beijing journalists that he knew of, had been broadsided. "Ethan," Jasper said, "we got caught with our pants down."

At 4:00 p.m., a handout from the PSB was distributed. It stated that the Falun Gong concerns were noted, and it reaffirmed the Three No's policy. Everyone should go home. But the handout said nothing about the "Tianjin 45." The practitioners stayed.

At 5:00 p.m., practitioners saw a black limo come out of Zhongnanhai with an unsmiling man looking out at them. It was Jiang Zemin, the chairman of the Chinese Communist Party. The limo circled slowly around Zhongnanhai a few times, Jiang staring hard at the practitioners, all so neatly lined up like a dress parade.[20] That night, Jiang would write a letter claiming that Falun Gong was more disciplined than the PLA itself.

At 9:00 p.m., Li Chang, a practitioner representative, came out of Zhongnanhai and announced that the Tianjin detainees were being released. The practitioners listened, questioned him a little, and then left, taking every speck of garbage with them, even the cigarette butts of the police.[21]

Throughout it all, for fourteen hours, no record, film, or plausible account suggests that the Falun Gong practitioners did anything that could be construed as even faintly provocative. Even by the party's hair-trigger standards, there was no pretext that could justify the use of the troops waiting by the Forbidden City.

That evening, Jiang Zemin released a letter to the politburo and other relevant leaders, making three claims: First, that April 25 had constituted the most serious collective action and the most potent threat to the regime since the Tiananmen demonstrations ten years prior.[22] Second, that Falun Gong's impressive mobilization capacity, discipline, and organization could well be the product of foreign influences.[23] Third, along with the usual attacks on superstition and the obligatory incantation of the Marxist belief in atheism and materialism, Jiang reportedly ended with an angry flourish: "If the CCP cannot defeat Falun Gong, it will be the biggest joke on Earth."[24]

Jiang's use of war terminology—"defeat"—opened up the PSB's floodgates to what practitioners would ultimately call "the persecution." But clearly Jiang Zemin would not have felt empowered to pen such a letter without tacit support from other members of the party.[25] And Jiang's decisiveness was also contingent on the optics of April 25—optics that are based on a series of myths that the majority of the Western press, and a surprising number of Western academics, simply swallowed and regurgitated.

Practically every major objective history of Falun Gong begins, not with 1992, but with April 25, 1999. This would not be a problem—one has to start somewhere after all—except that authors work from a set interpretation, a prefabricated picture. Out of the clear blue sky, ten thousand majestically disciplined and centrally controlled Falun Gong practitioners surrounded Zhongnanhai, disrupting social order, blindsiding the Chinese leadership. While Western analysts tend to look at Falun Gong's actions more as a strategic mistake rather than the party's depiction of a moral and legal provocation, party myth and Western common wisdom are surprisingly close. Given the urge for balance that any intelligent reader brings to a complex situation such as the Falun Gong repression—the sense that Falun Gong must have done *something* wrong to bring down the wrath of the Chinese government—April 25 has clearly become Falun Gong's original sin.

To sustain the myth, a series of conditions have to hold. The first is that the Chinese leadership was *surprised* by the demonstration (and thus in some indefinable way, victimized by it). Let us clear away the brushwood; PSB surveillance of Falun Gong began as early as 1996. By early 1999, practitioner sites always had a plainclothes observer-cum-participant present, and Falun Gong was riddled with PSB spies. But to avoid being surprised on April 25, the party didn't need to consult spies; there were plenty of practitioners to question within the party hierarchy. Given the Falun Gong edict to be truthful, the authorities would have received reasonably straight answers. Practitioners from the Public Security Bureau had already dropped off their phone numbers at the gates of Zhongnanhai on the afternoon of April 24—a highly unusual action, a signal of what was going to occur on that very street. It's fair to say that the people who were the most severely blindsided on April 25 were the foreign journalists of Beijing and an American attending a wedding. Journalists hate that. They *despise* being the only ones who do not know what is going on. Yet on Fuyou Street, on April 25, that was a reality. It may seem petty, but it appears that to avoid losing face, the foreign press corps preferred to believe that everyone was taken by surprise. Few attempted to dig further.[26]

The second myth is that Falun Gong "surrounded" (that's Associated Press and Reuters) or "besieged" (that's Agence France-Presse) Zhongnanhai. There are writers, whom I otherwise respect, who mock Falun Gong for advancing an alternate "conspiracy" theory: that Luo Gan fully intended for the practitioners to surround Zhongnanhai.[27]

Surely there is nothing conspiratorial about reviewing the basic facts: The Tianjin University authorities inexplicably changed their mind about a correction on He's article. Police throughout China blocked practitioners from coming to Tianjin. The Tianjin police acted with unusual brutality, spilling blood for the first time in Falun Gong history. The Tianjin police told the practitioners to go to the appeals office in Beijing. Police, cameras, and armed troops were assembled in Beijing. No matter how Falun Gong may have bungled the optics, the appeals office was the goal, and there were plenty of locations where the police could have herded the overflow of Falun Gong practitioners—into the hutongs, to Chang'an Avenue, or along Wenjin Street to the northwest—other than placing them in a half circle around the Zhongnanhai compound. As for the claim that practitioners had blocked traffic; no photographic or witness evidence of such an event exists. Thousands witnessed a small motorcade, carrying Jiang Zemin, do full circuits around Zhongnanhai and its environs without obstruction.

The only evidence offered for the "surrounded" thesis is that in the days following April 25 Falun Gong sources had a tendency to downplay the original goal (the appeals office) in favor of phrases such as we "gathered peacefully at Zhongnanhai to present facts to the Chinese leaders." Yet these statements were made in an atmosphere of practitioner afterglow; the evening announcement that the Tianjin practitioners would be released was greeted with quiet relief and optimism. Subsequent Falun Gong official statements either were attempts, however clumsy, to match the imagined new harmony with the party, or were retroactive attempts to take credit for a perceived success no matter how accidental it may have been.[28] But naïveté, hubris, spin control, and the Falun Gong tendency to fight their media offensives with the propaganda tools that they have learned from living in a police state do not call into the question the basic credibility of my witnesses. There is simply no evidence that they were attempting to overthrow the government.

The one area where the party's discussion of April 25 may have a kernel of validity is the role that Li Hongzhi and Falun Gong coordinators played in planning the demonstration. Li had a stopover on the twenty-second and twenty-third in the Beijing Airport on his way down to Australia (ostensibly to save money on airfare). Using the data of Kang Xiaoguang, a researcher in the Chinese intelligence agency (whose sources cannot be verified), the party ultimately promoted the idea that Li's presence in the Beijing Airport was part and parcel of his stage managing both the Tianjin and Zhongnanhai protests. Falun Gong spokesmen—in what seems like a case of excessive zeal to protect Li's image from appearing to be political or controversial or perhaps imperfect in some way—would deny, on at least one occasion, that Li discussed Tianjin or April 25, or had even ventured an opinion about what was to be done at all.[29] That claim seems as improbable as the idea that the PSB was surprised by April 25. It's no great leap to assume that Li discussed Tianjin and the next steps—and that he probably concurred with Falun Gong coordinators on the ground: *Appeal* explicitly meant the National Appeals Office. The usual protocol was to be followed—no chanting, no slogans, exemplary behavior. As always, it would be left up to individual practitioners whether they chose to participate.[30]

And yet even that level of leadership cannot be simply assumed. Numerous interviews that I've done with run-of-the-mill practitioners independently describe that after three years of unbroken demonstrations (or gatherings or truth clarifications), with a no-loss record until Tianjin, practitioners didn't need a lot of startup or direction for the same game plan that the coordinators were espousing—it was simply second nature by this point. The only difference was that in Beijing the stakes were much higher. Everyone knew that the arrests in Tianjin set a frightening precedent. Some practitioners believed it was better to stay home; they justified their decision in the usual way—Master Li had said that practitioners should avoid politics. Others argued for action in the usual way: the truth had to be defended; the law was on their side.

Much has been made about the demonstrators' motives: Some were true believers who were undoubtedly ready to die. Some were political naïf's who believed in the Chinese government and that it was all a big misunderstanding. Some were simply rote followers of Li Hongzhi and believed that is what he wanted. And some saw this as a rare opportunity for spiritual consummation.[31] There's a practitioner out there for every caricature, but in the majority of cases it boiled down to the attitude expressed by a serious young girl, whose bus had been stopped by the police in Siping en route to Tianjin, Jiang Xinxia.

Xinxia had recently joined the Chinese Communist Party, yet she felt this afforded her no particular shelter from the storm. As she said to me, "I thought it was right for the practitioners to go to Zhongnanhai. Today it was this group of practitioners that were beaten. Tomorrow it might have been me."[32] This was a novel feeling for Xinxia. A year before, in her discussions with practitioners who were also party members, they had agreed that there was no conflict between serving the party and practicing Falun Gong. Certainly, there was nothing preordained about a crackdown. Now, even as a young party member who had little contact with Beijing, Jiang Xinxia felt the presence of a fault line, that the leadership configuration in early 1999 was extremely precarious for Falun Gong.

We cannot see inside the souls of the top Chinese leaders in 1999. All of them were products of party culture; all of them shared the view that, at the very least, Falun Gong's morality was out of step with the New China. But we can draw some individual sketches.

Start with Jiang Zemin. It is practically gospel among practitioners that Jiang was "jealous" that Falun Gong could recruit and bond with new

90   **THE SLAUGHTER**

Thumbnail sketch of key leadership attitudes towards Falun Gong in 1999

Jiang Zemin	Li Peng	Zhu Rongji	Luo Gan
President, People's Republic of China	Chairman, National People's Congress Standing Committee	Premier, State Council	Secretary, Political and Legislative Affairs Committee
Actively negative	**Passively negative**	**Passively neutral**	**Actively negative**
Personally ordered Falun Gong (FG) repression in 1999	*Hardliner but dogged by rumors of family ties to FG*	*Initial sympathy: no evidence of mitigating influence*	*Ordered PSB to begin full surveillance of FG in 1998*

Photos from Baike.com.

members in a way that the Chinese Communist Party, with all its coercion, money, and power, could not. The jealousy theory, or more accurately, the narcissism theory, shouldn't be dismissed; I used to work with a former aide to Jiang who would tell me hilarious hotel-room tales of Jiang's anxiety over which outfit to wear to a meeting—a bit like Tom Brokaw's legendary dithering over his trench coat before an outdoor stand up. Jiang's vanity was equally obvious to the Chinese public; he pushed the "Three Represents," his quasi-spiritual directive for the new Communist man, way past the point where it was politically advantageous to do so. Yet there were two good political reasons for Jiang Zemin's proactively seizing the Falun Gong issue. First, recall Minister X's revelation of one of Jiang's first directives: *Make June 4th go away.* As Falun Gong was the first tangible movement to come out of the China black box, ten years on, why wouldn't Jiang see this as the opportunity to renew the Tiananmen lesson of absolute power while simultaneously changing the subject to a new enemy? Second, recall Jiang's career and his advance to the politburo. During the Tiananmen crisis, Jiang, then Shanghai's municipal secretary, boldly went out and spoke sympathetically to Shanghai student protesters while secretly preparing a swift and decisive local crackdown. The gamble worked; now he would gamble again using the same tactic of providing reassurance (exploiting Zhu Rongji's popular reputation) while simultaneously sharpening the knife—presumably with vastly improved odds.

Li Peng, arguably the second most influential leader in China in 1999, was far more notorious—dissidents called him "the butcher of Beijing" for his role in the Tiananmen massacre. So we can reasonably speculate that he saw the same opportunities as Jiang to apply his skill with the knife. Yet it was common knowledge among Falun Gong coordinators that Li Peng's wife was a practitioner. The depth of her commitment is not known—could she have been "outed"? Was Li in full control? Again we don't know, but clearly the optics of an active role for Li in the crackdown could become very complex. It was easier to lead from behind.

To Chinese citizens, Falun Gong or otherwise, the Chinese Communist Party is necessarily a sort of parental figure. Thus, when the state does something immoral, there is a slightly irrational tendency to see a good parent and a bad parent rather than accepting that the entire family might be dysfunctional. Zhu Rongji was the repository of practitioner dreams—the good mommy, if you will. Practitioners did not dream alone; for Western businessmen and reporters, Zhu embodied forward-thinking reformist leadership that represented the future of China. That may be true from a trade perspective, but for Falun Gong, there is simply no evidence that, aside from a few ambiguous comments to Jiang Zemin on the night of April 25 (quite unverifiable), Zhu took any tangible action to mitigate the repression.

When it comes to Luo Gan, it is extremely tempting to read a personal element into his Falun Gong vendetta. Luo may have genuinely believed that Falun Gong posed a threat to the New China; thus, He Zuoxiu was not just his brother-in-law coconspirator, but a man who spoke to Luo's soul and his deepest concerns. Yet again, political gain probably trumps speculative psychology; Luo Gan wanted to build a superagency in the form of the Political and Legal Affairs Committee (PLAC). Ultimately he would succeed; under his predecessor Zhou Yongkang, the PLAC became China's functional equivalent of the CIA, the Federal Bureau of Investigation, and the Justice Department under a single command. So if there is ever a case for the theory that state security muscles must be used or they will atrophy, Luo's actions personified it. More than any other single individual, Luo Gan would drive the Falun Gong repression, employing creative bureaucratic and law-enforcement configurations to do so.

As James Tong, UCLA professor and premier scholar of the Chinese state documentation surrounding this period, has acknowledged, "No planning document for the anti-Falungong [sic] campaign is available for the research community outside China."[33] Yet we can look at actions and postulate that from the leadership configuration that I have described, three active principles emerged.

* * *

The first was to *avoid a moving target*. Freeze Falun Gong in its current configuration. Give assurances in public. Prepare a surprise attack.

On April 26, Auntie Sha read the official state media report. "They said: 'Falun Gong gathered at Zhongnanhai'; they didn't say we 'surrounded' Zhongnanhai. It also said that there is freedom to practice or not practice as one wishes."[34] April 25, 1999, in the minds of the practitioners, was becoming a sacred event. In the following weeks, practitioners, ever the optimists, tended to ignore Jiang Zemin's duplicitous handling of the Shanghai student protesters ten years before—and that, more recently, Jiang had stared at them from his limousine as if they were an alien life form. They preferred to believe in the power of Zhu Rongji's memo, the one that no one had ever seen. The good feeling didn't last. In the first week of May, Jennifer Zeng was approached by a colleague at work, who casually asked her whether it was true that that Falun Gong practitioners were planning to go to Fragrant Hill (a park area outside Beijing) to commit mass suicide on May 13, Master Li's birthday. Jennifer was shocked. Obviously her colleague knew nothing about Falun Gong's edicts—suicide was considered to be violence and was therefore strictly taboo—and the whole idea was so bizarre on so many levels. Falun Gong wasn't being persecuted exactly; true the PSB surveillance at practice sites was no longer hidden, and many practitioners had taken to hiding their posters of Master Li, but ... thinking it over, Jennifer wondered if the Fragrant Hills rumor was some sort of plot to make Falun Gong look like a cult.[35] In the weeks ahead, no suicides materialized. Yet strange urban legends like this—combined with tangible events such as the arrest of a Liaoning Province practitioner for distributing six thousand copies of Li Hongzhi materials on June 4—led to widespread practitioner fears that the government was in fact planning a crackdown.[36]

On June 14, Xinhua News Agency took the extraordinary step of publishing a dispatch denying that any sort of attack on Falun Gong was in the works; the Three No's still applied; large gatherings that disrupted public order were illegal, but people were free to practice Falun Gong or not as they wished.[37]

To make sure this soothing corrective didn't create any actual confusion among the party elites, ten days later the top two leading newspapers (*People's Daily* and *Guangming Ribao*) ran a series of dog-whistle editorials that did not mention Falun Gong by name but urged the party to support atheism and eradicate superstition.[38]

* * *

The second principle was to *cleanse the party leadership*. Forbid all Falun Gong association within the party ranks and associated structures such as the military.

After a long stint as a secretary of Chinese economic affairs during the 1980s, Zhang Yijie was named division chief at the General Office of the Ministry of Commerce. By the standards of Beijing society she was a high-level success, and her son and daughter appeared to be on a similar trajectory. She also made no secret of the fact that she had been practicing Falun Gong since 1994. After April 25 the other officials at the Ministry of Commerce began approaching her, in a friendly way, simply seeking assurances that she would drop the practice and quietly renounce her beliefs. Zhang made it clear that she would desist from any public embrace of Falun Gong but that what she did in her own time, what she believed—this was not open for discussion.

Zhang stood firm. The situation deteriorated. Eight months later she would be expelled from her position and from party membership itself: "I left the ministry and went to work at the International Business and Commerce Research Institute. My daily employment duties consisted solely of filling the thermos tanks with hot water, sweeping the floor, and getting the newspapers. I was under constant surveillance."[39]

Amy Lee is a young woman with a gorgeous smile who lives in Queens, New York. There was a time when she had it all. A good degree from the Institute of International Relations. A perfect home in an area of Guangdong that resembled Manhattan. A sleek black Mercedes. A PSB husband.

On the night of May 12, 1999—she remembers the date because she was preparing to celebrate Master Li's birthday with other practitioners— Amy and her husband were driving home from a hotpot dinner with a couple of friends from Beijing. They were all laughing about something when her husband heard a ring coming from his big clunky cell phone— the one where you could hear both sides of the conversation.

"Yes? I'm driving."

"It's me. I just called to tell you not to go to the big group practice for your master."

"Why would I go to the practice site? I don't practice Falun Gong, so don't mix me in with them."

"Well, don't let your wife go."

"Look, I'm a Communist Party member, so I can execute your order. But my wife is not. She has her own beliefs. How can I prevent her from going?"

"I'm just saying..."

"Why shouldn't she be allowed to go?"

"It sounds like you are in a bad situation now, yes?"

Amy's husband was livid and the party mood in the Mercedes was spoiled. But even if the bureaucrat who placed the call was enjoying twisting the knife a bit, he was also carrying out a directive that, seen from the party perspective, was deeply humane. The purge of Falun Gong from their ranks—by choice if possible, by force if necessary—was not purely a punitive exercise but a Noah's ark project, an attempt to save favored individuals from the coming storm. People were free to practice or not practice as they wished; Amy could avoid jail, the destruction of her marriage, and exile from China, or she could choose to attend the "big group practice."

Amy attended. Jail, divorce, and exile followed. Yet what seems strange to me now is that Amy, and others who were in the elite, never fully depressed the alarm button.

Rumors were passed around that the state-run media was filming a hit piece on Falun Gong in Wuhan (in fact, it was the public security agencies of Jilin Province, and they were filming *Li Hongzhi: The Man and His Deeds* in Inner Mongolia as well).[40] In Liaoning Province local practitioners even set up a second string of coordinators who could take over should mass arrests become a reality. But they were the exceptions; there was no effort to take Falun Gong offline, to cover tracks, to remove names from phone lists. Perhaps it was a testament to the decentralized nature of Falun Gong. Or maybe it was a testament to magical thinking. But whatever practitioner leadership remnants still existed in the high party levels failed at the critical moment.

* * *

The third principle was to *create an entity with the sole function of eradicating Falun Gong*. Give it command over state resources and encourage advanced methods. Above all, give it freedom to fight an unrestricted campaign.

The 6-10 Office was created on June 10, 1999. However, from a Chinese legal standpoint, nothing was actually created that day. The closest approximation we have in the Western experience is a special intelligence unit created under wartime powers. Yet that doesn't fully capture the full secrecy, or the fact that the 6-10's office was illegal according to

Chinese legislation, or, to put it in qigong terms, the extraordinary powers of the 6-10 Office.[41]

If it's inappropriate to make a pun when describing such a deadly organization perhaps we can try to define the creation in terms of a hierarchy or flow chart: The 6-10 Office was under the jurisdiction of the Central Leading Group on Dealing with Falun Gong. Or we can just say that the Central Leading Group was run at all times by a member of the Politburo Standing Committee—Li Lanqing, then Luo Gan, then Zhou Yongkang.[42] But the 6-10 Office was not created to be part of an administrative flow chart. Its raison d'être emerged on June 7 when Jiang Zemin gave an internal speech calling for the urgent disintegration of Falun Gong. The actual shape of the thing sprung from Luo Gan's long-standing conception that entire branches of the military, China's major media and propaganda organizations, and even China's legal apparatus should subordinate themselves to the cause of destroying the party's enemies (not just Falun Gong, but fourteen kinds of qigong and a similar number of religious groups, especially Eastern Lightning, a House Christian splinter group). The 6-10 Office would grow to have over one thousand nodes in China, and yet the original plan was not bureaucratic growth but blitzkrieg, marshaling the power of propaganda, arrests, sentencing, and rehabilitation under a single command while still preserving the ability to be light footed and improvisational.

No flow chart can capture the Chinese Communist Party's culture in 1999; no single party leader, not Jiang Zemin, not even Luo Gan, was wholly responsible for the 6-10 Office's birth. There is first-hand evidence that a PSB entity that had some of the same functions as the 6-10 Office had been in existence since at least 1998. Hao Fengjun, the Tianjin policeman, was recruited into the Tianjin 6-10 Office in October 1999. Over a series of interviews, spread out over several years, Hao told me his first impressions: "At that time [in 2000] our monitor room already had a comprehensive record and data on the Falun Gong practitioners. These things are not something that can be done and collected in just one or two years."

From 1996 on, human intelligence—in the form of a spy, a neighborhood watchdog, a boss—was the backbone of state security's knowledge of Falun Gong. On April 25 electronic surveillance came into its own. For example, "Auntie Jun" standing in front of Zhongnanhai received a call on her mobile phone in the early afternoon from one of the Falun Dafa Association's main coordinators, Wang Zhiyuan, looking for Auntie Jun's sister. In September 1999, Auntie Jun would receive a phone call from the PSB, which clearly indicated knowledge of Wang, Auntie Jun's sister, and everyone who had been mentioned in her conversation that day. The PSB had not mastered seamless cell-phone interception, voice-pattern recognition, and precise GPS just yet, but by 1999, the PSB was already experimenting (with an assist from several Western companies) on early forms of facial recognition—ergo the cameras that Auntie Dee was so justifiably scared of.[43] At the same time, the Chinese Internet's growth was exploding and Falun Gong was getting online, too. The Shenyang authorities claimed that they had compiled a list of over one thousand core Falun Gong based on a combination of human assets and web-based techniques.[44] Ultimately the 6-10 Office would become the primary mover in China's hacker initiatives. But back in 1999, all that was just a gleam in the eye of the 6-10 Office and a few Western corporations.[45]

Following the creation of the 6-10 Office, the only thing holding up the surprise attack on Falun Gong was the Chinese government's schedule. Already packed, it had been disrupted by the US bombing in Belgrade, the ten-year anniversary of Tiananmen, the issue of Hong Kong, then Taiwan, but late July looked promising. Travel and public appearances by the top leadership were quietly curtailed and filler articles were reserved for the front-page slots of *People's Daily* on July 21 and July 22.[46] The flexibility built into the timing came in handy, as the internal announcement of the Falun Gong ban within party organizations was leaked on the nineteenth. To cut off the inevitable protests, the 6-10 Office went into action a day early.[47]

On the evening of July 20 PSB agents fanned out to homes across China and arrested every Falun Gong coordinator they had identified or could find based on on-site interrogation, the crackdown continuing into the early morning of the next day. By afternoon, as ordinary practitioners began assembling to protest at local government buildings across China, some practitioners came back to Fuyou Street, including Luo Hongwei, the young newlywed who had marveled at the swish-swish of the cars going past on April 25.

> July 21 was like April 25. We lined up on the street waiting for an official to come so we could talk to them. But no officials came. Instead these huge trucks, one after another, came with police officers and took us away.[48]

I remember them as buses, but I got there late. On the afternoon of July 21 a few reports from the Western press that something was occurring at Zhongnanhai were making it through the Chinese press silence. I left my office, loaded up my bike basket with guidebooks so I would look like a lost tourist, and rode past the police barricades at the top of Fuyou Street. I saw perhaps five or six buses leaving. They were all packed. The last bus was held up for a minute as an old woman waved her arms around wildly trying to resist two policemen. They gave up on trying to put her in a restraint hold and simply body slammed her through the doors. The bus took off as the cops sat down on the curb to eat box lunches that had gone cold.

I don't mention this as if I had witnessed an extraordinary incident—it was actually quite routine—but because the Chinese authorities officially claimed to have *arrested only one hundred fifty practitioners in all of China by July 22*. I have no way of knowing how many buses or "huge trucks" came to Fuyou Street or anywhere else in China. But in less than five minutes, assuming each bus contained say forty practitioners, I had witnessed two hundred arrests at Zhongnanhai alone.[49]

The true numbers must have been breathtaking. I interviewed over ten practitioners, geographically dispersed, who were arrested from July 20 to 22. They all reported that by July 22 their local detention centers were no longer capable of handling the crush. In every major Chinese urban center athletic stadiums were transformed into vast holding pens for Falun Gong. In Harbin, for example, there were over ten thousand practitioners detained.[50]

Obviously, practitioner recollections were deeply personal, but the pattern from one stadium to the next was fairly similar: Practitioners were unloaded and marched into the playing field. Free of the stifling heat of crowded transport, reassured by the sight of so many other Falun Gong, many practitioners describe an initial euphoria, as if they were participating in some sort of festival. One practitioner even recognized his stadium as a location where he had marched, clad in yellow silk, in Falun Dafa celebrations a few years back.

It was incredibly hot that July. There was not enough water to go around and no food at all. As the good feelings evaporated, the police worked hard to push the practitioners into some sort of line so they could begin individual interrogation. The practitioners would organize a mass Falun Gong exercise. The police, clearly under orders, broke it up—shoving and pushing people around until they stopped. In several stadiums practitioners retaliated by singing or reciting in unison from Master Li's scriptures, much harder for the police to control. The practitioners, feeling their numbers, sensed that they had the whip hand. Yet they all thought of themselves as good citizens of the state, so it was a stalemate; at best, if an elderly woman collapsed in the sun, the practitioners could get the police to ship her out for medical attention, but the idea of disarming the police, knocking over the registration tables, escaping—these were unthinkably violent acts.

Hour by hour, the police would work through the registration process with each practitioner—name, address, occupation—then the admonition against practicing Falun Gong and the order to sign a statement affirming that. Those who signed the statement were sent home. Those who refused to sign stayed on the field. A new shipment of fresh practitioners would arrive and the cycle would begin again.

On the afternoon of July 22 I received the big news, like everyone else in China. Several coworkers burst into my office saying that they were talking about Falun Gong on television, and I rushed out to the reception area with them to watch what at first appeared to be a CCTV emergency broadcast. These were my raw impressions at the time:

The news anchor, his eyes unnaturally wide and his voice raised several steps for emphasis, stated that Falun Gong was now illegal. Chinese citizens were forbidden to gather for exercise or to practice Falun Gong in their homes. As we watched the screen, we heard a kind of scratchy shouting from the window. Sound trucks were driving around Fuhua Dasha—and apparently all over Beijing—announcing that Falun Gong was now an illegal organization. A few of Wei's female producers began laughing nervously, burying their face in their hands, muttering that they had not seen such a thing since the Cultural Revolution. The CCTV anchor moved on to the next order of business: a special investigative program would expose the danger that Falun Gong posed to the Chinese nation. As the report began flashing across the screen it was clear we were watching a highly sophisticated indictment of the movement, rivaling *Inside Edition* in production values, cinematic tone, and narrative structure. There was a series of story-lines about "ordinary" Falun Gong practitioners' lives—how they became involved, the growing obsession with Falun Gong, how they lost control of their lives, and stopped caring for their families. And finally, the minutiae of self-immolation—how they destroyed themselves through medical neglect or, in several cases, outright suicide. The bereaved spouse would act as a kind of narrator, only to abruptly break down in bitter tears that capped off each segment. (Many older Chinese can shed tears when it is politically imperative for them to do so—another by-product of the Cultural Revolution).[51]

The stories were filled in with ridicule of Li Hongzhi and Falun Gong: belief in flying saucers, Armageddon, and extraordinary powers. In fact it was an indictment of the entire qigong boom culture, supplemented by the charges that the Falun Gong splinter group had made back in 1995: Li Hongzhi was a swindler who paid no income taxes on his vast profits from lectures, books, and videos. Li could not heal anyone, but he claimed to be God. Li had forged a birth date corresponding to the Sakyamuni Buddha's. Yet the real accusation was that Li was dangerous, a power-crazed agent of American imperialism who had phoned in the order to attack Zhongnanhai from his Beijing Airport hotel suite. Everything that Falun Gong espoused was actually the opposite: compassion meant destroying themselves and their families. Truthfulness meant denying Li Hongzhi's hidden agenda. Forbearance meant that Falun Gong could not tolerate anyone questioning their beliefs. The female handed it back to the male news anchor and the cycle began again, word for word.

One of the women in my television studio actually started weeping during the broadcast. But nowhere was the sense of shock and betrayal more keenly felt than among those practitioners who were party members. One of the most interesting Falun Gong practitioners I ever met was "Lotus," if only because she meets the party standard so well in most other respects: organized, attractive, levelheaded.[52] A lecturer at North East Normal University in Jilin province. A party member since 1971. Even as a refugee in Thailand, Lotus still had a bit of the school teacher feel to her; the kid who came from a politically advantageous "Red" background—her dad was a party member—and did everything right. She had started practicing Falun Gong because it seemed to combat physical illnesses better than other forms of qigong and because she was impressed by the morality shown by practitioners in everyday life. As someone who was inclined to clean the hair out of sink traps wherever she went, when she first started living around a practitioner in 1997 she was astonished to find that someone else had stuck their fingers in there first.

In two years Lotus became deeply committed to the practice, so when she heard the rumors of an imminent crackdown on July 22 her assumption was that it was a horrendous misunderstanding, and she joined a silent vigil outside of a Jilin provincial office. After a while, the police brought out speakers, balanced them on top of the police cars, and started blasting the CCTV audio:

> The sound of that broadcast reminded me of when I was seven or eight, of the scenes when a murderer was taken out to be executed . . . these people were very bad . . . and they were about to die. . . . Their head was pushed down . . . a very scary face. The announcer's voice was like: "These are the worst people in the world. These people ought to die." The same tone as the voice coming out of the speakers. It was the kind of voice that would even make the person's family members . . . not feel even a little sorry for him. The same terrifying tone.

Inside the stadiums, the police brought in large-screen televisions and played the program over and over again. But over the next couple of days, the stadiums slowly emptied out. The practitioners who would not sign the renunciation papers were handled as individual cases. Some were sent to detention. Some returned home but remained under careful neighborhood watch in a form of house arrest. They came back to a different environment: All the papers were running investigative reports, and fully eighty-one anti–Falun Gong books had hit the bookstores by the end of August.[53] All Falun Gong organizations had been dissolved. Every Falun Gong practitioner was forced to register with local party committees and the PSB. In Jinzhou City, Liaoning Province, this included handwriting samples, fingerprints, and headshots (a resource that would likely be exploited by the Jinzhou PSB in their medical experiments beginning in 2003).[54]

As fall began, a new television special was released on the silent gathering at Zhongnanhai, identifying April 25 as a day of infamy, with ominous pans of the Falun Gong apartment where the plot was hatched; a sinister slow-mo of the practitioners, the dark soundtrack welling. A single data point, that Li Hongzhi left China for Brooklyn, decoded as an American conspiracy to topple the Chinese government. In the upbeat ending, schoolchildren paint big banners attacking the "evil cult." An anti–Li Hongzhi cartoon competition is held in Beijing. Leaders of China's state-run religions—priests, Muslims, Daoists, and Buddhists—denounce Falun Gong. Doctors wheel practitioners into mental institutions to cure them with drug therapy. Students burn Falun Gong books in the middle of campus. Workers throw Falun Gong materials into the sewer. And soldiers stand at attention, armed and combat ready.[55]

The upbeat ending was, at least on the surface, accurate. The PSB under the 6-10 Office destroyed Falun Gong books, DVDs, paintings, and posters in the tens of thousands. Much of this was, in fact, done publicly on July 29—the "Eliminate Pornography Office" set up a sort of national day of hate, where local officials gave speeches, the event climaxing by a steamroller crushing Falun Gong materials.[56] The resemblance to a Nazi book burning should have been obvious to any educated Western citizen, had it been brought to their attention. But when it came to Western media, overseas practitioners were lost in the American wilderness.

Into the fire: Falun Gong books and posters are publicly burned in the fall of 1999. Source: Minghui.

Falun Gong practitioners in America simultaneously watched two screens, a Western one and a Chinese one. For them, China would always be the default, the focus of their ambitions and emotion. Yet fear of the party's manipulative abilities runs deep (which is why we see the alienating public torture displays and the Buddhist and Daoist demarcations of good and evil—again, aimed at the mainland—to this day). But the most damaging effect in 1999 was that they were crippled in their efforts simply to define themselves for a reporter on deadline. To avoid the Public Security Bureau's long knives, Falun Gong practitioners during the 1990s had learned, by trial and error, to define themselves with their own version of the Three No's: We are not a religion, not political, and not an organization. In the fall of 1999, practitioners repeated this almost verbatim to Western reporters. The definition was a vacuum, a black hole, which non-Chinese practitioners desperately tried to fill by floating unconvincing phrases like "spiritual exercise practice." But because no one in American society believed that practitioners were dying for an exercise—who dies for Pilates?—the overall impression was of deceit. Sensing the opening, by October 1999, the party had pushed its own message to Western reporters: *They won't tell you what they are because they are hiding something. But we'll tell you what they are—they're a cult.*

The best that Western practitioners could hope for was that some reporters would split the difference and use the more neutral-sounding (but still offensive to the practitioner sensibility) term *religious sect*. From the Western cultural standpoint this was not so bad; it indicated that Falun Gong might be deserving of religious freedom and the legal rights and protections that the West universally supports. But practitioners rejected that, too, and the shorthand perception of a cult permeated American society. Congress avoided using Falun Gong practitioners' testimony in hearings, while the administration concentrated on the human rights of "traditional" Chinese dissidents and the occasional House Christian. Hollywood stuck to the Dalai Lama.

The dissident community does not like change and competition, but they particularly don't like it when a group appears to be trying to reinvent the whole dissident identity. In Falun Gong's case, not only did they reject the term dissident—they wouldn't even identify a real enemy. Chinese practitioners hated Jiang Zemin but still held out a fading hope for rapprochement with the party. From the perspective of the Tiananmen crowd, activists like Harry Wu, and the Tibetans—the big kids on the dissident block—Falun Gong was selfish, terribly naïve, and did not play well with others.

So there were a lot of empty rooms in the West. First, there were endless rented halls: carefully prepared, decorated with banners, lotus flower Falun Gong bookmarks carefully placed where each reporter would sit (as if a door prize would be handed out at the end). The press conferences would drone on with not a journalist in sight. The failures mounted: from the attempt to convict Jiang Zemin for crimes against humanity in a Chicago court to Falun Gong spokesman Zhang Erping freezing up under Ted Koppel's steely voice of conventional wisdom on *Nightline*.[57]

AN OCCURRENCE ON FUYOU STREET 105

The other empty rooms could be found in the dormitories and temples painstakingly constructed in upstate New York. Like driftwood on an ancient coastline, these artifacts testified to a dramatic "bridge too far" plan, put together when Falun Gong realized that the world did not plan to intervene in China. The structures were built to house the orphans of practitioners, Buddhist monks, and nuns, the multitudes that some practitioners intended to save by organizing a small Dunkirk operation off the coast of China. The day came but the fleet never materialized.[58]

At the end of October the party officially applied the cult label. Thirty local practitioners of Beijing fought back by holding a press conference in

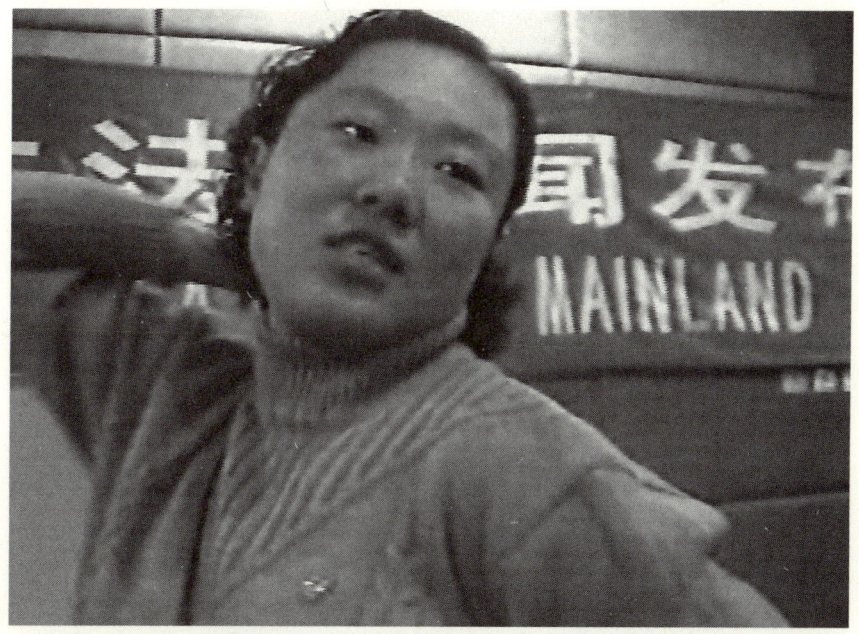

Ding Yan, a hairdresser from Hubei Province, demonstrates a police shackling procedure. The footage is from an illicit press conference held in a secret Beijing location that Ding helped to organize in October 1999. The Falun Gong event attracted press from the New York Times, the Associated Press (AP), and Reuters, but participants suffered consequences: the practitioners were arrested, a Western reporter lost her job, and press freedoms were rolled back across China. Two years later Ding died rotting in a water dungeon within Chengde City Prison. She was thirty-two years old. Source: Minghui.

October for Western journalists in a secret location. An AP intern was interviewed on camera and expressed sympathy for the plight of Falun Gong. She was fired. In fact any Western reporting on the Falun Gong crisis was either so carefully balanced and lacking in depth that it ended up subtlety legitimizing the Chinese government's wilder claims or, in the case of critical investigative reporters such as John Pomfret from the *Washington Post* or Ian Johnson from the *Wall Street Journal*, the writing was simply blocked on the Internet and literally cut out with scissors from the print editions sold in Chinese hotels. Without fear of Western contradiction, the Chinese media was free to seamlessly splice graphic images of corpses and funerals with doctored statements by Li Hongzhi and his overzealous followers to create a portrait of a cult run amok.

But something in the Chinese security establishment was surely running amok, too. First, in mid-August there was the case of Chen Ying, a freshman high school student. Because Chen had died from complications after jumping off a moving train, CCTV leapt on the chance to portray her death as a typical Falun-Gong-makes-you-crazy suicide.

First blood; Chen Ying, the escape artist, with her mother. Source: Minghui.

Chen had gone to petition in Beijing in late July, shortly after the crackdown. She was caught, but she evaded her police escort. Chen was caught again, formally arrested, and this time she was beaten up in custody for good measure. Somehow, she slipped away. Identified and arrested once more, the police began escorting Chen back to her home province of Heilongjiang, but this time she lost them in a train station. Now, after weeks of cat and mouse, she had been captured for a fourth time in Beijing—and in the early afternoon of August 16 she found herself back on a train home. She asked permission from the police guard to use the toilet. "Okay, but leave the door open," she was told. Minutes later, the police discovered that Chen had jumped from the bathroom window. When she was found, the local doctors claimed that Chen's hopeless physical condition justified cutting off her oxygen supply. We will never know Chen's physical condition; however, one point is intuitively obvious: jumping off a moving train is dangerous but survivable. Chen's leap was not meant to be a suicide, but her fourth escape. This one went horribly wrong.[59]

A rash of equally suspicious deaths followed: On September 11, Dong Buyun, an elementary school teacher in Shandong, was arrested in Beijing and detained in a school building. According to the police, she jumped out the window in the middle of the night and died on impact. Twelve hours after the incident the police had ordered the cremation of Dong's body. The window in question was on the second floor.[60]

Zhao Dong, a twenty-seven-year old male from Heilongjiang Province was also arrested in the Beijing protests. On a train back to Jixi City on September 29, the police beat him up. He leapt off the train and died. His corpse was still wearing handcuffs.[61]

On October 7, a fifty-year-old woman from Jinzhou City, Zhu Shaolan, died in a hospital following a four-day hunger strike. She was originally detained for signing a Falun Gong appeal letter.[62]

In Shandong Province, a middle-aged peasant woman named Zhao Jinhua had been arrested while working a field in late September. After nine days of beatings, electric shocks, and sleep deprivation she was pronounced dead on October 7, the first confirmed case of death by torture.[63]

Finally on October 17, a male of unknown age from Jilin Province, Wang Guoping, was reported to have jumped out of a Beijing detention center window. It was also reported in Minghui that he was tortured and had his head pushed into a toilet.[64]

On April 25, 1999, the party, in what can be compared to a superbly executed judo throw, had used Falun Gong's size against them. After the crackdown, Falun Gong had employed at least a small fraction of its numbers; three thousand practitioners had been arrested petitioning in Beijing in October.[65] But as November began, there were six dead practitioners by Falun Gong's count (the Chinese state counted only three; two dead by natural causes, and Chen by suicide).[66] Even recognizing that the information surrounding these cases was incomplete at best, a pattern was forming; what Falun Gong was beginning to call "the Persecution" had clearly entered a toxic new phase. A chill ran through the now-fragmented practitioner community. Those with passports fled to Hong Kong, Taiwan, Australia, and America, or thought about it hard. The vast majority of casual practitioners simply dropped out, avoiding any association with Falun Gong at all. By Christmas, the 6-10 Office had pinned the practitioners to the mat and Falun Gong no longer appeared to be a mass movement.

The remaining practitioners, surrounded by a world that had seemingly rejected them, faced a kind of death by emotional solitary confinement. Jennifer Zeng walked to a windy park entrance where she formerly performed Falun Gong exercises with a hundred others every morning and made a point of performing the Falun Gong exercises alone, in full public view of Beijing morning traffic, as her legs shook uncontrollably.[67]

4

SNOW

She made it through customs without incident. Now Ma Lijuan was feeling the absurdity of coming into China with nothing but a cell-phone number. She couldn't even recall the face of the Falun Gong practitioner who had given it to her; he was just some mainland refugee at a California experience-sharing conference. Maybe the guy who owned the cell phone—it had a Beijing prefix, but no one actually knew his name—was already gone.[1]

She chose the most isolated public phone she could find and dialed. Someone picked up on the first ring.

"Yes?"

"I'm a practitioner . . . I just have this number. I don't know you, but I have this number. Are you a practitioner?"

"Yes. Hang up. Right now. Don't use this number, it's not secure. I'll call you back."

Ma hung up, her head spinning. Then she waited, and she felt her heart rate beginning to slow to normal. After ten minutes, the phone rang.

"Where are you?"

"Beijing Airport."

"How many are you?"

"Just myself."

"Who are you?"

"I come from America. I'm a software engineer."

"What do you want to do?"

"I have no idea. I just want—tonight I want to go to Tiananmen Square. I just want to do exercises," she added timidly. "Look, I just want to do whatever I can do."

"It's three. You have some time until midnight. If you want to share, if you want to talk it over with some other people, I can tell you where to go. I'll tell you what bus to take and where to get off."

"Great, great."

"Maybe tonight you make a decision," the voice said.

The directions were hard to follow. It involved three transfers, and then riding a municipal bus to the end of the line, a late-Mao-era terminal at the edge of the city. As everyone got out, Ma felt a sinking, unsettled feeling. She was a bit tall for a mainlander, and she didn't want her foreign clothes to attract attention. She waited until the passengers, mostly peasants, cleared away with their heavy bundles and ratty suitcases. She had expected that someone would meet her, but there was only a village and fields and plastic bags tumbling in the cold, dry wind. Then, at the edge of the moldering concrete plaza, she noticed a free-standing public phone.

She called the landline the voice had given her. Again, it picked up on the first ring.

"Take the same bus back," the voice said. "At the eighth stop, get off. Someone will be there."

The line went dead.

As Ma got back on the bus, it hit her that the whole tedious exercise had a purpose. She was supposed to figure out if someone was tailing her. To her relief, none of the faces getting on the bus looked familiar. She got out at the eighth stop as planned, and this time, faintly illuminated in the falling light, Ma saw a middle-aged man leaning against a lamppost. She stared at him, but he seemed to look right through her. She walked to a nearby public phone.

This time the voice said simply, "The man at the lamppost."

As the line went dead again, Ma looked back. The man at the lamppost was smiling broadly now, satisfied that the American woman was not being followed, and he gestured wordlessly toward a motorcycle with seats tacked onto the back and the characters for taxi spray-painted on the gas tank. She got behind him, and he swung quickly by a large police detention center with a prominent lookout tower then into a hutong neighborhood of twisting alleys and dirt roads. The man parked on a side street, and then he led her on foot into a dead end. Smiling again, he pointed to a big gray door. Inside there was a sitting room that doubled as a makeshift office, and Ma found herself being quickly introduced to seven people, practitioners from across China: Shenzhen, Guangzhou, Hubei, and Anhui Provinces. One was a company manager, another worked at a bank. The remaining ones were students, some at the graduate level, others just starting out.

Ma sunk into the well-used plastic couch and was given a mug of tea. Her arrival had obviously interrupted an intense discussion about tactics and how they related to the theology in Li Hongzhi's book *Zhuan Falun*. One faction, the younger students and the company manager, were in favor of going to Tiananmen Square to demonstrate against the ongoing persecution of Falun Gong. They reminded everyone—Ma was pretty sure they actually mentioned it for her benefit because she was from overseas and thus assumed to be out of the loop—that practitioners Wang Huachen and Zhao Jian had been killed in police custody just a couple of weeks ago. They also repeated the rumor that more than a hundred thousand practitioners had disappeared, probably to labor camps—no one actually knew the real number.

The other faction objected to using the term *demonstration* at all, preferring the term *gathering*. It wasn't the risk that bothered them, they explained. As practitioners, we should be able to gather and practice Falun Gong wherever we like, but doing Falun Gong exercises at Tiananmen Square—even if the right to demonstrate is guaranteed under the Chinese constitution—it's just too provocative, too publicity conscious. They call us the "Falun Gong Movement." Falun Gong isn't supposed to be a mass movement at all, but a personal cultivation practice. Yes, a great reckoning is taking place between the forces of good and evil, but we can influence the outcome even as we practice in silence. The persecution is bad enough; under its strain practitioners are becoming too political, too much like an organized religion. That isn't what Master Li wants. It's what the Communist Party wants. Then the police have an excuse to crack down even more, to kill even more.

For a moment, Ma reflected on her own risks. United States immigration had made a rare—but temporary—exception to the terms of her visa status. Her state-side managers had only agreed to hold her job until January 22, 2000, less than three weeks away. But, as the conversation continued, she watched these thoughts disappear like a view from a speeding train. She had not come all this way to avoid risks, but to tell the Chinese government the truth about Falun Gong.

The Tiananmen faction fought back: We are not political. We are not coordinating with anyone. We don't know who will be on Tiananmen Square and whether any other practitioners will be there at all. But the point is: as practitioners, as cultivators of the Fa, aren't we bound to save sentient beings? Isn't that what compassion means? Well, the Chinese leadership—yes, yes, maybe even Jiang Zemin—aren't they sentient beings, too? Chinese Communist Party members—sixty-five million of them—shouldn't they have the chance to position themselves in accordance with the universe's own law of truth, compassion, and forbearance? If they oppose it, they will be punished by the heavens at the end of the day. As practitioners we know this is true. They don't. They simply don't understand that Falun Gong is good, that it is not a threat, but an opportunity—a point that brought universal nods of agreement around the room, and the factions, such as they had ever been, seemed to dissolve before her eyes.

Everyone had strong opinions, but Ma was impressed by how selflessly, how quickly they had resolved the argument. Death focused the mind. Practitioners in America would go round in circles for hours on these sorts of issues; on the mainland they didn't have that luxury. She gave up trying to guess which one of them had been the voice on the phone and simply basked in the sense of being back in the bosom of Falun Gong.

Now somebody was standing up and shouting: Let's go to Tiananmen! As everyone rose up together, Ma was hit by a wave of sweat and nausea. She placed her palm across her forehead. It was burning up. She collapsed back into the couch, and with a last glance at the faces she knew she would never see again, fell into a dreamless sleep.

* * *

Angel was on her last stop of the night, a shoebox apartment building in a sprawling residential area of southern Beijing's Daxing satellite district. Maneuvering past the bicycles, she sprinted up the three-flight stairwell in the faint glow of the streetlights on the bare walls. A warm somatic scent lingered alongside the steam from boiled noodles and a hint of Xinjiang vinegar. She fumbled to find the right key, color coded by district and postal code, and released the lock. Awkwardly balancing her squat torso against the hallway, she side stepped past what looked like a miniature tent city of neatly arranged shoes.

Inside, bathed in what seemed to Angel to be a golden light, was a large room with low ceilings. Blinds covered the windows, while the opposite wall was stacked with suitcases. In front of a massive backdrop of Dayglo green and pink floral-patterned quilts, carefully folded into tofu-like squares, women wearing padded coats were sitting on the floor in large groups talking quietly or earnestly reading together. Many looked up somnolently as Angel gently shut the inner door, nodding to some faces that she recognized. A poster of Master Li in meditation looked down from the wall just behind Angel, with a bowl of fruit placed before it, in the style of a Buddhist offering.

A middle-aged woman hurried up to Angel, breathlessly telling her in a pungent Beijing accent that three people had left this morning, but that another five had come in by the afternoon. So there is no wasted space as you can see, she said giving a quick laugh. As for the blankets, no problem, no problem. Of the five that just came in, one was twelve years old and would bundle with her mother. The men would make do, she said, waving toward the entrance to the next room.

Lowering her voice to a whisper, the Beijing woman added that the new group didn't really have anything to give and that she sensed they might want to stay a little while, maybe a week, maybe more. But, well, she didn't want to pressure anyone. It was okay, right?

Angel took off her thick glasses and smiled reassuringly, saying, "Right, right. Of course it's no problem."

Angel knew that someone else would pay more and would be happy to do so. As for the space constraints, she knew that practitioners were like water; they would fill any given volume evenly. The Beijing woman reassured Angel that the mood was good; the newcomers said that they could hear it. Angel knew that the "it" the old woman was referring to was *Pudu*, a slow, metronomic meditation music that some practitioners thought of as a Falun Gong soundtrack. Many practitioners said if they listened carefully, it was always there, softly playing throughout the apartment.

The Pudu discovery had been a kind of miracle, the sort of sign that Angel had craved for last August. Back then, Angel had no goals, no real plan, just a stone in her heart.

All through that month, the Beijing practitioners held meetings, sometimes in groups of seventy to eighty people, to discuss how to validate the Fa. Something had to be done—everyone recognized that—but the Beijingers had little clue as to how to coordinate with the country practitioners flooding into the capital city. Increasingly the Beijingers were looking inside, saying, "If you don't first move your heart, nothing around you will move." The peasant onslaught was seen by many of the Beijingers as an "artificial response" to the crackdown—an attachment to action and emotion that cultivation should have overcome. One local practitioner casually referred to the people from the countryside as "terracotta warriors," a phrase that seemed to take in their habitual blank expressions as they swarmed, antlike, to Beijing's center as if they were constructing a new imperial tomb—everyone knew that if imperial history repeated itself, they would be dumped into the earth and buried alive when the construction was complete.

Angel found herself spending less time at the meetings and more time riding her bicycle, wandering grimly through central Beijing looking for out-of-town practitioners who might need to stay at her apartment. Many did, but even that tiny operation ended with Angel's second arrest—her boyfriend's first—at the rough hands of a plainclothes policeman (Angel stupidly misread his open-eyed stare as a peasant practitioner's shock at the big city). After a month of watching practitioners of all stripes take cold-water showers and endlessly scrub the floor of the detention center, Angel was released, but now her eyes were open, too.

How radically the Beijing practitioners had changed! When the persecution started, they would go a whole day and not feel hungry, sleep a few hours every night and not feel tired. Now the Western journalists had stopped following their furtive leads; even the one autumn success, the secret press conference on torture, was organized outside of Beijing. So what role did the Beijing practitioners play? Worn down by avoiding the constant surveillance, nobody even knew they existed anymore. The older practitioners serially invoked the hopelessness of the Cultural Revolution. The middle-aged ones, Democracy Wall. The younger ones, Tiananmen. Like some sort of forgotten collective of aged cadres, they nurtured each other's fears, masking their world weariness with false sophistication and endless talk. Wringing their hands and arguing in the shadows—they were the tomb dwellers, the terracotta warriors.

And the provincial practitioners from the countryside? The stone in their hearts could lead this thing like a wrecking ball, smashing the cheap scaffold of lies that the government had erected around Falun Gong. In the meantime, they just needed somewhere to stay. It was all so obvious.

Angel secretly withdrew the ten thousand yuan from the savings account that her mother had given her for college and explained to landlord after landlord throughout the Tongzhou and Daxing districts that she was a student who no longer wanted to live at home. Paying for the security deposits and the first month's rents up front, she acquired the leases on seven apartments in seven different neighborhoods.

Angel could never get a bead on just how many practitioners were flooding into Beijing every day—she knew that there were at least four mirror operations throughout the city—but she kept careful track of her own supply chain. Each apartment had at least two rooms, sometimes three. Any single room could sustain at least ten practitioners, perhaps as many as twenty. So the rule of thumb was a minimum of thirty practitioners per apartment, usually ten males and twenty females, for a total of just over two hundred practitioners at any given time.

Of course it never worked out that way in real life. The rooms she could provide were way too few, really. The third room (practitioners were always talking about how nice it would be purely as an exercise or experience-sharing room) always ended up accommodating the overflow—always women, there were always more of them. So it was actually more like two hundred fifty practitioners at any given time, occasionally gusting to three hundred. Practitioners were healthy—of course they were—but when an apartment got too crowded, the probability of everyone getting the flu went up. Somehow—another miracle, really—they never had an outbreak of scabies, crabs, or lice. If it ever happened, Angel figured they would have to boil the blankets, and the cheap material would probably fall apart in the pot, like overcooked dumplings.

By January her money had run out, yet the apartments had become self-sustaining—to a point. Just give whatever you can really afford: that's what Angel always said, because the turnover made it impossible to calculate anyone's fair share. The donations from overseas practitioners—she never took more than she needed—filled the gap.

Security was the real problem. Early on, an apartment was busted because it was so obvious to the neighbors that it was a Falun Gong safe house. Yet the incident had a silver lining; the landlord kept in touch with Angel—even after he was questioned by the police—because she and others convinced him that Falun Gong were essentially good people. It was a double happiness; he was not only a potential sleeper agent, but a saved being.

Following the bust, Angel laid down strict rules. No more than two practitioners could exit or enter an apartment at any given time. Noise must be kept to a minimum. No phones; a practitioner who had to make a call would have to walk to a public phone, even if it was miles away. And she assigned a native Beijinger, usually a woman, to each apartment to help the country practitioners find their way and watch over things (including trying to ferret out potential spies, although a Public Security Bureau agent would have to be a world-class actor to blend into one of Angel's safe houses for any length of time). Only the appointed Beijinger and Angel had a set of keys. No exceptions.

Beyond that, there were no rules. The country practitioners would validate the Fa; no central plan would tell them how to do it, and as much as the apartments served as a base camp or a staging area, Angel didn't want to think about her people in a cold, logistical way.

A few stayed as long as a month, writing up their experiences for Minghui, or helping others record their arrest. A standard method was for three practitioners to go to Tiananmen; while one would pretend to be a tourist taking pictures, the second one would pose as a tourist smiling for the camera. Just behind the smiling "tourist," the protestor would unfurl the banner and wait for arrest. If the team was lucky, the camera would capture both the unfurling and the arrest. Because the protester might never be seen again, the unfurling pictures were valuable for relatives, friends, and Minghui, and the arrest pictures were valuable for the foreign press—or so it was believed.

The vast majority of practitioners stayed only a couple of days. They just needed a brief rest, to share a little, to catch their breath, before ... well, increasingly it was a big dark question what lay on the other side of arrest. Rumors were growing up like weeds poking through freshly dumped landfill, but all Angel knew was that these days only 5 percent of the post-arrest practitioners ever came back to her safe houses.

While Angel had been walking around the apartment looking things over, her thoughts kept returning to the twelve-year-old girl. She was out with her mother, making a call. Too bad. She would have liked to have met her. Angel had appointed the Beijing woman to anticipate and handle any security breaches and, incidentally, to assess whether anyone was mentally unstable. Recently, the biggest trouble of that nature centered on her undisciplined boyfriend; he kept bypassing the informal egalitarian ethic of the apartments, buying fancy fruits for himself. To tell the truth, it was becoming a kind of joke. He was young, that's all. Many of the practitioners were in their late teens. But she and the Beijing woman both knew that the presence of anyone much younger than that was a gray area, a potential problem.

Angel felt herself being pulled in two directions: imagining the trauma ahead, particularly if—really, it was more like when—the girl's mother was interrogated. And would they use the girl to make the mother recant? Of course they would. Yet Angel knew that no practitioner would force a twelve-year-old to be here. So she had to admit that she actually felt deeply moved by the girl's sacrifice—and it was precisely because of the girl's age that Angel felt moved, and she could not deny that either.

Angel reiterated to the Beijing woman that the most important thing was that all the practitioners were sure of what they were doing, that they were in a good place when they went; be sure to probe the twelve-year-old girl's motives in the next experience-sharing session, and make sure her cultivation was sufficient for what lay ahead. They both paused to let her words resonate. Then Angel added—how many times had she said this today?—that the second most important thing was not to go as a group or they might be arrested before they even reached Tiananmen.

Angel had finished her rounds. Top-floor Daxing was okay tonight. Tomorrow would be another day of battle, but Pudu was playing softly and the women were starting to pull the blankets down in perfect time.

* * *

Ma woke up hungry. It had been three days since her collapse, in and out of consciousness. The seven practitioners had not returned, she knew that—and there were three women who seemed to run the house. They had been present in the room; they had been looking after her, she was sure of that, too. Now, they were smiling down at her, relieved to see that she was awake and feeling better, and they quickly began serving her steamed bread and tea. After Ma had finished, they casually mentioned that they were leaving for Tiananmen that morning. Ma raised her eyebrows in concern, but they cheerily assured her that they had all been arrested before. Did she want to come?

"Yes," Ma said. But the sickness had given her time to think.

As she first entered the square, she noted that the swarm of tourists from the countryside, students, and pensioners could not hide the fact that practitioners were scattered across the square. There were hundreds, she guessed. Yet the pro-Tiananmen faction had been right. There was no coordination; they would randomly announce their presence by beginning the standing exercises or unfurling a banner while other small groups huddled, like a football team, waiting for—what? A sign that the police were overwhelmed? A pause in the action? No, it was more like they were waiting for a signal from the heavens; or perhaps, like people who have decided to step off a cliff, the cue, the knowledge of when exactly to take the step, emerges from some mysterious inner resolution.

The police had no such restraints. They had obviously divided up Tiananmen Square zone-coverage style with each defender—a squad consisting of plainclothes police, regular police, and a van—responsible for controlling a set amount of territory. In turn, the squads were coached by an unseen eye that swiveled the surveillance cameras and barked orders and coordinates into the walkie-talkies. The objective was never to let protesters reach critical mass like they had back in 1989.

A concealed camera records the Battle of Tiananmen in the winter of 2000. Screen capture from footage smuggled out of China. Courtesy of New Tang Dynasty Television.

That was the clinical impression anyway. But Ma found herself drifting back into a fever dream. Ten feet from where she stood, a young girl in a pink coat was tackled by a plainclothes policeman, her head cracking against the stone with a sickening pop. Cameras were being smashed on the pavement behind her, the shattered plastic pieces grazing her ankles. A municipal cleaner was nonchalantly sweeping it up. Manic laughter drifted by, mixing with practitioners screaming *Falun Dafa Hao!* in the distance, their calls ultimately drowned out by police sirens. Ma quickly lost sight of the women she had come with and found herself staring mutely at old people, even entire families shoved into vans. A bunch of American students from Beijing University were standing next to her puzzling over the mass arrests.

"Who are those guys? Did they steal something? It must be some kind of scam."

Ma butted in: "No, no, they are good people, good people. They practice Falun Gong."

She tried to smile at the American students, but she was trembling uncontrollably, fighting against a churning in her guts. A policeman began staring at this act of fraternization (although Ma suspected he didn't understand a word of English) so Ma drifted away.

It was all so pointless. If you moved your hand the wrong way they would arrest you. And it was getting hard to breathe. Saliva was gushing into her mouth and the air felt thick—a contagious animal stench. She didn't know what to do next. Beside her, a practitioner who had been handing out Falun Gong materials was being led to a van, his arm pulled behind him. In a final gesture, he used his free hand to toss the stacks of printed leaflets high up in the air. They came down like snowflakes as Ma wandered out of the square, a corpse walking.

* * *

Three days later, Ma woke up to an unnatural hush. Snow was falling, real snow, a rare occurrence in Beijing, and she could see through the little window above her bedroll that it was beginning to come down heavy. The other practitioners had already left, adding to the feeling that time had stopped. She lay in bed a little longer.

There was only one place where Chinese citizens could legally complain about their government; the seven practitioners that Ma had met the first night talked about it—the "National Appeals Office." One of them—Ma thought it was a student in the anti-Tiananmen faction—even advocated going there. No one supported him. Where was it anyway? Nobody found it on Fuyou Street back in April 1999. And April led to July and the persecution—that was the association—and that trauma, that negative conditioning; no matter how arbitrary, the mainland practitioners could not seem to shake it. Now they believed that to speak out, to be seen by the Chinese leaders, to have an impact, this meant Tiananmen.

But there was no impact, and the authorities said it was illegal. So what? Everything was illegal now. Even an unauthorized letter to an official could get a mainlander arrested in the current climate. But Ma was no longer a mainland girl, not completely anyway. Her US visa had to count for something. Perhaps the appeals office was only built as a symbolic pressure valve to bolster the fiction of government accountability. And yet, perhaps ... she knew she was circling around the tree again only to end up at the same branch ... perhaps the only way to expose the government's hypocrisy was to protest in the most legal, acceptable, and formal venue available.

Ma threw on her professional clothes and sprinted out of the hutong to find a taxi. She told the driver to take her to the National Appeals Center, and he nodded curtly.

After an hour, somewhere in the Andingmen neighborhood, the driver pulled over next to a series of small shops.

"Why are you stopping here?"

"The snow," the driver said, gesturing vaguely. "Just walk up the street."

"The snow is no deeper here than anywhere else. Why are you stopping here?"

The driver shook his head and gestured up the street again wordlessly.

Now Ma saw the beige institutional structure—the appeals office?—about a block away with a gauntlet of shiny police cars angle parked down the block, as if a superior alien race had landed in this old-fashioned Beijing neighborhood. For a beat, Ma hesitated, gazing at the gently falling snow. Then she shook it off, throwing open the door and striding purposely up the block.

Five men suddenly appeared around her matching her pace. Ma ignored them, but a fat, heavy-set man at least six inches shorter than her, sprinted in front of her and suddenly turned around, catching her eye. She slowed. He stopped, nodded, smiled, and said in a garbled southern accent: "ID?"

Ma decided to stay silent.

"Let's see some ID," he repeated firmly.

"I don't have ID. I have a passport."

"Fine. Show me your passport then."

"Why should I show you my passport?"

"Your ID. Show us your ID right now," the fat man hissed.

Ma almost laughed: "You have to tell me who you are and why I should show you my ID."

"I'm a policeman," the fat man said.

One by one, the casually dressed men pulled out police ID. She glanced at the unfamiliar cards, all from provinces far from Beijing: Hubei, Anhui, Guangzhou.

"Okay, okay, you have seen our IDs, right?" The fat man said triumphantly. "Now, can we see your ID?"

She pulled out her passport, and the fat man snatched it from her hands, glanced at the first page, and called out: "Shanxi Province!"

"Shanxi! Shanxi! Shanxi!" the policemen began bellowing up the street. Other police a hundred yards off joined the cry, as if they were in a cattle auction.

A middle-aged policeman had been sprawled out inside a police car with the engine idling. Now, looking like a film director enraged by a botched take, he leapt out, tossed his cigarette on the ground, and waved his hands dismissively for the benefit of the street. To Ma's interrogators, he explained in a low voice, "The Shanxi guy's not here; he didn't come in today because of the big snow."

He rolled his eyes at them meaningfully.

Then he turned to Ma and sternly asked what her purpose was in coming here.

"I want to talk to the government. I want to tell them about a very important issue."

"What issue? What kind of issue? Falun Gong?"

"Yes."

"Okay, okay," he said to the other policemen, "let her go. Even if she goes inside, she can't come out."

"Come on," he said to Ma, "here's your passport. Go on. Go!"

Ma was beginning to put it together. Each policeman represented a different province. Each was running interference to make sure that Falun Gong practitioners from their province didn't get into the appeals office. Perhaps it was embarrassing for their province if a Falun Gong practitioner actually filled out a written complaint, perhaps there was some sort of penalty to the local government, she didn't know. Perhaps the other policemen actually wanted to embarrass the Shanxi officer or get him in trouble. But whatever it was that kept the Shanxi guy home that day—the snow, the flu, or just sleeping off a hangover—it was a divine gift, because now she was throwing open the door and an old lady was handing her a form with a gesture toward a series of tables for people to write on. There were ten reception windows and two neat lines of people waiting to talk to the uniformed representatives. Ma headed to a corner table to fill out the form: age, birthplace, education, purpose for coming. Five police ambled over and began craning their necks to see what she was writing.

"Falun Gong," they whispered to each other. Then they turned to her: "Hey . . . so you are Falun Gong, right?"

"Okay," she said, staring them down. "You already know I'm Falun Gong. Why are you watching me?"

They just kept smirking as if it was a big fat joke. She kept filling out the form, but it was getting on her nerves. Finally she looked up at them and said: "You want to watch me write? I can read it for you."

Ma started reading as she wrote, top volume, as if she were giving an introductory lecture on Falun Gong to a university audience.

The policemen really cracked up now: "You waste your time! You waste your time!"

"It's okay. You can say I'm wasting my time, but I still want the Chinese government to know the real story."

One of the policemen, an older guy with a hangdog look, lowered his head to Ma's line of sight and said in a reasonable tone: "Look, I'm telling you, you're wasting your time. Just go to that room."

He pointed to a door at the end of the hall.

"Go to that room. Don't waste your time. Go there! That's your place."

Ma pushed past him to join the first line. A petitioner had just joined the second line, a tall young man with a leather jacket, holding his form. As they waited, Ma's eyes met his for a second. Then, slightly embarrassed, they both looked away. *He's so handsome*, Ma thought. And something about the motion of his eyes—simultaneously hard and sympathetic—suggested that he was a practitioner.

The hangdog policeman sidled up to her again. Pissed over the arrogant, casual way she had ignored his command, he barked, "Don't stand there. Go. Go to the Public Security Office."

"No. I have to tell the government what's going on."

"You know, you should listen to me. You don't understand. You do anything like this—you are just wasting your time because the government has already decided that Falun Gong is an evil cult."

"No, you don't understand. You don't understand what Falun Gong really is. Millions of people practice Falun Gong, not just in China, but all over the world. I live in the US. Many people practice there. It's no problem there."

The policeman unconsciously took a step back and blurted out, "Are you sure? Are you telling me the truth?"

"Why should I lie? Why would I come back? Just because in China the government lies, they declare war, they control the media. People don't know anything. That's why I came back."

The policeman looked at her seriously, trying to decide if this was some sort of strange propaganda trick. He repeated her words: "Western people practice?"

"Yeah, not just Chinese people, Westerners, too."

"Are you sure? I never felt like . . . I never heard of any Westerners doing Falun Gong."

"So . . . what have you heard?"

"I heard they already banned it. Falun Gong has disappeared. It doesn't exist anymore."

"No, that's wrong. Outside of China, in lots of countries, lots of people practice."

The policeman went quiet now. He looked her in the eye for a last second as if he was committing her face to memory, then he walked away. Ma was certain that she had forced him to think. He was a proud man, an experienced man. Now he would feel cheated by the government.

An old man standing in line just ahead of her had been squirming throughout the exchange. Now he swiveled his head back toward her, trying to remain inconspicuous while he whispered: "Quickly, run. You should run. Those people . . . they are just waiting for you. They are waiting to arrest all Falun Gong people. Quickly, run, otherwise you cannot go at all. They will arrest you—"

Ma matched his whispered tone: "No, I came from the US. That's my purpose, I want to tell our country, the top people, what Falun Gong really is. So—"

"You know, you know . . . they beat people. They arrest people and put them in jail."

"Yeah, yeah, I know that."

"You're not scared? You are not afraid to die?"

"No, not really. I don't think so."

The old man turned away, muttering under his breath, and the laughing boys started in.

"Where do you come from?"

"You come from the US? Why are you so stupid?"

"You came from the US for what? For Falun Gong?"

"You are putting yourself in a dangerous situation. Do you know the situation in China?"

"Yes, yes, I know."

A senior policeman marched in and pointed at her.

"You. You there. Get out of the line."

Ma stared at the old man's head in front of her. Then she began firmly: "No, I don't want to. I didn't come here looking for a policeman. I came here to—"

"Did you hear me? Get out of the line."

"No. I heard you. But no, I won't. Why should I get out of the line? I come from far away. I want to talk to the government."

Ma's voice was rising, and she tried to scale it back, to stuff it back in her throat. But the policeman was relentless.

"Enough! You talk to me. You don't need to talk to the government."

"No! I'm not a criminal. I didn't do anything wrong. I'm still a Chinese citizen."

The laughing boys moved in, yanking her arms behind her back, and Ma instantly realized her mistake—a Chinese citizen. She had mindlessly thrown away the foreign status, the invisible force shield. Now she was naked and everyone was staring as the laughing boys marched her down the hall to the office of public security. She glanced back at the lines. The boy with the leather jacket was already gone.

* * *

Inside the door was a vast, dark, human holding cell, big enough to hold a small army. Constructed far beyond a tall man's reach, one long safety-wired window spanned the wall facing the street, revealing only the quickening snowfall and the fading of the late afternoon light. The gray concrete floor—once painted key-lime green, judging by the few remaining flecks—also reflected a glow from the naked light bulbs in the policeman's offices, filtered through sheet after sheet of yellowed and scratched Plexiglas. The reception itself was a fortress of the stuff, with a pass through for documents, as if the Public Security Bureau had been carefully studying the design of liquor stores in the Bronx. At the same time, the reinforced door that led to the offices, barracks, and individual holding cells stood wide open, indicating the policemen's sanguine assessment of their current customers.

Without furniture, a radiator, or even a ledge to lean on, the thirty or so practitioners, old, young, urban, and rural, walked around, stretching their legs, talking about what they had written on the form, laughing, and exchanging information on how practitioners were doing in different provinces. Ma caught sight of the boy with the leather jacket, his large eyes fixed on an older woman loudly proclaiming that she was not afraid of detention and that she had made a specific point of writing that fact in her form. One by one, Ma worked through the crowd. A young girl, perhaps eighteen years old, was a veteran. She had gone to her local government, been arrested, and gone on hunger strike. Ma asked how they responded, and the young girl said they had handcuffed her and tortured her "in a very brutal way." The movement of her eyes indicated to Ma that she didn't want to talk further.

A public security representative was also making his way through the practitioners, taking down personal information, name, home province, and family history. Practitioners—being practitioners—cheerfully cooperated. Yet the fact that they were taking down the same information a second time indicated to Ma that the authorities had simply thrown away the original appeal forms. The laughing boys were right: she had wasted her time.

When the official approached her, Ma said that her parents were in the states (they were still in China). Ma was acutely aware that this lie conflicted with the truthfulness requirement of Falun Gong, at least the way most practitioners interpreted it. Practitioners might not cooperate, but they would seldom lie, although unlike the early stages of the persecution, the authorities now had to ask extremely specific questions. Yet Ma rationalized that the whole appeal process had become a sham anyway, so why should she risk getting her parents in trouble?

One by one, over the space of hours, the authorities started calling practitioners from the holding area. Ma stood next to the open door and listened to a sort of bidding process. The Public Security Bureau officers would only release the practitioner to the local police from the practitioner's province after a price had been reached, usually through a lot of screaming back and forth. It was hush money; if public security recorded the incident, it was like points on a license, and eventually the local mayor or other Communist Party officials would be replaced. Practitioners were going for an average of about five hundred yuan, an annoying expense for a local police department. Falun Gong as a protection racket; no wonder they had intercepted her before she reached the appeals office. She wondered absently how much she was worth to Shanxi. Perhaps the plainclothes policemen outside would even get a quiet little kickback from the Public Security Bureau for letting her in and making Shanxi pay.

Ma found herself face to face with the boy with the leather jacket. A little awkwardly at first, they introduced themselves. His name was Zhao Ming, and like Ma, he was a sort of foreigner, a student in Dublin, he explained in a soft, low, almost languid voice. He had started practicing when he was a student at Tsinghua University but, like Ma, he had not been in China when the persecution started. Many of his practitioner friends had gone to Tiananmen, but given his foreign status, he had come here because it was the only legal place to launch an appeal. Like her, he wanted to give the government a chance. But all of them had made a pact that they would not sign any "guarantee"—a written statement that they would not practice Falun Gong or anything like that—no matter what happened. Today he had carefully filled out his form, testifying to his benefits from the practice and how the government was *totally wrong* to ban it. He had handed it in while the police were hassling Ma, and the representative had simply asked for his passport, confiscated it, and told him to go down the hall. Ming was expecting to be met by some official he could talk to, instead, he said laughing, they were in "the hip of the tiger."

When Ma asked him about his home province, he explained that his parents still lived in Changchun. He hadn't disguised this on the form; he hoped to get a chance to say goodbye to his mother. Ma listened to all this without meeting his eyes much. Ma rarely felt competitive with practitioners over the Falun Gong practice, but this was different; not only did Ming carry a sort of effortless charisma, he was obviously in a very high state of cultivation; although he was clearly rational and sincere, he felt no fear, no attachment.

She let the conversation drop and sat down on the floor in the middle of the room, feeling in some intangible way protected by Ming's presence. There were only a handful of practitioners now, and it was getting quite dark, save for the falling snow, which was picking up a yellow glow from the lights along the street below. After an hour, the last practitioners were called, leaving Ming and her—the two foreigners—alone in the room,

Ma sitting in the middle, Ming standing near a corner. The Public Security Bureau officers were quiet now. Ma wondered if any of the provincial police would be traveling to the appeals office tonight in this blizzard.

Slowly, without ceremony, Ming began the first exercise. Looking up at the darkness and the hypnotic falling snow, Ma had a brief fantasy that the world had disappeared, leaving Ming and her like an old married couple who didn't feel the need to speak to each other.

After nine minutes, Ming began the second exercise, holding the wheel. Ma heard signs of life in the police office, then a voice say distinctly: "Someone is doing the exercises." It was followed by footsteps running toward the room. *Here they come*, she thought. *Surely Ming will stop.*

A young policeman shot across the room and struck Ming's cerebral cortex with doubled-up fists. Ming flew into the corner, coming down on his back, his limbs flailing, his head falling toward Ma.

Ming is dead, she thought, and then she had the distinct impression that he was counting the bits of green paint on the floor. And then he got up.

It was uncanny. He didn't drag himself. Ming got up very peacefully, as if nothing had happened. He walked back to where he had been standing, turned his back to the policeman, and resumed the second position, holding the wheel. The policeman, a half foot shorter than Ming, stood there for a second, his mouth open. Then he began beating Ming, systematically this time, not trying to knock him down, simply aiming punches to the teeth, to the stomach, and then bringing his knee up hard against Ming's balls. Ming went down and the policeman started aiming kicks at his sides. When the policeman started stomping on Ming's head, Ma looked away.

She knew what she should do, but she could not do it. She had lied to the old man. She was afraid to die. She noticed her face was wet, and there was a taste of salt in her mouth, and there was silence now, only the faint echoes in the empty room telling her that she had been unconsciously moaning. She glanced back to the corner.

Ming was standing up. In a steady voice he began to reason with the policeman: "I didn't do anything wrong. I just do exercises. I'm a practitioner. My job is being a student. With the rest of my time I just do exercises and read *Zhuan Falun*. I didn't do anything to interrupt your job. I'm standing in a corner. What's wrong with me doing exercises?"

Then Ming walked back to his spot and turned to the policeman, smiled, and gently touched his shoulder while he said lightly: "Doing this is not good for you in any way."

"If you touch me again . . ."

"I have no ill intention at all."

"If you do that you are a witch. I will take care of you."

The policeman started in on Ming again.

Again, Ma turned away, rocking back and forth, trying not to listen. Her flesh felt vulnerable, the concrete felt hard, she needed to pee, and the smell of sweat had invaded the room. She heard Ming's body hit the floor, and this time, it went on and on. Then silence, and for the third time, she glanced back. Zhao Ming had resumed the second position, his body inches from the policeman.

Ma was in shock. *It must be a trick*, she thought. The policeman, panting for breath, turned and walked out of the room. Without thinking about the police, or her fear, or how badly she had to pee, Ma stood up and took her place next to Ming, holding the wheel with him.

After a minute she heard a voice in the office: "So that guy is still doing the exercises? You're such a fucking idiot."

Before they finished, two plainclothes policemen from Changchun marched into the room and handcuffed Ming.

"Well," Ma said quietly, "we don't know when we will see each other again."

"Don't worry," Ming said, smiling through his swollen lips. "We will meet again."

Shanxi paid. Three days later, having signed a statement that she would never return, Ma was on a plane to California.

5

THE EVENTS ON DRAGON MOUNTAIN

Ming had scheduled his flight back to Dublin for the day after his visit to the appeals office. He would not make it. Yet the next beating—after he said goodbye to Ma Lijuan he was resigned to the fact that it was imminent—did not come either.[1]

In the police car parked outside Beijing's National Appeals Office, Ming found himself improbably squeezed in with a couple of chatty women wearing fur coats, local girlfriends of the Changchun police. The police drove them to a hotel where a couple of suites served as the Changchun police station in exile. The minute they were removed from official Beijing, the officers became surprisingly friendly. As they walked into the suite together, one of the policemen casually offered Ming a way out:

"Just sit down and write something saying you won't protest anymore. Then you can go. You know, just write a guarantee. State that you were misled."

"No. I was not misled. Falun Gong is not just something being practiced by uneducated people to improve their health. Intellectuals practice, too. In fact, it is you who are being misled by the government's propaganda. The constitution states clearly...."

The police just rolled their eyes at Ming and batted away any further discussion. They would relax tonight. If Ming was a problem for the state, let him be someone else's problem at some other time. Ming had heard that he could only be held for thirty-eight days without a specific charge under Chinese law and that many practitioners were getting out of detention without signing anything. Transforming practitioners—getting them to reject Falun Gong, confess their errors, and thank the party for bringing them back to their senses—was not yet obligatory. Ming was right, at least in his case. One good beating and a few weeks later, Zhao

Ming found himself released in Changchun, back among family and old buddies but wildly adrift.

Ming tried to retrieve his passport—he couldn't leave China without it—but the policeman who had beaten him back in Beijing (and who now assumed an air of friendship) told Ming in hushed tones: "Look, Ming, let's say you killed somebody. Well then, maybe you would have a chance of getting your passport back. But for a Falun Gong case? Right now? There's just nothing we can do."

Ming had flown into Dublin in February 1999, a year earlier; yet the dream of escape and empowerment that Ming had worked so hard to realize—the gently worn stone buildings of Trinity College Square, the hybrid vision of Western civilization, freedom, and Irish romanticism, not to mention his degree in data management and engineering—none of these had gotten started really. Starting on April 25, 1999, Ming's new world shrunk to a computer screen tracking Falun Gong's vital signs. He attended the Falun Gong European experience-sharing conference in June, but the Chinese practitioners who made it to Paris told him—as much by the way their eyes would stay fixed as by anything they had to say—that the constant monitoring on the mainland was becoming unbearable. Back in Trinity's O'Reilly Institute, Ming would stay online for eight hours at a time—never eating, drinking, or using the bathroom—obsessively punching refresh on the Falun Dafa sites, decoding the chatter and carefully phrased information about plainclothes police. He called the mainland but the voices on the other end did not dare to speak. In the reverse tidal wave that began on July 20, coordinators he knew intimately—Gao Qiuju from Dalian, Yuan Jiang from Lanzhou City, and just about every coordinator in Beijing—disappeared forever. The remaining Falun Gong voices grew, crested, and shorted out as practice sites, towns, universities, and finally entire cities went to black.

Ming responded by drafting a protest declaration for the Falun Gong practitioners of Europe. In August, he led demonstrations outside the Chinese embassy in Dublin, garnering thousands of Irish signatures on petitions. Throughout the fall, he helped to create a slick European version of Minghui, the Clear Wisdom website, which acted as a spiritual lifeline for practitioners everywhere by publishing writing that was smuggled out from the mainland. But exile was excruciatingly painful, particularly as so many practitioners posted passive, cautious interpretations of Master Li's writings. Such defeatism bewildered Ming: *Yes, Master Li had gone silent shortly after the beginning of the crackdown; yes, it was imperative to interpret the silence correctly. But didn't Master Li say that the practitioners who protested at Beijing TV in 1998 were correct? So what had changed in 1999? Truth is being defiled. We must stand our ground and defend this practice.*

By returning to China, by going to the National Appeals Office, Ming could say that he had stood his ground, technically anyway. It wasn't like he felt cheated out of some sort of great conflict with the Chinese state; the initial beating was horrible, and he had been herded onto public trains bound in handcuffs like a common criminal. But he had found no great spiritual meaning in sleeping on floors, and had anyone actually heard the things that he had come back to say?

At least he would not drift alone. In the early spring of 2000 Ming headed down to Beijing with several practitioners and formed a Falun Gong cell, which basically meant arguing—quietly, without the neighbors hearing—about what to do next. Over time, they found rough consensus.

Too many practitioners had sacrificed themselves at Tiananmen Square to abandon the front. They would *not* retreat. They would *not* go away. But they needed to make that fact clear to the Chinese leadership. Perhaps they just needed *one big push*. If one could add up all the practitioners who had come to Tiananmen, they suspected the total would actually surpass the student and worker demonstrations of 1989. If the practitioners were all there on the same day could it force the Chinese leadership to open a dialogue? April 25, 2000—the beauty of that target was that all the practitioners instinctively understood its spiritual and historical significance. Communication was unnecessary. Like migrating birds, everyone would simply show up.

On the appointed day, Zhao Ming and his small gang split up and approached Tiananmen from eight different directions. Instantly Ming saw the flaw in the plan. There was no unguarded entrance left; a wolf pack of buses and unmarked vans circled the square. The informal checkpoints manned by plainclothes police—clearly they were forewarned by the spies that permeated the remaining Falun Gong community—were so thorough that only a fraction, perhaps a hundred practitioners, Ming guessed, had actually made it onto the square. Yet something even more elemental conspired against them. It was the air: Perfectly still, yet there was something noxious floating in it, something yellow and nauseating and brackish, with tiny particles you could feel, as if a massive baby was picking apart a cheap foam mattress. Inside this blizzard the practitioners revealed their locations in a slow motion haze. Even the cries of *Falun Dafa Hao!* as practitioners succumbed to the security officers sounded as distant to Ming as if they were shouting it in Dublin. In the muffled stillness, the Falun Gong banners drooped and fell.

His own banner carefully wrapped in his shirt, Ming sat down by a lamppost, defeated. A white van screeched to a halt in front of him. Two sets of eyes—PSB eyes—stared fixedly, challenging Ming, waiting for him to exhibit the tell-tale signs of the practitioner—the inappropriate excitement, the shiftiness, the motions of fear. Ming just gave them a languid half-smile, his face revealing nothing more than a sincere indifference. After a while, the van drove away, heading out of the square. On a sudden impulse, Ming got up and headed the same direction. He had never truly believed in the Tiananmen plan. It was too limited—lambs to the slaughter. Now the thought that they had all been avoiding had emerged, and he was suddenly seeing the depth in every face, every hard corner, the intensity of every color. Ming walked out of the square grinning like a village idiot.

He took a bus to a vast shopping center in western Beijing, teeming with families, children, people laughing and shouting and running and eating snacks. Ming chose the most central spot in the crowded square, turned toward the crowd like a street performer, elegantly whipped the yellow silk banner from his shirt, and thrust the words *Falun Dafa Hao* high over his head, looking into their eyes.

People stopped and went mute as if a woman had bared her breasts publicly for the whole world to see. Then a murmur grew up in the crowd, argumentative, questioning, disturbed—yet distinctly not hostile. One elderly couple loudly proclaimed their respect for the courage of the young man before them. A young boy on a bicycle approached Ming:

"Hi. Are you okay? Isn't Falun Gong bad for you?"

"Hello. Yes, yes, I'm okay. No, it is not bad at all. The government has told people many lies. I know that Falun Gong is actually very good for you."

The child gave him a shy smile, the look of a boy who would tell this story many times. But Ming knew he had to keep moving, and he caught sight of a massive highway overpass at the edge of the shopping center. He sprinted through the crowd for the entrance ramp. Holding the banner over his head with one hand as he ran—the wind had come back of course!—he made his way to the top of the structure and held the banner aloft, now flapping exuberantly in the breeze, so that hundreds— no, thousands—of Beijing drivers could see it. To Ming's satisfaction, people in the cars began pointing and the traffic began to slow down. He found he could actually manipulate the speed of different parts of the intersection by pointing the banner at different angles, as if it was a light traced against the glass of a tropical fish tank. Then out of the corner of his eye, at the bottom of the tank, Ming noticed a police cruiser crossing the lines of the highway, breaking from the pack to pursue him. In his state of *satori*, his radiant moment of enlightenment, Ming made a lucid calculation as to how long it would take the cruiser to manage the thicket of traffic crowding the interchange. Ming sprinted back down the ramps. In the end, he made it look easy, leaping inside a taxi and flicking the magically folded banner back into his shirt.

Inside the cab Ming could suddenly put it all into words: *Stop going to the government. They have had their chance. Stop it now. Go to the people. This is the unbeatable strategy. We are everywhere. We can help everybody. They cannot destroy us all. We are the people!*

Ming took the taxi straight to the safe house and began writing up an article for Minghui arguing for the new strategy. It would be widely read if not instantly followed; the Tiananmen demonstrations would continue like a perpetual motion machine, the paralysis of the Beijing practitioners would continue, but for many practitioners—including a few who were already hatching plans up in the northeast city of Changchun, Ming had given a rationale to a practical, local method of resistance. By May, some Chinese practitioners were going door to door distributing leaflets. Among them was a double-sided newspaper titled *Falun Gong: The True Story*, which included a section called "Practitioner Jail Jokes" that Ming had specially compiled.

Ming had no illusions that his actions had changed anything. He had planted seeds, that was all. Yet he would never get to see them grow; eighteen days later, while Ming was visiting a friend in an Academy of Social Sciences dormitory, plainclothes police stormed into the room and took Ming into custody. With the influx of Falun Gong into the penal system nearing peak—probably a million at a minimum—the short-term detention centers and black jails were no longer physically viable, and practitioners across China were being led into prisons, psychiatric and drug rehabilitation centers, and most of all, labor camps.[2] Ming's resistance would play out in a very different setting than he had planned.

* * *

When Han Guangsheng graduated in 1982, he rejected teaching in favor of a career in law enforcement.[3] Han might have been a good teacher—he looks the part: he has the height and the robust build of a Manchu, the technocratic wire-rimmed glasses, and the calm, systematic mind. Over a dinner of Harbin-style cuisine, he gives me a thoughtful tour of modern China's political horizon. At times, he speaks painfully of his own responsibilities within that world.

Han sizes me up early. It's a survival mechanism. He is a man fighting for asylum, and perhaps for his life; if the Canadian immigration authorities actually send him back to China he could be executed for "revealing state secrets." I don't ask if he or his lawyer came up with Han's made-for-tabloid characterization as the "Chinese Schindler," but, thankfully, there will be no repetition of that phrase over the next twenty-four hours.[4] Instead he will calibrate his remarks to what I and my research assistant can actually consume—not too hot, not too cold.

The former director of Longshan Labor Camp; Han Guangsheng in Toronto. Photo by the Epoch Times, *December 2006.*

Coming from a dreadfully impoverished family, Han chose the masculine road of a uniform and a pistol. He took nothing for granted; every career advance was a sort of miracle, an escape from shame. There were bumps in the road, that's all: in 1989, as his force was used to round up Tiananmen movement participants, his ability to self-deceive reached a breaking point. The slogan that he lived for—"serve the people"—was blatantly being used against the people. It was not in his nature to live as some sort of secret, smoldering dissident, but when the crackdown was over, he vowed to try to use the power in his hands as wisely as he could—*to serve and protect people, to catch the rascals wherever they might be, to uphold justice.* He had that slogan drawn up in beautiful calligraphy and he hung it above every desk he occupied. By 1994, he had become deputy director of the Public Security Bureau of Shenyang, the second most powerful man in the capital of the northeast province of Liaoning.[5]

Under normal circumstances, the structure of the Chinese Communist Party's control at the provincial level is built like a factory with five departments. These departments share a specific work flow—a series of steps—that leads toward one of three outcomes: rehabilitation and release, permanent incarceration, or execution.

The first step belongs to the Public Security Bureau or PSB, which investigates, arrests, and interrogates the target. The second step is the Procuratorate, or prosecutor's office, which checks up on the PSB's work and either withholds approval, forcing the PSB to reinvestigate, or approves and then publicly prosecutes the target in court, including sentencing. The third step belongs to the Court of Justice; a lawyer is assigned to defend the target, and a formal decision is made on sentencing. The fourth step, actually detaining or rehabilitating the target, is controlled by the Judicature Bureau. The fifth and final step is the oversight of the National Security Bureau, but only if it is an international or high-profile case rather than a domestic crime. All these mechanisms collectively make up the party's innocuously labeled "Politics and Law Committee," but the main force, the front line, is the PSB.[6]

In 1996, Han requested a step back from the front line to the fourth level—the Judicature Bureau. Here the emphasis was on paperwork and presenting an image of order rather than the often-chaotic, snake-pit world of the PSB. His university background and even temperament prepared him well for this niche, yet as Han explains it, wherever he went, the snakes seemed to follow.

As the anti–Falun Gong campaign took shape in the summer of 1999, there was suddenly a sixth department in the factory, the 6-11 Office (so named because Shenyang's 6-10 Office was created the day after Beijing's). Headed up by the deputy secretary of the Municipal Party Committee, the 6-11 Office contained representatives from all of the five departments as well as officials from the party committee. Everyone quickly recognized that the 6-11 Office had upset the entire pecking order. Directives would come down mysteriously from higher-level authorities—Han did not even see them—and be instantly transformed into operational missions: intercepting Falun Gong practitioners who were on the way to Beijing to appeal, detaining and brainwashing practitioners, and sentencing them to labor camps. The PSB, still the front line, but with far less flexibility in these wartime conditions, had three specific forms of detention: one for vagrants, another for criminals, and a final one for the special cases. Practitioners were clearly special, but it quickly became obvious that the space was inadequate. With the central directive that each region was responsible for containing practitioners and preventing them from going to Beijing (a certain degree of slippage was expected, but if it went over quota the province would have to pay a financial penalty), the steps leading to long-term incarceration were streamlined beyond recognition. It was a coup.[7]

Han had no dog in the fight, legal or otherwise. He first noticed Falun Gong on April 29, 1999, when a small group of Falun Gong practitioners gathered in front of the Liaoning provincial office in Shenyang, but they didn't make much of an impression on him. Why should they? He had never been curious about qigong and he had left the PSB to stop spying on people. So he simply ignored the whole campaign until his female supervisor, Zhu Jin, called him in and told Han to set up a new reform center exclusively for Falun Gong women.

Zhu spoke of small numbers of inmates initially, but Han could see the project unfolding in his mind's eye. His bottom-line task as a director of such an institution would be simply to keep the Falun Gong from escaping. They were nonviolent, so that would make it easier. *But religious prisoners are hard to handle*, Han thought. *Criminals, those who have actually committed serious crimes—they know they've done something wrong. They are obedient. Even when they are beaten, they know it's really their fault that they are there in the first place, so they will tend to do what the police say. Religious prisoners resist. First, in their minds. Second, they want to read and recite and pray and exercise. But how can a labor camp be a place that allows prisoners to do such things? The police are used to handling the worst people in China. Their permanent, unshakable rule has to be: whatever I say, that's what you'll do. Falun Gong? They'll just respond that they didn't commit any crimes and shouldn't be in there. Worse, the police* know *they shouldn't really be in there.*

Han looked at his supervisor and blurted out the truth:

"My department shouldn't be handling them. Look: Falun Gong are not the sort of criminals that we should be putting into detention. We simply can't incarcerate them. Let's deal with real criminals."

"Han, this is an order from the top. If there are any problems you'll be held responsible."

Han nodded, but he went behind Zhu's back and escalated the matter, calling his supervisor in the court.

"I can't agree with this. A reformatory center is not the place to lock up Falun Gong practitioners. You should give me a document saying that we can't arrest these people. Then I can say—you see, the court doesn't allow us to lock them up."

The court official agreed, and a week later the court sent Han a document. But the document said *you can arrest them*. And the orders came from Jiang Zemin.

Han thought about it: *Okay, if I must set up a brainwashing center, at least maybe I can establish it in a remote location. That way I can keep them under my control and conditions will be a little better than in other places.*

In an obscure valley surrounded by hills not far from Shenyang, there was a small "re-education center" for males with the romantic name *Longshan* or Dragon Mountain. Han noted that there was plenty of room to build. *Quiet: that was important. Isolation was important, and time was important, too.* To re-educate these women, Han determined to use their families; rather than using torture or hard methods, he would play off their loneliness and their maternal instinct. He could still serve the people.

The practitioners arrived in October 1999. The sign greeting them read "Longshan Compulsory Study Class," and Han firmly instructed the guards to tell the practitioners on the very first day: *You are not criminals. We will not regard you as criminals.*[8]

A few nights after Longshan Labor Camp had opened for business, Han drove in for a surprise inspection. Above all, he wanted to make sure that the male guards were staying well away from the women's sections after dark. Han entered one of the rooms in which the practitioners were locked, said hello, sat down on a bunk, looked them all in the eye, and posed the obvious question:

"Why do you insist on practicing Falun Gong? You have children. You aren't home to look after them. You have elderly parents. You have husbands. Why aren't you at home taking care of them?"

"Yes, yes, Mr. Han, but once I started practicing Falun Gong, my life was raised to a new level."

"Mr. Han, do you see me? Look at me. All the illnesses I had before I started practicing are now gone. I don't even need to take any medicine. Even if you were to pull a gun on me right now, even if you were to threaten to shoot me—I'm not afraid of you."

"Come on ladies. I wouldn't dare to pull a gun on you. I wouldn't do it."

In spite of all the spiritual machismo being thrown around, Han noticed two things: First, it didn't matter if they were peasants, workers, professors, or students, their group cohesion was solid. Second, they were all essentially good people. Many of them were clearly from well-educated families, too (the fact was that Han would never have talked to ordinary criminals in such a gentle way). Yet Han had not come into the "Women's Group 1" cell unprepared. He had seen their files. Some of the women had children who were still breastfeeding. They left the kids at home anyway and went to Beijing to petition. They knew they would be arrested. Han didn't understand that. But he knew if he couldn't refocus the women, his maternal-instinct theory of transformation would be in jeopardy.

Han's theory would never get a fair test because the lab conditions kept changing; it was said that there were only five hundred practitioners in the Shenyang Laogai system, but the amount of women coming into Longshan—mostly picked up at Tiananmen or on their way—dwarfed the numbers he had agreed to take. The other camps were already asking if they could park their practitioners in Longshan during the Chinese New Year Festival.

Longshan already had a contract to produce Christmas hats for Western export. Han needed skilled prisoners—yes, and he needed quiet and isolation—to make that quota on schedule. Instead he would get distractions: lice, infectious diseases, and backed-up sewage. And he had lost the time element, too. The only way to reduce the overcrowding was high turnover; the first group of women had to transform, to reject the practice, to sign the *three guarantees* (a series of promises and rejections of Falun Gong that the party required) to make room for the next group. Otherwise cells that were meant for two would have to accommodate ten or more. Crushed together like that, ordinary prisoners might turn on each other, but Han suspected the practitioners would bond, and then, like a reactor core, go critical.

Longshan Labor Camp checkpoint. The paper on the tiled floor next to the guard's table is actually a popular poster of Li Hongzhi, the founder of Falun Gong. Visitors and family members were told to step on it or they would not be permitted to enter. Source: Minghui.

* * *

In terms of the practitioner death-rate, Liaoning Province, home to Shenyang and Longshan, is high; during the first four to five years of the Falun Gong repression, 341 confirmed fatalities by torture are recorded. That number is undoubtedly a gross underestimate, but it places Liaoning in perspective as the third most deadly province, at least in terms of conventional deaths, out of thirty-three provinces or administrative regions in China.[9]

The word *Laogai* translates as "labor-reform." It means labor camp. When we speak of the *Laogai System*, we are referring to a patchwork of long-term detention centers, jails, prisons, "black jails," custody and drug rehabilitation centers, shelters, psychiatric hospitals, and labor camps.[10] While any legal process was a hit-or-miss proposition for Falun Gong at best, practitioners tended to fear labor camps in particular because they could be committed for a three-year term without any trial at all. Liaoning Province had a robust Laogai System and several institutions have a particular resonance for practitioners: Dalian Reformatory, Dabei Jail, Zhangshi Reformatory, and above all, Masanjia Labor Camp.[11]

Masanjia deserved its fearsome reputation. It not only contained vast amounts of practitioners, but it was also clearly in the vanguard of transforming practitioners—a 90 percent transformation rate. Han could not compete with that; unlike Masanjia, Longshan practitioners were not integrated with violent criminals, making it a softer camp than many of the others. Yet, from the party's perspective, Longshan could be said to be in the lower range of statistical respectability—not in terms of transforming practitioners, but in terms of torturing them.

Following an initial round of what might be called *shock orientation*, Han's deputy publicly announced to the Longshan practitioners on November 25, 1999, that there would be no further use of electric batons.

Yet I can make the following statement with reasonable confidence: throughout Longshan's first year of operation, from October 1999 to October 2000, sixteen out of sixty individuals, all Falun Gong women, reported that Longshan's guards used high-voltage electric batons to shock and burn their skin. The ratio of electric shocks, approximately one out of every four women, corresponded to the widely held belief among the guards that 75 percent of the women were victims who had been callously misled by Li Hongzhi, while the other 25 percent of the women were "diehards" with their own mini cult (while I do not agree with the guard's characterizations, their ratio is roughly congruent with my own observation that the majority of practitioners were transformable whereas roughly 25 percent of them, those who were able to withstand pain for various reasons, could be considered—initially, at least—to be "nontransformable"). In the majority of the Longshan cases, the electric baton was aimed at the woman's face, particularly the mouth, occasionally the nipples, and on at least one public occasion, a woman's exposed anus. The sexually charged nature of these sessions was made explicit in at least three cases where a clothed male guard forced female practitioners to simulate fellatio on him while he administered electrical shocks on their backs; the same guard is reported to have forced a twenty-seven-year-old woman to extend her buttocks and perform the motions of sexual intercourse.

While Longshan male prisoners were not forced to make explicit sexual displays, they did not evade pain and physical injury. Yu Pan, a male practitioner, attempted a lawsuit against Bo Xilai, then governor of Liaoning Province, on the basis that the guards had shocked Yu with a forty-thousand-volt device that appears to have been acquired in New Zealand. Yu claims that he was brought to the point of death. It is also noteworthy that Longshan rivaled Masanjia in its organized reaction to hunger striking. While Masanjia guards favored force-feeding by a plastic tube extended down the throat, Longshan brought in skilled doctors who accomplished the same end simply by using brute force and two metal spoons.[12]

Director Han's intention to use the maternal-instinct method of reuniting families was a bust—not because the women were particularly callous or detached but because their family members reported massive police harassment in their homes. The constant reports of suffering and public embarrassment alienated everyone in the family, goading the prisoners toward the Falun Gong equivalent of civil disobedience—reciting the Fa and exercising in full view of the guards. The police would respond to this breach of discipline with electric batons. The practitioners would refuse food. The guards retaliated by using the "medical method" of feeding to shatter their teeth. The entire downward spiral was accelerated by the extremely crowded conditions—by the end of the first year, approximately twenty women per cell would commonly sleep like a row of industrial spoons (in the West a similar cell would house only two people). The hunger striking was promoted by the general sense that the

THE EVENTS ON DRAGON MOUNTAIN 145

food, consisting of brackish, contaminated water and buns made with spoiled flour, wasn't worth eating anyway. By the summer of 2001, Longshan was hit by a massive diarrhea epidemic, which ended only when the Falun Gong practitioners were allowed to take over the cooking.[13]

The sign at Longshan now read "Psychiatric Correction School."

According to a letter smuggled out of Falun Gong in China, in October 2000 Masanjia guards stripped eighteen female Falun Gong practitioners and threw them into the men's cells to be raped. This practitioner woodcut consciously employs older popular resistance conventions to depict the scene. Similar allegations have emerged suggesting that female practitioners were transported from Longshan to the all-male Zhangshi Reformatory, although the timing of that event may have occurred after Director Han left China.[14] Source: Minghui.

* * *

Han Guangsheng received a call from the deputy commissioner of the Liaoning Province Judicature Bureau. There were ten female Falun Gong practitioners at the Masanjia Labor Camp. It was "not too suitable" for them to stay there. Come and get them.

Han received a grim satisfaction from the call. Ever since the autumn of 1999, Han, and every other labor-camp director in the province, if not in all of China, had been told that Masanjia was the model for transformation—it had even won an award for fifty thousand yuan. Following Masanjia's lead, the transformation rate for all camps was going to be 90 percent starting in 2002—an ambitious target. (But what did it mean? Would anyone really check? And if a practitioner was transformed but started distributing truth-clarification materials upon release, was he or she really transformed in the first place?) The bottom line was that all the other camp directors were expected to *learn from Masanjia*. Sick of hearing about Masanjia, Han sent his assistant director, Zhang Xiansheng, "to learn." Zhang reported back:

"As I see it, Director Han, Masanjia's experience in transforming practitioners consists of just one thing: using electric batons. We can do the same."

"Zhang, mental problems cannot be solved through beating, and I absolutely forbid you to use electric batons."

Zhang's "findings" were utterly banal. Everyone knew what Masanjia's stellar reputation was based on; it was like those predictable meetings hosted by Deputy Commissioner Lin Bizi. The officials would be seated around the circle according to the size of their cities—Shenyang, Dalian, Anshan, and so on. Then Lin Bizi would say: "Today we are here to hold a meeting to summarize how we have done in the last period in our work of transforming Falun Gong practitioners. Let us exchange experiences and talk about how to do the work going forward." The Masanjia director would speak up: "At Masanjia we 'strictly supervise'; we make 'strict requirements'; we are 'carrying out transformation'"—all euphemisms for flat-out torture. Han felt the personal pressure—it was always the other directors being invited to speak first. Whatever seniority he had accumulated over his years of law enforcement was worthless compared to any young upstart with a cattle prod.

Yet Han was also annoyed by his informal meetings with practitioners. They would solemnly quote Jiang Zemin saying: *If a practitioner dies, call it suicide.* Well, Han reasoned, it was possible that a small number of policemen said this while delivering a beating, but Han had never heard such a quote through any official channel. *Anyway,* Han thought, *Jiang wouldn't say such a thing. Nor would Luo Gan or any other official. These things can't be stated without embarrassing China in front of the world.* Learn from Masanjia—*that said everything just fine.*

Now Masanjia was sending Han its factory rejects, the ones who couldn't be transformed. Han saw a glimmer of opportunity, both for curbing Masanjia's methods and for taking the director down a peg, so Han eagerly strode into the camp one evening to meet with two practitioners, Zhao and Ren, average-looking women probably in their thirties. Han shook hands with them and said:

"Sit down. Let's chat. You've suffered a lot in Masanjia, haven't you?"

They started sobbing immediately and began recounting how they had been tortured. They had to crouch half standing and half sitting in the bathroom, had to walk barefoot in the snow, and so forth and so on. Han ordered the police to give them both pen and paper and told the women to please write down everything they had been through.

That night, as Han drove home, it all caught up with him. His heart felt heavy. *We say "serve the people," but how could people be treated like this? Masanjia is such an evil, evil place.* After a week Han received a thick pile of paper from Zhao and Ren. He read it and was suddenly angry again— *Masanjia is just so inhumane!* But it was pointless to actually complain about the overall campaign against Falun Gong, so he thought, *I'll just do this one little bit for the women.* Han attached a note to the practitioners' accounts, saying: "I'm just passing on these two statements from Falun Gong practitioners, please take a look." And he had the entire package delivered to the head of the Liaoning Province Judicature Bureau.

What had Han hoped to accomplish in his note? The meaning of it

148   **THE SLAUGHTER**

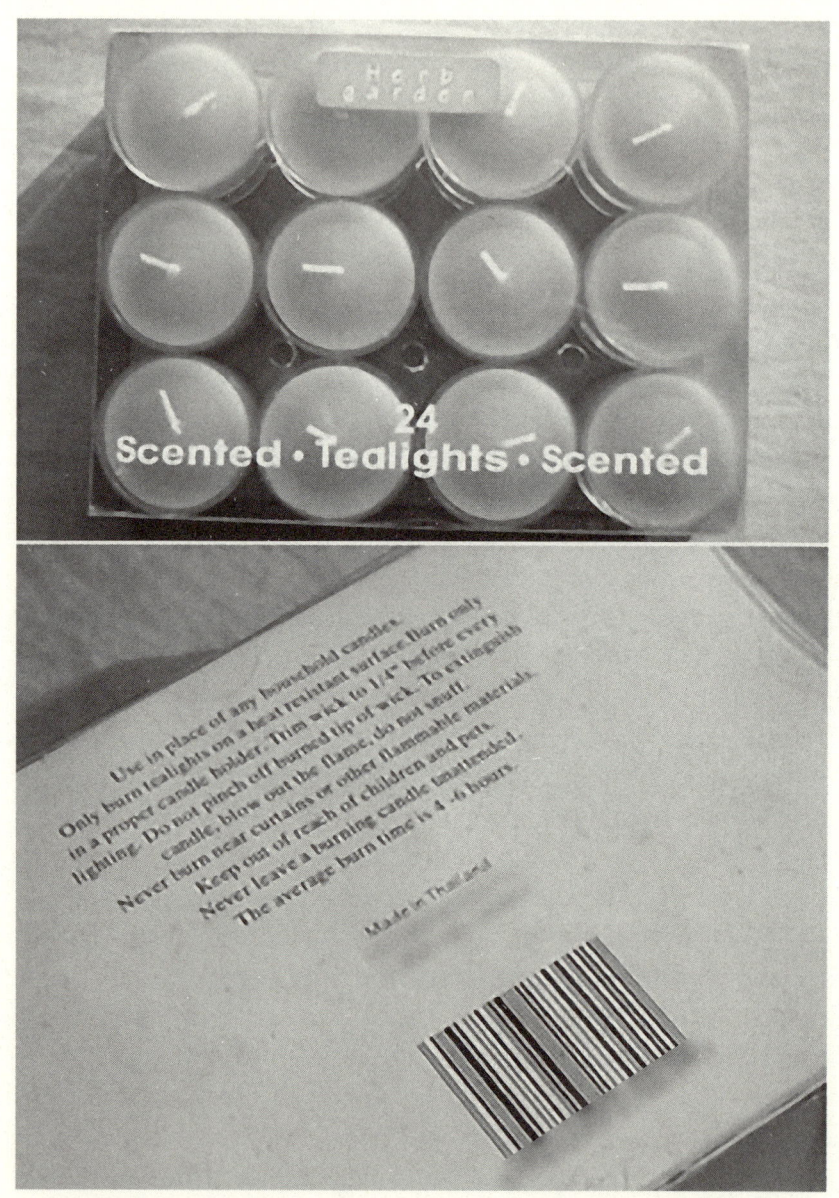

"Scented Tealights" marked "Made in Thailand" produced in Longshan Labor Camp. Under Director Han, Longshan began wax processing and candle assembly in July 2001. According to the prisoners, the transparent glue that they used to seal the boxes of candles was toxic. Source: Minghui.

was: *I can't control what happens in Masanjia but you should.* Did it work? In the end, Han reported: "The head of the Liaoning Province Judicature Bureau was very unhappy with me—and, for example, didn't give me the holiday bonus that I should have received, while others received it."

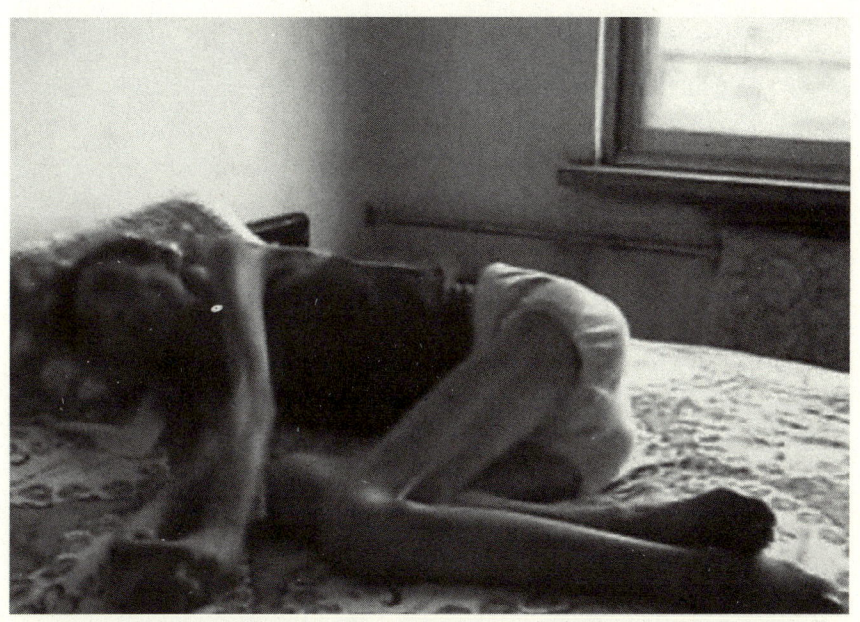

The Longshan candles were placed in large boxes that had to be carried out to a loading zone. Ren Shujie, shortly after her release in December 2004 from Longshan, gave a brief interview as she lay in bed. "I carried forty boxes in one day," she said. Nine months later, at the age of forty-two, Ren was dead.[15] Screen capture from footage smuggled out of China for New Tang Dynasty Television. Courtesy of New Tang Dynasty Television.

※ ※ ※

Director Han was furious. It was mid-summer 2001 and a flunky had just dropped the news that there were over forty Falun Gong women who were not eating or drinking at Longshan. Han had to pry the rest out of him: Fifteen year old girl. Wouldn't sign the guarantee. Electric baton. Taken back to the cell. Han erupted. "Right, well, what did you expect? How many days ago did this happen exactly?"

On the drive over, Han thought about how stupid the whole system was. The news had to trickle up through six levels of officials in order to reach him in the chain of command, like the military. And it was like herding children; you tell them *you are not allowed* to take other people's things, *you are not allowed* to fight. *But one of the kids takes something from someone else or starts a fight. But no, he won't dare tell you about it because he knows you will take away his stuff. So he shuts up everyone else, too. Yes, the electronic batons are there in the center—standard equipment normally found in Chinese detention centers. There are guns, too, but that doesn't mean the equipment is there for the policemen to play with.* Han had been explicit on that point. *Well—now they will lose their toys.*

When he arrived at Longshan, Han went directly to the hunger strikers: "I want to criticize myself. I do not stand before you."

The hunger strikers had two demands: No more electric batons. And remove the deputy head of the center, Bai Suxia.

"I will do both right away."

Han went back to his office on July 15, 2001, and filled out the paperwork transferring Bai Suxia to another reform center that had no practitioners. And he gave an internal order that all the electric batons should go back to storage.

* * *

Few details have surfaced about the fifteen-year-old girl, Han Tianzi. The story of how a minor ended up in the interrogation office of a labor camp has never been satisfactorily explained. It was said that she went to Beijing to protest, possibly to the National Appeals Office. The Longshan guards clearly knew the girl's real age; they publicly threatened to send her to a youth reform school.

One practitioner who was present in the same interrogation office describes Han Tianzi as a sort of model nontransformable, firm about not signing the guarantees and prone to repeating certain phrases—"Falun Dafa is a righteous Fa. Restore my master's reputation. Release all the detained Dafa practitioners unconditionally"—even when a Longshan policeman brought out an electric baton and cleared the office.

Han Tianzi told the policeman that she was a minor and had certain protections under the law. The policeman ignored her precocious appeal and used the remaining three to four hours in his shift to torture her with the electric baton. The policeman's bellowing and the girl's screams and moans could be heard quite clearly throughout the women's quarters, so when Han Tianzi suddenly went quiet, many practitioners became frantic with anxiety. Han Tianzi had not died. She had simply lost consciousness, so the guards escorted her back to the cell. Yet the state of the girl's body was so appalling that most practitioners were too upset to eat the camp supper. The girl's abuse ignited the spontaneous hunger strike that ended only after Director Han's unusual intervention. What ultimately happened to Han Tianzi remains a mystery.[16]

About a month after Director Han's Longshan "correction" there was a new incident: a practitioner in her early fifties named Tong Chunshi was tortured so severely through force-feeding that her esophagus was permanently damaged. Tong died of complications in 2006.[17]

On August 22, 2001, the Longshan guards released Wang Hong, a thirty-nine-year-old nontransformable to her family, with a single command: collect her body. Wang was alive, but she was covered in black and purple bruises. Nine days later, Wang was pronounced dead from acute kidney failure.[18]

* * *

Assembling scented tea candles and snowflake decorations were decent long-term contracts for Longshan, but too seasonal. In August 2001, Han went to the United States to drum up new business. I asked him if anything happened while he was away.

"A female practitioner jailed in Longshan named Wang Hong died of a serious illness nine days after release. Had she been beaten or not beaten? I didn't know. Anyway, I was very sad. Even though I wasn't at my work unit at the time, I was, after all, the director."

Han returned and left again in mid-September 2001, this time for an international legal exchange in Canada. It was a well-earned junket for Han; in previous human rights talks between the People's Republic of China and the United Kingdom, the head of the British delegation had asked Han to lead a tour of Longshan. The British had apparently left with a good impression. So while the other camp directors might look at Han as a bit of a squish, the higher ups in the party saw him as a potentially useful ambassador for the Laogai System. Han claims that all the while he was debating whether or not to leave China for good. But the decision may have been made for him. On September 29, Han's role in the case of Han Tianzi was revealed on the Falun Gong site Minghui.org. The effect on China's international image of a fifteen-year-old girl being tortured with cattle prods could have disastrous potential if it were to be picked up by the mainstream Western press (predictably, it was not). But the potential impact on the party's internal propaganda war of a weak director surrendering to some crazy women was far worse, particularly where it was continuously claimed that victory over Falun Gong was just around the corner. Han had no clue as to how the news had gotten out of Longshan—one wonders if Wang Hong's body also contained a written message—but it didn't matter. The potential effect on Han's career was incalculable. He would never return to China.

There is much that Han does not know—or possibly chooses not to think about—when it comes to his final year as Longshan's director. Why were 90 percent of the practitioners moved out of Longshan within his last year if the transformation rate was a fraction of that? Where did they go? Why were medical doctors called in to administer force-feedings?

Han sidesteps this sensitive line of questioning. It's understandable; what possible advantage can there be for a man without a country to speculate on forced, mass disappearances? And Han reads me correctly: I know that Longshan was only a mid-level camp in terms of its brutality, compared to big brother Masanjia. Han's claim to be a restraining force has some credibility, too, given the numbing horror of what the Longshan guards did to practitioners such as Gao Rongrong after his departure.

Yet Han cannot stop his own mind completely; he is a man quietly haunted by the micro-world of Longshan, by the practitioners who died

THE EVENTS ON DRAGON MOUNTAIN 153

The legacy of Longshan; inmate Gao Rongrong was subjected to extreme electric shocks in May 2004. A year later she was dead. In the West, Gao's face would became the first truly effective symbol of the Falun Gong repression. In this Epoch Times *photo, two practitioners in Los Angeles publicly display before and after pictures. Photo by Epoch Times, December 2005.*

under his direction. So he does something for us both, something that makes the room feel comfortable again. He pivots to the macro-term "the persecution"—consciously using the Falun Gong phrase, invoking the sense of great historical forces at work, implicitly transferring the accumulated guilt from the individual to the party itself:

> To be an official under the Chinese Communist Party there is a precondition.... If one has a conscience or a human heart, it's impossible to carry out such work for a prolonged period.... In the beginning, many people are like me—they have good intentions, they want to be an honest and upright official, they want to do their best for the people. But once they become officials? It's like jumping into a river ... you can't go against it. You can only go with it. If you swim well, if

you go with it, you will move forward.... You see the sky is very dark. It's about to collapse. But you can't to do anything to keep it up. You want to protect your area, put it under an umbrella, don't let the people below get drenched. But you can't do it—your umbrella is too small; it cannot block wind and it cannot block rain. And since you can't block it, you just destroy yourself.

For Christmas 2001, Longshan Labor Camp was awarded a four hundred thousand Yuan bonus.[19]

* * *

By 2000, Officer Hao Fengjun enjoyed all the perks of the Tianjin 6-10 Office: personal command over eighteen regional public security bureaus, a lavish budget, high-end computers, and unusually sophisticated software, far superior to that found in any Chinese police department.[20] For years, practitioners of Falun Gong thought of themselves as protected by the amorphous floating world in which they traveled—a world without membership lists, authority, or hierarchy. Yet they were being watched, infiltrated, and studied. Before 1999, Falun Gong practitioners hadn't systematically used the Internet as an organizing tool either. But now that they were isolated, fragmented, and searching for a way to organize and change government policy, they jumped online, employing code words, avoiding specifics, communicating in short bursts. But like a cat listening to mice squeak in a pitch-black house, the "Internet Spying" Section of the 6-10 Office could find their exact location, having developed the ability "to filter and jump automatically" as a result of what Hao describes as a joint venture between the Shandong Province Public Security Bureau and a prominent American technology company.[21] What emerged was a comprehensive database of people's personal information—including 6-10's Falun Gong lists—and a wraparound surveillance system that was quickly distributed to other provinces. The Chinese authorities called it the *Golden Shield*, and Hao used it on a daily basis. "As far as following practitioners," he says, "the Golden Shield includes the ability to monitor online chatting services and mail, identifying IPs and all of the person's previous communication, and then being able to lock in on the person's location—because a person will usually use the computer at home or at work. And then the arrest is carried out."

Hao's job was to round up specific high-profile practitioners who had "slipped the net." The 6-10 Office usually had amassed camera surveillance of the individuals, taped at various public gatherings, which could be matched up with real-time surveillance cameras using advanced facial recognition technology. These, in turn, could be linked to the individual's personal history or *danwei*. "As long as we had . . . video footage of the people involved," Hao told me, "we would be able to get their personal information from our computer system." Hao's responsibilities ended with the target's capture, and he had little involvement with the practitioner interrogation process. Surfing the Internet—unlike most Chinese, he could access anything he liked—Hao closely examined the graphic photos of torture victims that increasingly were showing up on overseas Falun Gong websites. He concluded they were all simply clever fakes.

Late one evening in early 2001, Hao's director called and said there had been some sort of problem with a practitioner over at the interrogation center. It had been snowing hard that day, so Hao's drive over was tense. Inside the dark compound, the interrogation room was blazing with light. The policeman in charge was just sitting there with a blank expression.[22] Next to him, on the table, was an iron bar used at construction sites, grooved, about a foot long.

"I'm Hao Fengjun. From the 6-10 Office. I'll be taking over this case. Please step out now."

The policeman nodded and casually walked out of the room, leaving Hao alone with a diminutive middle-aged woman, her legs tied to a metal chair, her face twisted down, and her hair strewn across her eyes as if she was trying to avoid the light. Then, like a cornered animal suddenly looking for an opening, her head jerked up and their eyes locked.

It was his mother.

"What is your name?"

"Sun Ti."

The illusion had lasted but a fraction of a second; Hao chalked it up to the sudden movement and something familiar (and wretchedly sad) in her eyes. But Sun was just a middle-aged woman, about his mother's age and build, so Hao stuck to protocol:

"Do you have any injuries?"

Sun started crying and shaking: "You can question me. But you can't beat me like this."

"Where are you injured?"

"My back hurts pretty bad. Please take a look."

"I'll step outside. I'll call a female policewoman to come in and look you over."

A lot of Sun's clothes were off already. Now she started pulling off her shirt.

"Look, I'll step out and call a policewoman in."

"It's okay. I'm old. I don't care about you seeing me. I want to show you what they did."

"I want to step out."

"No problem, no problem, just come here. Take a look."

There was a four-inch gash on her shoulder, oozing dark blood. All the way down to her waist was a swollen mass—the skin wasn't gray or brown or purple, it was all just crazy black, even under the harsh light. Hao didn't get it; he'd seen overseas photos of Falun Gong practitioners who were beaten to the point that their skin turned black and purple yet in his entire law-enforcement career, no matter how he beat people, it had never turned that color.

"How did they beat you?"

"They used that iron rod. This afternoon."

"Who did it?"

"That policeman who was sitting there."

"Auntie, I'll take you to the hospital right away."

He nearly had to carry Sun to the squad car, and driving slow on the icy roads, they made it to the hospital around one in the morning. The doctor on duty treated and bandaged the wound. Clearly the infection had just started and the fever would come later. Hao drove Sun back to detention.

The fever built overnight, and by the next day she was back in the hospital. Hao visited her. Then he came the next morning, too. Then it became a routine, where Hao would stop by every day just to comfort her. Initially Sun would only talk about Falun Gong. Hao thought that was weird, then he thought it was boring, then, after a few more days, he had to admit he didn't really mind it. Anyway, as Sun grew to trust him, she talked more about her husband, already in prison for practicing Falun Gong, and above all, her fourteen-year-old daughter, "pretty and smart" but now homeless and alone on the streets. Sun would end up begging Hao to stop them from persecuting Falun Gong, to stop ripping a mother apart from her daughter—"just be human," she would say. Hao nodded, but he told her there was really nothing he could do. Day by day, Sun's fever was receding. When she was well enough, she would be sentenced to eight years in prison.

Hao's fever had just begun. There was nothing weird about Sun; she was normal. But Hao knew, from the moment their eyes had met, that he no longer was. It would take four years for the infection to become acute, but the defection germ had entered his system.

6

ALIVE IN THE BITTER SEA

I'm not quite sure which eye Wang Yuzhi is using on me tonight.[1] One of them was dislodged during a session with the Public Security Bureau, and it doesn't really focus anymore. Anyway, she's easily the toughest dissident I have interviewed. Her voice is chesty. Her body, which appeared willowlike in some of the early post-labor-camp photos, now carries the robust health of a peasant girl meeting her first tractor. She doesn't smile often, but when she does it's incredibly open, appealing, and somehow carnivorous. She catches me staring. "These teeth are fake," Wang says bluntly, "I bought them overseas." The guards knocked out the originals during force-feeding.

Wang was born into an accomplished Chinese family in the far northeastern city of Harbin. Yet she forged her own entrepreneurial success. Harbin Eastern Electronics, her computer and office-supply store, used to fetch Wang a million yuan in profit every year. She claims Falun Gong was good not only for her health and her relationship with her husband and her ten-year-old son—it was also good for her business reputation; the customers knew she wouldn't rip them off.

For the next several days, Wang is going to give me a very accurate, just-the-facts account. She's got a flair for comedy, but she's not the dramatic type: no tears, no unnecessary dwelling or obsession. She moves on, always. I suspect that is part of the reason that she is still alive. So it seems slightly incongruous that she wants to talk about her dreams. She leads off with a premonition.

When Wang was a little girl during the Cultural Revolution, the Red Guards accused her father of harboring foreign connections. He refused to sign a confession statement, and because he was going to be there for a long time, Wang was allowed a brief visit at the prison. She had never

160 THE SLAUGHTER

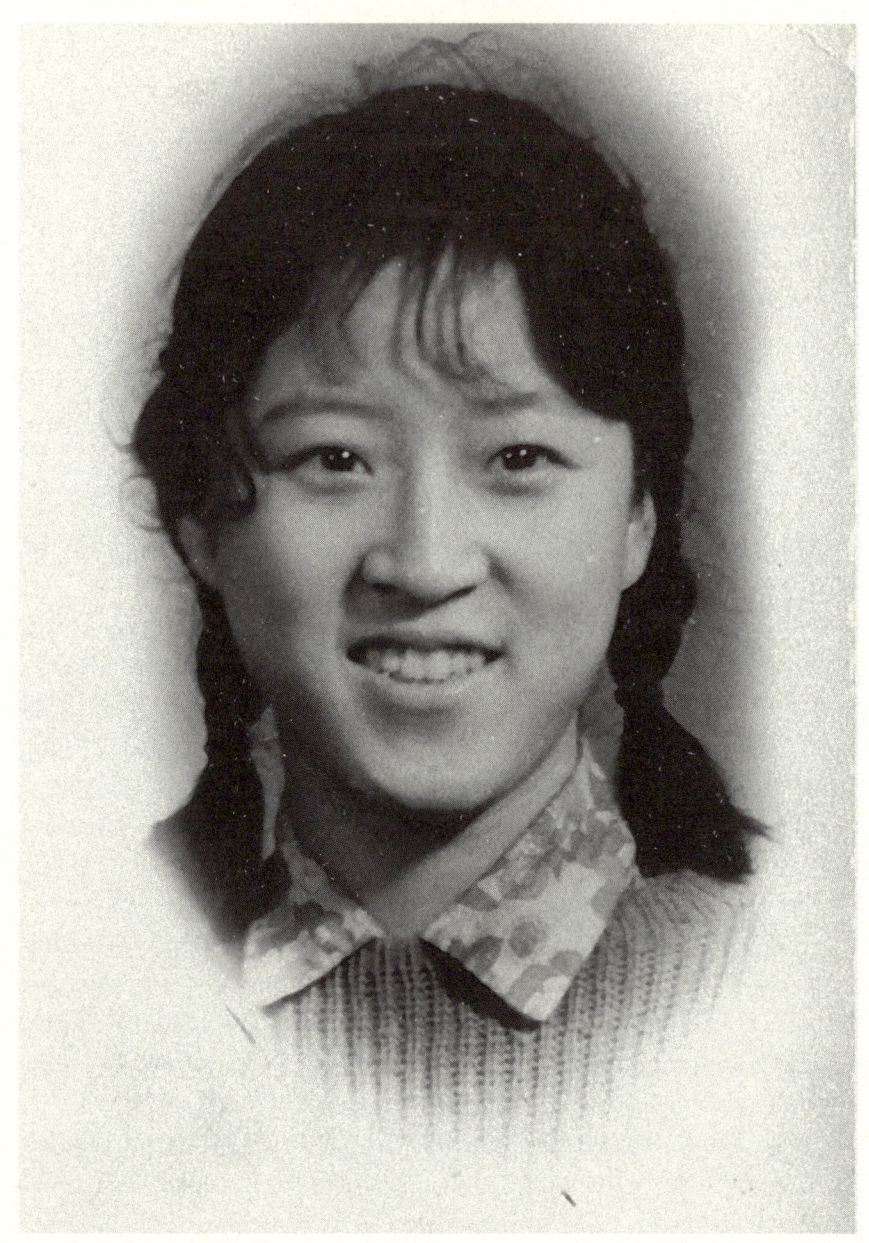

Wang Yuzhi at the time of the Cultural Revolution. Courtesy of Wang Yuzhi.

seen one before, and just as her dad was led in, the guards grabbed a prisoner and smashed his head into the bars inches away from her face. Like an immortal dismissing the illusions of the world, her dad's face remained calm, reassuring, filled with love for her.

If the prison incident imprinted, or if resistance simply lay buried in Wang's genes, nothing emerged until the Falun Gong crackdown. On the twenty-first of July 1999, Wang was arrested in the Harbin city railway station as she tried to board a train to Beijing. When she entered her first holding cell, a cop suddenly threw a practitioner into the bars and Wang was hit with an overwhelming sense of déjà-vu, as if her entire life had been a dream and she had just woken up.

These were early days; Wang would be released, arrested, and released again over the next twelve months. Wang took advantage of her relative freedom by renting out a basement apartment in an obscure area of Harbin, cramming it with computers and industrial printers that could produce massive amounts of *samizdat*, or as Falun Gong call them, "truth-clarification materials." But Wang needed content. The online world of Falun Gong was not only sparsely populated, but monitored. Wang recruited a young college student studying computer science to teach her how to communicate anonymously and get around the Internet blockade one step at a time. On October 1, 2000, China's National Day, Wang printed one hundred thousand flyers directly attacking Jiang Zemin and exposing how many high-ranking party officials actually disagreed with the persecution. The handouts spread quickly from Harbin to cities around the periphery of Heilongjiang—reaching schools, residential areas near labor camps, and the relatives of Public Security Bureau personnel. That night, exhausted but happy, Wang fell asleep on the floor of her printing factory.

Wang was looking out toward where the sun had dipped below the horizon. In the deepening twilight, from a great distance she could see men slowly walking toward her, first just a few, then many, filling her vision. Suddenly she understood they were all policemen. They were carrying guns. They were going to kill her, but she ran and hid.

THE SLAUGHTER

Wang woke up in the dead of night, sweating and thinking about where she could hide in the basement. It was not the fear of being arrested or beaten that worried her as much as the idea that the printers would be seized. But the dream's message was unmistakable; and, in fact, the official retaliation to Wang's flyer distribution had been as comprehensive as the distribution. Harbin practitioners had been arrested, interrogated, and tortured with the efficiency of a speed-dating event. While Wang had slept and dreamed, her name and photo were posted online and on telephone poles throughout the city along with a fifty thousand yuan reward for information leading to her arrest.

The next morning there was a knock on the basement apartment door. Wang did not open it. Instead, she slipped silently out a long-forgotten coal door in the back of the apartment. The police—it was them, of course, and although there weren't as many as in her dream, they moved much faster in real life—pursued Wang through the Harbin traffic to the train station. There, like a prop in a movie, a train stood at a platform belching out white smoke. Wang ran to it and stood in the center of the smoke, occasionally craning her neck out and gasping for fresh air, praying for the smoke to continue while the police searched the station. Then the train lurched and Wang grabbed on to its rail, throwing herself on the last carriage. She entered the train through the still-unsecured door and collapsed onto a hard seat.

Wang was walking on the shore of a vast sea. The sun was reflecting off the ocean; the sand was moist and warm, and she could see fresh footprints. Many people had walked here before her. But there was something in the waves— discarded wooden shoetrees, bobbing like cicada shells on the dark surface. When the waves hit the shore, the shoetrees would be violently carried along, rushing onto the beach like a mindless swarm of wasps. Suddenly she was seized with a fear that something had gone wrong and that the sea would swallow her up. She saw a big wave rushing in and she dashed forward as it broke behind her. Just ahead a dark wave, exponentially larger, was preparing to break, the shoetrees clattering together in their excitement. She tried to run, but her feet were sinking into the sand with a low moaning sound.

Wang woke, clammy, slightly nauseous. *Something is about to happen. I can't go back now—I have to keep moving. I can't be swallowed up by this big sea.*

A month later, she made her way back to Harbin anyway. In the wee small hours she snuck into her home to get some things and maybe kiss her son's cheek. Like a waking dream, she suddenly heard police sirens and saw searchlights dancing through the windows. She ran out the backdoor and circled around the police positions. As a wet snowstorm blew in, Wang began hauling ass across the city. Shuffling through the blizzard with nothing but a backpack and a heavy down coat, Wang thought miserably about how close her bank was from where she was standing. She had to get her son out of Harbin, to relatives or a private school. But how? And how would she pay? Her bank account had over a million yuan, but she didn't dare walk into her branch.

Now it was getting light. Now they would see her.

She started running again—the backpack lurching against the small of her back, the sweat pouring down the inside of her coat. Nowhere to hide—it would be so easy for the police to find her at a friend's apartment. Panting like an animal, Wang finally stopped and sat underneath the awning of a store that had not yet opened, the wet snow seeping into her trousers, the clammy plastic coat sticking to her skin. Maybe tomorrow morning she could get train tickets. *Tomorrow*, Wang thought—*Beijing, Shenyang, Guangdong—but where to sleep tonight, what to eat?* Then she couldn't think anymore. *When will this persecution end? When can I stop?* She had been fooling herself. She was truly, utterly homeless, adrift in the bitter sea.

* * *

Until 2001, based on the reporters I knew in Beijing and subsequent interviews with practitioners, I estimate that about half of the Chinese public never really bought into the party's campaign against Falun Gong. There was no way to actually observe this, of course; for a Chinese citizen to make a gesture of support for Falun Gong was potentially very dangerous. Every profession had its ritual criticism sessions. In some companies employees had to pretend not to notice, memory-hole style, when fellow workers became un-persons. Every neighborhood had some form of obligatory anti–Falun Gong activity, with a special emphasis on schoolchildren, designed not just to assist the capture of practitioners but to make everyone in Chinese society in some tiny way complicit. Those who subsequently complained were open to accusations of *lies*, of *hypocrisy*—epithets beloved by the party.

While I'm reluctant to commit the ultimate journalist sin of using my Beijing driver-on-call as evidence, it was striking how often he used to spout off on how stupid the repression of Falun Gong was. He knew I wouldn't report him, but he wasn't playing up to me either; I represented the American Chamber of Commerce Committee for Government Relations, so I kept my trap shut about ultrasensitive Chinese affairs when speaking with Chinese nationals. At the same time I knew that people like my driver were a problem for the party, because their irritation was real. *Falun Gong is a dangerous cult, Li Hongzhi is like Hitler, practitioners kill themselves and they are planning to do it on Tiananmen Square*—such charges were repeated over and over for months on end. The campaign had become so tedious for the state-controlled media that they had turned to "former practitioner" Fu Yubin who had the ability to cock his head like a cat with an ear infection while serving up gleeful descriptions of how he had killed his own father "for being a demon."[2] All this theatrical excess simply led many Chinese to wonder: Why exactly is the party so deeply threatened? Why don't they just leave those people alone?

Then, on the afternoon of January 23, 2001, Falun Gong seemingly committed its own theatrical excess. Five protesters (later claimed to be seven, including a mother and her twelve-year-old daughter) walked onto Tiananmen Square, doused their bodies with gasoline, and set themselves on fire. The footage, including grisly interviews with the burn victims, played for weeks. Some of the "practitioners" were said to have recovered, some were said to have died, but this time, the public disgust, including my driver's, was unmistakable. Fifty percent latent support collapsed to perhaps 10 percent in a single week. The "self-immolation" was a green light for the 6-10 Office; any remaining inhibitions about fair treatment for incarcerated practitioners were replaced by death quotas and mass disappearances. Falun Gong was finally being erased.

Most practitioners assumed the entire incident was faked because Falun Gong forbids suicide as strictly as it forbids violence. The self-immolators were clearly supposed to be doing Falun Gong exercises, but the moves and postures appeared to be taken from military drills. Yet the Chinese media had laid the groundwork: Falun Gong was said to be responsible for thousands of suicides—yes, that number appeared to be pulled out of thin air, and the math actually indicated a lower rate of suicide among practitioners than in the general population, but this time the mud could stick because in the midst of the crackdown Li Hongzhi wrote an article stating: "It is in fact time to let go of your last attachments. As cultivators, you already know that you should, and in your actions you have, let go of all worldly attachments (including the attachment to the human body) and have made it through the process of letting go of life and death."[3] There were several ways that practitioners interpreted these phrases: as a battle cry in the midst of the largest scale public security crackdown since the Cultural Revolution, as a balm to the sorrow that practitioners were experiencing over fellow congregants tortured to death, as an entreaty to assume a higher spiritual level in a world of arbitrary pain. Perhaps Li meant all of these things. But in the context of the self-immolation Li's words (shorthanded in the Chinese media as Li Hongzhi commanding practitioners "to give up your attachments to life and death") suddenly sounded sinister. Nor was that interpretation purely based on party propaganda. As the line between life and death for a mainland practitioner was growing increasingly fine, it was conceivable that a minority of practitioners, isolated from mainstream Falun Gong thought and discussion, could have leaned toward a darker interpretation. Thus, the robust party storyline of the self-immolation could only be refuted by facts about what had actually happened that afternoon.

The Chinese state press showed unprecedented speed, releasing the immolators' names, personal histories, and motives within (a rather absurd) two hours. By contrast, China Central Television did not present footage of the incident at all. Yet about a week later, selective portions were shown in spectacular style. Simone Gao, presently a New Tang Dynasty Television anchor but with extensive experience in mainland television journalism, told me of her reaction to the footage. She was fully aware of the surveillance cameras located at regular intervals on the square, but she remembers being puzzled by the zooms, the intimate camera angles suggesting it had all been choreographed like a CCTV Chinese New Year's Special.[4] That's not so far-fetched. The deputy director (ultimately director) of the 6-10 Office, Li Dongsheng actually had no experience in law enforcement. According to Stephen Gregory of the *Epoch Times*, Li came directly from CCTV where he had worked for seven years in popular newsmagazine-style shows.[5] Possibly to avoid acknowledging the ubiquitous surveillance on the square, or to give the coverage a more objective veneer, CCTV claimed that the footage was from CNN.

In a nice safe Hong Kong location, I had a talk with Rebecca Mackinnon, former Beijing bureau chief of CNN, about what happened that day.[6] To her, one fact was indisputable: everyone, from the Public Security Bureau to the police stationed on the square to most major Western news organizations, *knew* that there was going to be some sort of important demonstration on that particular date, the eve of the Chinese New Year. Considering that Falun Gong was riddled with spies by 2001 and the police were brandishing fire extinguishers less than a minute after the bodies were lit on fire makes it exceedingly difficult to refute the obvious: at a minimum, the Chinese authorities were aware of what was going to take place and did nothing to stop it from occurring.

When the five individuals burst into flame, the CNN cameraman was on the far side of the square. He began shooting, using his standard method. Shoot five seconds of tape. Then, run toward the action, pull tape, hide the tape on his body, and slap in another tape. Shoot five more seconds of tape, pull, hide, slap, and repeat. He made it perhaps fifty yards down the square before the police jumped him and took his tapes. But they didn't search his crotch, and that tape was shown on CNN—burning figures, but from a long way off. CNN's cameraman never made it close to the action.

The CNN footage claim was only the first of the party's unforced errors. The oversell came swiftly: a CCTV reporter with no surgical mask and a bacteria-laden camera crew storming into a burn unit where all the victims—actually, it's far from clear they were the same people who had been on the square—are apparently convalescing, buddy style, to ensure cross-infection. Like a Monty Python sequence, the camera pans over to a gurney where a self-immolator appears to be wrapped in an immense amount of gauze, resembling a full body cast, a treatment which would quickly lead to rapid infection and death in an actual burn victim. The twelve-year-old girl would ultimately give an interview to CCTV, even singing a heartrending song, although we are informed that she has just had a tracheotomy. Western journalists were, of course, prevented from interviewing any of these "survivors."

But the central lie, far beyond CCTV's shenanigans, was exposed by *Washington Post* reporter Phillip Pan.

For the Chinese public, the real issue in the immolation had never really been the burning practitioners—there's a long tradition of Buddhist monks burning themselves in protest, as the Tibetans have recently reminded us. No. It was that a mother, Liu Chunling, had seemingly set her twelve-year-old daughter, Liu Siying, on fire to satisfy a spiritual madman. While it is highly unclear whether Liu Siying was actually there or the whole thing was made up after the fact—the CNN cameraman claims he didn't see any children, and the dramatic footage that CCTV released of the girl calling for her mommy as she is loaded into an ambulance doesn't fully resolve the issue—Pan traveled to Kaifeng, where the mother had made her home for many years. Pan's diligent questioning revealed that Liu was known both for beating her daughter and for working in a karaoke bar as a dancer; that is, Liu was a common prostitute. No one who knew Liu had ever seen her do any Falun Gong exercises. Nor could anyone remember her ever saying anything about Falun Gong at all.[7]

There are still many unanswered questions. Were the other participants really practitioners? If not, how exactly were they induced to set themselves on fire? Threats? Money? Through the assurance that Hollywood stuntmen consider setting themselves on fire to be relatively routine as long as it is extinguished quickly? The mind reels; investigative journalism may be a lost art in mainland China, but there's a great book waiting to be written for the Chinese reading audience. For the time being I can comfortably state my perspective: The police knew what was going to happen, and the centerpiece of the tableau—a Falun Gong mother forcing a child to burn on Tiananmen Square—was an outright deception.

* * *

When Wang Yuzhi heard about the immolation she lay in bed for a couple days weeping.[8]

The party tells people that Falun Gong is an evil religion that makes people jump out of buildings and commit suicide. Now this. Now people won't believe anything we say. I don't know the facts, and anyway I have only one mouth. I have already been arrested twice. My home is a stake out. But I know how to make leaflets. I know how to get printing equipment. But only in Harbin.

Wang snuck back. But it was a different Harbin, where all the practitioners Wang knew had fled, been fired from their jobs, or incarcerated. The remaining ones were homeless, their families broken up by the PSB, and they had been reduced to a hand-to-mouth existence. Wang cobbled together a production run of leaflets and flyers. She didn't sleep, and it was three times bigger than last time. It felt heroic, but once the materials were printed there was no money left. Even the equipment was borrowed. So in the middle of July 2001 Wang rolled the dice. With a straight face, Wang walked into her bank and filled out a withdrawal slip. The bank officials called Wang into the office and told her gently that her account was now frozen. She started to get up, but a security guard was already behind her firmly pressing her into the seat. A minute later, the police strode into the bank and told Wang she was under arrest. When she asked them what the charges were, they replied: "linking up with overseas forces"—the same accusation thrown at her father during the Cultural Revolution. There was no arrest, no paper trail, no trial or lawyers.

The police simply escorted Wang into the interrogation room of Harbin City No. 2 Detention Center and chained her to a chair. Then the officers started in:

"Wang, who did you give these flyers to? What are their names?"

"Look, we know you made these flyers. Here's one. See? You printed them out. You know how we know? Because other practitioners turned you in. That's why you're here. Because they fucked you, Wang. So you should give us their names."

"Answer the question, Wang. You say you practice truthfulness, compassion, and forbearance—but you don't answer truthfully, do you? You think sitting there saying nothing is truthful? Who did you give these flyers to?"

"Wang, listen to me: If you don't tell us, we'll torture you. So don't be stupid. Don't think you can get out of this. We followed you from Harbin, through Shenyang and everywhere you went. We found all your relatives. They all talked. It cost one million yuan just for us to get you. So a hunger strike won't help. Nothing will help. So don't be fucking stupid. One of your Falun Gong—she was seven months pregnant—we hung her up to the ceiling. No problem. Her husband watched. He was crying. He kept saying stuff like 'please don't beat her anymore,' but we—"

"Officers, I know what you did. I know all about it. I wrote about what you did and I put it in the leaflets that got passed out in the street. So put your minds at ease; I'm not going to give you any names."

That night Wang was given half a bowl of pig feed. There was a layer of sand at the bottom. Then she tried to do the exercises, but the criminal inmates—they had been prepped—started cursing her. Then they took turns shoving her, and then they just started hitting her in the face. Finally they strangled her until she passed out.

The next morning Wang woke up early, wedged and twisted herself out of the line of bodies spooned against each other, trying not to disturb anyone. She sat on the concrete floor in a corner of the cell, meditating.

Wang saw a realm in which people were celebrating and looked happy. Then she heard heavenly, celestial music. The vision faded and the music drifted away. Divine beings walked into the cell. They were Western gods, about forty to fifty years old, wearing white robes. They stood there looking down at Wang. The first god gave Wang a bunch of flowers, and the other handed her a bunch of green onions.

She came out of the vision with her partially closed hands above her head, as if she was still holding the flowers in her left hand and the green onions in her right. But the gift was a command; the Chinese word for *onion* is homophonous with the word for *rushing out*. So obvious, so direct: *Go quickly*. But she could not transform, nor would she sign their papers. The only way out was to starve.

* * *

Thirteen men would come for her in the early morning. She would be sleeping and they would grab her and drag her outside and strap her to the wooden board. They would force her mouth open with the spoons and push a little tube in—that's when she would start gagging, and her powerful jaws would start bending the metal spoons so they had to do it all over again with a horse clamp. And then her throat contractions didn't matter, but her moaning was loud and crazy now, and they would bring the big tube out of the trough, a long thick tube like for siphoning gasoline, and they would start pushing it into her mouth, and it would hit the back of her tongue hard, but there wasn't anything to bring up, so she would just spasm around it, and they would wait and nothing would come up, and they would push it back, deeper into her throat. That's when she felt like a bug pinned to the board, and they would keep sliding the tube down her throat until it hit the bottom of her stomach, and they would be cursing at each other to get the mush ready. Corn meal in salty water—they would pour it and plunge it while the others stirred the tube at the bottom of her stomach. That's when her body would heave again, really hard this time, and she would puke it all—mush, phlegm, juices, blood, and bits of teeth—up her throat, into her nose, around the tube, out of her mouth, and right into their faces. And they would yell at her that she was a crude fucking bitch and then pull the tube out hard now, all smeared with blood. And she would scream "Falun Dafa Hao!" good and loud, over and over so that everybody in the detention center could hear it. Then they would do it through the nose. They had another tube, smaller this time, and they would push that in and put the mush in until that shit got backed up and her eyes started popping. And the whole time she was screaming, "I see your face! I know you! The world knows! You'll go to world court!"

After a while some of the thirteen men started hiding their faces and even the doctors wouldn't do it anymore.

*　*　*

In 2001, Hao could read e-mails within China and intercept e-mails to and from overseas, but he couldn't read overseas to overseas.[9] Students, businessmen, and Chinese expats served as the party's eyes and ears abroad. But from the Chinese leadership's perspective, such assets were no longer sufficient if China were to fight its way out of a defensive crouch. Thus, when the patriotic hacking movement—the Green Army followed by the Red Hacker Alliance—began its spontaneous growth, the Chinese leadership chose to channel it rather than to crush it. Notwithstanding the hackers' swashbuckling self-portrayals on their websites, the state had kept them on a leash that was slackened only for largely symbolic skirmishes with Taiwan, Indonesia, Japan, and a few high-profile defacements of American websites after China's Belgrade embassy was bombed. When state security became aware that the hacktivists planned a major assault on American networks in 2002, the movement was temporarily shut down by a Chinese leadership that was not ready for a potential confrontation with the United States. Falun Gong was a different matter.

On the surface, Western practitioners were still in the wilderness. In desperation, young non-Chinese practitioners had turned to a gesture that conveyed equal parts futility and courage: Thirty-five non-Chinese practitioners, the majority from North America, materialized on Tiananmen Square, unfurled a Falun Gong banner, and waited quietly for violent arrest. (Leeshai Lemish, who would eventually become my researcher and translator, was among them. Throughout our travels he could predict when it was going to rain by the throbbing on the right side of his jaw socket, a relic of his violent interrogation by the PSB). Yet for all the public desperation, practitioners in the West had a penchant for documentation and numbers. They were quietly counting: practitioners tortured, practitioners lost, in what jail, tortured by whom. The names, the addresses, all the information that would be needed someday if justice came to China (and that concept of justice would eventually become the impetus for Falun Gong to unequivocally break with the Chinese Communist Party with the publishing of the "Nine Commentaries"[10]). These practitioners tended to have strong technical skills, weak support from the media, and very little money, so they put it all on the web (including the sites that Hao first perused and rejected). So as the internal war with Falun Gong dragged on, as its overseas practitioners stubbornly kept putting up verified accounts and graphic photos of torture—images that were increasingly capturing the eyeballs of the international legal community—the party felt that it had no choice but to seriously widen the campaign. According to Hao, this explains why the first examples of hacking leading to widespread, sustained network disruption outside China were not aimed at the Pentagon or Wall Street. China's first prolonged "denial of service" attack—essentially exhausting the bandwidth capability of a website until it becomes unavailable—was carried out from servers in Beijing and Shenzhen against Clearwisdom.net, the main Falun Gong–practitioner website, hosted by servers in North America. The technical signature suggested a primitive, neophyte army; not long after the attacks took place, the origin was traced directly back to the address of the Public Security Bureau in Beijing.[11]

On June 26, 2003, according to Hao, the internal 6-10 Office merged with state security overseas operations. In Tianjin, the combined forces laid out a three-year plan to undermine overseas Falun Gong and other groups such as Chinese democracy advocates. Hao began directly working on international spy operations, the most critical being the creation of fake refugees—young, trained to mimic Falun Gong behavior, and holding paperwork confirming time in the Laogai System. "No matter how clever the Australian or the American government is," Hao told me, "they have no way to distinguish the real ones [Falun Gong refugees] and the police officers."

To create friction between Falun Gong and other dissident groups, the refugee-bots planted themselves in dissident media centers, particularly in New York and Sydney. Even if many were ultimately unmasked, it created havoc for Falun Gong's internal network security.[12] I also talked to Chen Yonglin, who was a Chinese diplomat based at the Sydney consulate until 2005, when he suddenly requested protection from the Australian government. We met in a private home in the suburbs eighteen months later. Careful and media savvy, Chen began by authenticating his point that there were more than a thousand Chinese agents on Australian soil. He went on to explain that the vast majority were employed not to go after military technology, but to monitor Falun Gong and other dissidents (the so-called five poisons: Uyghurs, Tibetans, Falun Gong, democracy activists, and advocates for an independent Taiwan) in the Chinese communities of Melbourne and Sydney.[13] China's internal wars had widened into the Chinese diaspora. The goal was to turn anyone of Chinese blood into a de facto supporter of the Chinese Communist Party.

Judging from the witnesses I interviewed in the United States, Canada, Australia, and the United Kingdom, it was as if the battle for the Chinese diaspora had already been ceded. In the United States the intelligence community was distracted by terrorism and pacified by occasional Chinese military and intelligence cooperation on terrorist networks—even if the information given was sketchy and unclassifiable, as in the case of the alleged Uyghur jihadists. With no one blocking them, Chinese hackers began carrying out successful denial-of-service attacks in Taiwan in 2004. The so-called Titan Rain attacks of 2005 targeted military contractors, the Department of Defense, the State Department, and the National Aeronautics and Space Administration. From 2007 to early 2009 the "Ghostnet" attacks featured impressive break-ins of government centers around the world, including the Dalai Lama's government in exile. No explicit action or sanctions followed.

So any pretense of surprise or outrage in Washington following Operation Aurora or more recent mainland hacking attacks is in my opinion a case of too little, too late; US intelligence may prefer to think of this as ancient history, but if Hao and Chen's testimony tells us anything it is that Chinese hacking flowered not only because of the party's imperative of disrupting overseas Falun Gong but because of the United States government's own studied passivity in the face of such illegal attacks.

Hao Fengjun defected to Australia in 2005. He was never asked to testify in Washington.

* * *

No matter how global the conflict would ultimately become, the emotional foundation of Falun Gong resistance to the Chinese state was forged within the Laogai System. Falun Gong would protest in Tiananmen Square in the hundreds of thousands, and Ming would urge practitioners to take the struggle to the people, but it was here, in the cells and interrogation rooms of China, that no practitioner could go through the motions. The legalities, the political nuances, the crude perceptions of an often-apathetic and brainwashed Chinese public did not matter. Only one's will and the ability to tolerate pain mattered.

Some practitioners thought of resistance in prison as standing up for the truth; others simply didn't want to let down the team; some even believed that by keeping the prisons overcrowded they might contribute to the end of the persecution. But there was a small cadre of practitioners—Ming was one of them—who, once they were incarcerated, didn't give tactics a second thought. To Ming, it was all binary. A practitioner cannot falsely renounce belief. The weight of the party was used to make them renounce that belief. So nothing but resistance, expressed with the purest dignity a practitioner could manage, was acceptable. A realm that none of them could see, this was the power of the powerless. Ming, perhaps more than any other figure in the Laogai System at that time, and perhaps because he was already a hybrid of Chinese and foreign resistance, would come to embody this stance.

Following his arrest, Ming was shunted through a series of institutions, staying at each one for an average of two weeks: in Haidian District Detention Center, where Ming held his first hunger strike, he was nearly killed by violent detainees trying to force-feed him—until the authorities stepped in and put him on an intravenous drip.[14] In Daguang Detention Center of Changchun City, the guards employed Ming's father in a failed effort to persuade Ming to sign a guarantee. In the drug rehabilitation center at Weizigou in Changchun (now cleansed of actual drug addicts and exclusively stocked with Falun Gong), Ming got a rare chance to physically mend, but the Beijing City Detention Center was a replay of hunger striking and convicts trying to jam things in his mouth. In the Beijing Labor Camp Prisoners' Transferring Center Ming was ordered to walk through the courtyard naked and received his first taste of the electric baton.

If these procedures had provided calluses, it was in Beijing's Tuanhe Labor Camp that the heavy lifting began: two weeks of sleep deprivation combined with relentless transformation lectures. Asleep at 3 a.m., up at 5. When that failed, the police turned Ming over to what they called the "Wild Room": sixteen hardcore criminals, all led by a little guy with a dark, malevolent face.

The Wild Room boys played many games with Ming: airplane, squats, ass-slap, trip-the-practitioner, but they eventually got tired of Ming's screams, gasps and little-girl fibrillations, and just watching him fall down over and over. The little dark guy ordered Ming to squeeze under a low bed folded at the waist, face against his knees. One by one, the inmates plonked their fat asses down on the camp bed. Then they began to bounce and jump on it, laughing really hard like they were at a frat-boy slumber party. The challenge for Ming was not to panic, even while he knew that this exact procedure had killed other practitioners. He was just slim enough from hunger striking to survive. When the prisoners saw that Ming was breathing, the little guy got pissed off all over again and ordered a straight-up beating. When Ming faced torture with a predictable beginning and end, he would employ little distraction devices such as reciting the Fa. During an unpredictable assault like this, he would simply let his mind go blank, as if he were asleep. But even in the haze, Ming noticed that they didn't aim for his upper body. Maybe they wanted to keep the marks off his face.[15] After the bed-sit, Ming could barely crawl, let alone use the squat toilet. So he held it for two weeks. The Wild Room boys left him alone while they worked over other practitioners. They all broke and signed, although one of them had to be repeatedly sodomized first. Three weeks later, the labor-camp guards started in on Ming again—yet it was all reason and party principles this time; the government says you must renounce, that's the law, and so on. Ming debated in cold logical terms. At 4 a.m. the guards' false patience ran out and the electric batons appeared. Shock. Talk some more. Shock. Repeat.

Ming's confidence was frayed. He signed a statement; it did not renounce Falun Gong exactly ... but it did grant that his detention was justified, that he had broken the law. A few days later, Ming renounced his previous statement in a new written statement. Like a boulder tumbling back down the mountain, the several remaining practitioners who had transformed suddenly followed Ming's lead and formally renounced their own statements, too. Somehow, everyone was back where they started. It had gone awry. The Wild Room and the little guy had gone too far. Crazy torture, sodomy—illegal acts like these made the police nervous, but worse, they hadn't worked. So simplify. Centralize. The police moved the practitioners to a single floor and took control of the torture process again, selecting practitioners one by one, always choosing the weakest, the ones with the least reserves. Again, some renounced. But at the end of 2000, even more practitioners arrived in Tuanhe. In the delivery were several guys who had never renounced, guys who had an unusual ability to put up with pain. They were thrown in with Ming's gang.

Most practitioners in Tuanhe would ultimately "transform," perhaps even 90 percent. About half of them would go right back to practicing Falun Gong and spreading leaflets the minute they were released. But Ming and his friends were becoming living symbols of the idea that long-term resistance within the Laogai itself was in fact possible. It was a rough way for those who aspired to it, but the idea was spreading not just in Tuanhe but throughout the Laogai System of China. To avoid further contamination, quarantine was necessary. The six men deemed most nontransformable, including Ming, were chained up and driven the short distance to Xin'an, a woman's labor camp.

As Ming suspected, it was a move to softer methods: cells that previously belonged to male teenagers, and a group-therapy method of transformation. The phases were simple: (1) torture, (2) sign, (3) study and further renunciation of belief, (4) renounce belief before all the labor-camp detainees, and finally (5) renounce before the whole country (usually on videotape, but occasionally before a live audience).

Female practitioners seemed to respond well to this gradual method. The second stage of transformation, signing, was often followed by manic behavior—hysterical laughter, crying, begging forgiveness. This was a deeply dangerous point, a twilight zone. Handled stupidly, it would lead to a reversal and further radicalization of the practitioner. Angel, the girl who had run a series of safe houses in Beijing, spent several hours describing to me how she had developed an almost obsessive maternal love for her party handler during a similar scenario of transformation. She compared it to Stockholm Syndrome; clearly some practitioners were particularly vulnerable to the acting out, the exaggerated surrender, the submission. The idea in Xin'an was to use the loss of belief, the gap, in a radical way. Give prisoners love; give them a new mission immediately. Strengthen their transformation by involving others who had also transformed. Make the transformed practitioner not just complicit but directly responsible for transforming others. Then take the show on the road: lights, camera, action. Ming thought: *Then it's not a trick anymore, you have made a statement that people believe. You have joined the evil.*

Ming had come into Xin'an at a special time. "Mr. Hua," a former practitioner, had just arrived, and the entire camp was gathered to hear him speak. Hua was a charismatic; he had designed an array of popular Falun Dafa teachings that he interpreted, all in intricately styled Falun Gong language, to show that they were actually in accord with the Chinese Communist Party's objectives. In the hothouse, asylum-like environment, the women were desperate to hear something spiritual, and they were equally desperate for an explanation that could free them from exhaustion and torture. To Ming's shock, As Hua preached, the women began standing up and crying and screaming. Some guards said about 90 percent of the women transformed that day—a new high for Hua. On his labor-camp speaking tour it was touted that he had brought the average transformation rate from 50 percent to over 80 percent. In the wake of Hua's miracle conversion, the camp directors took the six nontransformable men and put them in the visitor's center with the newly transformed women. Ming did not hesitate to engage them:

"You are so vigorous, so strong in trying to get me to renounce—so, why did you pick up the practice in the first place? What were you thinking about?"

"I had health problems," a woman said.

"What kind?"

"Breast cancer."

"Your second life was given by Falun Dafa. You are denying your own life."

There was no answer. Ming believed that she was just too afraid to let others know that she was holding a clear mind. Many were like this; clear in their conscience but just too afraid of further torture.

One of the women who worked on him was Jennifer Zeng, the young professional from Beijing who had participated in the Fuyou Street vigil.[16] She addressed Ming as a well-educated person. Ming recognized that even as Jennifer was urging him to give up Falun Gong, she did not work for the police, and there was something subversive about her. When the others left on a bathroom break Jennifer quickly whispered that her intention was to get out and reveal these things to the world. In the days that followed, Ming would occasionally give her a careful, well-calibrated look, so subtle that others did not see it. But Jennifer lived for that softer look in his eye.

It was a strange meeting: the ghost of resistance past meeting the ghost of resistance future. Jennifer had transformed because she intended to get out and write a book—or so she thought. Yet when she saw Ming sitting, like a rock, with the waves of women's voices crashing against him, she was overtaken by feelings of profound guilt (in fact, for years practitioners across the world would be highly critical of Jennifer's transformation maneuver) and naked admiration for Ming's accomplishment. Without Ming knowing, she anonymously wrote a deeply effective article for Minghui about Ming's resistance.[17]

I've spoken with Jennifer many times. I suspect that article was an important personal step for her, for Jennifer was better than her whispered words to Ming. Even though Jennifer had experienced less torture than many other practitioners—the guards quickly figured out that sleep deprivation was enough—her book *Witnessing History* is, in my opinion, the most effective labor-camp memoir that has emerged from the Falun Gong diaspora.[18] Perhaps Ming's resistance helped her at a critical time.

And for Ming, too, help would come, but from an unexpected source.

The nontransformed Ming was transferred back to Tuanhe, which now held more than two hundred practitioners. Then, in early March 2002, Ming was taken upstairs to the director's office where a crowd of guards waited. They asked him to sign. Ming refused. Suddenly they tied him down on a plank and all of them simultaneously began shocking him with electric batons. After half an hour, his leg went into a spasm, and Ming felt like he couldn't hold on. "I'll sign," Ming said. And he did. And the director of Tuanhe told Ming he was going back to Dublin.

The Irish minister of foreign affairs had, in fact, made a public announcement back in January that the ministry's firm pressure (which had been inexorably pushed by street demonstrations in Dublin and the unyielding resolve of Trinity College) had led the Chinese to agree to release Zhao Ming imminently. The final torture, the signing of the guarantee, was counter to the agreement with Ireland. Perhaps it was the party having the last word. Perhaps it was the Tuanhe director's attempt to save face. Either way, at the end of the day, unlike so many other larger and more powerful European nations that would simply go through the motions, little Ireland did not forsake her adopted son.

* * *

180   **THE SLAUGHTER**

Lotus (Wang Huilian) in Bangkok, waiting for asylum. Photo by the author, 2008.

Lotus, the kid who did everything right, would not only lose her Communist Party membership but also her right to a passport.[19] In 2006, she bribed her way across an obscure stretch of China's border with Burma. Traveling on a motorcycle with two other practitioners and a crying baby, Lotus made it to Thailand. I interviewed her in Bangkok while she waited for a country to accept her as an asylum case.

Lotus was kidnapped by the Public Security Bureau and detained illegally four times. This was one of them.

As the repression of Falun Gong intensified back in 2000, Lotus had become an organizer of the resistance, urging the practitioners of Changchun to fan out across the provinces of China to gather the sleeping practitioners into a coherent force that could come out from the shadows. Her activist phase didn't last long; in a train station on the way back from Guangzhou she was picked up and detained for three months. Her detention had been honorable; she had refused to divulge any information, not even her name, and she was able to get a letter telling of her experiences smuggled out through one of the regular prisoners. It was published in Minghui, anonymously, in March 2001. Given the references in the article, the police quickly figured out that Lotus had written it. Yet they seemingly did nothing for several days.

On Saturday morning, the police suddenly carried Lotus out to a car, cuffed her hands and feet, put a bucket on her head, and threw her on the floor in the back seat. Then they drove for about two hours and carried her into a cold room. When they took the bucket off Lotus saw about twenty male plainclothes policemen and two policewomen in uniform standing around her. The room was cramped, primitive, and even though they hadn't bothered to shut the door, incredibly quiet. Batons, ropes, and some tools that she did not recognize were neatly hanging from the wall. Clearly they were in a very remote area. Something about the way the men had formed themselves into two groups told her that about half of them had traveled from another district just to be there.

"What's going on? What did you do? Who did this?"

They were all shouting at once.

Lotus stayed silent. There was a pause then two of the plainclothes police expertly tied her handcuffs with a rope and pulled it onto a hook in the doorway. Another rope was whipped around her legs and, with a jerk, her feet were hoisted off the ground. An icy wind was whistling through the doorway, but Lotus immediately broke into a sweat. The sensation of being ripped apart was extraordinary, a level of pain that seemed insane, unthinkable. Any torture she had experienced before—handcuffs too tight, beatings, being slapped around—was nothing compared to this. She was gasping and shaking and mumbling and could see her own sweat and tears dripping off her taut stomach onto the concrete floor.

Lotus began to recite spiritual poetry, anything to concentrate her mind. A baton smashed her mouth hard. She believed the blow had dislocated and cracked her jaw. At the same time another policeman pulled the rope up further. Now she was hanging from the ceiling, stretched out as if she were on a medieval rack, closing her eyes because looking at her puddle was making her sick. Suddenly it was all clear to Lotus: she was not going to make it, she was going to die here. She started screaming uncontrollably. Like an echo, a dog, very far away, howled back. The police let Lotus and the dog howl for a few minutes more, then, all at once, they dropped her on the floor.

"There's no point in screaming like that," one of the policemen said in a comical voice. "No one can hear you —just that dog of yours."

They chained her arms and feet, with weights this time, and stuck her in front of a table with a copy of the Minghui article.

"Did you think we didn't know about this? Actually we know everything about where that article came from. We've already interrogated many other people. They spat it all out. There's no need for you to put up a fight."

Lotus didn't answer. They shrugged and made it perfectly clear that very soon she would go back up to the ceiling. But it was break time, so they took a kind of professional delight in showing her some of their gadgets, which had obviously cracked subjects in previous PSB interrogations: an electric baton with a wire net about the size of a TV screen that could be used to electrocute a large portion of the body, and a bright light about six inches in diameter. As soon as they shined that light in her face she was blinded and couldn't see anything. But they could see everything about her very clearly, even subtle facial expressions and shifts in mood.

Blinded, Lotus could still understand their system. First they wanted to terrorize you. That was the most striking thing for Lotus at the time— not how painful it was, not even the sensation that her body was being permanently, irreconcilably damaged, but the feeling that she was actually going to die. Then, after a while, they would let her fall, then resurrect her and sit her down for a talk. Then they would hang her up again. No sleep, no change. For three days.

They would ask a question, knowing what their next question was going to be. Sometimes they would glance at each other in a certain way and then step outside to discuss things between them. When they would come back in, the policewoman on duty would suddenly appear concerned.

"Does it hurt? Are you hurt anywhere?"

"Are you okay? Don't be like that—why don't you just speak?"

"Do you miss your family?"

"What's your name? What's your last name? How many characters are in your name? Where about does your family live?"

Lotus knew the plan. During those three days their purpose was just to get her name. She always had the image of being lifted up again—she could hear the dog howling and smell her own sweat—and it was this fear that was more painful than her now-useless limbs. Because the torture and sleep deprivation was so intense, Lotus knew her endurance was going fast. She found herself looking at the policewoman with gratitude—maybe she could slow things down, perhaps she was secretly aligned with Lotus, she just couldn't fully show it to the others.

Then, during a quiet stretch in the middle of the night, one of the guards confided to her that this case was a big blunder for them; a prisoner managing to smuggle out a letter while in detention and get it posted on Minghui? They had orders from above to find out who's responsible. He posed the question to her calmly, almost as if Lotus was a colleague: "If you can get away with smuggling letters out like that, well, what if, in the future, we have some kind of high-profile white-collar crime case and the inmates smuggle out letters—then what do we, the PSB, amount to? What are we worth?"

Her last line of defense collapsed. With the policeman's gesture, that tiny glimpse of respect, she could understand them a little—just for a second—and she thought: *You know, that makes some sense. I can see now why they would torture me like that. Maybe I'll just say my name, what's the big deal? So what if I tell them my name?*

On the third night, Lotus came out with her name and her work unit. "Okay, we are done for the day," the police replied. And they let her sleep. Just like that.

The next day, they started in on her about the person she had been arrested with, the man who had also refused to give his name. Five days of the exact same torture followed until Lotus blurted out: "Wang Baogang."

Lotus knew that she would rather die than transform, than sign a guarantee, than slander Dafa. And she held out for that principle. But her betrayal of Wang, her shame—well, this is why Lotus is telling me her story.

Wang Baogang would receive three years in a Changchun Labor Camp. Lotus would be sent to Changchun's Heizuizi Female Prison for a year and a half. But even if Lotus feels remorse over Wang Baogang (implicated by multiple sources, Wang was already in labor camp but he had never revealed his name), Lotus' perception that she was close to being killed—although it likely would not have taken place in the PSB interrogation center—was probably accurate all along. Not having a name made Lotus vulnerable to a fate far worse than ropes and chains and batons.

She never really did have the full story, maybe no practitioner did. Yet in her moments of failure, in giving up two names, Lotus may well have saved two lives.

* * *

Wang Yuzhi was outside the yard, facing the door to her mother's house. In past dreams she had tried to go to that door many times. There had been a pack of dogs in front of the house waiting, ready to raise the alarm and attack her and take her away. Now the dogs were gone. There were just kindly old people standing there smiling at her, just standing at her mother's doorway. Now they were opening the door for her.[20]

The question for Wang Yuzhi waking up was: Why was she still alive? They had been force-feeding her for months now. Just recently she wasn't getting tortured as intensely as some of the other practitioners—one of the women had a piss-soaked mop stuffed into her mouth the other day—but she wasn't getting off easy either. Still, on balance, she sensed a change in the air. She had become a problem to the detention center. She knew her screams were becoming legendary.

Martyrdom is the wild card of Chinese history. The Chinese leadership was torn between a final solution and trying to convert practitioners from Falun Gong through transformation. That's why it had become a chess game between the practitioner and the torturer. Both sides knew that each new practitioner murder had a chance of being reported, giving the state a pyrrhic victory at best.

But these games were not what the party wanted either. A woman like Wang had become toxic waste: difficult to bury, dangerous to keep around, and problematic to release.[21] The ambiguity of the government's position was expressed in an increasingly common procedure: the police would suddenly free a practitioner, having tortured him or her up to imminent death. In the early days that worked like the Sicilian warning of delivering a severed head on the doorstep of a village. Now, with global websites like Minghui.org, a severed head was potentially bad publicity.

Death quotas played a role, too, Wang knew. Every center had them: a certain amount of practitioners were allowed to die, but no more. But Wang wasn't at all sure that the quotas were as strict following the Tiananmen immolation. Maybe the reason she had survived was that the police still stood to gain a thousand yuan if they transformed her. Split up between thirteen guys—was that seventy yuan worth getting vomited on every day? No, Wang was sure that it came down to the martyr problem. And she had family abroad, so it was potentially global martyrdom. Even the guards knew that Chinese history was full of sudden revolutions and collapses. If Falun Gong was rehabilitated and the guards were identified … Wang wrote off 75 percent of the police as just plain evil—they actually wanted you to die. But about 25 percent of the police knew that the party creates these persecutions, these disturbances. And if the party falls, Wang knew that she would be a hero, a martyr. The evil guards would be incarcerated. Maybe a few of these policemen even wanted to see the party regime fall.

The detention center punted.

Wanjia literally means "ten thousand homes." It was a labor camp mostly for prostitution, robbery, and drugs. But Wang thinks there were over a thousand female practitioners detained there.[22] When Wang was transferred to Wanjia, she noticed that the regime had allocated funds for a new building. It was part of the Wanjia Hospital, but it had state-of-the-art facilities. Doctors and staff were on the first floor. There was a big monitoring room on the second floor. Most people in the wards on the second floor were female Falun Gong practitioners who had been tortured severely. The third floor was populated mostly by male practitioners who had been transferred from Changlinzi Forced Labor Camp.

Wang was driving a car. She drove it straight out of the labor camp.

Wang didn't wait for any more dreams, she simply refused all food from the moment she entered Wanjia. The cycle of force-feeding began again. But although her body was failing in every other respect, the morning routine had made her throat tougher, the muscle control slightly more accurate. So it was getting harder for them to get the tube in. During the periods when they were trying to force the tube down as she resisted, Wang started sending forth righteous thoughts, focusing the mind on eliminating all the evil forces in the cosmos.

Wang saw the Wanjia Hospital head. She knew he was one of the people in the ward in real life, but now it was just her and him. But there was something behind him: a huge, black, dog-like creature controlling his actions. The beast was enormous, the size of the entire room. At first it was a great horror when the beast began to talk, but then she started listening to the words. It was talking to her: "I know what you are doing," the beast said. "I know what you are up to." Then it paused, and its voice became somehow less accusing: "From today on," the thing said, "I will leave you alone."

It was a premonition that she would get out, the clearest one yet.

She had been on hunger strike so long that she paid no attention to the examinations the Wanjia Hospital head ordered for her. Wang knew she was on the verge of death, so even in her weak voice she would ask the doctors mockingly: "What are you examining me for? To see if I am capable of doing labor?" Wang knew that even if she died, she had already won. *My hunger striking has created too much trouble for them, too much manpower to deal with me. They want to get me out of here.*

The doctors ignored her and went on with their blood tests, examinations of her heart, and a urine test. Then a medical team probed her body, her groin, her stomach, her eyes, and her head. She thought they were measuring her brainwaves. They would ask her if she had any history of illness. Wang said she did, and she noticed that they were talking about her AB blood type. They took her different places for more physicals, but

Wang kept hearing the medical staff saying "this person is no good"; that is, she has no value. But the 6-10 Office wouldn't just let her go. They wanted to probe her body further; they still wanted to do physicals. The medical team examined Wang four times, always for an hour or two, and a little differently each time.

On the last examination she noticed something.

Passing from one room to another, Wang found herself suddenly walking alongside some practitioners that she knew, all dressed in patient gowns like her. When the doctors saw the look of recognition, they immediately separated them. It was obvious to Wang that the doctors were scared. Wang was *no good*, but many of the practitioners Wang recognized in the hospital center were men—healthy, strongly built men.

Wang was looking at two 6-10 police officers. Then two things fell out from their bodies. It was two pieces of meat. Without arms or legs, just pieces of meat.

On the edge of heart failure, Wang was escorted out of the hospital to freedom.

* * *

The doors to the caged balcony of Heizuizi Female Prison had not opened for a year, but it was a day in late March, and a warm wind had come in after the heavy snows of 2004.[23] The ice was melting and there was an irresistible, almost itchy feeling throughout Lotus's cellblock. The guards were even in an unusually good mood, as if they had some sort of secret. They kept looking at their watches. Then they abruptly walked the length of the cell to the end, unlocked the massive steel gates, and threw them open. Streaks of sunlight seemed to illuminate the entire cell and everyone, practitioners and regular prisoners alike, got up from their carefully demarcated spots and walked out to a long-forgotten balcony.

The floor was dusty from neglect. Up to the waist level, there was a concrete wall, and the top was sealed off by steel bars.

All the prisoners from seven cells stepped out at the same time. Lotus remembers how quiet it was. Everyone just breathing the air as if one could drink in traces of oceans and steppes and the Himalayas. Beyond the cell blocks and guard towers, vast clouds were tumbling across the horizon, and even the patches of grass waved exuberantly toward the sky. Under the golden light they could precisely make out every blade and even tiny white flowers pushing through the hard ground.[24]

For a change, everyone was together—all the practitioners, many with the scars of electrocution on their faces, some with enough accumulated shocks to the genitals to produce incontinence.[25] Standing among them were the hardened criminals, the drug addicts, the prostitutes, and the gangbangers who had served, at the urging of the guards, as the masters of routine punishment. Looking out at a world they could not attain, the criminals were diverted from their need for guarded expressions and set smiles. Under the warm light, Lotus remembers noticing that a few of them were actually very pretty.

A practitioner from Lotus's cell known as "Sun Shufen" had been trained on the stage. Spontaneously, softly at first, she began to sing in a spacious falsetto:

> *Coming from far away,*
> *Again and again, I come for you, I come for you . . .*

It was a Falun Gong anthem, and the four practitioners from Lotus's cell joined in, and Sun's voice swelled and trilled on the descents. Then some of the practitioners from the other cells began singing as well.

> *I come with love for you.*

All the practitioners in seven cells were singing along now, and when they reached the chorus . . .

> *Precious Chinese people, please listen to my heart-felt voice,*
> *Wonderful Falun Dafa, Falun Dafa Hao!*

... the regular prisoners joined in, too. Only half an hour ago they would have been forcing the practitioners to assume the airplane position as punishment for singing. Now, not quite knowing the lyrics other than the chorus, they hummed along.

> *See the truth behind those lies.*
> *Facing violence and danger ...*

But as they reached the bend, heading to the crescendo, they were singing along loudly again. And when the chorus came near ...

> *Again and again, I come for you, I come for you*
> *I come with love for you.*

... they began crying. Then everyone was. Across seven cells.
Then the guards said, "Okay, okay, get back inside." And everyone did. And the guards locked the steel gates and never opened them again.

7
INTO THIN AIRWAVES

A personal note: Back in 2002, I published my first report on China's big-brother Internet, documenting how Western companies were handing over key technologies to the Public Security Bureau of China that could be used to censor and track dissidents, mainly Falun Gong.[1]

These technologies, serviced and upgraded, would ultimately transform the makeshift *Great Firewall* into the sophisticated *Golden Shield*, a self-contained universe of online surveillance. I was often invited to present my research at universities, hearings, and public seminars. Over time I learned that at some point in the question-and-answer session, I would get *The Dismissal*, the eternal cry of the relativist, the sophisticate, the self-styled revolutionary: *China? It's just like that here.* The evidence consisted of stringing together words like *Patriot Act* and *Cheney* and referring to American public libraries where you aren't allowed to search for pornography or bomb recipes.

How the worm turns. How quaint my investigative research must seem in our post-Snowden world. *It's just like that here!*—is now the default attitude of the not-so-silent majority, not to mention a handful of my friends and colleagues. And yet, if NSA surveillance represents a potential threat to our way of life, is not China the living, breathing proof of it? We debate. We accuse. We project heroic traits onto Rorschach personalities such as Edward Snowden and Julian Assange. Yet China's global position has not diminished. Indeed the Chinese Internet has emerged as the gold standard of censorship, surveillance, and arrests based purely on Internet activity. Pity the China blog watchers: The largest electronic forum in the world is characterized by vast amounts of sound and fury signifying nothing all that subversive once the internal censors have done

191

192   THE SLAUGHTER

their job. So I still answer The Dismissal the same way: If you insist on believing that *it's just like that here*, if that's what it takes to make you passionate about defeating the electronic subjugation of the great and creative culture that we call China, well then, go forth. Read. Protest. Come up with a system.

It feels long ago now, but there was a time when the US State Department was eager to come up with a system to defeat the electronic subjugation of China; back in January 2010, Secretary of State Clinton gave a pay-any-price, bear-any-burden address calling for the liberation of the global Internet. The price Washington was willing to pay? It promised $50 million to groups developing "new tools that enable citizens to exercise their rights of free expression by circumventing politically motivated censorship."[2] The burden it would have to bear? The only group that had actually pulled this off was named *Falun Gong*.

Now, it is a fact that if you ever have the desire to see a Chinese administrator do a squirmy, unpleasant little dance, you have only to mention those two little words. But it is also a fact that the State Department reads *the New York Times*, which credited the Global Internet Freedom Consortium—essentially a group of Falun Gong computer engineers—with the creation of revolutionary web systems that not only enabled millions of Chinese citizens to surf beyond the Great Firewall, but also provided the platform for the vast majority of the citizen reportage that reached the West during the aborted Green Revolution in Iran.[3] By May 2010, the State Department, breaking a long-standing Washington taboo against sustained contact with Falun Gong, was reportedly ready to offer $1.5 million to the Global Internet Freedom Consortium.

Miraculously, for once, the squirmy dance apparently hadn't had its full intended effect. And for some Falun Gong practitioners, the timing seemed to carry a touch of divine justice, if not an outright Hollywood ending–for just days before the *Washington Post* reported the State Department's decision, the man whose ingenuity had spurred the group's work on Internet freedom died in China.[4]

* * *

All movements—even pocket-protector ones—have their legends and their origin myths, often set in an older, simpler place and time, as does this one.[5] But although he never won a Nobel Prize, the man who died was real. And in 2002, when China experts in the West universally judged that his cause was a failure, he commanded the most successful Falun Gong action ever undertaken on Chinese soil—the hijacking of a massive city's television signals for nearly an hour. Pulled off by a small gang with minimal experience or resources, the operation was strikingly uncharacteristic of Falun Gong at the time, but from it would grow far more sophisticated challenges to Chinese Communist Party control over information in the years to come. Television hubs would become Internet routers, guerrillas would be replaced by geeks, infocops and robbers would go virtual, and the brawl would spill out from China into Atlanta, Tehran, and the State Department. But it all started in the city of Changchun with a man named Liang Zhenxing.

Liang Zhenxing. Source: Minghui.

In the last known photograph of Liang—probably taken in mid-March 2002—his jaw is set and his eyes seem fixed on some point outside the interrogation room. Connecting the dots—the six head-level stains on the wall—some observers detect a trace of blood on Liang's left temple. Either way, Liang's posture speaks clearly enough: His run is through.

Liang could hardly have assumed that Westerners would see the picture. The Chinese police briefly published it online as a trophy—and a warning to the Chinese people—confident that no Western media outlet would bother to publish anything substantial on one more captive Falun Gong practitioner. Liang endured for eight more years, but he ultimately died in Chinese police custody on May 1, 2010, in Gongzhuling's Central Hospital. The cause of death was routine by Falun Gong standards: inexorable physical deterioration from beatings, electric shock, sleep deprivation, force-feeding. Under the strain, Liang may have accelerated things by throwing himself down a stairwell during a prison transfer, suffering a cerebral hemorrhage. In historical terms, Liang may have had an incredible run, but by the end he could no longer speak.

Falun Gong sources such as Minghui reported his demise, but no extraordinary efforts were made to promote his obituary. Perhaps there was an unconscious reluctance there; Liang's actions had once been considered to be controversial. And Liang himself had always been an outlier practitioner—a heartland Horatio Alger, a real-estate player, a mover and a schmoozer and a playboy, giving his sudden conversion to Falun Gong a cross-and-switchblade veneer. In short, Liang was a product of Changchun.

In the beginning of the second chapter, I described a gritty motor city to you, how it lies in the center of northeast China, and how, just south of Victory Park and north of Liberation Road, lies Changchun City Cultural Square where a naked cast iron man throws up his arms in triumphant despair. I described that spot because Li Hongzhi lived only a couple blocks away back in 1992, and that square was the birthplace of Falun Gong.

Liang Zhenxing lived a block away from Cultural Square, just across Liberation Road, in comfortable housing. Sometimes, in the half-light of an early winter morning, he would watch the masses of down coats and mittens hypnotically swaying in unison, right below the naked muscleman, while frigid winds whipped trash across the square. One cold morning in 1996, Liang woke up, threw on his coat, and walked over. Initially, the practitioners were nervous about Liang: his paunch (his full lotus was considered comical), his brash way of speaking, and his skeptical wife. But within a month Liang started bringing in recruits: family, real-estate contacts, intellectuals he met in the park, and working guys he met in dark clubs. Whatever passed for a hierarchy within Falun Gong quickly agreed to make Liang a coordinator, free to teach the exercises and run his own study group. Some practitioners whispered that Liang hadn't read enough or didn't have experience, but he was immune to gossip; he told a friend that the great thing about Falun Gong is that after three months you don't care about power anymore.

Yet in the eyes of the party, even the desire not to have power, if shared by enough people, becomes dark matter—a hidden gravitational force that pulls state enemies and party members alike into its orbit. By this point, you know what happened and why—how a few years later, on July 20, 1999, the arrests began in Beijing. Three days later, as the sun rose over Changchun's Cultural Square, Liang looked out. Only policemen stood beneath the triumphant muscleman.

Two months on, Liang made the acquaintance of his first interrogation room. Many Changchun practitioners had been there already. Liang had held back from public action, reasoning that the Master Li legacy meant Changchun security was abnormally high. Instead, Liang and a hundred other practitioners planned to go to the National Appeals Office in Beijing on October 1, National Day. Such a large group was easily infiltrated, and the police rounded them up before they boarded the train.

In detention, Liang refused to damage the cause by signing a public condemnation of Falun Gong or informing on his coconspirators. The police responded, as they did throughout China, by instructing the drug addicts and criminals to play tedious power games (Please may I eat? Please may I scratch? Please may I use the toilet?), where the practitioner, dedicated to compassion and nonviolence, becomes a hapless object of amusement and torture. Most practitioners quietly endured, believing that humiliation and pain have spiritual value. They hoarded indignities like money in the bank. Liang hated this, so when the criminals told the practitioners to shout party slogans as they marched in the courtyard, Liang said he wouldn't shout anything, and he took the beatings that followed. Yet what really pained Liang was that no practitioners joined his mini-rebellion. He analyzed his failings: He had the will, yet he couldn't quite articulate why his resistance mattered. Still flabby in spite of his hunger strike, he didn't inspire physical courage. But Liang had heard of someone who did.

Liu "Big Truck" Chengjun. Source: Minghui.

Liu Chengjun was a practitioner from a small town in Jilin Province not far from Changchun. As a stockroom clerk, he was just another migrant worker in the big city, but he had access to a truck. Liu's response to the Falun Gong crackdown was to load his truck with "truth-clarification" pamphlets and drive them up highway 302 to his home in Nong'an and to the surrounding villages, which, as a country boy, he knew well. That, and the fact that he was unusually large, strong, and even-featured, won him the nickname "Big Truck."

Like Liang, Big Truck didn't go along with the prison games. But he went further; other practitioners would get their legs kicked out from under them if they moved a muscle during roll call, but Big Truck would casually stroll over to the nine-foot wall of the detention compound. Confronted, he didn't raise his hand or bare his teeth. He didn't need to; the frank stare and unyielding posture, like a warrior in a Peking opera, warned the guards of untold consequences if they dared touch him. The guards developed myths: Big Truck was connected; Big Truck ate pork buns in a single bite; Big Truck was a go-to guy for organized crime. Flitting in and out of prisons and detention centers, Big Truck would carry the reputation with him.

On July 12, 2000, Liang was transferred to a labor-camp cell shared by Big Truck and a skinny little guy with glittering eyes who never seemed to shut up. Big Truck whispered to Liang that little smart-smart was a radiologist from Chuncheng Hospital, Changchun. His name was Liu Haibo, but everyone called him "Great Sea," both as a play on his Chinese name and because of his uncanny ability to memorize swaths of Master Li's writings in a single night, a data retrieval system that could seemingly have other applications. Liang was initially unimpressed with Great Sea's story: Changchun practitioner '96, two arrests, two Falun Gong renunciations, two rejections of his renunciations, never met his newborn son, Tianchun, and so on. Yet there was one incident that stood out.

Shortly after the crackdown, some party apparatchik had put up an exhibition of Falun Gong "atrocities" at a Changchun elementary school. Liang knew of it; that the authorities had forced children to see practitioner "suicides"—practitioners hanging from nooses or with their guts hacked out—had turned like a knife in his own stomach. "But don't worry, the exhibition is gone now," Great Sea said. Great Sea related that he had walked in, ripped the posters down, and thrown them away. "They were poison," Great Sea said, without a trace of anger or drama. Liang realized that Great Sea was that rarest of birds in China: a scholar without fear.

Liu "Great Sea" Haibo. Source: Minghui.

They were an odd trio, Great Sea, Big Truck, and Liang. Initially they had no plans, no journey to the West in mind. Instead, larger events would conspire to bind them together on their personal pilgrimage. By 2001, practitioners—perhaps a hundred fifty thousand or more—had gone to Tiananmen Square to protest the Falun Gong ban. It hadn't been effective; they wafted in about five hundred a day, gusting up to four thousand or so on special occasions. Even then, they unfurled their yellow banners according to some internal conscience clock rather than a preconceived strategy, making them easy pickings for the security forces. But for all its shortcomings, Tiananmen had given practitioners—so different from each other in terms of class and education level—a focal point, a commonly respected means of sincere expression that dated back to imperial China.

On the afternoon of January 23, 2001, five to seven people, and with them all the hopes of the practitioners' Tiananmen strategy, burned before their eyes in what state-run television called the self-immolation. Yet the key participants—the mother and daughter combination that ignited widespread public disgust toward Falun Gong—were not practitioners. Incarcerated in Changchun's Chaoyang Guo Prison, Liang's gang's discussions about the holes in the immolation story probably weren't all that different from mine, or so I like to think. There were rumors in practitioner circles that CNN hadn't provided the footage, as the authorities claimed. The strange camera angles and inexplicable police behavior was apparent to anyone who cared to look, not just media experts. But the real reason that they had a grip on the story was due to Great Sea, the voracious reader with the perfect recall. He related a story to them, a samizdat piece about a translation of a *Washington Post* article that reported on the discovery that the burning mother was actually a whore.

The three men had all used "truth-clarification" techniques: Liang liked tapes and remote loudspeakers. Big Truck swore by his mountains of pamphlets. Great Sea favored slogan balloons. All seemed faintly ridiculous now. Yet an article on "broadcast interruption" in Minghui had caught Liang's eye while in detention. The article spoke of the theoretical possibility of intercepting television transmissions by climbing up telephone poles, splicing into wires, and connecting DVD players. No specifics, but Great Sea's experience in radiology gave him some purchase on the electronics. Meanwhile, Big Truck worked on getting back into shape.

One chilly morning in late October 2001, as everyone slept, Big Truck got up, leapt to the edge of the wall, and pulled his massive body up and over.[6] The guards retroactively claimed they had released Big Truck, but when Liang woke up and heard about the escape, a thought flashed across his mind: he had found his general. Liang and Great Sea stopped hunger striking immediately and adopted a cooperative attitude. They were soon released.

Reunited in Changchun, the three men hit the streets and immediately began assessing transmission lines. It seemed impossible at first—just a series of lines running in every direction. But Liang's familiarity with Changchun's geography kicked in, and he noticed that each neighborhood appeared to have a box. Tracing the wires, he wondered if each box was an electronic hub. Big Truck scaled a conveniently placed wall and confirmed it. Yet even if they could map the system, there were many hubs, only three pairs of hands, and walking around craning their necks heavenward had already attracted curiosity, never mind climbing a wall (even Big Truck was afraid to climb a pole). They began sniffing around Changchun for young, athletic practitioners who were prepared to risk their lives.

Liang found three. The first was a twenty-six-year-old named Lei Ming, the little brother of the gang. Changchun at this time was a hotbed of Falun Gong activity; practically every street had a Falun Gong cell involved in making pamphlets or video discs or banners. Lei had drifted in from Jilin City, with his black leather jacket, black shoes, black pants, and a couple of T-shirts. Previously a short-order cook of northern cold dishes like pig knuckles, he was remarkably good with his hands, and he wore a perpetually self-humoring look that could morph into a strangely ominous stare if a stranger showed undue interest. Most of all, Lei was perfectly fit, in part because he'd spent less time rotting in cells than the others. After he unfurled his banner in Tiananmen, he had outrun an entire phalanx of cops, ultimately losing them in the nearby hutongs, the spider-web alleyways of Beijing.

Lei "Little Brother" Ming. Source: Minghui.

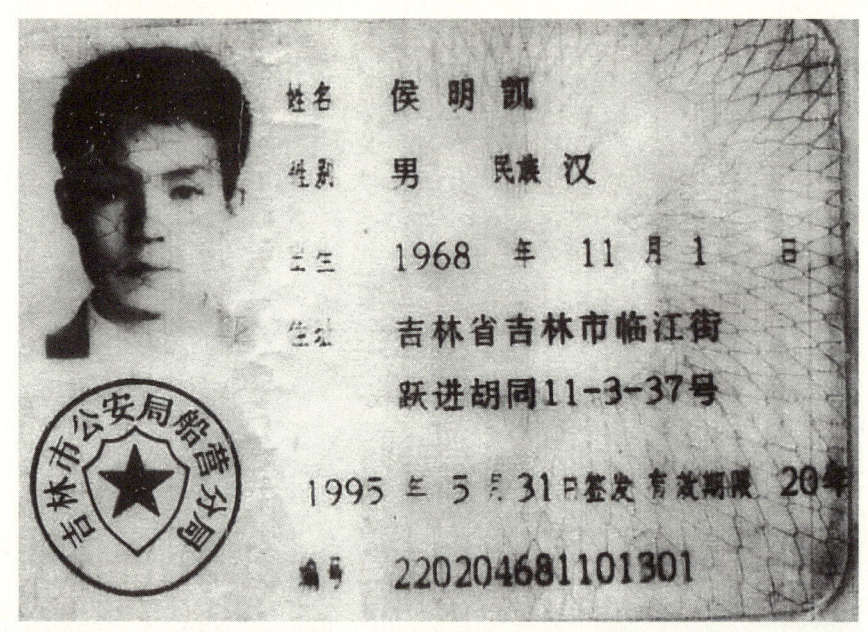

Hou "The Monkey" Mingkai. Source: Minghui.

The second recruit was thirty-two-year-old Hou Mingkai. Unlike the others, he was selected by a local coordinator because of his electrical acumen, his extraordinary fitness, his proven ability to withstand torture, and his charisma. For his part, if Hou felt any misgivings about leaving his lovely wife and daughter to go to the mattresses with Liang, he masked it by playing the court jester—or, in Chinese terms, the monkey. He had learned how to hustle at the foot of his parents' fried dough-stick stand—the entire city knew they were "long and tasty." Now Hou's absurd impersonations of interactions with police and peasant bystanders as he craned his neck to map the transmission lines (*Dude, a storm is coming. Seen my pigeon? Man, what a crap massage.*) even had Big Truck cracking up.

Finally, there was Zhou Runjun, who came in as the group's cook. Zhou also excelled at one other essential Chinese feminine activity: nagging and pestering. Great Sea always wanted to talk, theorize, and hold meetings, but Zhou would storm in from the kitchen snarling that they were all just too chicken to climb. One morning she walked in with a bundle of lineman hooks, twisted a pair onto her boots, and scaled the pole in the backyard, screeching at them as she went. Rather than listen to Zhou call them sissies all day, they followed her example. By evening, even Liang had done it once.

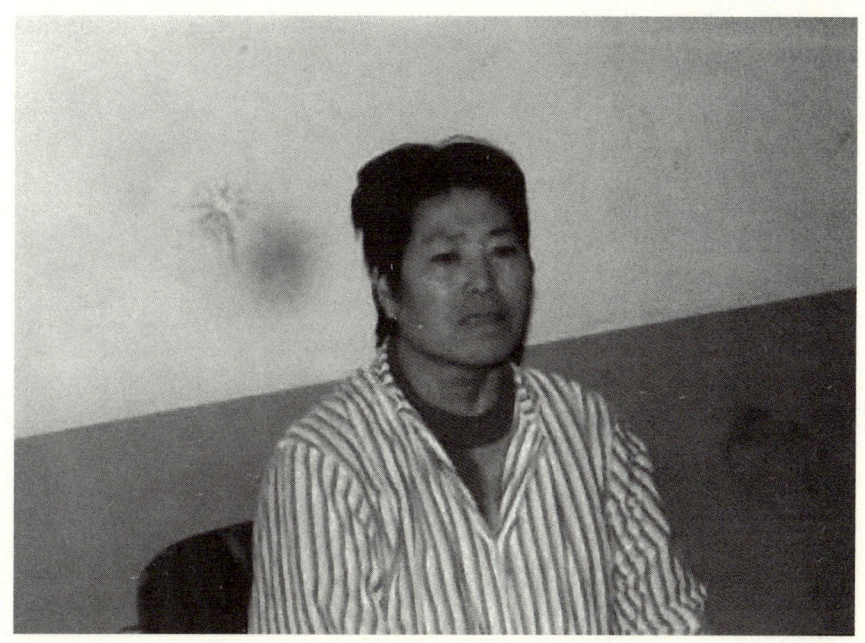

Zhou "The Cook" Runjun. Source: Minghui.

They were getting close now. During the day, they would practice on an abandoned hub pulled out of the junkyard. By night, they would scale poles in strange neighborhoods, always in pairs, with Big Truck, Monkey, or Little Brother scrambling to understand the hub configuration while Great Sea, Liang, or the Cook distracted the neighborhood watch—the old women wearing red armbands.

On the night of February 16, 2002, Liang received word that some television screens in the steel town of Anshan, a five-hour drive southwest of Changchun in Liaoning Province, had briefly flickered, gone black, and been replaced with a Falun Gong spokesman clarifying the self-immolation. It was only on cable, and it hadn't lasted more than seconds—a practitioner had been shot or a wire had short-circuited—but it could be done, and now the police would know that, too. The rehearsal schedule would have to be cut short. Liang designated the evening of March 5 as zero hour, following the kickoff of the National Party Congress, the Chinese state's equivalent of Holy Week.

While they feverishly mapped the lines, Liang faced a rearguard action. Liang kept his cell small, enforcing a no-talk zone with the practitioner community, but word had spread. Even if Liang's plan didn't involve taking over television stations with guns (as rumor briefly had it), most Changchun practitioners were dead set against the hijacking. Cutting wires was illegal, and people would hate Falun Gong even more if they missed their favorite show—yet it all came down to the practitioners' belief that it was purity of motive that counted, not worldly results (a logic that had led to millions of practitioner arrests throughout China). Even in 2002, Liang's plan sounded suspiciously like organized political action. Hadn't Master Li said that practitioners shouldn't get involved in politics? Chinese politics was a filthy business—lies, murders, graft, and karaoke bars. By that standard, Falun Gong was still as pure as white snow—the red blood of the martyrs only highlighted its radiance.

Tang Feng, a tall and stately Changchun practitioner who commanded universal respect for his convictions, was sent to Liang's hideout to talk them out of it. Liang listened carefully. Then Liang pounced: *The Tiananmen get-your-spiritual-card-stamped approach is finished—permanently contaminated by the self-immolation. So stop begging the party for mercy and go directly to the people. How people position themselves between Falun Gong and the party will determine their spiritual fates, right? Maybe the people are even with us, but not without the facts. Should only Anshan receive the facts? What about Changchun? There will never be another chance.*

Following the meeting, Tang Feng quietly informed the other practitioners that he had failed to talk Liang out of it. "Actually, I would join the hijackers myself," Tang said, "but my skills are better employed writing about these events for Minghui. And perhaps everyone should be more discreet about Liang's operation from now on."

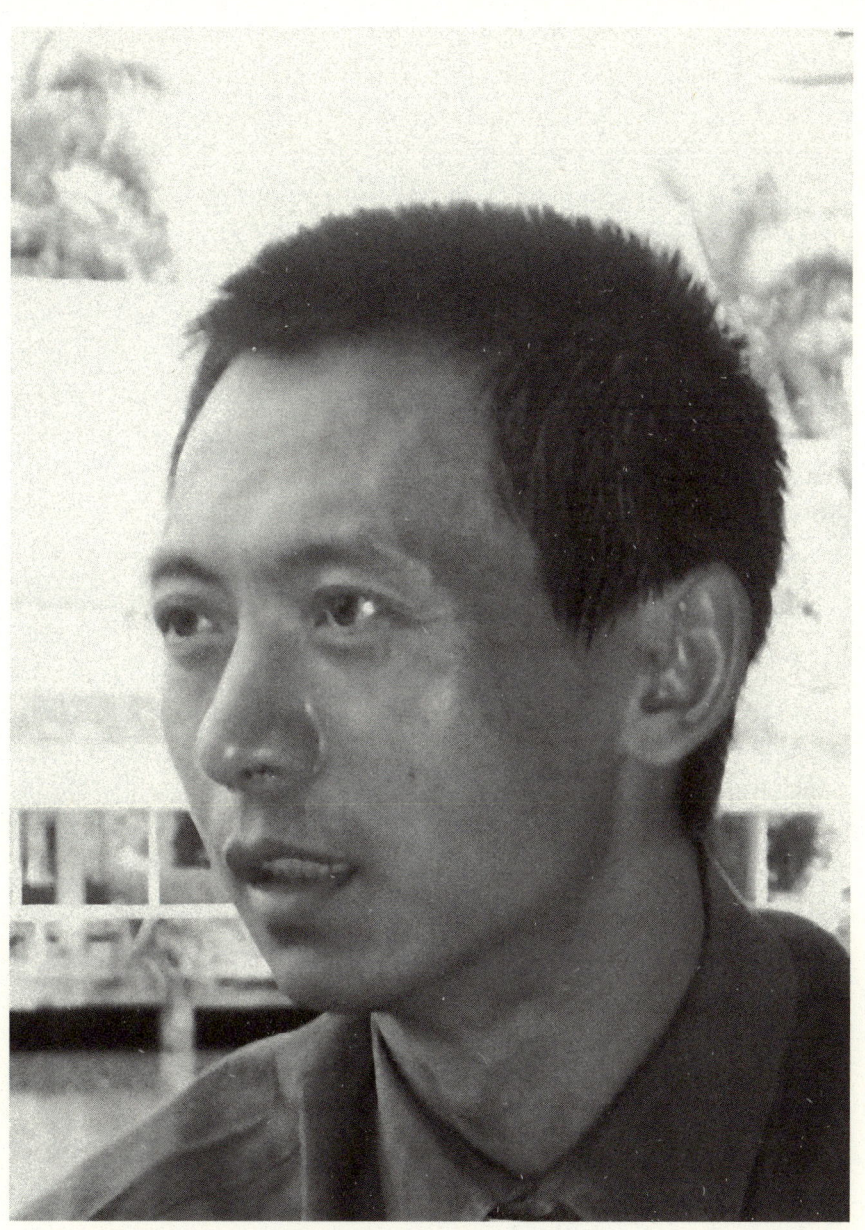

Tang Feng. Source: Minghui.

On March 1, Liang was woken up by a real-estate buddy asking him to sort some papers ASAP. Liang appeared at his former office an hour later and was suddenly surrounded by police. They drove him back to the now-familiar interrogation room.

That night the gang ate Zhou's dinner waiting for the policemen's knock on the door. It never came, so they went out mapping. Great Sea and the Monkey had finally cracked a method of splicing wires in advance so that only a last-minute adjustment would be needed. Over the next three nights they would transform every hub into a truth time bomb. Using bicycles and cabs, within fifteen minutes, they could launch across Changchun simultaneously. But it came down to the interrogation room. Maybe the police knew nothing of the hijacking plan. But they would torture Liang for names, activities, and locations. Somehow, Liang had to hold on.

Four nights later, Tang Feng went into a convenience store at a big intersection near People's Square. People were standing around watching TV, but with a curiously hunched, agitated posture. Tang looked up. A television program was wrapping up, a sort of bearded Chinese Goldstein calling the self-immolation at Tiananmen Square a "false fire," a lie, and a criminal propaganda campaign by President Jiang Zemin. Then a new program showed vast parades of yellow silk passing under the Eiffel Tower, past Big Ben and the US Capitol, explaining how Falun Gong had spread around the world and is welcomed in other countries. "What happened to the TV?" a man asked. "Maybe a neighbor is watching a video and the store is somehow picking up the signal," the owner replied, flipping through the channels. They were all showing the same program. A few people started speculating that an anti–Jiang Zemin faction had taken over the state.

Tang watched with them, feeding off their excitement, his eyes welling up, a lump growing in his throat: *Liang had held on. Now people can finally know the truth about Falun Gong. They can learn about how Falun Gong is treated in foreign countries. Their eyes are so wide open!*

Then the screen went dark, and there was no signal. After a while, Tang knew there would be no more. *They must have been discovered.* As he walked home, far in the distance, almost imperceptible, Tang thought he heard shouts coming from the direction of Cultural Square.

The Falun Gong broadcast had played on eight channels for fifty minutes, garnering an audience of over one million people, the ratings building as word spread, people calling each other, saying they should turn on their TV immediately. In some neighborhoods, local party officials grew desperate and cut the power, plunging streets into darkness. In others, such as those near Cultural Square, people spilled into the streets to celebrate. *The ban is over! Falun Gong is rehabilitated!* A few practitioners emerged from factories and hideouts, openly handing out literature. Neighbors, children, random strangers, even the old ladies with the red armbands approached them, everyone talking at once, bubbling over, laughing, slapping them playfully, congratulating them. A few suspected it had not been a government broadcast, but still they smiled broadly and whispered: "How did you do it? You Falun Gong are so amazing!" And it was almost beginning to seem as if they had been rehabilitated after all, and the euphoria and laughter did not cease, not even at 10 p.m., when the first practitioner got a phone call from a military friend saying they had orders to round up Falun Gong.

Now we're getting to the part in the story that's a bit more difficult. The ascent of the mountain, the view from the top, is interesting, perhaps even inspiring; the descent, the transformation of individuals into howling animals, less so. At this point in the book you may be weary of it too. Yet far more detailed testimony exists about the latter events, because—understandably or perversely, depending on your perspective—it is intensely important to practitioners, several of whom were even present—for example, tied to a heating pipe—to witness the moment of death.

I'm going to summarize.

Lei Ming, the little brother of the gang, was captured at 10 p.m. on March 5. Over the four days that he was bound to an iron chair, he may or may not have informed on his colleagues. Little Brother was ultimately released early and died of meticulously documented spinal injuries on August 6, 2006.

208   **THE SLAUGHTER**

Little Brother attempting to walk; screenshot from footage smuggled out of China shortly before his death. Courtesy of New Tang Dynasty Television.

It's unclear whether Jiang Zemin actually gave an order to "kill [Falun Gong] without mercy." Yet there is far less debate over whether the Jilin City head of the 6-10 Office said: "This time we will tear their skin off." It is a fact that Changchun and Jilin City officials were warned that they would lose their jobs if another hijacking occurred. The PSB and the TV Broadcast Department ordered control rooms across China to keep "eyes glued to the screen, hands glued to the buttons." Plainclothes police were mobilized to stand by television transmission poles throughout Changchun. Western television reporters were ordered not to film any Chinese television sets. And the police rounded up between two thousand and five thousand Changchun practitioners while Little Brother was tied to the iron chair.

On the evening of March 9, Great Sea was arrested in his home along with Tang Feng. The police trussed Great Sea to his living room chair and broke his ankle in front of his wife and his two-year-old son. Transferred to the Central Changchun Police Station in the early hours of March 10,

Great Sea was stripped naked and a policeman named Huo, now living in the United States, observed two police staff members forcing a high-voltage electric baton into Great Sea's rectum. A few minutes later, the policemen began calling around the station that Liu Haibo's heart had stopped. Great Sea was officially pronounced dead at Changchun Central Hospital.

Great Sea's son, Liu Tianchun. Source: Minghui.

Big Truck—always the country boy—headed back up 302 to the Nong'an area where he had relations. It is said that his young nephew was fascinated with Big Truck's cell phone. Big Truck explained that he never turned it on anymore, but the boy asked if he could keep it for a day or two. Playing with a friend on the twenty-fourth of March, he took out the phone, and the friend persuaded him to turn it on—just for a second, just to make sure it worked. When darkness fell, over sixty police officers drove into the village, surrounded the sprawling woodpile that Big Truck employed as his hideout, soaked the pile with gas, and lit it. When Big Truck emerged, they shot him twice in the thigh. It is said that the fire spread throughout the village. As the police drove Big Truck to the station, the van overturned. Practitioners like to think that Big Truck maintained the principle of nonviolence; I'm not a practitioner, so I like to think that he punched someone's lights out. Anyway, police vans don't routinely overturn, so perhaps we can split the difference and just say Big Truck attempted to escape.

Big Truck in detention. Source: Minghui.

A police photograph taken shortly afterward shows that Big Truck could no longer sit vertically. A shirt is just draped over his torso, suggesting that his arms are broken. Soon after, Big Truck spurned a China Central Television crew's attempt at an interview. From that point on he was seen being carried between incarceration centers by stretcher. Big Truck was ultimately sentenced to nineteen years in the No. 2 Prison in Jilin City, but he died of injuries with his family present on Boxing Day 2003.

On September 20, 2002, the Changchun Intermediary People's Court sentenced the Cook to twenty years in prison. It is believed that she died in labor camp.

Hou Mingkai, "The Monkey," was the last to be caught. Having escaped to neighboring Jilin City, Hou attempted to repeat the hijackings. Failing, he stayed true to his monkey persona by climbing a tree and placing loudspeakers denouncing Jiang Zemin within the Public Security Bureau compound. A bounty of fifty thousand yuan was placed on his head. On August 21, Hou was arrested in Changchun, taken to Qingming Police Station, and beaten to death by 4 a.m. the next day. The police officers then held an impromptu celebratory meal. It's unclear whether the dough sticks they ate were particularly long and tasty, but the circumstances suggest they may have been purchased at the Hou family stand.

The hijacking and its bloody aftermath galvanized a vast wave of copycat attempts, most of them failures, a few wildly successful. But it was a one-trick pony. The Changchun effect would never be repeated; with all the publicity surrounding the hijackers' arrests, no one would ever believe again that Falun Gong had been rehabilitated. But no one would ever quite believe the government's version of the Tiananmen self-immolation either. Changchun turned certain checkmate into perpetual check, but there was no international chess federation, or none that cared anyway, to enforce the draw.

It took a small cadre of Chinese practitioners in the West—elite, highly educated, cool—to realize that Chinese television, and indeed propaganda and counterpropaganda, were mere foothills. The mountain had moved.[7]

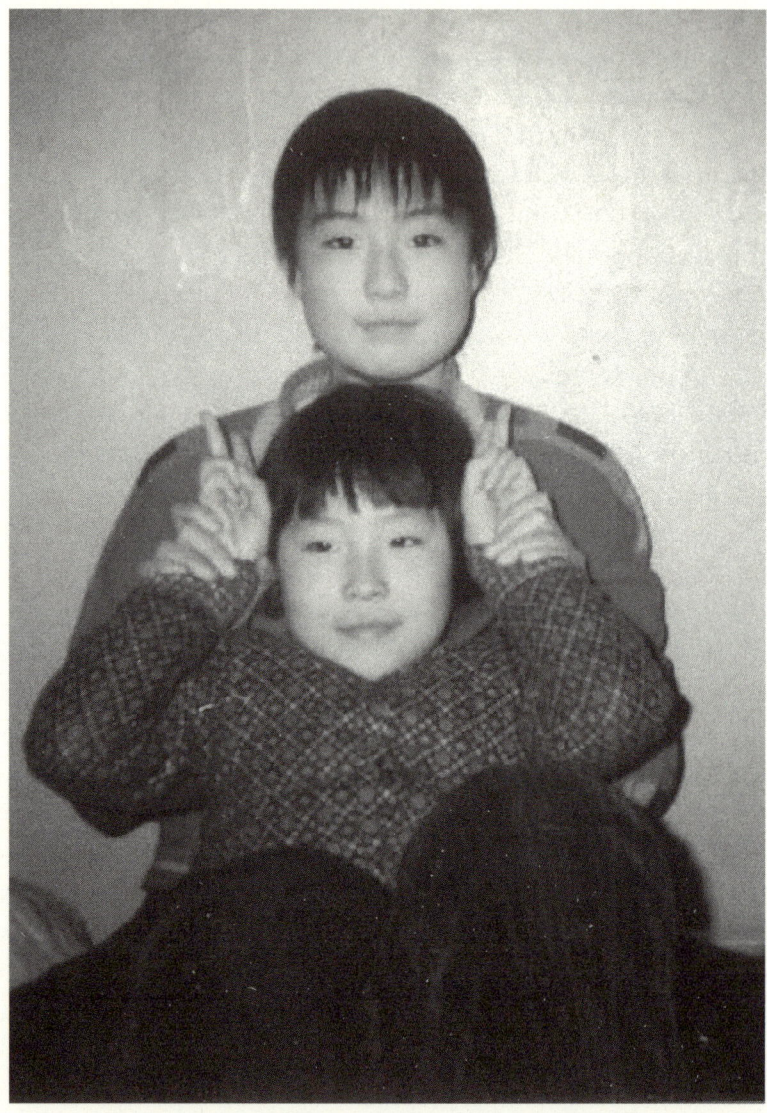

Hou Mingkai's wife and daughter. Source: Minghui.

The majority of activist practitioners in the West were dedicated to simply getting the Falun Gong story out to the greatest number of people in the shortest amount of time. Since Western journalists were not really interested, practitioners built their own media outlets—the *Epoch Times*,

New Tang Dynasty Television, Sound of Hope Radio, and Shen Yun Performing Arts. Yet all these outreach projects had various degrees of technical difficulty getting through to the mainland audience. A couple of practitioners operating out of the North Carolina suburbs looked at the problem differently; every scrap of this media could be carried on the web. Instead of explaining and defending Falun Gong, simply puncture a hole in the Great Firewall. Chinese users were hungry for alternate news sources. Perhaps they would surf for porn, or perhaps they would, in due course, find the Falun Gong websites. Either way, it was a first step.

Their engineering training dated back to the early days of the Chinese web. Because the Chinese Internet was constructed like a company barracks, in orderly blocks, the Falun Gong engineers, by looking at a seemingly meaningless series of numbers, could tell with reasonable certainty if an address was state connected. With this knowledge they could track state security behavior as if it were a dog being led around the perimeter on a daily walk. Eventually they discerned patterns—corners where the dogs gave only a cursory sniff. They built special programs simulating those corners, but with hairline cracks in the firewalls, and then used those cracks to send truckloads of uncensored news, the "Nine Commentaries" (Falun Gong's Ur-condemnation of the party), and instructions for Chinese users to set up their own wormholes.

It was a dynamic process. Bill Xia, the public face of the engineers, remembers waking up one morning to find that party censors had disabled the system. He corrected it. Ten minutes later, it was down again. And so it went for months, like salvos between the trenches, with activity falling into a lull over the Chinese New Year Festival then starting up again after the party guys got back to the office. The Falun Gong engineers introduced new weapons: spam attacks on a vast scale, dummy websites that would proliferate automatically, and evolutionary algorithms that could change Internet addresses many times within a single second yet somehow bookmark normally.

These caused havoc for the party censors—they ended up blocking Chinese government news sites by accident, and there were days when the entire Chinese Internet slowed to a crawl with incalculable losses to

Chinese ecommerce. The Falun Gong engineers soon gathered diverse reinforcements: Ultrareach, Freegate, and the other dissident systems. On a "Quit the CCP" website, millions of Chinese citizens clicked a button that renounced their party membership. Most of those who clicked probably weren't party members, yet for all the Falun Gong hype and wishful thinking, these were significant promissory gestures from Chinese citizens of all backgrounds and beliefs. More than that, the consortium became a lifeline for the underground network of Chinese activists and a conduit for uncensored information, metastasizing from the Chinese Internet into printouts and pamphlets dropped off by real people on real doorsteps across the villages of China—usually in the dead of night to the sound of an all-too-real barking dog.

To avoid the 6-10 refugee-bots, the consortium's staff was purposely kept small. But they held a lot of cards—essentially a series of proxy systems that could be played in lightning succession, confusing and counteracting the Chinese censors. They also held doomsday programs that could light up China's network like a Christmas tree in a crisis. In this manner, small cells of practitioners, operating out of offices in northern California and living rooms in North Carolina, began the process of climbing over the great Chinese firewall and forging a permanent Internet connection to China from the West.

In response, or perhaps out of simple frustration, the party's operational landscape widened. In 2004, a car full of Falun Gong legal-activists on their way to serve papers against party officials in Pretoria, South Africa, was strafed in a drive-by shooting on a highway outside the Johannesburg Airport.[8] Break-ins and vandalism of *Epoch Times* offices followed in Hong Kong and Taipei.[9] In 2006, as it became clear that Falun Gong was no longer playing for stalemate, Liu Jing, vice-director of the 6-10 Office, verbally passed down a secret fatwa on Li Hongzhi. The North American systems administrator of Falun Gong, Dr. Peter Li, was rolled into a carpet, beaten, and left bleeding in his suburban Atlanta home by a couple of Chinese hit men with mainland accents.[10] That same year, practitioners formed the Global Internet Freedom Consortium. A few years later they posted an intro page written in Farsi and—well, you know the rest.

Did Liang understand what he had wrought? It's far from clear that he was informed of any of this, or even that he would have understood the full implications had anyone told him. Whenever he was allowed fleeting contact with a practitioner, he always asked, in hushed tones, "Did our story make it into Minghui? Do they know?"

Yes, the practitioners know. But the story didn't work out quite as some had hoped. After Liang's death, the State Department balked at actually funding his Internet successors. Instead, Internews, essentially a media-training NGO, and the well-established research organization Freedom House got most of the money, thus rewarding the dual principles of political safety and utter irrelevance to the task at hand. In 2011 the State Department caved and finally sent approximately $1.5 million to the Broadcasting Board of Governors (BBG) to give to Ultrareach and Freegate. From there on out, Congress changed its strategy and started giving BBG half the Internet freedom money, which it dutifully allocated to these two companies as well. It's not enough to overwhelm the firewall, but it's a start, particularly because it has become increasingly clear that the State Department's original stated goal of liberating the Chinese Internet was essentially a feint to try to get the Chinese to negotiate an end to their own serial hacking attacks on systems in the West. But Falun Gong's howling commandos didn't die for Western network security, and they wouldn't have done it for the provincial visions of Edward Snowden or Julian Assange either.

So the Hollywood ending is delayed. But I keep hoping that somehow the hijackers' story may not be quite over. Every couple years, a new generation of Western hackers, thinly employed code writers, and angry young men emerge from the woods. They rally round the campfire of Internet freedom, feeding the fire with scary stories and fresh vows. Then they drift away in the early light, while the coals are still warm. There is a chance, remote perhaps, that some night they will get liquored up enough to leave the warmth, the humblebrags, and the laughter behind, that they will strike out into the darkness and find their way to the mountain. Perhaps they will even summon up the guts to climb it.

8

THE NAMELESS

The jeepney driver sizes us up the minute we climb in. My research assistant is a healthy, young Israeli dude, so I must be the one with the money. He addresses his broken English to me: "Girl?"

"No. No girls. Take us to the—"

"Ladyboy? Kickboxer?"

"No. No ladyboy, no kickboxer, thanks." I may be a paunchy, sweaty, middle-aged white guy, but I'm here to—well, actually, I am on my way to meet a Chinese woman in a back alley. She is going to tell me intimate stories of humiliation, torture, and sexual abuse. And the truly shameful part is that after fifty or so interviews with refugees from the Chinese Laogai System, I won't even be listening that closely.[1]

I'm in Bangkok because practitioners of Falun Gong, particularly those without passports, tend to head south when they escape from China. They make their way through Burma on motorcycles and back roads. Some have been questioned by United Nations case workers, but few have been interviewed by the press, even though, emerging from Chinese labor camps, they are eager, even desperate, to tell their stories. With the back-alley Chinese woman, I intend to subtly direct my questions away from what she'll want to talk about—persecution and spirituality—to something she might barely remember, a seemingly innocuous part of her experience: a needle jab, some poking around the abdomen, an X-ray, a urine sample—medical tests consistent with assessment of prisoners for organ harvesting.

My line of inquiry began in a Montreal community center, listening to a heavy-set middle-aged Chinese man named Wang Xiaohua, a soft-spoken ordinary guy except for the purple discoloration that extends down his forehead.[2]

He recalled a scene: About twenty male Falun Gong practitioners were standing before the empty winter fields, flanked by two armed escorts. Instead of leading them out to dig up rocks and spread fertilizer, the police had rounded them up for some sort of excursion. It almost felt like a holiday. Wang had never seen most of the prisoners' faces before. Here in Yunnan Forced Labor Camp No. 2, Falun Gong detainees were carefully kept to a minority in each cell so that the hardened criminals could enforce discipline.

The practitioners were forbidden to speak to each other, and other than quick little comments on the pretext that a shoe was untied or a belt was loose, they complied. But the guards could not stop the practitioners' eyes from searching around for the held gaze, the raised eyebrow, the quick nod—the universal signs that they had not been broken, that their defense of the Fa was steadfast. As the guards motioned for them to begin walking, Wang felt them fall into step as if they were old comrades. He looked down at the red earth, lit with flat gray light, streaked with straw and manure to the barren mountains on the horizon, and Wang found himself exulting in the moment. Whatever lay ahead, Wang knew they were not afraid.

After twenty minutes, he saw a large, gleaming structure in the distance—maybe it was a hospital, Wang thought, maybe a good thing. The summer of 2001 had been particularly brutal in southern China. After working for months in the burning sun, Wang's convict-shaved head had become deeply infected. Perhaps it was getting a little better. Or perhaps he had just become used to it; lately he only noticed the warm, rancid stench of his rotting scalp when he woke up.

Wang broke the silence, asking one of the police guards if that was the camp hospital ahead. The guard responded evenly: "You know, we care so much about you. So we are taking you to get a physical. Look how well the party treats you. Normally, this kind of thing never happens in a labor camp."

Inside the facility, the practitioners lined up and, one by one, had a large blood sample drawn. Then a urine sample, electrocardiogram, abdominal X-ray, and an eye exam. When Wang pointed to his infected scalp, the doctor mumbled something about it being normal while motioning for the next patient. Walking back to camp, the prisoners felt relieved, even a tad cocky about the whole thing. In spite of all the torture they had endured and the brutal conditions, even the Chinese government would be forced to acknowledge that practitioners of Falun Gong were extraordinarily healthy.

They never did learn the results of any of those medical tests, Wang says, a little smile suddenly breaking through. He can't help it. He survived.

I spoke with Wang in 2007, and even then his story was not new. Two prominent Canadian human rights attorneys, David Kilgour and David Matas, outlined his case and many others in their "Report into Allegations of Organ Harvesting of Falun Gong Practitioners in China," published and posted on the web in 2006.[3]

By interviewing Wang, I was tipping my hat to the extensive research already done by others. I was not expecting to see Wang's pattern repeated as my interviews progressed, nor did I expect to find that organ harvesting had spread beyond Falun Gong. On both counts, I was wrong.

I was equally surprised by the scale. In retrospect, I shouldn't have been. Numbers tend to be big in China, and it was a truism among practitioners at the time that Falun Gong was the biggest issue in China. Yet even that doesn't quite capture it. My numerical estimates of the dead, my assumptions, my methods, are all laid out in an appendix at the end of this book, but at this point, I'll just set out a few key numbers for the years 1999 to 2005.

The 6-10 Office, the entity actually charged with eliminating Falun Gong, used an internal working figure of seventy million practitioners in 1999, approximately one out of every twenty human beings in China. Following the July crackdown, Falun Gong practitioners began mass protests from provincial capitals to Tiananmen Square, and by the beginning of 2000, many of those same practitioners were facing extended incarcerations, about three years on average. If the Laogai System of China holds three to five million people at any given time, Han Guangsheng and other witnesses from inside the system suggest that Falun Gong briefly constituted the majority of the Laogai System in 2000 and 2001.[4] Regardless of the actual Falun Gong percentage, the party clearly considered the overcrowding to be a problem, and the raw numbers of Falun Gong within the system were reduced by pressure on the Laogai captains to use harsher methods to achieve transformation, methods that received tacit public support following the "self-immolation" in 2001.

The transformation rate of practitioners was internally touted as 90 percent, but Hao Fengjun of the 6-10 Office observed to me that individual "relapses" were so pervasive that he thought the real rate was more like 50 percent.[5] That squares with my interviews, and I estimate that the number of incarcerated practitioners stabilized at approximately half a million to one million practitioners at any given time. The methods of transformation appeared to stabilize as well, if we examine the confirmed deaths by torture—fully three thousand dead practitioners by 2005. That's a lowball figure rooted in what Falun Gong investigators based in the United States believed would stand up to scrutiny and the real figure is undoubtedly higher. Yet just to reach a conservative, defensible count, one that named individuals and something of their incarceration history, demanded a massive effort by practitioners. One of these practitioners is a woman I'll call "Crystal."[6]

It wasn't glamorous work. Sitting on the floor of Crystal's Canadian public-housing flat late into the evening, listening to her colloquial accent, I felt that she was a diamond in the rough, an embodiment of the sort of care and professionalism that any dissident movement desperately needs but can never recognize publicly. Originally trained as a nurse in the mainland, Crystal makes do with the simplest of tools, a landline, a recorder, a series of tricks to make her calls untraceable, and a jerry-rigged computer on which she meticulously records the status of Falun Gong practitioners for the Minghui website:

> Sometimes you had to make dozens of calls just to verify one death. Take the case of a practitioner from Northeast China: I called the police department. They said "let me call the detention center and find out for you." The detention center claimed that he was doing well—actually I believed them. But after two days, I decided to make a few more phone calls to the practitioner's workplace. He was, in fact, dead.[7]

In the autumn of 1999 the Western press was still covering the repression of Falun Gong. As the media lost interest in 2000 and 2001, the party didn't bother to contest these individual death cases. It would have been easy for Crystal to inflate the numbers a little, but she never took advantage of that opening. Even if the overall numbers of death in confinement are low, the trajectory seems plausible.

Start with 58 confirmed deaths in 1999. As Falun Gong flooded into the system, 228 deaths were recorded for the year 2000. In 2001, the death rate per year doubled again, just short of 500, and then it stayed stubbornly around the 500 per-year mark for the next several years.[8] In other words, once the Falun Gong repression ramped up, it stayed ramped at an extremely high level. Arrests, sporadic sentencing, and whatever took place in the detention centers, psychiatric institutions, and labor camps were not following any established legal procedure or restraint. Throughout the system, everyone, from Luo Gan to the prison janitor, understood that it was hazardous for one's career to not appear enthusiastic about the hunt for Falun Gong. The party's dilemma was that as Falun Gong evolved it became a moving target. While stubbornly holding to nonviolence, Falun Gong's growing activism—the grassroots efforts to influence public opinion against the party, the hijacking of television signals, the Internet penetration, and the martyr displays—was perceived as a grave danger.

Yet practitioners in captivity were increasingly vulnerable. As we saw with Lotus and her friend Wang Baogang,[9] to avoid getting other practitioners in trouble, as an act of passive resistance, but often just to avoid endangering their families, many Falun Gong began withholding their names from the police en masse, identifying themselves simply as "practitioner" or "Dafa disciple." When asked for their home province, they would answer "the cosmos." According to Crystal, for these, the nameless ones who didn't relent under torture, whose families had no way of tracing them or agitating on their behalf, there may be no records at all.

* * *

In early 2006, the first charges of large-scale harvesting of the organs of executed Falun Gong practitioners emerged from Northeast China. The *Epoch Times* ran a series of stories focused on a hospital outside of Shenyang, in the satellite city of Sujiatun. It was alleged that in 2001, accounting department employees noticed that requests for food, toilet paper, and specialized hospital equipment rose dramatically without a corresponding increase in patients. By 2002, this logistical increase represented a discrepancy of perhaps a thousand people or more.[10]

One of the accountants was also concerned about her husband, a surgeon at the hospital—his long hours on the graveyard shift, unusual amounts of cash, and signs of mental breakdown. After a year, he confessed to her: there were extra "patients" in the subterranean depths of the hospital and some makeshift operating rooms down there, too. When his cell phone rang, it meant that a "patient" had been wheeled in and given a small dose of anesthesia (the hospital had a limited supply). Then he and the other doctors—some hired from the outside, each with a specialty, all constantly on call—would come in and remove the patient's kidneys, skin tissue, corneas, and other organs, to order. The remains of the "patient" would then be carried down to the old boiler, which doubled as an incinerator. The staff helped themselves to the occasional watch or ring as a tip. The "patients" were Falun Gong practitioners—often with no arrest records. There was no need for paper work.

Several objections were quickly raised, which can be just as quickly dismissed.

The first was that Sujiatun was not legally a member of the class of hospitals that were authorized to do transplant work.[11] Yet the witness spoke of organ harvesting, not transplants. In any case, in the new entrepreneurial China, organ transplants at hospitals of a similar classification had been openly featured on Chinese state-controlled television without any apparent repercussions.

A second objection came from the US State Department. Officials from the regional consular office visited Sujiatun and "found no evidence that the site is being used for any function other than as a normal public hospital," which awarded a massive victory to Chinese propagandists.[12]

Yet three weeks had elapsed between the publication of the first story in the *Epoch Times* and the consular visit—an eternity by Chinese construction standards. There were many hospitals that one might have profitably toured three weeks after the *Epoch Times* report (particularly if one were posing as a potential patient); logically, given that its force shields were up, Sujiatun should have been on the bottom of that list.

However, a third objection—the veracity of the sources themselves—remains a legitimate question to this day. For if one wanted to create an ideal composite of the most ineffectual vehicles for such serious allegations, the witnesses, known by their aliases "Annie" and "Peter," came close to achieving it.

Truth, lies, and first witnesses. "Annie" and "Peter" at an outdoor rally across from the White House during Hu Jintao's visit. Photo by the Epoch Times.

Although Peter claimed to be a reporter, his rapid-fire release of sensational information—a SARS cover-up, a snuff tape of a Falun Gong woman being raped by Chinese police, and, by the way, a death camp named Sujiatun—made him look more like a three-card Monte dealer. Annie, the actual witness from the Sujiatun accounting department, was more nuanced. In my brief interview with her in the darkness of a parked van, I sensed that Annie was pretty shaky on the numbers, but that she had heard things in her former workplace that genuinely scared her.[13] Yet as I thought about it over the next few months, I wondered why Annie never took her dark glasses off—not even in the darkness of the van—as if the PSB of China was incapable of piecing together her identity. It was a tell. Annie was a modern-day Madame Bovary, a woman in love with her own dramatic role. She imagined her confession would galvanize flashy congressional hearings—the Hollywood version of Washington—and her urgency and outright petulance played into the *Epoch Times* decision to prematurely release the Sujiatun allegations. Tragically, this shut down the only opportunity to independently confirm the story without alerting the Chinese authorities.

It also alerted the dissident community, most notably Harry Wu—first among equals among overseas dissidents at that time—who had formidable research credentials in organ harvesting. Wu and his Laogai Research Foundation may have been a natural choice to lead the investigation but for a lot of reasons that have never been satisfactorily explained, the relationship between Wu and the *Epoch Times* devolved into a warring states period at precisely this time.[14] Wu wrote a "Dear Colleague" letter to Congress actively discrediting the *Epoch Times* investigation into the harvesting of Falun Gong in China and casting aspersions on the credibility of the practitioners themselves. They say that first impressions are everything, but the damage went beyond that; reporters searching for a skeptical voice would go back to Wu time and time again to demonstrate their "objectivity" about the organ harvesting story. Few bothered to read the actual works of the Laogai Research Foundation; if they had, they would have noticed that in 2009 Wu had unexpectedly circled back to the "worrying possibility" that Falun Gong and other prisoners were being harvested for their organs. Wu specifically referenced my work as credible evidence.[15]

THE NAMELESS 225

Indisputably, the winner of all these initial skirmishes was the Chinese Communist Party. I dredge, not to stir things up again, but because my responsibility is not to "Annie" or Harry Wu or the *Epoch Times*, but to you, the reader. If you have ever wondered about the lack of mainstream press interest in tackling the organ harvesting story, keep in mind it was this initial hand, an exceedingly weak one, which was dealt to every investigator who followed.

Sujiatun District officials mock allegations of organ harvesting—this official is holding a photograph of the boiler room in Sujiatun—at a victory-lap news conference held at the State Council Information Office. Photo released in April 2006. From facts.org.cn.

Sitting on the floor of her public-housing flat, Crystal, the Falun Gong death-case investigator, reviewed the facts: accounts of mass disappearances and unusual movements of practitioners throughout the Chinese labor camps, even the odd harvesting allegations, had been surfacing for several years. Yet Crystal was not truly convinced of Annie's credibility. On impulse, not even bothering to record the conversation,

Crystal dialed a Shenyang hospital not too far from Sujiatun, and a nurse came on the line. Crystal asked if the hospital performed kidney transplants. The nurse, perhaps sensing the intensity of voice on the other end, immediately assumed that Crystal needed a transplant.

"Yes, we have kidneys. All of them are from living young people. You should come quickly. The wait is only one or two days."

"Where do you get these people?"

"They're death-row criminals."

"Where do these death-row criminals come from?"

There was a distinct pause before the nurse said politely: "Please don't ask such questions."

Crystal felt like she was on the edge of something: *China is different from other countries. In other countries patients wait for organs. In China, organs wait for the patient.* Crystal explained to me that if a kidney actually belonged to a death-row criminal, the nurse would have to mention certain delays: there would have to be a court order to set a date for execution, the prison guards would have to produce a signed statement indicating the criminal's willingness to donate his body. The nurse said: "Two days." Many death-row criminals are old. Many, perhaps a majority, of their organs are unusable. The nurse said: "Living young people." She said: "Come quickly."

Those phrases gave Crystal the confidence to launch an unprecedented investigation. She would pose as a hard-to-please buyer and ask tough questions in her aggressive, almost abrasive style: *Are they alive? Are they young? How young? How do you know they are healthy? Where are the prisoners from? What did they do?* Crystal, along with a few other recruits (including Wang Wenyi, the Chinese-trained pathologist who would ultimately scream bloody murder during Hu Jintao's speech at the White House Rose Garden), would target eighty hospitals scattered across China. They would strike pay dirt—recorded conversations that positively affirmed that the hospital was harvesting Falun Gong—in seven medical centers.[16]

Here's a short sample of Crystal engaging a doctor in Tongji Hospital in the city of Wuhan[17]:

"Do live transplants, for example, use organs from live people who practice Falun Gong?"

"Sure."

"At your place, for example, prisoners, like those who practice Falun Gong, can you guarantee enough live supplies from such people?"

"Yes, sure! When it's convenient for you, come over and discuss the details."

Here's another recorded conversation excerpt from Zhongshan Hospital, affiliated with Fudan University in Shanghai:

"I have to have a fresh and healthy kidney. And it should be alive. You are not going to give me a kidney from a dead person, are you?"

"Of course we will give you a good kidney, how could we give you a bad one?"

". . . Do you have ones from people who practice Falun Gong? I heard that they provide very good ones."

"All that we have here are of this type."

As part of her sick-woman pose, Crystal had been explicitly told that she could get a transplant at any of six hundred medical centers across the country. Therefore, with a hit rate of roughly 10 percent, one could premise that about fifty centers were harvesting Falun Gong. I asked Crystal whether she would have received a higher hit rate in her phone calls if *Epoch Times* had not publicized Annie's claims? "I would have got 80 percent," she shot back, her eyes blazing.

It lasts less than a fraction of a second, then Crystal is patiently explaining that it wasn't just the *Epoch Times* that warned the Chinese medical establishment to stop talking about harvesting Falun Gong; Chinese practitioners had spontaneously sent missives condemning organ harvesting to hospitals across China. Crystal's frustration comes down to the "deleted scenes," the conversations that had to be left on the cutting room floor because without the little intonations, the pauses, they would look ambiguous on the printed page, and yet *both parties knew they were talking about Falun Gong*. The doctors wanted to reassure Crystal of organ quality and speed without explicitly breaking their muzzle order. A few split the difference; the First Affiliated Hospital of Qinghai University said it had Falun Gong organs but did not dare to use them now. The phone was the great inhibitor: "Often the doctors would say: Look, the news about Falun Gong is really big overseas. If you want to know more, you come over here. We'll talk face to face."

As the *Epoch Times* put out new articles with highlights of Crystal's phone investigation, the collective effect was to set off a quiet storm in the human rights community. Yet what initially drew most fire from skeptics was the claim that organs were being harvested from people before they died.

For all the Falun Gong medical theatrics being acted out on the streets of New York, there was nothing outlandish about that claim.[18] Any medical expert knows that a recipient's immune system is far less likely to reject a live organ; any transplant dealer will confirm that buyers will pay more for one. As we saw in Xinjiang, live-organ harvesting has been around experimentally since at least 1994. That the procedure was still active in 2008 was confirmed by a defector referred to as "Mr. Chen." As a non–Falun Gong prisoner, he was given the job of accompanying convicts to execution: "Instead of being executed, the prisoner was shot near his ears. The prisoner would lose consciousness but not be dead. Then the doctor would remove the prisoner's organs, and after that they would shoot the prisoner to death. They think they can hide it, but in fact we witnessed the process clearly."[19] Live-organ harvesting of prisoners is, in fact, routine. No, the real problem was that the charges came from Falun Gong—always the unplanned child of the dissident community. Unlike the Tiananmen student leaders and other Chinese prisoners of conscience who had settled into Western exile, Falun Gong marched to a distinctly Chinese drum. With its roots in a spiritual tradition from the Chinese heartland, Falun Gong would never have built a version of the Statue of Liberty and paraded it around for CNN. Indeed, to Western observers, Falun Gong public relations carried some of the uncouthness of Communist Party culture: a perception that practitioners tended to exaggerate, to create torture tableaux straight out of a Cultural Revolution opera, to spout slogans rather than facts.

Wei Jingsheng, the prominent dissident who had famously posted his essay "Fifth Modernization" on the Democracy Wall in Beijing in 1978, had his own litany of complaints with practitioners: "Initially Falun Gong said that they don't oppose the Communist Party. They were constantly waiting for amnesty. So we tried to help the Falun Gong not to wait for amnesty. But they snapped at us and told us not to help them."[20] Yet Wei defended Falun Gong within the Chinese prodemocracy community: "There's no chance that the Communist Party will end the persecution. So even if the Falun Gong doesn't want to oppose the Communist Party, they'll oppose it in the end. We need to give people time." Wei's prediction was right. Falun Gong irrevocably rejected the party in 2004 with the publication of the "Nine Commentaries on the Chinese Communist Party."[21] Ironically, even as Wei gave me an unvarnished view of Falun Gong in his Washington office, the person who was actually relating his words, his full-time translator, was a Western practitioner.

Even if Falun Gong has achieved a grudging acceptance in the dissident community, the credibility of persecuted refugees has often been doubted in the West. In 1939, a British Foreign Office official, politely speaking for the majority, described the Jews as not, perhaps, entirely reliable witnesses. During the Great Leap Forward, emaciated refugees from the mainland poured into Hong Kong, yammering about deserted villages and cannibalism. Sober Western journalists ignored these accounts because they were clearly subjective and biased.

Perhaps sensing that the yammering of a spiritual revivalist apparently counts for even less than the testimony of a peasant or a Jew, the Coalition to Investigate the Persecution of Falun Gong, with 501 (c)(3) status in the United States, formally asked David Kilgour and David Matas in their capacity as human rights lawyers to conduct an independent investigation.[22]

David Kilgour was a Canadian parliamentarian for twenty-seven years and had acquired high-level China experience as secretary of state, Asia-Pacific. David Matas, highly respected as a prolific and trusted source on a wide range of human rights issues, also possessed solid affiliations—senior legal counsel for B'nai Brith Canada and director of the International Centre for Human Rights and Democratic Development.

Both Kilgour and Matas had some previous involvement with Falun Gong human rights cases, but what really clicked was the yin-yang combination. Kilgour exudes active warmth, humor, and a sort of mercurial moral passion, while Matas is even-keeled, effortlessly systematic, and unwaveringly practical. Together, they compiled, analyzed, and verified the accumulating evidence on Falun Gong harvesting in a single report titled *Bloody Harvest*, which can fairly be called the Ur-stone of the harvesting investigation. It included transcripts of the recorded phone calls with Chinese doctors, written and transcribed testimony from the mainland of practitioners' experiences in detention, ads with transplant prices from the Chinese web, an extended interview with Annie, and comparisons of international waiting times for organs, with international customers waiting as little as a week for a tissue match (in most countries, patients waited over a year).

One of the questions Crystal posed to me was this: "There are six hundred hospitals in China that are involved in organ harvesting. The amount of organs they can provide vastly exceeds the number of death-row criminals being put to death each year. Isn't that something important that should be investigated?"

The sustained attention of the international medical community came down to the research by Kilgour and Matas on Crystal's question. Extrapolating from published Chinese numbers and casual statements that ended up on the record, Kilgour and Matas were able to clearly demonstrate that there had been an explosion in organ transplant activity that coincided with the increasing incarceration rate of Falun Gong practitioners over time. Then Kilgour and Matas compared the execution rate in China (essentially constant, according to Amnesty International) and the number of reported transplants. It left a discrepancy of 41,500 unexplained organ transplants over a five-year span. Kilgour and Matas theorized these organs could have come from no source other than Falun Gong practitioners.[23]

Bloody Harvest has never been refuted point by point—even the Chinese government only took pot shots at it, such as jeering at Kilgour and Matas for a mislabeled province—yet the vast majority of human rights activists kept their distance. Since Falun Gong claims were suspect, their allies' assertions were equally tainted. Transplant doctors who claimed to have Falun Gong organ donors in the basement? They were just saying what potential organ recipients wanted to hear. Written testimony from practitioners? They'd been prepped by activists. The rise in organ transplant activity? Maybe just better reporting. Anonymous tips from a military doctor? If it came from the *Epoch Times*, it was unreliable. The discrepancy between executions and transplants? As a respected human rights scholar asked me, why did Kilgour and Matas use Amnesty International's estimate of the number of executions in China to suggest the execution rate had stayed constant for ten years? Even Amnesty International acknowledges that its numbers might represent a gross understatement. There might be no discrepancy at all.[24] Finally, why had no real witness, a doctor or nurse who had actually operated on Falun Gong practitioners, come forward? Without such proof (although such an individual's credibility can always be savaged, even with supporting documents), human rights advocates argued there was no reason to take the story seriously.

The critics had hinted at legitimate points of discussion, but since they didn't debate the points openly, it's hard to credit them without drawing up an imaginary conversation (that's not my style, and, in any case, over the last two years several organizations, most notably Amnesty International, have begun to reframe their attitudes—although when discussing the possibility that organ harvesting of prisoners of conscience exists they will often affirm it through the use of double negatives).[25] Yet the initial political effect was chilling—for example, President George W. Bush did not mention organ harvesting in his human rights speech on the eve of the Beijing Olympics. The thaw is interminable as well; the British Foreign Service was still quoting a skeptical Congressional Research Service report from 2007 as an excuse for inaction in 2013.

Yet if there was one major player that indisputably reacted to *Bloody Harvest* it was Beijing. Fresh off the slip of the tongue in 2005 that organs were being harvested from ordinary death-row prisoners (the Chinese government officially admitted it in March 2006), and after issuing its ritual denials of harvesting organs from Falun Gong, within a month of the *Bloody Harvest* report's release in July 2006, Beijing abruptly passed a law forbidding the sale of organs without the consent of the donor. At a minimum, the Chinese leadership was implicitly recognizing that many prisoners were being executed and harvested without a consent form. In practice, the new law had as much force as serial Chinese anticounterfeiting laws—little more than a signal for major suppliers to consider relocation. So I read the party's actions as a rather weak attempt at damage control before the Beijing Olympics, but no matter how you interpret it, three things happened. The organ supply tightened. Prices doubled. And transplants continued. So unless there had been a dramatic cultural shift since 2004, when a Chinese report found that only 1.5 percent of transplanted kidneys were donated by relatives, the organs being sold had to still come from somewhere. Let's assume it was mainly regular prisoners and theorize that the new law was a signal: get your consent forms and stop harvesting from Falun Gong. For now.[26]

And the critics had one thing exactly right: precision is an illusion. No taped conversation with a mainland doctor is unimpeachable. All witnesses from China have mixed motives, always. And, again, no numbers from China, even the ones in the last paragraph, can be considered definitive.

As a former business consultant in Beijing, I carry a legitimate distrust of Chinese official numbers. I used to advise my corporate clients that even if they are looking at tapioca production figures, mainland numbers are often coded political messages that reflect reality selectively. Yet Kilgour and Matas made their calculations of Falun Gong harvesting working from figures that emerged before there was extreme political sensitivity regarding the topic. At times, Kilgour and Matas were privately disparaged because there was variance in their Chinese sources on the number of organs harvested over time. Yet to my mind, that very lack of consistency suggests that the numbers might not be party-driven propaganda.

But there is a way to bolster that claim, too, and it involves going off piste. That's what I did. There were times when I was lost, and one witness seemed much like another, just as trees do when you are skiing down a mountain by yourself. But over time I started to see a pattern, and a landscape. I expect you may see it, too.

* * *

Qu Yangyao, an articulate Chinese professional, holds three master's degrees. She is also the earliest refugee to describe an "organs only" medical examination. Qu escaped to Sydney in 2007. While a prisoner in China in June 2000, she refused to "transform"—to sign a statement rejecting Falun Gong—and was eventually transferred to a labor camp. Qu's health was fairly good, though she had lost some weight from hunger strikes. Given Qu's status and education, there were reasons to keep her healthy. The Chinese police wanted to avoid deaths in custody—less paperwork, fewer questions. At least, so Qu assumed.[27]

Qu was thirty-five years old when the police escorted her and two other practitioners into a hospital. Qu distinctly remembers the drawing of a large volume of blood, then a chest X-ray and probing. "I wasn't sure what it was about. They just touch you in different places … abdomen, liver." She doesn't remember giving a urine sample at that time, but the doctor did shine a light in her eyes, examining her corneas.

Did the doctor then ask her to trace the movement of his light with her eyes, or check her peripheral vision? No. He just checked the health of her corneas, skipping any test involving brain function. And that was it: no hammer on the knee, no feeling for lymph nodes, no examination of ears or mouth or genitals—the doctor checked her retail organs and nothing else.

I may have felt a silent chill run up my spine at points in our interview, but Qu, like many educated subjects, seemed initially unaware of the potential implications of what she was telling me. Many prisoners preserve a kind of "it can't happen here" sensibility. "I'm too important to be wiped out" is the survivor's talisman. In Qu's case, perhaps it even worked.

I asked Hao Fengjun, the 6-10 officer, if he had come in contact with these sorts of examinations. No, he said. But it wasn't his department: "Physicals would be administered through the jails. Usually when people enter a jail or labor camp they'll be given a normal examination. . . . But if large blood samples are being taken, X-rays and other stuff, that's definitely abnormal." Then he slowly added: "There's nothing that the CCP is not capable of doing. In jails and labor camps, prisoners are guinea pigs. They might as well be livestock."[28]

Falun Gong practitioners are forbidden to lie. That doesn't mean they never do. It's tempting for an individual to serve the cause by giving me what he or she thinks the world needs to hear (not because people have been "prepped"—practitioners actually tend to keep each other honest). In the course of my interviews I've heard a few distortions, mainly because an individual has suffered trauma. To repeat, the best way to guard against false testimony is to rely on extended sit-down interviews. The majority of my subjects were aware of the organ-harvesting issue, but they had no clear idea of the motivation behind my line of questioning or what were the "right" answers.

In all, from a sample of just over fifty Falun Gong refugees from labor camps or extended detention, I interviewed fifteen Falun Gong refugees who had experienced something inexplicable in a medical setting. Leeshai Lemish interviewed an unambiguous case (Dai Ying) while she was in Sweden, bringing our total to sixteen.[29] If that number seems low, consider the difficulty of survival, release, and escape from China.

Just over half of the subjects could be ruled out as serious candidates for organ harvesting: too old, too physically damaged from hard labor, or too emaciated from hunger strikes. Some were simply too shaky in their recall of specific procedures to be much help to us. Some were the subjects of drug tests at the time. Some received tests that were obviously configured to detect the SARS virus. Some received seemingly normal, comprehensive physicals, though even such people sometimes offered valuable clues.

For example, Lin Jie, a woman in her early sixties living in Sydney, reported that in May 2001, while she was incarcerated in the Chongqing Yongchuan Women's Prison, over one hundred Falun Gong women were examined "all over the body, very detailed. And they asked about our medical history."[30] Fine. Yet Lin found herself wondering why "one police per practitioner" escorted the women through the physical, as if they were dangerous criminals. Practitioners of Falun Gong can be many things—intense, moralistic, single minded—but they are strictly nonviolent. Clearly someone in the Chinese security system was nervous about these tests.

Or take Jing Tian, a female refugee in her forties, then in Bangkok.[31] In March 2002, the Shenyang Detention Center gave a comprehensive physical to all the practitioners. Jing watched the procedure carefully and saw nothing unusual. Then, in September, the authorities started expensive blood tests (these would cost about $300 per subject in the West). Jing observed that they were drawing enough blood to fill up eight test tubes per practitioner, enough for advanced diagnostics or tissue matching. Jia Xiarong, a middle-aged female prisoner who came from a family of well-connected officials, told Jing outright: "They are doing this because some aging official needs an organ."

But Jing sensed something else in the air that fall, something more substantial: prisoners were arriving in the middle of the night and disappearing before dawn. There were transports to "hospital civil defense structures" with names like Sujiatun and Yida, and hundreds of practitioners with no names, only numbers.

It was not a good time to be an angry young practitioner, according to a refugee in her thirties recently arrived in Hong Kong. She has family in China, so let's call her "Chen Jiansheng."[32] Back in 2002, Chen noticed another pattern. When the blood tests started, she said, "before signing a statement [renouncing Falun Gong] the practitioners were all given physicals. After they signed, they wouldn't get a physical again."

Chen was a "nontransformable" with an edge. Not only did she refuse to renounce Falun Gong, but she shouted down anyone who did. Chen was getting medication three times a day (possibly sedatives), so drug testing can't be absolutely ruled out. Yet as her resistance dragged on, the police said: "If you don't transform, we'll send you away. The path you have chosen is the path of death." For eight days, efforts were made to persuade Chen to renounce Falun Gong or gain her submission by torture. Suddenly, the guards ordered her to write a suicide note. Chen mocked them: "I'm not dead. So why should I sign a death certificate?"

The author with former prisoners. This picture, taken in Bangkok, is a pretty good mathematical representation of Falun Gong refugees. All these women were incarcerated in the Laogai System. All of them were tortured. One of them was sexually abused. And one of them was a candidate for organ harvesting: Jing Tian, on the left, was given suspicious blood tests over an extended period of time. She also identified several locations in Liaoning Province as organ-harvesting centers. Lotus is on the right. Photo by Leeshai Lemish.

The director brought in a group of military police doctors wearing white uniforms, male and female. The labor-camp police were "very frightened" at this point, according to Chen. They kept repeating: "If you still won't transform, what waits for you is a path to death."

Chen was blindfolded. Then she heard a familiar policewoman's voice asking the doctors to leave for a minute. When they were alone, the policewoman began blatantly pleading with her: "Chen, your life is going to be taken away. I'm not kidding you. We've been here together all this time, we've made at least some sort of connection by now. I can't bear to see this—a living person in front of my eyes about to be wiped out."

Chen stayed silent. She didn't trust the policewoman—why should she? In the last eight days, she had been hung from the ceiling. She had been burned with electric batons. She had drunk her own urine. So, the latest nice-nice trick was unconvincing. Then Chen noticed something dripping on her hand. It was the policewoman's tears. Chen allowed that she would maybe *think* about transforming. "That's all I need," the policewoman said, and following a protracted argument with the doctors, they all left.

Practitioners like to talk about altering the behavior of police and security personnel through the power of their compassion. It's a favorite trope. Just as a prisoner of war is duty-bound to attempt escape, a Falun Gong practitioner is required by his or her moral code to try to save sentient beings. In this spiritual calculus, the policeman who uses torture destroys himself, not the practitioner. If the practitioner can alter his behavior, through moral example or through supernatural means—just as when a prisoner of war completes a tunnel—there's some natural pride, even if the tunnel never gets used, even if the practitioner still gets tortured.

But practitioners vary. Chen did not tell her story with composure. Under a Hong Kong streetlight, she screams the whole thing out cathartically in a single note of abrasive, consuming fury. It's also relevant that Chen is not just stubborn, impossible, and a little mad, but young, attractive, and charismatic. She gave her account of the policewoman without braggadocio, only abject, shrieking shame at having finally signed a transformation statement. As Chen's voice echoes back through the Hong Kong night, I sense that the policewoman might have felt like she had met a fellow warrior. Tears are plausible.

The presence of the military doctors in Chen's account also jibes with certain structural mysteries that Crystal had come across.[33] As Crystal explains, local armed police and people's courts are in charge of putting criminals to death. In this case, we can also assume that one of the people present during Chen's torture was from the 6-10 Office and gave the go-ahead for Chen to be selected for harvesting. The People's Liberation Army does not ordinarily get involved in executions, and yet Crystal asserts that not only were the military hospitals the vanguard of harvesting Falun Gong, it was usually the military doctors who performed the surgery. This division of labor worked relatively seamlessly when a policeman shoots a prisoner in a nonlethal way and then a military surgeon takes the living body and goes to work. But as organ harvesting turned to more advanced "surgical" methods of execution such as light anesthesia followed by lethal injection—the timing of Chen's proposed execution could still be considered to be on the cusp between the two methods—the military surgeons could theoretically have had Chen's organs, and any profits that came from transplanting them, all to themselves. Although it is not commonly understood in the West, the Chinese military, and its associated assets, such as real estate and hospitals, are permitted, and even officially encouraged, to behave as capitalist enterprises whenever possible. Deng Xiaoping ordered the army to start paying part of its own freight, and it has never stopped doing so. As one Taiwanese doctor who had studied the situation closely put it, "China's Department of Health can't control the military. It's always been like this—for sixty years the government cannot control the military. The Department of Health has many regulations, but these cannot be carried over to military hospitals."[34]

At the same time, the organ harvesting procedure was not a normal capitalist enterprise but a hybrid between medical profiteering and state imperatives; harvesting of Falun Gong can be said to exist in a space that is neither fully legal nor illegal. Crystal observed that while the surgeons are almost always military, the armed police hospitals often provide the hospital infrastructure, including the actual gurneys. Yet if that is correct, this doubles the chances of information leaking out.

We can only theorize. One possibility is that the police continued to stay involved in organ harvesting out of bureaucratic inertia or simply to help manage the overflow from the military hospitals. Or perhaps Falun Gong practitioner organs are simply seen as valuable assets and the police compete with the military to carve them up. According to Crystal, the courts also got in on the action as paid arbitrators: "If the police give more money to the court, then they will receive more organs. If the police give them less, then they will receive less." Bolstering this theory is Crystal's observation that when the police oversaw the operations themselves, they tended to keep it strictly in-house; in an armed police hospital in Shanxi

Province, Crystal was told "there will be a room with only a few people inside, and they will pick the donor... saying they must draw some blood for testing. If the donor does not allow them to do so, a few policemen will pin the person down by force.... Under these circumstances, sometimes they will operate on seven or eight people in one single day."

Dai Ying is a fifty-year-old female refugee living in Norway.[35] As 2003 began, 180 Falun Gong practitioners were tested in Sanshui Labor Camp where she was locked up. The usual our-party-especially-cares-for-you speech was followed by X-rays, the drawing of massive blood samples, cardiograms, urine tests, and then probes: "They had us lie on [our] stomachs and examined our kidneys. They tapped on them and ask[ed] us if that hurt." And that was it—organs only, hold the corneas—a fact that Dai, almost blind from torture at the time, remembers vividly. Corneas are relatively small-ticket items, worth perhaps $30,000. By 2003, Chinese doctors had fully mastered the liver transplant, worth about $115,000 from a foreign customer.

To meet the demand, a new source of supply was needed. Fang Siyi is a forty-year-old female refugee in Bangkok.[36] Incarcerated from 2002 to 2005, Fang was examined repeatedly, and then, in 2003, she was picked out for special testing in the Jilin Detention Center in northeastern China. Fang had never seen the doctors before: "Upon arriving, they changed into labor-camp uniforms. But what struck me is that they seemed to be military doctors." Twelve prisoners had been selected. Fang estimates that eight were Falun Gong. How did she know? "For Falun Gong, they called them, Little Faluns." Who were the other four? "[The staff] would say—Here comes another one of those Eastern Lightning."

Eastern Lightning are Christians—fringy, out-there Chinese Christians to us; incurable, nontransformable deviants to the party. Jing, too, remembers Eastern Lightning being given blood tests in 2002, but Fang remembers the Jilin exam as far more focused: "The additional examinations would just be blood tests, electrocardiograms, and X-rays, nothing else. It was just Falun Gong practitioners and Christians."

Fang Siyi with her child following a public parade in Bangkok. In 2003, she was examined repeatedly with other prisoners who the guards referred to as "Eastern Lightning." "[The] examinations were blood tests, electrocardiograms, and X-rays, nothing else. Just Falun Gong and Christians." Photo by Leeshai Lemish.

* * *

The Tibetan government in exile sits perched on the upper reaches of the Kangra Valley, on the edge of the Indian Himalayan Region, in a town called Dharamsala. If you have never heard of it that may say less about your knowledge of the world than about your age. Every year, droves of hip young Westerners, armed with backpacks and phones that can do clever tricks, brave long-haul train rides and gastric upset to make their way to Dharamsala. They go because it's interesting and it's a place to hang, but above all, they go to seek spiritual awakening.

Jaya Gibson was young. He was also a jack of all human rights trades, including film production, legal activism, and research. Having arrived the day before, Gibson was settling into a serious exploratory mission:

to interview and record Tibetan refugees from China's labor-camp and prison system, particularly those who had experienced unusual medical treatment while in Chinese captivity. Thus, Gibson had no plans for any sort of "awakening," but as he walked by the storefronts along Bhagsu Road in the mountain village of Mcleodganj, he got one.[37]

It was at the DVD rental shop—hanging in the front window, in a sort of massive grid, were perhaps forty DVD sleeves, most of them documentaries: Tibetan culture, the Dalai Lama, the colorful monasteries, Buddhist teachings—check, check, yeah, yeah—*but the hook was always Tibetan human rights*. Jaya had interviewed two refugees the day before, and he was pleased that he had hit the ground running. The conversations had been very emotional and intense . . . but now, staring at the DVDs, Gibson could feel the blood drain from his body: *Oh, my God. This has been done before. Done to death.*

Gibson had listened to his friend Gutmann describe the raw hunger of the Falun Gong refugees in Bangkok, the desperation to tell every aspect of their story. With practitioners in Singapore, Gibson had experienced this, too. But here? In the most authentic place—authentic-looking place, anyway—on earth, the Tibetan refugees were gorged on media, bathing in it, so used to the documentary crews—there were three in town right now—that they had their entire spiel down pat: Sit down. Talk for thirty minutes. Done.

But damn it, Gibson didn't need their sound bites, their tears, their disposable tales of woe—that's all he really got yesterday—but their long-form story, the facts, including the dust balls of memory taken from the most arcane and boring days they had ever spent with Chinese guards and doctors. No wonder his subjects had looked slightly offended yesterday; they felt like they were being interrogated all over again.

A few nights later, in a café, Gibson watched a young American ostentatiously lecture a couple of monks how the Dalai Lama should be podcasting and employing social media—two ordinary monks who probably have never even met the Dalai Lama, two monks who have been in front of cameras more than any of us have. *How perfectly naïve we all are*, Gibson thought.

Gibson needed a new method to establish legitimacy. The Tibetan Center for Human Rights and Democracy interviews every refugee who comes into Dharamsala, about two hundred a month on average. So Gibson sat down and read the briefs carefully. Then, face to face with the witness, Gibson would tell the cameraman to stand down before soberly explaining that there were some further questions to be asked about his or her experience. He found himself depersonalizing the interview process, almost like he was a government bureaucrat. If he stayed focused and firm, the witnesses would eventually follow.

Gibson interviewed approximately forty subjects over a ten-week period. Unlike Falun Gong, the majority were not recent prisoners; they had been incarcerated in the 1990s. The one consistency: blood testing, often in large enough samples (350ml) that it may have been actual blood banking, particularly in the notorious Gutsa Detention Center in Lhasa. Only one out of ten prisoners had never been tested.

One refugee remembered a huge blood-taking operation in the 1990s, when military doctors came to a prison and took a pinprick sample from some seven hundred prisoners, then lined up all the prisoners according to blood type and age, fourteen lines, and took a large amount of blood from each. Several witnesses mentioned that this was being carried out by military doctors of the "Zheng Ye" military hospital, an elite facility built in 1991 specifically for military officers and CCP officials. The blood extraction process occurred on a twice-monthly schedule, always on the day prior to prison transfers.

Rather than interpreting this as a harvesting scheme, Gibson notes that no medical exams were given prior or after the extraction. But there was a purpose; one witness with a rare blood type mentioned that he was once recalled to Gutsa from Drapchi Prison and held for another month so blood could be extracted two more times. An important military or CCP official may have needed his blood type urgently. The explanation given for the blood-banking practice was "you need to pay for your food with blood," and the prisoners did not question it. In 1994, the explanation shifted to "this is a medical examination for your benefit." That same year, there were rumors of harvesting for the first time. This may have signaled the beginning of harvesting Tibetan prisoners of conscience—three years ahead of the confirmed harvesting of Uyghur political prisoners—but Gibson is skeptical that it took place on any significant scale during the 1990s:

> On one hand it's clear that the Tibetans were completely unaware of what could possibly be happening to their people—in terms of organ harvesting and medical experimentation.... Yet one of the reasons that the Tibetans haven't been harvested on a scale that's been easy to recognize is proximity to medical facilities. They are far, and even further away from the patients. From a marketing perspective: There's a supply, but perhaps not the proximity demand that you see in other parts of China. I think it's that simple really.

By 2002, when organ harvesting of Falun Gong was becoming more common, one of Gibson's witnesses mentioned an old prison in bordering Sichuan Province, housing about eight hundred inmates, suddenly receiving an upgrade in the form of an unusually large, state-of-the-art hospital facility. Gibson notes that Kilgour and Matas (and indeed Crystal) have identified Sichuan as a potential organ-harvesting hotspot. The prison was also unusual because it had not only Tibetans, but Falun Gong.[38] According to a second witness, by late 2003, a Tibetan doctor began independently investigating whether Drapchi Prison in Tibet proper was harvesting Tibetan activists. The doctor's fate is unknown.

A Tibetan witness, who has to keep his identity secret, told Gibson the story of a family member who got sick and went to the doctor to get help. He was in and out, but he died in a fairly short time. The Tomden, a sort of shaman or specialized butcher who prepares the body and carries out the Tibetan funeral rites, broke with precedent and allowed the witness to see the body before he began his work. Both kidneys had been removed.

Two conditions shifted after the Tibetan uprising of 2008: First, the transfer of Tibetan prisoners to Sichuan and Qinghai Province (another organ-harvesting hotspot according to Crystal) increased. Second, the construction of advanced hospitals in Tibet expanded dramatically.

Lhamo Kyap was still in Chushul Prison during the Tibetan uprising, having been captured (arrest would be too formal a word) in May 2006 and incarcerated for three years. He was given a suspicious physical exam followed by what he terms a "deliberate beating." It was tactical, aimed at one side to protect the organs. While he lay on the floor, the prison guards tried to coerce him into surgery and asked him to sign something he couldn't read. Kyap managed to escape. He believes the surgery was a pretext to take his organs: "Everyone knows that they do this to kill high-level lamas and political dissidents."

The last case, and the one that Gibson believes is most significant in terms of conforming to the organ-harvesting physical examination pattern is that of a monk named Tenpa Dargyay. After the March riots in Tibet in 2008, Dargyay and other monks were moved to locations in Sichuan or Southern Gansu Province. One day, the monk was escorted from the prison with about eighteen others. Each monk had a soldier to one side and a police officer on the other. On the bus, they were told to look forward and not to look out the window. Arriving at what appeared to be a hospital, the monks were hooded and led inside. Dargyay described it as a shockingly high-tech facility—the stuff of dreams. He was a given a scan, what Dargyay describes as a chest or abdominal examination, done standing. Then the doctors took 100ml of blood. There was no reflex check, no tongue, no ear, no nose, no throat, no genitals or lymph nodes. Very quick, and they all went through the same procedure. The hospital was in a town, so he did not believe it was a military hospital, but a private one. Then the monks were escorted back to the prison, an armed man on each side again. The monks were told this was for their own good, but Dargyay thought the whole thing was very strange. He doesn't recollect if there were disappearances following the exams. In general, Dargyay describes a very fluid situation: prisons (not labor camps), no formal charges, no trial, just thrown in there, taken out, and moved around. Brute force and blood tests were the only constant.

Overall, three subjects had organs-only exams, all appearing in a cluster after 2005, and were witness to approximately thirty-three other prisoners receiving the same exams.

THE NAMELESS 245

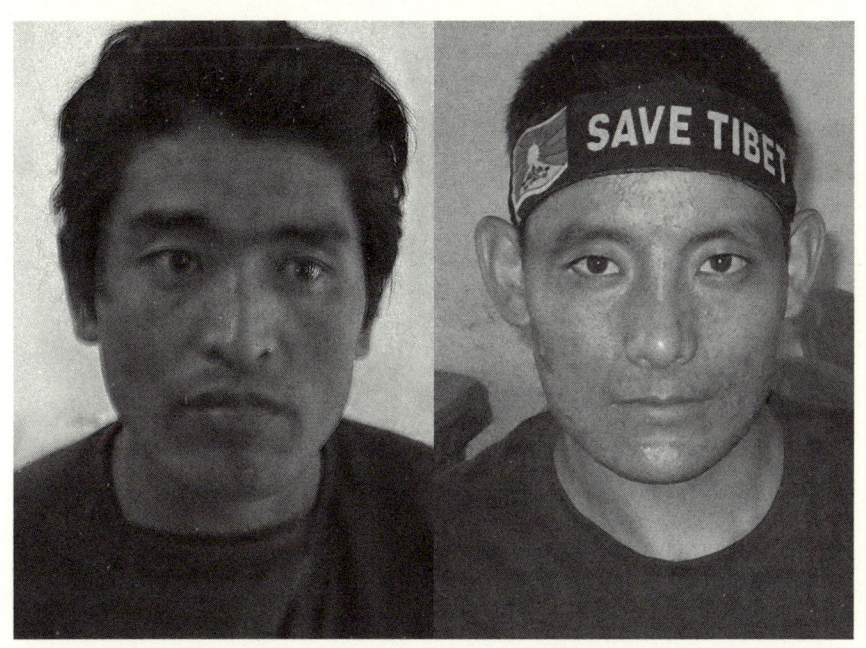

Two who came back alive: Lhamo Kyap (left) and Tenpa Dargyay (right). Photos taken by Jaya Gibson in Dharamsala.

Gibson took his findings to the human rights center, to the prime minister, and to the Dalai Lama himself. At the human-rights center, Gibson was met with an initial blast of shock, followed by a state of denial, then a period of soul searching as to why they had never really asked medical questions in their debriefings before. Finally, with some reluctance, they approached Gibson with a practical question: *How do we start asking these questions in addition to the comprehensive surveys we already do?* It was a paradigm shift for the caseworkers. When Gibson met with the Dalai Lama, he was supportive and brought up stories of children being snatched for possible organ harvesting; he even offered eight million rupees (about $135,000) to fund a documentary to get the word out. Yet Gibson quickly realized that members of the higher staff at the political level still had their heads in the sand: *No, no, no. We don't want to look at it, we don't want to touch it.* The policy of dialogue with the Chinese leadership came first, and they would not want to have the Dalai Lama connected with the research. And like a typical episode of the satirical British sitcom *Yes Minister*, the staff won.

246　THE SLAUGHTER

His Holiness and Jaya Gibson. Courtesy of Jaya Gibson.

Approximately seven hundred to one thousand monks were rounded up in August 2008 and sent to a military detention centers, the most prominent based in Golmud, close to the First Affiliated Hospital of Qinghai University. Hundreds have not returned.[39] There are many murky aspects to the Tibetan case, many mysteries that will never be fully solved, but we can say that the ongoing Tibetan policy of dialogue with China appears not to have inhibited the harvesting of Tibetan prisoners of conscience. Neither did the increased scrutiny that accompanied the 2008 Beijing Olympics. For now the party policy of Tibetan exploitation and extinction appears to be in full swing. Perhaps I'll be proved wrong and that policy will change, but for hundreds of Tibetans, that correction may come too late.

* * *

Compassion fatigue seeping in? I'll keep this short. "Masanjia Confidential" has family in China, so prudence dictates mentioning only that she's about forty and was in Bangkok during our interview.[40] Her experience takes us into what I call the "Mature Harvest Era" of 2005, when many practitioners seem to have been whisked off to wham-bam organ exams and then promptly disappeared. When I asked her if anyone in Masanjia Labor Camp actually received medical treatment, she responded without missing a beat: "If people came in on a stretcher, they were given cursory treatment. In good health, a comprehensive exam. They needed healthy people, young people. If you were an auntie in your sixties or seventies they wouldn't pay attention to you." Were there military personnel present at the physicals? "They didn't need them. Masanjia is very close to Sujiatun—a pretty quick drive. If they needed someone, they could just tie them up and send them over.... Usually they were taken at night."

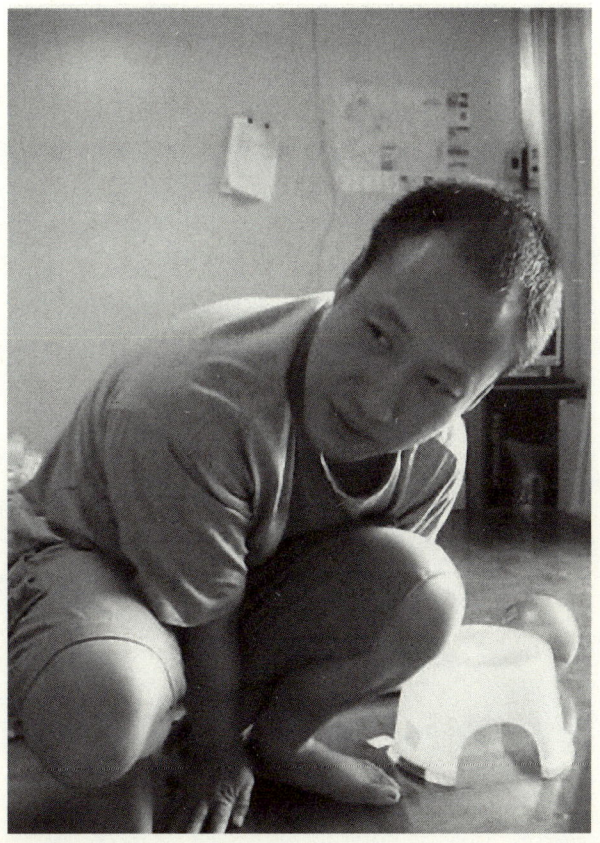

"Even before you die, your organs are already reserved": Yu Xinhui in Bangkok. Photo by Leeshai Lemish.

248 THE SLAUGHTER

In 2007, Yu Xinhui, free after five years in Guangdong Prison, signed himself, his wife, and their infant son up for a foreign trip with a Chinese tour group.[41] Upon arriving in Bangkok, they fled to the YMCA and applied for United Nations refugee status. Yu is in his thirties, the picture of robust health. While in prison, he was tested repeatedly, finally graduating to an "organs-only" exam under military supervision in 2005. Yu makes a good show of indulging my questions, but to him it was never a big mystery: "There was common knowledge of organ harvesting in the prison. ... Even before you die, your organs are already reserved." Criminal prisoners would taunt the practitioners: "If you don't do what we say we'll torture you to death and sell your organs." That sounds like a stupid game, but everyone knew there was a real list: prisoners and practitioners alike would be taken away on an annual schedule. Yu knew which month the buses would arrive and where they would park in the courtyard. He gave me a tour of the exact spot on Google Earth.

Guangdong Prison seen from Google Earth in July 2008. According to Yu Xinhui, the buses to collect prisoners selected for organ harvesting would arrive in the center of the compound, at the lower right-hand corner of the empty field. Map data from Google Earth, 2008.

When Falun Gong's claims about organ harvesting surfaced in March 2006, Yu still languished in prison, incommunicado. So it's all the more interesting that he vividly remembers a large, panicky deportation of prisoners (perhaps four hundred people, including practitioners) in May 2006. "It was terrifying," Yu says. "Even I was terrified." The timing is consistent: with all the bad publicity, mainland doctors were hinting at a close-of-business sale on organs at exactly this time.

By 2007, the consensus was that the Chinese government had shut down Falun Gong harvesting to avoid any embarrassing new disclosures before the Olympics. So my final case in this chapter must be viewed as borderline, a comprehensive medical exam followed by . . . well, judge for yourself.

Liu Guifu is a forty-eight-year-old woman who arrived in Bangkok in 2008.[42] She got a soup-to-nuts physical—really a series of them—in Beijing Women's Labor Camp in 2007. She was also diagnosed as schizophrenic and possibly given drugs.

But she remembers her exams pretty well. She was given three urine tests in a single month. She was told to drink fluids and refrain from urinating until she got to the hospital. Was this testing for diabetes or drugs? It can't be ruled out. But neither can kidney-function assessment. And three major blood samples were drawn in the same month. Was the labor camp concerned about Liu's health? Or the health of a particular organ? Perhaps an organ that was being tissue matched with a high-ranking cadre or a rich foreign customer?

The critical fact is that Liu was both a member of a nontransformable Falun Gong brigade (with a history of being used for organs) and considered mentally ill. To the party, she was useless. She was also alone, the closest approximation we have to a nameless practitioner, one of the ones who never gave their names or home provinces to the authorities and so lost their meager social protections.

There were thousands of practitioners identified by numbers only. I've heard that number two hundred and something was a talented young female artist with nice skin, but I don't really know. In over a hundred interviews I only met one nameless practitioner who made it out of China alive. Her organs were even more worn out than my own.

250   THE SLAUGHTER

According to Crystal, the doctors' euphemism for the nameless ones was the "homeless."[43] Crystal used the expression, too. It was a way of establishing a sort of code, an understanding with the doctor so that he or she could relax and talk more freely. The doctors told her that if a practitioner was "homeless," if "they don't have information on the family, they just handle the bodies themselves." If they identified a practitioner's province and family members, the procedure was "to have the organs harvested and then inform the family [of the death]. After cremating the body, they would give the ashes to the family."

Certain cremation centers stand out in Crystal's mind: the Changchun factory site where dozens of corpses were uncovered by earthmoving equipment. Zhenjiang City in Jiangsu Province where, according to the staff, "the military sends over carloads of corpses with missing organs to be cremated."

Sometimes the hospitals just sent small plastic bags with human remains to Zhenjiang. Of course the family would want to know that the whole body had been cremated but "the staff said that any part of the body can be used: the internal organs and the skin for transplant. Even the hair can be made into wigs. So the intestines are the only thing that's left."

* * *

I confess that I felt a touch of burnout when Crystal presented that image to me. It's an occupational hazard. It's why I told that one-night-in-Bangkok joke in the first paragraph—just to get on with the writing. But what's really laughable is the foot-dragging, formalistic, faintly embarrassed response of so many in the human rights community, for so many years, to the murder of prisoners of conscience in China. Some will fight hard to read these on-the-ground accounts with skepticism. To verify the shape of the landscape, they need confirmation not just from below, but from above. Well—me, too. And the next chapter will provide that. Yet the real essence of their resistance is based less on evidence, and more on an accusation: that those who work on this sort of primary research are dreamers, not doers. After all, *you* don't have to negotiate with the

Chinese Communist Party. *You* don't fight to save individual lives like the American businessman John Kamm or Amnesty International. *You* won't get a tour of a labor camp like a UN representative. *You* won't even get an entry visa.

I acknowledge their point, and as someone who worked in Beijing for years, that acknowledgment is not simply politic. We all have to live with the Chinese Communist Party, for now. For that matter, we can console ourselves that there is no irrefutable physical evidence, no bones, for now. There will be none until the party falls and the Chinese people begin to sift through the graves and ashes.

Until that time, as I said in the first chapter, investigating harvesting puts us in the position of the early dinosaur hunters. Our findings threaten an established orthodoxy, a faith, not in Genesis, but in slow-but-certain economic and social progress, China's progress. Just as paleontological experts like Richard Owen had to coin the term *dinosaur*, a word that literally means "terrible lizard," we have to make up terms to explain our findings—*nontransformable, nameless ones, organs-only, Xinjiang Procedure*....

We are all allowed a touch of compassion fatigue—it's understandable. But make no mistake: There are terrible lizards. And in spite of all of Beijing's serial promises of medical reform—turning scalpels into ploughshares, labor camps into drug rehab centers—they roam the earth today.

9
ORGANS OF THE STATE

There's a set moment in an interview when both sides feel out each other's intentions, and initially, I thought I was the problem. I wasn't quite ready to explain to Dr. Ko Wen-je—a senior surgeon at National Taiwan University Hospital—that Leeshai had obtained his name through the Taiwanese medical grapevine by asking for someone who might know something about mainland transplants... in short, that our sitting down together was an absurd long shot.[1] Nothing about Dr. Ko's demeanor, his urbane manner, even the sophistication of his gentle handshake suggested mainland rigidity or some sort of prejudice, but the air felt distinctly ominous, as if a thunderstorm was imminent. It didn't help that both of us—I'm a big guy and Ko's unusually tall—were perched on two flimsy plastic chairs inside a cramped little office, close enough to smell each other's sweat. I blandly opened by telling Dr. Ko that I was interested in any information he might be able to provide about organ harvesting in the mainland.

Dr. Ko dismissed my quest as futile. With impatient authority, Ko laid down all the confining features: There is no centralized database of organ donors in China. Instead, doctors use an informal eBay-style system because it's an entrepreneurial business that operates in a gray market. Hospital staffers use their personal connections to acquire donors and recipients alike. Advertising for organ transplants appears not only on the web (bait for foreigners, and I'd seen some of those sites) but also at the street level for potential Chinese patrons—stickers in phone booths, ads in little trade newspapers, flyers on bulletin boards.

The similarity to escort services ran through my mind. Perhaps a minute flicker of disgust crossed my face. Perhaps not. Either way, Dr. Ko appeared to take the silence as a challenge, and his voice rose slightly.

"You really don't understand, do you? You can do whatever you want in China. Cut someone up. Cut their dick off if you like."

He showed his teeth as he presented me with a smile that wasn't pleasant. This was unsettling. Yet my real fear was not that he would call me a stupid foreigner again but that he would shut down the interview. I had no choice but to be perfectly candid:

"Look, I am not from a government agency. I can't make you talk about this. I'm just a writer. I have no power to prosecute you or cause trouble for your practice. And I know that you care about your patients. By going to the mainland for transplants, you are saving lives."

Leeshai jumped in:

"I've just come from Israel. The government has banned organ tourism to China because there is no way of determining whether an organ comes from a legally executed criminal or a prisoner of conscience."

"Do you want that to happen here?" I added. "It will, if it's not cleaned up. . . . So is it true? Aren't prisoners of conscience—Falun Gong, perhaps others, being harvested?"

What happened next was something I thought only occurred in the movies. Ko's body seemed to simply retract, his jaw, his shoulders collapsing. His eyes gazing at the emptiness of the wall, he fell into a barely audible hiss. "Yes," Dr. Ko said, "Yes, they are doing that. Yes, it's true."[2]

* * *

A few years before we showed up at his office, Dr. Ko began thinking about going to the mainland to acquire human organs.[3] It wasn't a pleasant decision; he was a conscientious and careful surgeon, not a gambler. But the waiting period for a liver or even a kidney in Taiwan could be as long as two or three years. Time enough for many of his elderly patients to simply waste away. And if Chinese hospitals could perform the soup-to-nuts services they claimed on the web—donor to order, tissue match, surgery, observation, drug therapy, recovery—patients who could barely be loaded onto a plane might come back as human beings who had successfully digested their airline meal, weren't sure they actually needed the wheelchair, and tearfully hugged their grandchildren. Taiwan was a death sentence: mainland Chinese hospitals were blatantly advertising a tissue-matched organ within a week or perhaps two.

He didn't particularly want to look behind the mainland curtain, that's all. Yes, you could do anything you liked in China. And castration

"All the organs will come from Falun Gong." Dr. Ko Wen-je, chairman of the Department of Traumatology, National Taiwan University Hospital. Photo courtesy of Dr. Ko Wen-je.

wasn't all that different from what he was trying to do; it was common knowledge that the organs were being taken from executed prisoners on death row. So if his job was to ride his fragile patients into the wild, wild east and bring them back alive, okay, but even that wasn't certain; the criminal lifestyle led to a high probability of drug use or promiscuous sex. Hepatitis, just for starters, was rampant. Labor camp led to stress and malnutrition. Any, or perhaps all, of these medical histories would now be given a second life in his patients' bodies. And what was the recourse if something went wrong in this highly competitive business fought out in a legal no-man's land? Nor were his patients rich. Taiwan was still an emerging tiger; his patients had lived interesting lives to be sure, but modest ones. A glance at the web established the foreigner price of $62,000 (US) for a kidney. Because the Chinese regarded the Taiwanese as slick foreigners wearing a Chinese mask, that would be his price, too. Yet native Chinese were paying half that or even less.[4] This injustice gnawed at him. Somehow, where so many Taiwanese businessmen before him had failed, Dr. Ko would have to convince the mainland doctors he was not a foreign devil but a brother.

Dr. Ko went to China and meticulously worked through the checklist of intimacy with his medical colleagues: The go-to-hell banquet. The karaoke bar. The cognac followed by the Mao-Tai. The subtle flattery and the jokes about his accent. And when the ritual was truly finished, and everyone had sobered up, the Chinese surgeons summoned him.

You are one of us. You are a brother. So we will give you the family price. But we are going to do more for you than that. We noted your worries and concerns about organ quality. And we trust your discretion. So you will have no worries for your patients. They will receive nothing but the best: all the organs will come from Falun Gong. These people may be a little fanatical, but you know? They don't drink. They don't smoke. Many of them are young, and they all practice healthy Chinese qigong. Soon your patients—they will be young and healthy, too.

And Dr. Ko smiled and thanked them politely, and the process began. But at the point of victory, Ko had felt no relief, only something that gnawed at him far worse than before. Something he could not speak of.

Even as he set up appointments for his patients on the mainland, Dr. Ko kept thinking that there must be a way to rationalize the system, to apply some oversight, some sort of technical fix. Now that the mainland doctors had blood on their hands there was no obvious path to medical reform. An open discussion would require dredging up the past. The party would never allow the slaughter of prisoners of conscience to be revealed to the world—in fact, his Chinese surgeon friends had already let him know discreetly that the harvesting of Falun Gong would be put on hold as the Olympics approached. *But don't worry*, they reassured him, *when the Olympics are over it will start up again!* Perhaps the way forward was to use that brief hiatus as an opening to implement good bureaucratic hygiene, something to raise the cost of keeping secrets?

There was plenty of talk about consent forms—making the prisoner sign a release donating his or her organ to the nation "as a final penance" or something like that. But the surgeon knew the labor-camp administrators could get anyone to sign anything. Reform had to start with the doctors' conscience and sense of self-preservation. On his own time, Dr. Ko labored to create a national database system, a mandatory electronic form just for the surgeon. For every organ acquired, the doctor would have to fill in details on individual donor health, medical background, blood type, address, arrest record, everything. Dr. Ko moved us over to his desktop computer, and we looked it over. It was beautiful actually—simple, clear, mainland-user friendly—something even a barefoot doctor could use.

Maybe he could even have sold the system to the Chinese medical establishment, even received some sort of compensation, and yet—that gnaw again—even if the mainland doctors adopted the system, "you would only remove 95 percent of the problem," Ko said, shaking his head.

Anyway, they rejected it. It was obvious in retrospect that it was okay for the mainland doctors to run a sort of informal auction for organ trading, done through e-mails and discrete online user groups, but Ko's forms would either cut out too many donors from the system, create too much of a level playing field, or perhaps simply leave too much of an electronic trail. It was too late in the day, and it was sickening; the rejection was passed on to Dr. Ko with the respect you give to a distant cousin who doesn't quite get it.

Dr. Ko was whispering now: "But something should be done. Something should be done."

A year or so after the database was rejected, Dr. Ko gave an anonymous interview to an American writer—well, we thought it was anonymous anyway—and the surgeon was banned from the mainland.[5]

* * *

Less explicit versions of Dr. Ko's testimony have surfaced; Dr. Francis Navarro, director of transplantation in France's Montpelier Hospital was invited to demonstrate his liver transplantation technique at Chengdu University in 2006. The Chinese organizers hospitably informed Navarro that they would have a liver ready for him on the day of arrival. If this was a sign that they were killing to order, Navarro's suspicions were confirmed by the director of a military hospital who mentioned that he was hurrying to finish his executions before the Chinese New Year.[6] Navarro duly reported on these incidents, but the French government has shown scant interest in curbing or restricting French organ tourism to China.

Dr. Franz Immer, chairman of the Swiss National Foundation for organ donation and transplantation, also went on the record with a similar story: "During my visit in Beijing in 2007, a hospital invited us to watch a heart transplantation operation. The organizer asked us whether we would like to have the transplantation operation in the morning or in the afternoon. This means that the donor would die, or be killed, at a given time, at the convenience of the visitors. I refused to participate."[7]

Dr. Jacob Lavee is a cardiac surgeon and director of the heart transplantation unit at the Sheba Medical Center in Israel. In 2005, a patient with a severe heart condition reported that his medical insurance corporation, essentially a health maintenance organization (HMO), had identified a transplant opportunity in China two weeks hence. Not only was the insurance corporation going to pay for it, to Lavee's surprise they had identified a specific date for the heart transplant—which clearly ruled out an accident victim. Lavee had heard of Israelis going to get kidneys in China for several years, but he had assumed that it was much like the conditions in India—some poor person, down on their luck, selling one of their kidneys to make some money. Yet this was prescheduled murder. After researching the work of Kilgour and Matas, Lavee went on to become a leading figure in Doctors against Forced Organ Harvesting (DAFOH), and in spearheading a quiet revolution in the Israeli organ-transplantation laws.[8]

The experiences of Doctors Lavee, Immer, and Navarro confirmed an acknowledged fact—Chinese prisoners are harvested for their organs, and they are executed to order. Yet in all three cases the personal element, the tangible rediscovery of a medical culture where anything was possible, led them to believe in the far more controversial and disturbing premise that prisoners of conscience are being harvested as well, and that led to varying degrees of personal activism. Dr. Ko did not go through this process. He fought for his patients, and following his winning touchdown the truth was dumped over his head like a bucket of cold Gatorade.

To understand Dr. Ko's minor collapse during our interview, a word about Taiwan may be germane. The Taiwanese and Chinese speak the same language and employ similar bargaining strategies, but crucially, Taiwan is a free society—and when it comes to Falun Gong, Taiwan and China might as well be orbiting around opposite sides of the sun. Yes, in recent years the Taiwanese police have tended to keep Falun Gong protesters at arm's length from mainland tourist groups (seen as a valuable revenue source), and like everything else in the cross-straits relationship, politicians dance carefully around certain mainland tripwires. But a few days before I spoke with Dr. Ko, I followed a small band of Falun Gong aunties through security into a Taipei prison and observed them teach the exercises to hundreds of convicts—drug addicts, gangbangers, and possibly even a few hit men, judging by their tattoos. A smiling prison guard even mentioned to me his enthusiastic support for Falun Gong as a form of penal rehabilitation. The next day I watched a dozen of the Taipei central district's finest, including the district police captain, gather at the end of the day, not to shoot pool and have a beer at their local, but to perform Falun Gong exercises—from the party perspective, a case of inmates taking over the asylum. There are estimated to be forty thousand people in Taiwan who identify themselves in some form as Falun Gong, and most Taiwanese clearly think of them as members of a legitimate religious entity rather than a cult.

As I write this in mid-January 2014, Dr. Ko Wen-je has apparently become a very important figure in Taiwanese politics. In fact, when this book is published Dr. Ko may or may not be presiding as mayor of the city of Taipei.[9]

Because Dr. Ko's experiences and actions can be exploited by his political opponents, I would like to add a personal observation. Dr. Ko faced a genuinely vexing moral dilemma. His patients would die without the transplants he had arranged, and there was little to be gained by informing his patients of the source of the organs. So although Ko can claim no overt political activism, his attempt to change the system from within through a standardized medical form had at least a whisper of a chance, and it was more than all the world's health organizations and doctors associations and transplant conventions can claim to have done. At the end of the day, Dr. Ko's willingness to speak candidly is evidence of a singular courage. His account is the smoking gun. It represents the culmination of a long quest to find medical confirmation of China's harvesting of prisoners of conscience from an unimpeachable source.

* * *

An additional confirmation of China's harvesting of prisoners of conscience came from within the Chinese leadership itself. It's a complex story. It began on the night of February 6, 2012, when the head of Chongqing's PSB dressed up as an old woman, got in a car, and drove to the American consulate in Chengdu. For approximately thirty hours, he spilled confidential information about his boss and long-term patron, the Chongqing party secretary, leading member of the politburo, and dark-horse contender to assume the presidency of China (or at least control of the security forces).[10] The informant's name was Wang Lijun and his boss was Bo Xilai.

What did Wang reveal? A combination of leaks and inference suggest that at least four areas were discussed:

First, Bo Xilai's wife, Gu Kailai, had been engaged in business with a British expat named Neil Heywood. When their affairs went sour, she had him murdered.

Second, Bo had siphoned off portions of Chongqing's public funds.

Third, in the guise of a popular anticorruption drive, Bo routinely performed shakedowns of local criminals and political opponents alike, sometimes ordering executions and incarcerations with minimal due process.

Fourth, Bo was secretly running surveillance on other politburo members.[11] As 2012 opened, the scheduled Chinese leadership transition was widely expected to go smoothly; the colorless Hu Jintao would step down in the autumn, while various factions—the so-called reformists and hardliners—would compete, quietly and efficiently, and settle unanimously on a new leader. Yet some hardliners were promoting Bo Xilai over Xi Jinping, the leading compromise candidate. Bo's spying indicated that he might even be thinking about aggressively seizing power with Zhou Yongkang, secretary of the Political and Legislative Affairs Committee (PLAC)—the agency that over the course of a decade had accumulated power equivalent to, in American terms, the Central Intelligence Agency, the National Security Agency, the Justice Department, and the Federal Bureau of Investigation rolled into one. Wang Lijun, Bo Xilai, and Zhou Yongkang, were all part of an antireformist faction aligned with former president Jiang Zemin. All of these men had enhanced their reputations through the repression of Falun Gong, and Jiang was perceived to be the supreme architect of that repression.

A power struggle had begun, a crisis that did not fully upend the planned Chinese leadership transition of 2012, but would threaten its legitimacy and delay the handover to Xi for months.[12] Yet Western audiences tend to find intrigue within the byzantine Chinese bureaucracy to be tedious beyond description, so most Western editors encouraged their reporters to simply pursue the Sopranos aspect, the alleged Heywood murder. With the Chinese press given exactly the same assignment

THE SLAUGHTER

(including the license to print preposterous rumors about Gu Kalai or anything else that could distract the Chinese public) the entire International Heywood Fishing Expedition was chasing a single red herring. Let's return to the evening of February 6 instead.

The faces behind the leadership struggle of 2012. Clockwise from top left: Wang Lijun (the would-be defector), Bo Xilai (the dark-horse candidate), Jiang Zemin (the architect of the Falun Gong repression), and Zhou Yongkang (the head of the all-powerful PLAC). All photos from Baike.com except Bo Xilai, from Wikimedia Commons/Voice of America.

Wang apparently spent much of his time arguing with consulate officials about sanctuary, a request that was complicated by the cell phone that Wang had foolishly brought along. Easily traced, Bo Xilai surrounded the Chengdu consulate with police cars. Confidential witnesses claim that Bo also tried to marshal armored fighting vehicles as a further demonstration of his power.[13] The US consulate ultimately surrendered Wang to the Chinese authorities, and Wang was whisked away to an undisclosed location where he was undoubtedly "debriefed."

Just over a month later, on March 15, Bo Xilai was fired from his Chongqing post. But the leadership struggle was hardly over.

Four days later, on the night of March 19, Beijing microblogs were rife with reports of strange police movements and armored vehicles on the streets of Beijing.[14] This was highly irregular; while Beijing is home to countless military units, they do not normally engage in competitive maneuvers, let alone in the middle of the night. This was, in fact, the apex of the leadership crisis.

The following day, March 20, certain blocked web searches suddenly became available on the search engine Baidu, the Google of China—specifically the phrases "live harvest" and "Wang Lijun live harvest."[15] For twenty-four hours, Chinese citizens could read Kilgour and Matas, *Epoch Times*, The World Organization to Investigate the Persecution of Falun Gong (WOIPFG), and congressional hearings on organ harvesting. For the Chinese people, this was absolutely unprecedented. It was also inexplicable unless a Chinese government faction wanted to expose—or just threaten to expose—a forbidden secret.

Three days later, on March 23, in a high-profile announcement clearly designed to produce front-page reports in all major Western papers, Huang Jiefu, China's vice minister of health, declared the country's intention to end "organ donations" from executed prisoners within three to five years.[16] There was no acknowledgement of harvesting prisoners of conscience. Nor did any Western reporters raise the topic. Most important, there was no answer to the questions: *Why the harvesting mentionitis? Why exactly now?*

The answer was buried in Liaoning Province where Bo and Wang had started on their road to power.

As a Princeling, the son of a high-ranking party official, Bo Xilai had achieved success early, being appointed mayor of Dalian, a leading coastal city in Liaoning in 1993. By 1999, Bo was widely seen as a brawler with broad populist appeal yet somehow charismatic, worldly and urbane—the sort of Chinese leader who would be comfortable running China's international affairs. With the repression of Falun Gong, Bo further established himself as a man who could keep time with the party drum, while his intelligent and attractive wife Gu Kailai was busy creating the nucleus of a prominent law firm and consultancy; if a foreign business wanted to set up shop in Liaoning Province it would be well advised to use her services. By 2000, Bo was promoted to acting governor of Liaoning, a critical position in the fight to eliminate Falun Gong.

Wang Lijun's rise was far more skin of the teeth. Born into a southern Mongolian railway worker's family in 1959, Wang joined the army in 1978 and entered the Liaoning police force in 1983. In 1987, he was given party membership and was stationed in Tieling, a city of about three million people about an hour and a half drive northeast of Shenyang. In 2000, Wang Lijun was promoted from deputy director of the Tieling City Public Security Bureau to director, a position he would hold until 2003. It probably didn't hurt him to be ethnically Mongol in a city where almost a quarter of the population is not Han Chinese, yet his promotion appears to have been genuinely earned. According to Chinese media reports he stood out as a dark, almost theatrical character (a television series based on his persona as a crime fighter was in the works until Wang's attempted defection in 2012). His reputation was that of an extremely tough cop with an educated twist: good English skills, and a serious and efficient demeanor. In 2009, *People's Daily* ran an unusual feature on Wang, describing him as a *cold-faced Yama*—in Chinese mythology, the king of hell itself.[17]

Up until this point in the story I have not leaned heavily on research by Falun Gong practitioners. But with the leadership crisis of 2012, Falun Gong investigators came into their own. A few days after Wang Lijun's trip to the American consulate in Chengdu, WOIPFG investigator Lisa Lee dug up a highly unusual 2006 quote from Wang, part of a speech given at a medical award ceremony:

> For a veteran policeman, to see someone executed and within minutes to see the transformation, in which this person's life was extended in the bodies of several other people—it was soul-stirring.[18]

It is fair to say that Wang would never have been at that awards ceremony without an assist from Governor Bo Xilai. In 2003, Wang was tapped to head up the Public Security Bureau of one of Liaoning's greatest cities: Jinzhou. Whatever resources the local PSB lacked in comparison with the great labor camps of Shenyang, it made up for it in terms of surveillance—the Jinzhou PSB not only claimed that it had managed to register 9,190 Falun Gong practitioners, but also that it had acquired fingerprints, handwriting samples, and photos of the majority of them. With two thousand "monitor messengers" (amateur spies) reporting, Jinzhou was a vital part of the province-wide elite network of sixty-five special agents who had supposedly collected more twenty thousand intelligence items on Falun Gong.[19] Such over-fulfilling-the-quota bragging was standard throughout China at the time, but Wang did not see arrest as the end of his responsibilities—rather than relying on the massive clearinghouse of Masanjia to sort out the practitioners, he constructed his own formidable medical/law enforcement entity: the Jinzhou City Public Security Bureau On-site Psychological Research Center.

We might not know much else about the center's history—it's not clear that it survived long after Wang's move to Chongqing—but Lisa Lee told me that an official webpage devoted to Wang Lijun receiving a medical innovation award had been carelessly archived. In the official account of the ceremony, Wang was feted for pioneering a lethal injection method, a solution to a problem that has plagued organ harvesting in China for a decade—how to extract still-healthy organs from the "donor" while the person is still alive.

I've written about live organ harvesting previously--how, like a flower stem cut under running water, it preserves the organ's viability and soothes the immune system of the new host. Yet one must cut a living being deep while avoiding the involuntary contractions of the body that could make surgery difficult. In a pinch, a shotgun blast to the chest can send the body into shock, but the reader may remember that in Dr. Enver Tohti's experience, contractions still occur. Anesthesia is problematic too, but according to Ren Jinyang, the secretary-general of the China Guanghua Science and Technology Foundation, Wang "created a brand new protective fluid, which is used to provide a perfusion treatment for liver and kidney . . . the recipient's body is able to accept the liver and kidney after such a treatment." After the organs are removed, a lethal injection is administered to the body. How many bodies? Wang oversaw "several thousand intensive on-site cases" of organ transplantation.[20]

These were not relatives sparing an extra kidney for a loved one. It was surgery to remove any physical part that carried retail potential from individuals selected by the state. Transplanted into new recipients, foreign and Chinese alike, a liver could go for $115,000, with hearts, lungs, and corneas fetching almost twice that at what might be termed a seasonal price.

Judging by the photographs in which he is shown clad in scrubs, lecturing surgeons while a patient lies on a gurney, Wang was a hands-on manager. Were the operations for which he was honored performed while the donor was still alive? Yes, because Wang received the award for the lethal-injection method following surgical extraction. Were the operations performed exclusively on death-row prisoners—murderers, rapists, and the like—as Huang Jiefu intimated in his famous statement of March 23? Given the context, that's logistically impossible. Dr. Huige Li, a professor of vascular pharmacology at Johannes Gutenberg University, points out that the expected number of executed prisoners (between 2004 to 2006, the award period) for Jinzhou City would be fourteen, not "thousands of cases." In fact, if one accepts Amnesty International numbers for the same period, then Wang Lijun's center would have harvested just under half of all of China's executed prisoners.[21] In addition, refugees from the Laogai System have consistently pointed to Liaoning Province, including locations such as Yida, Sujiatun, and Dalian Medical University, as the epicenter of Falun Gong harvesting. One final point. Four years ago, WOIPFG volunteers posing as party investigators called top Chinese officials in an attempt to confirm Falun Gong harvesting. Severely hampered by not having access to a secure line, and operating without the shield of an actual official inquiry, it was the investigative equivalent of a crank call, and WOIPFG received only passive confirmation. Every official contacted eventually realized that it was wildly inappropriate to be discussing harvesting on an unsecured line with a potential imposter. In April 2012, WOIPFG tried again—and the tone changed.[22]

One of the calls was to a key collaborative partner of Wang Lijun's: Chen Rongshan, the urology chief physician of the PLA 205 Hospital

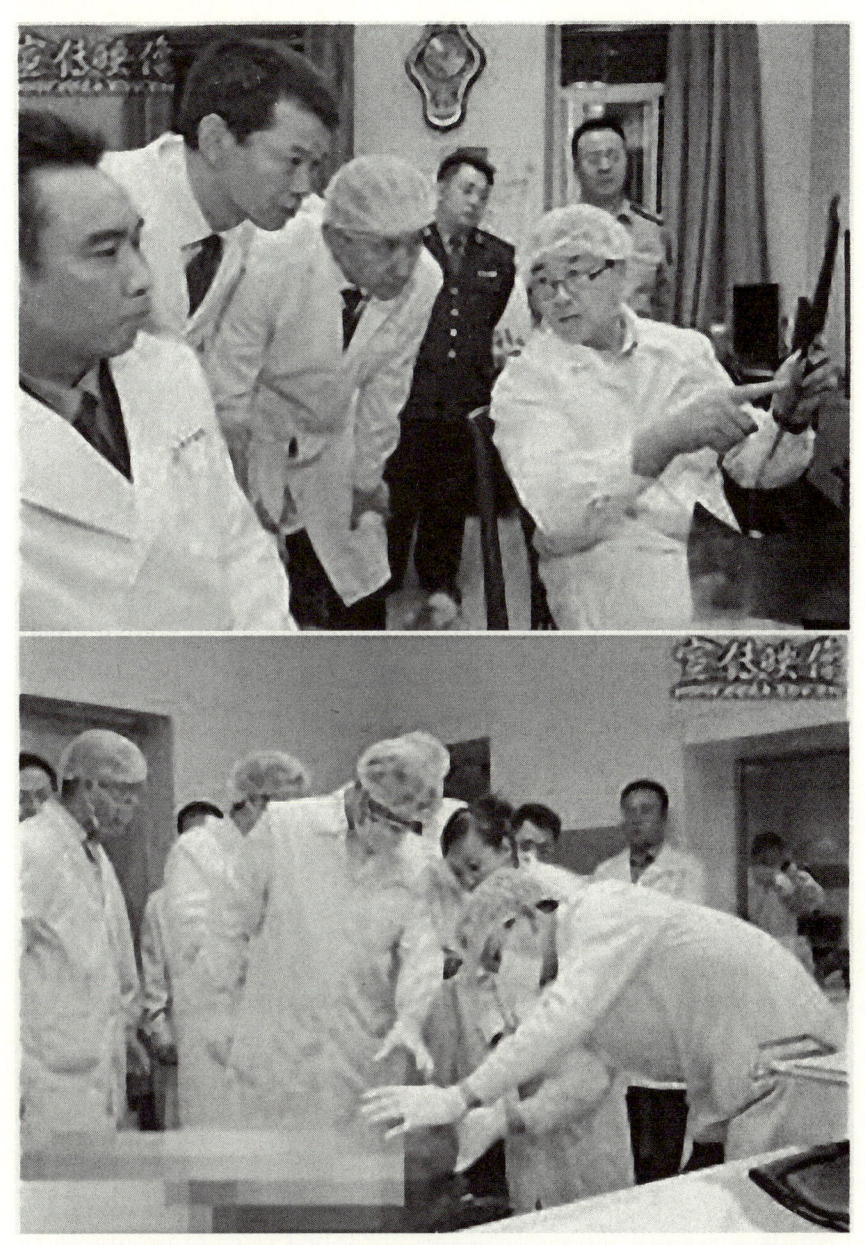

Wang Lijun (in glasses) directing organ harvesting at the Jinzhou City Public Security Bureau On-site Psychological Research Center. Photos courtesy of World Organization to Investigate the Persecution of Falun Gong.

in Jinzhou City, who had publicly been praised for having completed 568 cases of kidney transplants. The investigator asks: "Wang Lijun told us that some organ donors were jailed Falun Gong practitioners. Is that true?" Chen's answer: "Those were arranged by the court."

Another call implicates Bo Xilai and Zhou Yongkang. A WOIPFG investigator leads Li Changchun, former Politburo Standing Committee member and China's propaganda point man, into a discussion of using "Bo Xilai's involvement in murdering and removing organs from Falun Gong practitioners to convict Bo, right at this time." Li responded: "Zhou Yongkang is in charge of this specifically. He knows it."

Did Wang Lijun reveal the harvesting of living Falun Gong practitioners in the US consulate? Over a hundred US representatives sent a letter to Secretary of State Clinton asking that exact question:

> While at the US Consulate, it is claimed that Wang Lijun may have divulged information about the harvesting of organs from still living Falun Gong practitioners. If such evidence was received and brought to light, measures could be taken to help stop such abominable abuses. We therefore ask that the State Department release any information it may have that relates to transplant abuses in China, including any documentation that Wang Lijun may have provided to our Consulate in Chengdu.[23]

The State Department apparently made no response, but the party didn't know that would be the outcome. If you were in the party and you had "debriefed" Wang Lijun to the point where you knew every piece of information he revealed to the American State Department, how would you read that paragraph? Did Wang's revelations carry the potential to taint China's global medical ambitions in the lucrative pharmaceutical testing industry? Yet those concerns pale before the central problem. China is a surveillance state, but not everyone is watched that carefully. Like Orwell's *1984*, the telescreens are not aimed at the proles, but at the party members. And the military—including the military hospitals—are watched intensely. In an investigative phone call, Tang Junjie, head of the Political and Legislative Affairs Committee in Liaoning Province, was asked directly about the organ harvesting of Falun Gong. "Actually," Tang said, "Party Central is taking care of this." So yes, Party Central owns this. The leadership, including reformers who may not have approved, such as Wen Jiabao, had to be aware. Could the party's historic crime, laid before the world, and worse yet, before the Chinese people, upend the leadership transition?

Let's look at the sequence of events one last time.

- February 6: Wang Lijun goes to US Consulate
- March 15: Bo is fired
- March 19: Police movements and armored vehicles on the streets in Beijing
- March 20: Baidu unblocks search-terms "live harvest" and "Wang Lijun live harvest"
- March 23: Declaration to end "organ donations" from executed prisoners within 3 to 5 years

All the elements to cover up a crime are in place: A truncated game of chicken between factions (played out with armored vehicles and on the Internet). A pseudo airing of the harvesting issue that avoids the real subject (the public declaration to end "organ donations"). A couple of scapegoats (Bo, Wang, and now Zhou) to deflect responsibility from the party leadership as a whole. And, waiting in the wings, the architect of it all, Jiang Zemin, presently in ill health. Should he die, he could absorb any excess guilt (in the standard formulation, Jiang Zemin could be declared to be 70 percent right and 30 percent wrong).

The burial strategy needed one more component: Western approval.

The man who made the historic announcement on March 23, 2012, that China would end organ harvesting in three to five years, was Dr. Huang Jiefu. On paper, he was the perfect vehicle for this message: China's vice-minister of health since 2001, deputy director of the Health Committee (12th CPPCC National Committee), and deputy director of the Chinese Organ Transplantation Association.[24] From 1987 to 2001, Huang climbed the ladder at Sun Yat-sen College of Medical Science, ultimately serving as president from 1996 to 2001. By 2001 Huang had developed a reputation as a very prolific surgeon and an active proponent of liver transplantation (you may recall that Sun Yat-sen surgeons were among those harvesting executed prisoners in medical vans parked at an execution ground in 2002). After 2001 Huang became director of liver surgery at Beijing Union Medical College Hospital. There were rumors of Huang performing a special demonstration transplant in Xinjiang for Luo Gan, the PSB director and a cofounder of the repression of Falun Gong. But we don't need to rely on rumors. By Huang's own admission, he has personally performed over five hundred liver-transplant operations, from "donor" to recipient, from soup to nuts, mostly from prisoners.[25]

Huang was also a visionary; in late 2005, before any charges had publicly been aired, and when the Falun Gong community could still be fairly characterized as being in a state of denial, Huang clearly sensed that organ harvesting was becoming a problem for the Chinese medical community. China's exponential harvesting increase from 2000 to 2005 had been noticed, and the larger medical world might question the sourcing. Perhaps Huang even knew that the Sujiatun story would break soon. Falling on the lesser sword, Huang made statements in December 2005 confirming that death-row prisoners were, in fact, being used as a source of organs for transplant (ultimately he would admit that prisoners constituted 95 percent of the supply), while a ban on Western organ tourism was declared. I use the passive construction here because these were seen as little more than trial balloons. It was not until the Sujiatun story broke in early 2006 that Huang Jiefu emerged as the public face of the party's efforts to portray a specific image—a China that was rapidly reforming its organ harvesting system. And he assumed this position at exactly the time when it was convenient for the party: within weeks of the release of the Kilgour-Matas report. Initially the reform was aimed at making sure that all the prisoners who were harvested had signed proper release forms, and the ban on foreign organ tourists was repeated and amplified. But Huang went further, stating openly that he would phase out the organ harvesting of prisoners by encouraging ordinary Chinese citizens to donate their organs. He backed up the statement by encouraging the establishment of pilot donation programs in ten cities. Above all Huang made it clear to Western surgeons that he did not consider China's current harvesting environment to be an ethical one, and that he was trying his best to change it. The details of how this would occur were flexible, they had to be in a massive society like China's, but with the world's support, Huang promised he would end harvesting of prisoners in China.

Initially Huang and the Chinese medical establishment didn't have a deadline for the reform, but as new external challenges emerged—the first mention of organ harvesting by the *New York Times* in 2011, the paltry numbers coming out of the voluntary donation programs, and finally, the Wang Lijun revelations of 2012—Huang Jiefu increased his volume and his apparent determination to clean up China's transplant environment. With every new promise, Huang picked up greater public support from Francis Delmonico, the president of the Transplantation Society, or TTS, the international organization that acts as the beacon of ethical leadership to thousands of transplant surgeons around the world.

For a brief moment, Huang Jiefu's initiatives were even tacitly approved by elements of Falun Gong, particularly those who, perhaps subconsciously, longed for rapprochement with the party rather than its destruction. When Huang Jiefu made his statement on March 23, actually attaching a three-to-five-year deadline to the abolition of prisoner transplants, euphoria swept through the overseas Chinese Falun Gong community. Among those who had relatives, friends, and comrades incarcerated throughout China, it was hoped, and fervently desired, that practitioners were implicitly included in the term *prisoners*, and that Beijing's decision to air the issue could ultimately lead to a full reckoning of the history of organ harvesting. They even saw a continuum between Huang's initiative and Premier Wen Jiabao's consistent exhortations to reform the party, to turn China toward a democratic path, and to sincerely apologize for the party's mistakes. Cynical outsiders like myself read this as posturing, but Chinese insiders read it—particularly the apologies—as a meaningful wink: Wen knew the full extent of party crimes and was prepared to prosecute. Throughout 2012, as it became obvious that Wen Jiabao and the reformers would not be ascendant in the leadership struggle, these hopes faded.

Yet Huang Jiefu's optimistic tone did not change. He repeatedly emerged to make even more extravagant claims of imminent reform to an acquiescent Western press corps, continuously shaving the timetable for the ultimate abolition of convict harvesting. By 2014, he claimed, the harvesting of prisoners would be gone forever.

The TTS did not seem worried by Huang's shifting and often-contradictory time scale, or his ever-changing numbers (at times they were not consistent even within the same PowerPoint presentation). The TTS was focused on the fact that Huang had started a new regime with language modeled on its own. With Huang Jiefu's Hangzhou Resolution of 2013, approximately forty (again, the numbers aren't consistent) Chinese hospitals voluntarily signed a statement declaring that they would no longer harvest prisoners.

Yet Huang had no jurisdiction over military hospitals. And there was no verification, other than a photograph of Huang Jiefu, Francis Delmonico, and other Chinese medical luminaries celebrating the Hangzhou Resolution by grinning broadly and extending their hands like the three musketeers, that any of these reforms were actually taking place. Even as Huang Jiefu claimed that fewer prisoners were being harvested, and that the rate of prisoner execution was slowing, the overall numbers of transplants in China appeared to be steady. At the same time, reports claiming a sudden growth in voluntary donation appeared to be blatantly jiggered for Western consumption. Analysts such as David Matas premised that the expanding gaps in reliable transplant information could mean that even more Falun Gong were going under the knife, not less. Doctors against Forced Organ Harvesting brought these points to the TTS only to have Francis Delmonico make it clear in his private statements to associates of DAFOH that he did not believe that there was enough evidence to establish that Chinese military hospitals, or any other Chinese hospitals for that matter, were engaged in the organ harvesting of prisoners of conscience; the TTS would not publicly challenge its Chinese counterparts on the issue.[26] The point was not to get obsessed with issues such as prisoners of conscience, or military hospitals, or external observation and verification by foreigners, but to wholeheartedly support and reward China's historic road to reform, however bumpy the ride.

In late May 2013, an ABC News Australia team questioned Huang about his own medical practice. A bit lax from the softball Chinese journalism environment that he resides in, Huang somewhat shakily admitted that he had previously extracted organs from prisoners, an admission that backed him into defending the concept of Chinese prisoners donating their organs and repaying their debts to the state.[27] It was a body blow to Huang's reputation, but he had been lucky. Perhaps surprised that he had gone that far, ABC did not dare to ask the next logical but impolite question. A week later, Huang Jiefu and Shi Bingyi, a deputy chairman of the organ transplantation branch of the Chinese Medical Association, preempted that very question by giving an interview to a friendly state-run media organ during which Shi was asked if Falun Gong had been murdered for their organs. Shi responded that he "absolutely does not believe" that practitioners had been harvested.[28] Clearly, this was an inoculation strategy. Should a Western reporter dare to ask about Falun Gong in the future, the denial is now on the record. The question, and the answer recognition, would be stale news.

Huang had been showered with awards and honorary titles from Harvard University, MIT, Stanford, Southern Illinois University, the University of Sydney, the Royal College of Surgeons of Edinburgh, and the Transplantation Society. Doctors against Forced Organ Harvesting complained, but ultimately was shunted aside. To these Western entities, Huang was a reformer, a crusader. Even if he had broken the ethical practices of surgery that they had enshrined, some rules could be overlooked to be on the right side of Chinese history.[29]

There were tiny cracks in the façade but they were hard to see initially. Before Huang had officially shut it down in 2006, China's organ harvesting trade was not a charity, but a capitalist operation driven by demand, and largely supported Western organ tourists. Now that was over. But enter the strange case of Daniel Rose, a popular humor author who resides in Massachusetts. Rose had acted as the wingman for his cousin Larry's successful kidney transplant in China shortly before the

2008 Beijing Olympics, and he wrote a book about their adventures titled *Larry's Kidney: Being the True Story of How I Found Myself in China with my Black Sheep Cousin and His Mail-Order Bride, Skirting the Law to Get Him a Transplant—and Save His Life*.[30]

Well, fun is fun, and lots of reviewers found the book heartwarming, but I can't seem to resist making just two background observations: First, Rose is the descendant of Holocaust survivors. I didn't dig that out; he wrote a book about it. Second, and far more ominous to those who cared about the credibility of Huang Jiefu's reforms, there was nothing secretive about Rose's identity as a popular author, and the evidence from the book strongly suggests that the outcome of *Larry's Kidney* was approved by the Chinese Communist Party. Chapter after chapter is dominated by amusing, touching, and gauzy romantic stories about Rose's Chinese fixers "Cherry" and "Jade"—attractive young women with big hearts who selflessly facilitate the process of finding a kidney "donor" (yes, they are both party operatives). At one point—it's actually kind of a fluke that he mentions it at all—Rose wonders aloud to Cherry:

> "Can you also give me an idea of where the kidneys come from? Because we hear all kinds of things in the West about prisoners and religious sects and—"
>
> Cherry cuts me off with a general answer about the conditions of the kidneys, which she assures me, will be top-notch. Dr. X is renowned for this sort of transplant. Medical colleagues all over the third world send him their relatives to do.
>
> "Am I answer all your question?" she asks pleasantly.[31]

Rose doesn't bring it up again, so I guess Cherry answer all his question. When Rose finally meets with the organ-kingpin himself, "Dr. X," more hilarity ensues:

> "We are peppering very many documents for permission to go through," Dr. X continues. "Need strict order from high court. Paperwork in process for donor to sign, also his family, everyone be on the same page, no coercion."...

I can hardly contain myself. "You pepper all the documents you need," I say. "So do you mind if I ask who the donor is?"

"Bad-bad criminal," Dr. X says. "Thirty-one years of age and already kill many people. Break in woman's house, kill woman's father, then decide he want no witness so come back and kill woman and woman's baby. Very bad man!" he says with surprising vehemence. "I would kill him hundred times!"[32]

The "thirty-one-years" part might actually have been true. At any rate, Rose has no further questions. Instead he finds himself "in a triumphant mood that nothing can wreck."[33] The revelation that a bad-bad criminal has to die (or maybe someone who's not so bad-bad, he's not really fully convinced) "damages my mood only slightly. It's the equivalent of seeing a baby calf frolicking in the field and realizing it's this evening's veal piccata."[34]

Well, as the old Yiddish song goes: *How the winds are laughing*.

Enough fun. The point is that Rose's tacked-on warning-label gag ("Don't try to go to China for a kidney. We got the last one."), is only necessary because of the book's crystal-clear takeaway: despite laws against foreigners receiving transplants, the Chinese Communist Party wanted you to know that China was open for business in 2009.[35] But what about 2014? As I write this, in January 2014, Omar Healthcare Service, a Chinese organ broker "authorized by the Government of People's Republic of China," advertises freely to Western organ tourists on the web.

If I have quoted from a single source more than would seem justified, it's because gaining information from Western organ recipients is especially challenging. They are desperate individuals engaging in a highly unethical practice that they would prefer not to think about. They are emotionally prepped to cooperate with the atmosphere of secrecy and information withdrawal that is maintained in the Chinese military hospitals. Organ donor names and consent forms are not revealed to patients nor do patients demand to see them.[36]

Organ tourism numbers are particularly vexing. Testifying before the Scottish parliament last year, Kilgour, Matas, and I were asked how many Scots have gone to the mainland in search of human organs in recent years. We didn't know. Until Chinese organ-harvesting practices are uni-

276 THE SLAUGHTER

versally recognized as a crime that outweighs medical privacy laws, the composition of organ tourism to China will be the black hole, the mysterious island in the entire investigation.

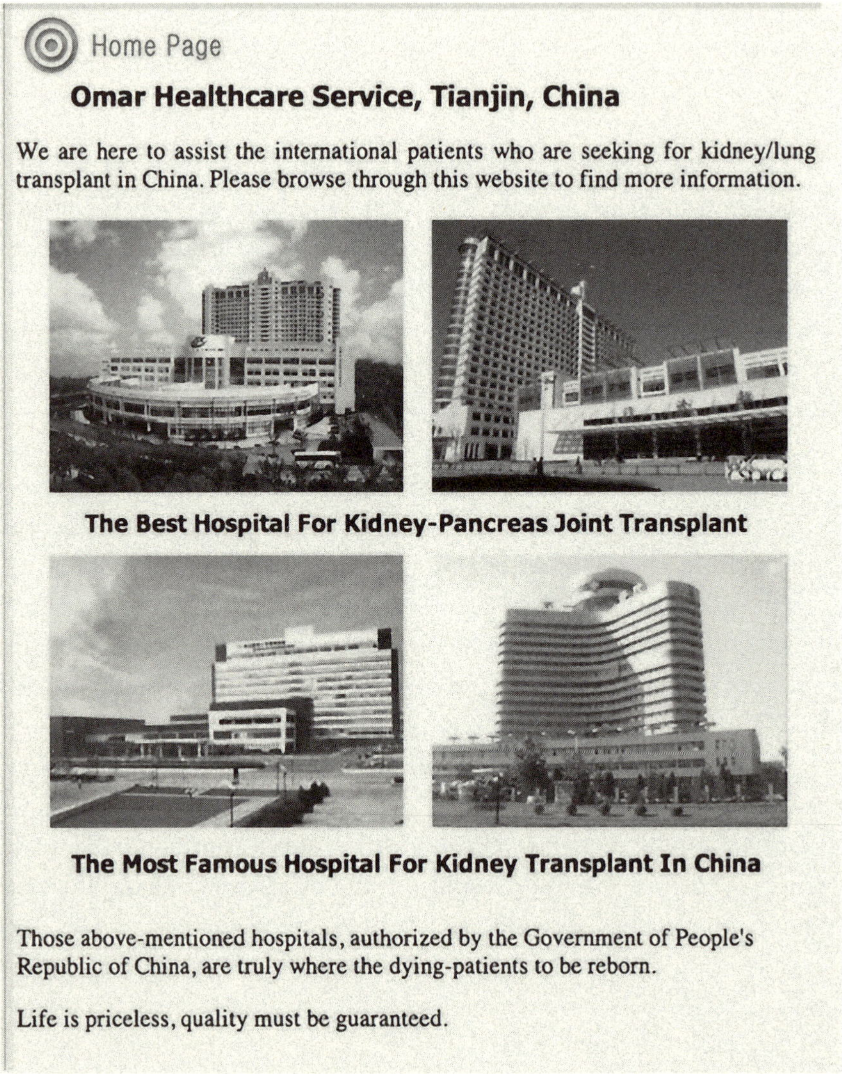

> **◎ Home Page**
>
> **Omar Healthcare Service, Tianjin, China**
>
> We are here to assist the international patients who are seeking for kidney/lung transplant in China. Please browse through this website to find more information.
>
> **The Best Hospital For Kidney-Pancreas Joint Transplant**
>
> **The Most Famous Hospital For Kidney Transplant In China**
>
> Those above-mentioned hospitals, authorized by the Government of People's Republic of China, are truly where the dying-patients to be reborn.
>
> Life is priceless, quality must be guaranteed.

We're baaaaack! Screenshot of Omar Healthcare Service, January 2014.

* * *

My research has focused on the mysterious "donors" rather than the recipients, Western or otherwise. If I might speak for Kilgour, Matas and myself, I would say that we have all felt a special sense of responsibility as the first full-time "Western outsiders" to investigate organ harvesting of prisoners of conscience. Each of us has our own methods of not going native, but we cannot help but be responsive to the needs of the Chinese refugees around us. And when it comes to a tragedy of this scale, human beings have a deep need for numbers.

We have all chosen to take a stab at how many practitioners were harvested in the early years. For them, it's from 2000 to 2005. For me, it's from the year 2000 up to 2008 and the Beijing Olympics. There are practical reasons for our respective focuses. During that period, in the beginning at least, the government had not fully constructed its shield of secrecy. Kilgour and Matas list fully fifty-two key points of evidence in *Bloody Harvest*, many of them based on Chinese official numbers. Chinese government figures are always problematic, inflated, and inherently political, but at least these medical estimates were released before organ harvesting became a major international issue. This was the also the period when Falun Gong refugees were still coming out of China at a reasonable clip (it's harder now that China has "rationalized" its passport system), and that's a critical aspect of my survey method of determining casualties. So yes, we do use different methods. In fact, we have never colluded on the numbers in any way, probably because we share a feeling that diverse sources and methods make the overall conclusions more robust.

There are many complications involved in making these calculations, but the ones I encountered are detailed in this book's appendix. To fully appreciate the calculations Kilgour and Matas made, you will need to acquire copies of *Bloody Harvest* and *State Organs* (where Matas has an excellent chapter that focuses on more recent trends in the numbers). Since Kilgour and Matas have a right to sell books and to present their own information, let me break their calculation down for you in simple terms. Let's just concentrate on kidneys. Kilgour and Matas report that in 2005 alone, China completed ten thousand kidney transplants (and four thousand liver transplants). That number, ten thousand, had practically doubled from the year 2000, tracking the upward trend in Falun Gong incarceration rates.

Crunching the harvesting numbers. Researcher Leeshai Lemish with an insider source, Dr. Huang Shiwei of Taiwan. Photo by the author.

Now there may be two kidneys per human being, but in China there are many reasons why the vast majority of those second kidneys never make it into a patient: the logistical difficulty of distributing several organs from the same individual when you are killing to order, the lack of a national organ-distribution system, criminal-code and consent-form problems, botched execution methods, and the difficulties of blood and tissue matching. The bottom line is that the baseline demand for kidneys is extraordinarily high, and (chiming in here with my own observation) not a single witness I have interviewed has spoken of the mass physical examinations of routine prisoners—or even death-row prisoners—that would be necessary to meet such a demand. So Kilgour and Matas are clearly on to something when they say that the rate of execution of regular prisoners (which reached a high-water mark of about three thousand in

2005 while showing no sign of any major increase, according to Amnesty International) could not conceivably have kept pace with the exploding rate of kidney transplants, which hovered around ten thousand per year in 2004 and 2005. As voluntary donation was statistically insignificant throughout the entire period, there must be another source. And given that the only independent variable is the stunning growth of Falun Gong incarceration in the Laogai System, Kilgour and Matas premise that the source of the organs was Falun Gong: 41,500 practitioner organs between 2000 and 2005.[37] If you extrapolate from the annual rates estimated by Kilgour and Matas, just short of 7,000 a year, the total becomes 62,250 Falun Gong organs harvested between 2000 and 2008.

By my estimate up to three million Falun Gong practitioners would pass through the Chinese corrections system. Approximately 65,000 would be harvested, hearts still beating, before the 2008 Olympics. An unspecified, significantly smaller number of House Christians, Uyghurs, and Tibetans likely met the same fate. I employ a survey method to reach that conclusion, and all the calculations are fully laid out in the appendix (and if you are skeptical, well, why not turn immediately to that section?). The basic premise of my survey method is that unlike organ tourists who don't want to talk, practitioners are desperate to do exactly that. And, unlike Chinese government numbers, I can cross-examine them. So these are not back-of-the-envelope calculations. Yet I don't like false precision either, so my findings are bracketed by dramatically different high and low estimates, allowing the reader—me too, actually—to employ some accumulated intelligence and think about the range of uncertainty.

Remember, too, that using the Kilgour/Matas method generates a result just over 62,250 *organs*, while I am premising the murder of 65,000 *individuals* for the same time period. So it's an apples-and-oranges comparison—but Kilgour and Matas did run across cases where the same wealthy foreigner was given one organ after another until one finally worked. And given the point that I have already made about the logistics of Chinese harvesting, I think it's fair to say that no matter how different our methods, we are collectively looking at fatalities above 50,000.

One last point. It is also germane that in 2012 Matas came out with a new estimate, writing that "the source of the 10,000 transplants a year in China is 1,000 from prisoners sentenced to death and then executed, 500 from living donor relatives, 500 from Tibetans, Uighurs and Eastern Lightning House Christians and 8,000 from Falun Gong practitioners."[38] Over the period from 2000 to 2008, that would amount to 64,000 Falun Gong practitioners murdered for their organs.

My original, rather bland assumption was that organ harvesting of prisoners of conscience started petering out after 2007. I mean how could it continue with Huang Jiefu constantly decrying how unethical the whole system was? I also thought our collective work—WOIPFG, DAFOH, *Epoch Times*—was having an effect. "Murder of innocents is harder in broad daylight," as Matas says.[39] The evidence for that was that Beijing has been on a public reform jag in recent years: most recently the supposed "closing of the labor camps" (although this actually seems to involve little but rebranding them as drug-rehabilitation centers, and no practitioners have actually been freed to my knowledge).[40] Pledges were made to reform the death penalty as well. Indeed the death-penalty rate has shown some signs of a downward slide—perhaps 30 percent since 2007. Yet David Matas points to a darker interpretation:

> In the abstract, from a human rights perspective, the reduction in the death penalty is good news. The news ceases though to be good if the decrease in the death penalty leads to an increase in the killing of Falun Gong for their organs. While the decrease in the death penalty has occurred at the same time as the increase of living donor transplants, the increase in living donor transplants has come nowhere near the estimated decrease in the death penalty.[41]

That pesky gap again. In truth, my survey method, which is partially contingent on bad passport control and a reasonable number of refugees, had lulled me into the sense that I was writing about history rather than current events. Starting in November 2013, three female Falun Gong refugees from China forced me to reconsider.

Jia Yahui was the deputy director of marketing for the *Liaosheng Evening News* in Shenyang, Liaoning Province. Arrested on April 25,

2008, at the age of thirty-five, she "received a blood test and other medical exams, including liver function, heart function, and blood pressure."[42] On June 4, 2008, she was sent to Masanjia Labor Camp. Jia said, "In 2006, the organ harvesting had already been exposed." And yet "everyone who was detained received a physical test [aimed specifically at testing the health of the organs] and blood test, no exceptions!"

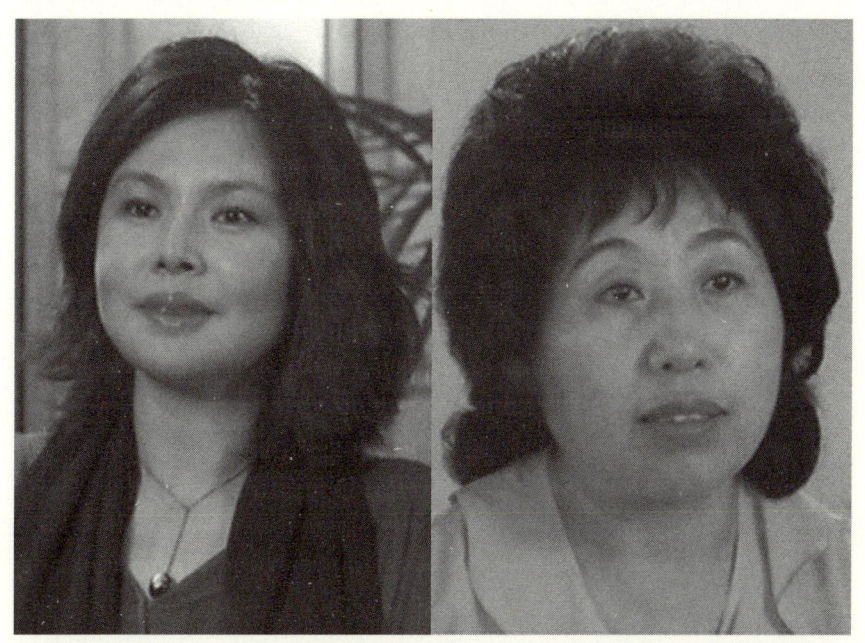

In the shadow of the Beijing Olympics: Jia Yahui and Wang Chunying were examined as potential organ sources and watched as other practitioners disappeared over time. Courtesy of Wenjng Ma.

Wang Chunying, a nurse from Dalian, was interred in Masanjia at the same time as Jia. One afternoon the captain ordered all the practitioners into the entrance hall of the clinic "for a blood test":

Wang asked the captain: "Why do we need the test?"

"For infectious diseases."

"What kind of infectious diseases are you checking for?"

"It is not your business to know."

"You don't have right to draw my blood. It is persecution to draw blood from Falun Gong practitioners. There are organ harvestings from Falun Gong practitioners. Why do you want to draw my blood?"

Wang was ordered to stand aside. The others were forced to have their blood drawn. Many of the practitioners tried to hold on to the door, but in the end, they were all dragged to the exam room where their blood was drawn.

Jia remembers the aftermath in Masanjia: "A lot of practitioners were sent there [Masanjia] from different places. After meeting in the camp, we never saw each other again. I don't know where they were sent. And I don't know what happened to them."

Those stories might feel a bit repetitive to the average reader at this point in the book, but I think that's actually the point. Everyone in the practitioner community knew of organ harvesting by this stage. If flight 93 was the first conflict of the post-9/11 world, then Jia and Wang are describing something similar. Except that they lost and the state won, and less than two months before the Olympics, China's "opening" to the world, it had *not* ended for Falun Gong.

That same year, on March 14, the Tibetan uprising began in Lhasa. The enforced disappearances of monks and activists were swift. By June an estimated one thousand Tibetans were unaccounted for, a number that would nearly double by the end of 2009.[43]

In July 2009, Urumqi exploded in street riots. The authorities massed troops, kicked out the Western journalists, shut down the Internet, and, over the next six months, quietly, mostly at night, rounded up Uyghur males by the hundreds. A captive Uyghur was able to get the message out that he had been given a physical examination unambiguously aimed at assessing the health of his retail organs.[44] As I write this in January 2014, enforced disappearances within the Uyghur population continue.

Let us close with the third case. In 2012, Zhang Fengying, a fifty-five-year-old woman, was arrested for handing out Falun leaflets outside of a Beijing marketplace.[45] She gave her name as "Dafa Practitioner" and settled down to serve some time in a local detention center. Zhang was given a blood test, but she didn't think much of it. Shortly after, in January 2013, she was forcibly escorted to Beijing Tiantanghe Women's

Forced Labor Camp. Upon entry blood samples were drawn from her arm and her earlobe, and she was also given X-ray, EKG and urine exams. She asked the doctors why they were taking blood again. The doctors didn't answer. Then, in May 2013, her "brigade" (over one hundred people consisting of 90 percent practitioners and 10 percent ordinary criminals) was marched to a large medical RV caravan where each prisoner received all the usual retail-organs-only tests again.

Live organ harvesting of political and religious prisoners was first used by party officials in Xinjiang in the aftermath of the Ghulja Incident in 1997. In 2009, the pattern appeared to be repeating itself as hundreds of Uyghur political demonstrators disappeared without a trace. In this photograph from Getty, Uyghur women, calling for the return of their sons and husbands, is broken up by Chinese armed forces. Photo by Peter Parks/AFP/Getty Images.

"None of us knew what these blood tests were for," Zhang says. Having given up her real name to the prison guards—time enough for her comrades to move the printing presses she'd been protecting—she was released not long after the tests in May. Zhang doesn't know if there were any subsequent disappearances, but she is certain that her brigade was just one of four brigades that were tested that day.

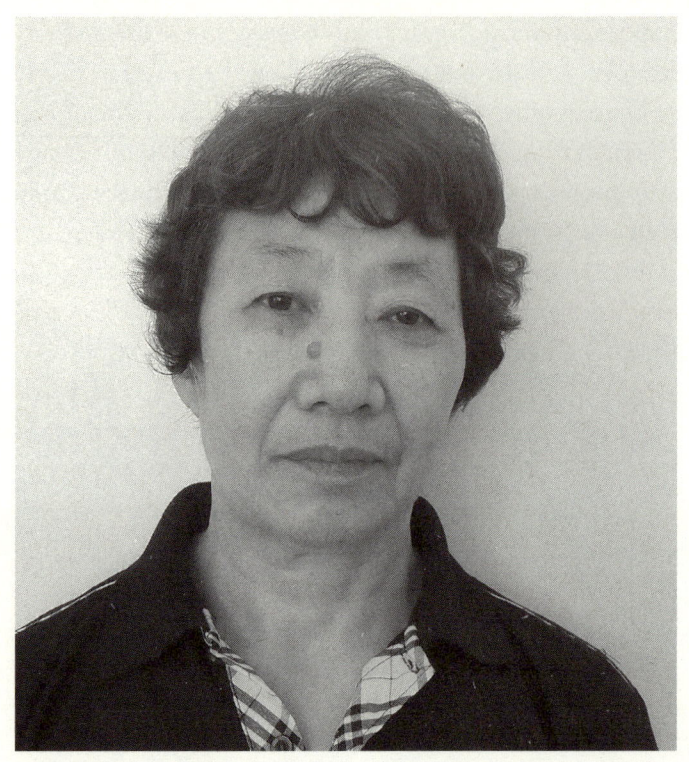

It never ended. In Beijing Tiantanghe Women's Forced Labor Camp, Falun Gong practitioner Zhang Fengying and hundreds of other prisoners were repeatedly examined using medical procedures aimed at assessing the viability of their retail organs. The most recent medical examination took place in May 2013, shortly before Zhang's release. Photo courtesy of Mrs. Fengying Zhang and Ms. Lisa Zhang.

* * *

I'm a slow writer. Falun Gong practitioners used to like to rush me. *You have to get that book out there*, they would say. Sometimes the reason was that the Communist Party was doomed and my poor book wouldn't be relevant anymore. Usually they said that I had to get the book out because *I could save lives in China*. Still, my sense was that I could sit back in my comfortable writer's chair and take my time because I was basically just writing history. But with the new testimony from Zhang Fengying, this sense collapsed.

And Huang Jiefu's transplant reform? Oh yes, that collapsed, too.

In early March 2014 Huang was quoted in the *Beijing Morning Post*, and indeed across the Chinese web, saying, "Judicial organs and local health ministries should establish ties, and allow death row prisoners to voluntarily donate organs and be added to the computer organ allocation system."[46] His colleague Wang Haibo, director of the China Organ Transplant Response System Research Center, went on the record a month later confirming to a German journalist that there was no plan to stop harvesting prisoners for their organs.[47]

The Hangzhou Resolution, all the pledges, all the press conferences, were swept aside. Apparently all along Huang just wanted accurate "voluntary" forms before prisoners were cut to pieces. And what of engagement? In its embarrassment, the TTS (which had surely gotten wind of the complete reversal) preempted, writing an open letter to Xi Jinping two weeks before Huang's new announcement, expressing its unhappiness with the general turn of events. And the TTS recently let it be known that, by gum, it won't be attending the usual China transplant conferences this year. But perhaps the TTS should relax; Western press coverage of all these events was practically nonexistent.

So we are right back where we were in 2006. Prisoners will get their forms. Organ tourists are banned, kind of. As for prisoners of conscience, somehow the TTS had managed to go through the entire charade without ever uttering those words—*prisoners of conscience*—and it didn't mention them in its letter to Xi either.

Well, points for consistency. On all sides actually. I still write slowly, and the harvesting of Uyghurs, Tibetans, Falun Gong, and House Christians continues.

10
A NIGHT AT THE MUSEUM

I have taken my first steps into "Body Worlds," an exhibition at Vienna's Museum of Natural History, and it has sparked a memory. The room in which I am standing—dark, somber, strangely hushed—exhibits fetuses at various stages of development, placed on blocks that evoke a pagan circle of standing stones. The show's mastermind, German doctor Gunther von Hagens has suctioned all the liquid and fat from the small bodies and filled the soft tissues with hard plastic through his ingenious process of "plastination." Usually, if you see a fetus in a museum, it is floating in a jar of liquid and is red or yellow and translucent. These bodies seem to be flat gray, and that is what ignites the flashback, a surreal freeze frame of my son, born a month prematurely by C-section. As the medical staff pulled him out of my wife's womb, just for a second, his flesh looked gray.[1]

Since all bodies, the living and the dead, the guilty and the innocent, can be "plastinated" through von Hagens's revolutionary process, I've traveled to Vienna with a critical eye, to question whether some of the bodies displayed in the latest version of this traveling show (first created in 1995 but massively larger now) could include those of political and religious prisoners in China. Yet von Hagens is drawing me in. Okay, I don't have a clue as to where von Hagens acquired a baby the size of my son, but the stated purpose of his exhibitions is health education, and I am hearing a whisper of scientific justification—*is this not the mystery of life? Your curiosity is good. It absolves you. Go farther. Step inside.* I consent and enter von Hagens's freak show.

Start with the man who's wearing nothing but boots and skis. He is performing a perfect split. His skin has been removed, revealing every sinew, every muscle. His eyes are intense, fixed on the horizon and—ready for the joke?—from the skull on down, his body has been split open, literally hacked in half.

288   **THE SLAUGHTER**

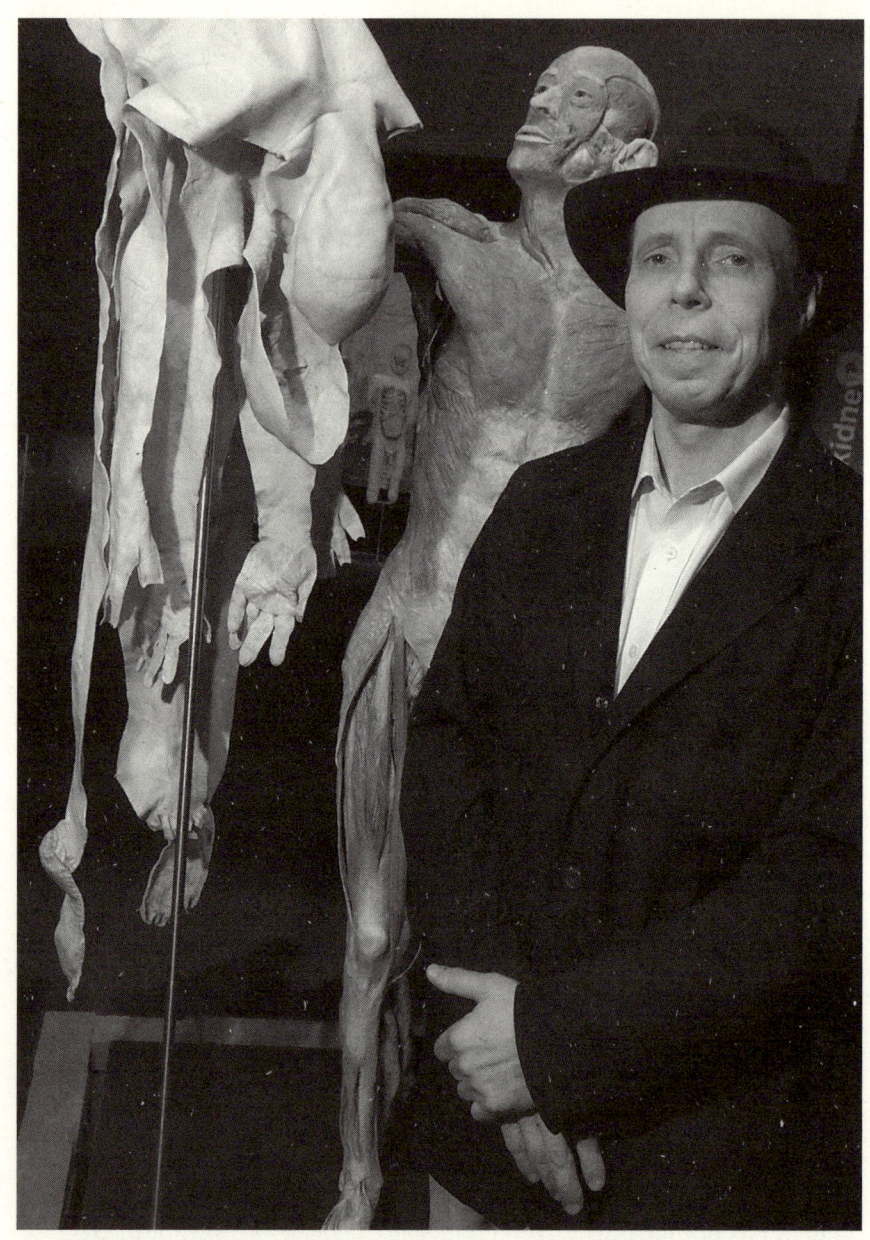

Gunther von Hagens strikes a pose next to a "Body Worlds" plastinated cadaver that holds its own skin. Photo by John McCoy.

Every apparently serious display in the exhibition is countered by another that smirks at you: instead of chipmunks playing poker, it's a lively troika of corpses in various states of corporeal undress. One is little more than a skeleton with—again, quite comical I suppose—foolishly bulging eyes. Naturally he has the winning hand—death always does—and you can imagine the giggles as they set this one up. Clearly, von Hagens wants to be seen as a wild and crazy lab guy.

And yet, after several rooms of bodies in sublime and macabre postures—for example, a corpse playing chess against an imaginary opponent (fill in the Bergman reference yourself)—it becomes obvious that von Hagens equally yearns to be appreciated as an artist. Naturally he must challenge my bourgeois inhibitions concerning necrophilia; at show's exit, suspended in air like the bodies in the medical thriller *Coma*, a couple engages in frozen sexual intercourse—"reverse cowgirl," since you ask. Porn directors favor the position because it allows the camera lens an unimpeded view of the genitals. And if you think I'm the one being prurient here, consider that von Hagens is not only the guy who hung the bodies so that the important bits are precisely at eye level, he also cut open the woman's womb and peeled back her vaginal walls so that the full penetration, the male presumably plastinated during rigor mortis, is permanently exposed.

Now it is a fact that there are ten year olds walking through this very room. But that's not my problem with the show. What's bugging me is that some of the bodies, the female ones in particular, have unusually short legs. And there's something about those legs combined with the small, refined skull and the slight frame that looks Chinese.

That's a problem because there really aren't supposed to be any Chinese bodies in the exhibition. But here's where the plot thickens slightly; there are actually two competing shows touring the world, von Hagens's "Body Worlds" and "Bodies: The Exhibition," managed by Premier Exhibitions, a US entertainment company. The bodies in the latter show are provided by von Hagens's very own sorcerer's apprentice, Professor Sui Hongjin.

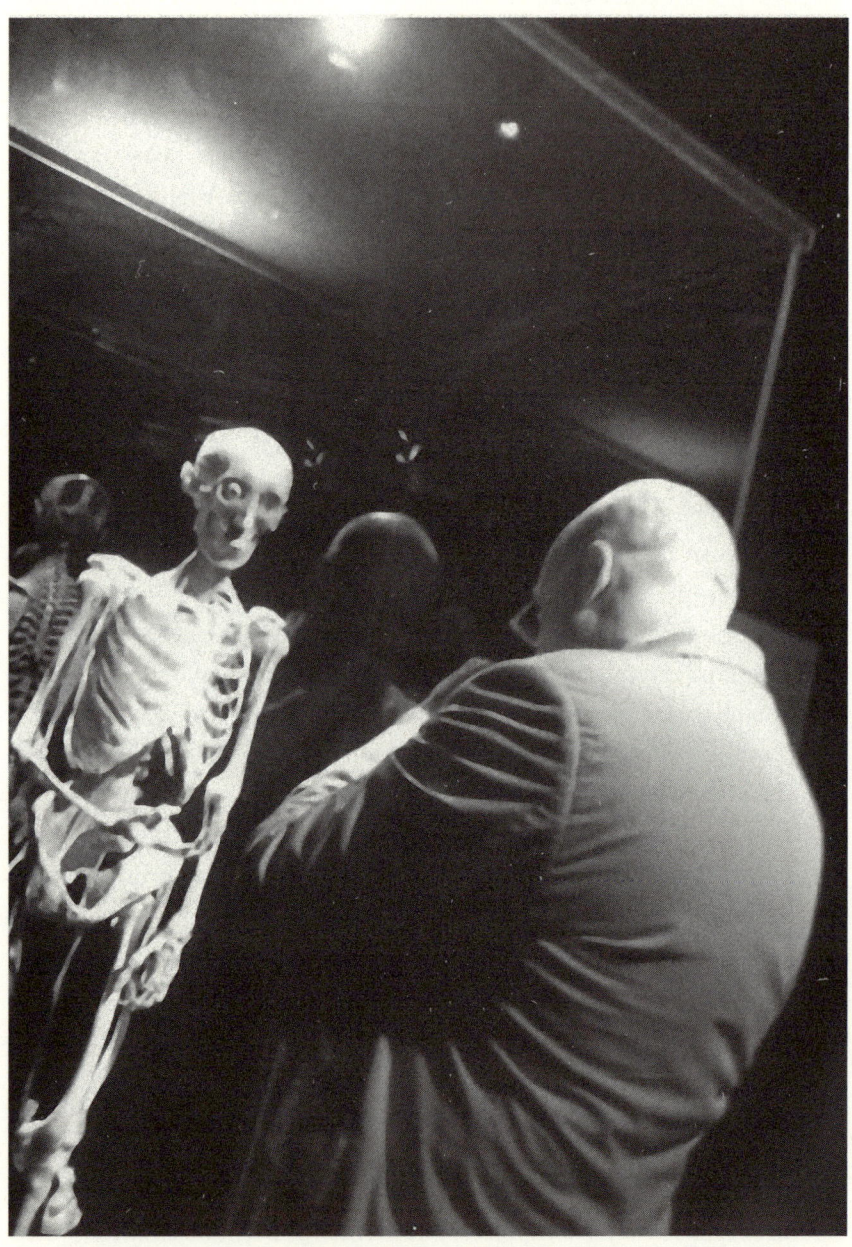

The author at the Körperwelten show in Vienna, June 13, 2013. Photo by Florian Godovits.

The story of the rivalry between von Hagens and Sui—a nearly perfect composite of the perils of doing business in China—is intrinsically fascinating but only relevant to this investigation inasmuch as it exposes tactical vulnerabilities for both men. In a nutshell: when von Hagens founded a Chinese plastination factory in 1999 (incidentally the same year that Falun Gong practitioners began flooding into Chinese labor camps and prisons), he hired Sui Hongjin as his general manger. After a couple years, Sui set up his own secret plastination company in the same city, Dalian in Liaoning Province. Von Hagens found out about the factory, fired Sui, and Sui took "Bodies: The Exhibition" on the road. In 2008, a "confidential informant" from the mainland, a man who claimed to be an operator in the black market for human bodies, appeared on ABC's *20/20* claiming that the specimens in Sui's show were executed Chinese prisoners. The informant later publicly retracted the claim, adding that von Hagens had manipulated him to discredit Sui.[2] Yet after political pressure in a number of US locations, Premier Exhibitions was henceforth obliged to post a disclaimer at the entrance to its show stating: "This exhibit displays human remains of Chinese citizens or residents which were originally received by the Chinese Bureau of Police. The Chinese Bureau of Police may receive bodies from Chinese prisons. Premier cannot independently verify that the human remains you are viewing are not those of persons who were incarcerated in Chinese prisons."[3]

Von Hagens himself avoided this obligation. He had closed down his Chinese operation a year before, and on *20/20* he tearfully claimed that he had unilaterally cremated all his Chinese specimens and replaced them with Caucasians who had legally donated their bodies to science.

Perhaps; doubtless some Caucasians have short legs. But by coincidence, at the show in Vienna, the facial muscles of these short-legged figures have been systematically stripped away, so no trace of an Asiatic fold or any other odd characteristic discernible to a sharp-eyed anatomist can be seen. In one case, other than the skeleton, all that is left of the woman's body is every intricate, spidery nerve. It's a breathtaking sight. Imagine how long it must have taken trained plastination experts to strip away every fiber of skin and muscle and inner organ from her corpse.

A year? Two years?[4] Now put yourself in von Hagens's mind-set for a moment: You've created art from corpses; you've named them and posed them and loved them. You've been photographed in every pose short of outright necking with them. So perhaps it is one of those fools-at-the-academy-don't-understand-my-work moments; would you really destroy your handiwork just because of that traitor, Sui? Maybe, maybe not.[5] How about because of a little protest by the officially despised group of dissidents from China named Falun Gong?

Over time, the questions surrounding the "body" shows—particularly Sui's, as he has sold an estimated one thousand Chinese plastinated bodies—have followed the long-term pattern of questions over Chinese organ harvesting, moving from concern over sourcing from death-row prisoners (murderers, rapists, and the like) to concern over sourcing from prisoners of conscience. But in contrast to the larger harvesting investigation, these questions are not likely to be about Uyghurs or Tibetans. Given the peculiar history of Liaoning Province, the questions are firmly centered on Falun Gong as the source.

Now it is a fact that elderly Falun Gong women have been patiently informing me for years that the bodies in Von Hagen's and Sui's exhibitions are Falun Gong practitioners being hideously displayed for people's amusement. My tendency was to nod politely and ignore them. *Too dramatic, too urban legend, too Falun Gong at the center of the universe*, I thought. Besides, it struck me as a sidebar issue; how could the "bodies" shows be relevant to investigating organ harvesting, which, numerically, is a far greater crime? Those feelings are still there, and yet, here in Vienna, I'm noticing that the liver and kidneys appear to be missing from some of the plastinated bodies—although there's a plastinated kidney right in front of me in a display case, so there's no obvious explanation for the omission. That's curious because von Hagens is fully aware that he could have slipped another human's plastinated liver and kidney set in there without anyone being the wiser. Are the organs missing because von Hagens—a virtuoso collector of a sort, with all the finicky attention to detail and authenticity that implies—considers putting a stranger's liver into one of his masterpieces a bit like putting a counterfeit exhaust manifold into a cherry Aston Martin DB5? Is it conceivable that these were dual-use bodies, the organs harvested before plastination? And could those kidney and livers still be alive inside some aged American, Japanese, or European who went to China for an organ a decade ago?

We can only read so much into plastic. The bodies are, for now, mute witnesses. The elderly Falun Gong refugees are operating on rumor. Confidential informants from China are always problematic. But if we take the few facts that have been dug up of how plastination unfolded in China and combine them with what we now know about Bo Xilai (through Wang Lijun's unscripted disruption of the Chinese leadership transition of 2012), we may yet shed some light on this mystery.

*　*　*

We also need to know a bit more about the father of plastination. Gunther von Hagens was born in the former East Germany in 1945. He actively fought Communism in his youth, and he has the humor and improvisational skills of an east-bloc youth—origins that may have given von Hagens a special ability to work within China's authoritarian system. It would also be fair to say that von Hagens does not think of himself as a scientist by nature, but as an adventurer. Like Toby Tyler, the boy who joined the circus, von Hagens declares his life has been "marked by defiance and daring." In 1974, after finishing his medical studies, von Hagens landed his first real job at the Department of Anesthesiology and Emergency Medicine at Heidelberg University, where he realized "his pensive mind was unsuitable for the tedious routines demanded of an anesthesiologist."[6] Over the next two years, he cycled through the university's anatomical institute and then into pathology, where he began experimenting with corpses. By 1979, he had cracked a method of preserving small specimens and body parts and was applying for a patent. But he dreamed of operating on a much larger scale.

It was during the late eighties—or perhaps the early nineties—that von Hagens met a student named Sui Hongjin (keep in mind that fixed dates that involve both men are often missing, vague, or contradictory).

294 THE SLAUGHTER

Certainly von Hagens and Sui have each retroactively tried to scrub the other out of their career histories, and they both share a talent for self-invention.[7] The critical fact about Sui for our purposes is that he claims to have been a visiting scholar from Dalian Medical University when he met von Hagens. Dalian is a well-managed city on the coast of Liaoning, and its medical university may be the key to understanding both von Hagens's, and ultimately Sui's, successful plastination business.

Three important things happened between 1992 and 1994. Von Hagens achieved the technical method to plastinate entire bodies. Sui convinced Von Hagens that plastinating bodies would be significantly cheaper in China. And finally, with Sui operating as a fixer, von Hagens paid his first visit to Dalian.[8]

Falun Gong morning exercises in Dalian's Xinghai Plaza in 1998. Dalian would ultimately emerge as a major organ-harvesting center. Source: Minghui.

By 1995, von Hagens had produced a small show of his first full-body specimens, which he exhibited in Japan. In China such an exhibit would be seen as an assault on Chinese cultural taboos and von Hagens was unlikely to make much in the way of admission fees. Even in Japan, he received mixed reviews—the controversy over the ethics of von Hagens's plastinated specimens appears right in the beginning—but the interesting question is: Where were these bodies produced? Von Hagens now claims that he had set up a donation system in Germany and a plastination center at the University of Heidelberg as early as 1993, but it's not clear that the German donation program was anything more than an effort to cover his tracks and the Heidelberg operation anything more than a place to hang his shingle. If it were otherwise, why didn't von Hagens hold the exhibition in Germany or at least in Europe? Japan was a natural choice for the first exhibition if the bodies had come from China and had been plastinated in the labs of Dalian Medical University. The evidence supports this scenario: in 1996, von Hagens was appointed as a visiting professor at Dalian Medical University, where he formally founded a plastination center—although von Hagens was clearly using Dalian Medical University merely as a launch pad for the company that would make him an extremely wealthy man: Von Hagens Plastination (Dalian) Co. Ltd.

In August 1999, the company was officially registered with the Dalian municipal government and von Hagens was approved to invest fifteen million.[9] Von Hagens was making a sizable investment that could help Dalian's burgeoning medical industry, and if foreign investment was a feather in the cap of any local party official back in 1999, a foreign investor in a city that was off the Beijing-Shanghai-Shenzhen-Guangzhou beaten track was worth at least two feathers. Still, that does not fully explain how the approval went to a solely foreign-owned enterprise—a rarity in a China full of joint ventures. How did this happen? Von Hagens appointed Sui Hongjin as general manager, and Sui was considered to be politically reliable. Von Hagens had gone to Dalian for cheap labor costs and material, a supply of cadavers, and an unfettered regulatory environment. But he also may have had a reasonable expectation of receiving miles of red carpet from the local Chinese political leadership. Back in 1999, the anxiety for foreign investors in a place like Dalian was less about whether they would be welcomed, but about whether the carpet was of good enough quality to support their venture. In 1999, Dalian was blessed with a mayor who could ensure that the carpet was both plush and very red: Bo Xilai. He would become governor of the province in 2001, and ultimately a competitor for the presidency of China.

You will recall that Bo's plans were fatally shattered by his long-term protégé, Wang Lijun, and Wang's fateful night ride to the American consulate on February 6, 2012. Ultimately, the consulate surrendered Wang to the Chinese authorities, Gu Kailai was charged with the death of Neil Heywood, and Bo Xilai would receive a prison sentence for corruption. But it was Wang Lijun and Bo Xilai's secret activities in Liaoning that constituted a far greater danger to the politburo.

The genesis of those activities began in 1999. We cannot reconstruct Bo Xilai's exact motivations with regard to Von Hagens Plastination (Dalian) Co. Ltd., but the company's sudden breakthrough suggests a close linkage to the Falun Gong repression that started in July.[10] In August, von Hagens received his approval from Dalian municipal, possibly with an assist from Bo's wife, Gu Kailai, and her consultancy firm. Finally, in September, Bo Xilai personally gave Gunther von Hagens an award certificate and medal at the Xinghai Friendship Award Ceremony (held in Dalian). According to Sui Hongjin, following the splashy ceremony, von Hagens bragged about his close connection to Bo Xilai.[11]

However, von Hagens faced a problem in 1999, specifically a shortfall of bodies. His business model was based not just on exhibitions, but also on selling plastinated bodies and parts to universities and other medical entities in volume. As von Hagens complained, the Chinese don't donate their bodies. A plastinator could perhaps use the unclaimed corpse of the odd homeless vagrant, but Chinese autopsy regulations required that such a body be held in the morgue for as long as thirty days to give the family a chance to identify it. Successful plastination requires the injection of formalin followed by silicone within about twenty-four hours of death, forty-eight hours at most (and even if exceptions could be made to the autopsy regulations, one wonders if homeless bodies might be too unhealthy to show).[12] Was it theoretically possible to use death-row prisoners if the Public Security Bureau played along? Perhaps. Yet according

A NIGHT AT THE MUSEUM 297

Figure 10.1: Key Dates for Bo Xilai, Wang Lijun, Gunther von Hagens, and Sui Hongjin

Bo Xilai

1993–2000	Mayor, Dalian
2000–2001	Acting Governor, Liaoning Province
2001–2004	Governor, Liaoning Province
2004–2007	Minister, Ministry of Commerce
2007–2012	Member of Politburo Central Committee

Wang Lijun

1995–2000	Deputy Director, Tieling City Public Security Department
2000–2003	Director, Tieling City Public Security Department
2003–2008	Party Secretary, Jinzhou City Public Security Bureau (PSB)
2004–2008	Director, Jinzhou PSB On-site Psychological Research Center
2006	lethal injection transplant method wins Guanghua Innovation Award

Gunther von Hagens

1993	von Hagens visits Dalian
1996	von Hagens accepts visiting professorship at Dalian Medical University
1999	Dalian municipal officials approve Von Hagens Dalian Plastination Co.
1999	Bo Xilai awards "Honorary Citizen of Dalian" to von Hagens
2003	von Hagens claims Dalian factory is responsible for 80% of his profits
2007	von Hagens shuts down Dalian production

Sui Hongjin

1993	Sui facilitates von Hagens's visit to Dalian
1999	Sui hired as General Manager, Von Hagens Dalian Plastination Co.
2002	Sui secretly sets up Dalian Medical University Plastination Co.
2004	after von Hagens termination, Sui creates Dalian Hoffen Bio-Technique Co.
2006	Sui signs $25 million agreement with US-based Premier Exhibitions

All photos from Baike.com except Gunther von Hagens, from Wikimedia Commons/A7babzorona.

to doctors and police that I have interviewed, using a bullet to kill the prisoner (with the family receiving the bill and so on) was still a sanctified PSB procedure in 1999, and such bodies would bear scars that would be difficult to explain—in fact, both Sui and von Hagens have made reference to purging such bodies from their exhibitions over the years. Adults between twenty-five and forty years of age, freshly killed, with no external wounds—that was the demographic that von Hagens required.[13] And he needed a steady supply of them.

The next few years brought in a vast wave of this precise demographic. Liaoning Province, in part because of its proximity to Jilin Province, the cradle of the Falun Gong movement, had an unusually high number of practitioners to begin with. After April 25, Jilin provincial officials accelerated spy operations and information gathering on practitioners throughout the province. Liaoning lagged.[14] But in autumn 1999, as Falun Gong practitioners flooded the Laogai System, doubling China's total prisoners and detainees by the beginning of 2001, Liaoning would make up for its slow start, and lift the political careers of Bo Xilai and Wang Lijun in its wake. From 2000 to 2004, when Bo served as Liaoning governor, he moved to the provincial capital Shenyang, but he appears to have retained his Dalian power base.[15] One of his first actions as governor was to authorize a massive capital infusion into Liaoning's prison and labor-camp capacity.[16]

On the outskirts of Shenyang lies the now-notorious labor camp of Masanjia. It was said that before Bo Xilai came to power, the camp had trouble paying the electricity bill, but in October 1999, the No. 2 Woman's Ward was opened for female Falun Gong practitioners. To incentivize this new facility, each prisoner was worth the equivalent of $1,500 in local matching funds, and the woman's compound and its associated assets would eventually encompass 330 acres. A million yuan, about $150,000 (US), for "environment enhancement" of Masanjia followed.[17]

In 2003, Bo Xilai authorized a billion yuan to expand the Laogai System of Liaoning. Fully half of the new money went to Masanjia, but it wasn't just to build more cells—Under Bo, Masanjia became the vanguard for Falun Gong "transformation" techniques—cattle prods, sleep deprivation, propaganda, and rape in the main. At the same time witnesses consistently report that Liaoning became infamous as a vast holding pen for young "nameless" Falun Gong. The other half of the money was largely distributed between three cities. In Shenyang, it was Longshan and Zhangshi Labor Camps and the massive egg-shaped compound that practitioners commonly refer to as "Shenyang Prison City."[18] In Jinzhou, it was an expansion of Jinzhou Prison. In Dalian, it was Nanguanling and Wafangdian Prisons, Dalian Labor Camp, and the Yaojia Detention Center.[19]

Shenyang Prison City. The egg shape comprises the First Provincial Prison, the Second Provincial Prison, the New Inmates Prison, the Women's Prison, and a general hospital. Imagery © 2014 CNES/Astrium, DigitalGlobe; map data © 2014 AutoNavi, Google.

The earliest confirmed reference that we have to an operational organ-harvesting center in Liaoning is in 2004. Recall that Bo Xilai's lieutenant, Wang Lijun, was running the Jinzhou City Public Security Bureau On-Site Psychological Research Center, where Wang oversaw "several thousand intensive on-site cases" of organ transplantation.[20]

Shenyang Military General Hospital and Hospital #2 of Dalian Medical University. Photos from Minghui and Baike.com.

There were other suspected organ-harvesting sites in Jinzhou, such as the PLA Number 205 Hospital.[21] But they pale before the fact that Wang was running one of the largest chop shops in all of China. That revelation led to the strange dance of veils by the Chinese leadership that we saw in the winter of 2012—admit anything about organ harvesting as long as it is not prisoners of conscience—that has continued into the present day. But Wang was just part of a larger pattern. Falun Gong labor-camp refugees that I interviewed consistently pointed to Liaoning, including specific locations in Shenyang, Dalian, and Jinzhou, as the geographic epicenter of Falun Gong harvesting from 2001 to 2006. There is little reason to doubt them, particularly as practitioners all across China heard a fairly similar refrain, especially in 2004 and 2005: *If you don't behave, we will send you to the Northeast.*[22]

But when it comes to specific organ-harvesting centers, the most persuasive evidence on actual locations emerged from Crystal's phone-bank operation back in early 2006 (see chapter 8). The first specific confirmed location of organ harvesting with a full stable of tissue types (although here it was based on actual witness accounts rather than phone calls) was Shenyang Military General Hospital.[23] The second was Hospital #2 of Dalian Medical University, where the wait for a liver donor was said to be as little as *three days*—yes, the same Dalian Medical University that had granted professorships to Gunther von Hagens and Sui Hongjin and served as their plastination production base.[24]

While we know that Shenyang Military General Hospital and Hospital #2 of Dalian Medical University were performing organ harvesting in 2006, and we know that Wang Lijun's center was performing it as early as 2004, we cannot say with assurance if any of these organ-harvesting operations had been running in 2001. Perhaps Sujiatun and Yida (both in the Shenyang area) were more prominent harvesting centers in the earlier years. But we can say that there was not a single Falun Gong practitioner in Liaoning who had been charged with a capital offense, even under the arbitrary standards of Chinese law.[25] And we can say that in 2001, under von Hagens's direction and Sui's management, receipts indicate von Hagens's factory began spitting out plastinated bodies at a good clip, with some medical institutions paying hundreds of thousands of dollars for a single specimen.[26]

Meanwhile, Sui secretly set up his own highly productive plastination factory—probably in 2002. Again the dates are murky—but we do know that he named the company "Dalian Medical University Plastination Co. Ltd.," thus linking plastination directly into a highly regarded Chinese academic entity that also happened to be performing organ harvesting.

Five essential elements flourished in Liaoning of value to both organ harvesting and plastination.

First, fresh bodies. Bo Xilai's carceral expansion program—I call it "The Liaoning Triangle"—acted as a magnet for Falun Gong prisoners, particularly nameless ones and nontransformables, the problem cases that a premier, forward-thinking institution like Masanjia was specifically designed for. In many cases these were prisoners without records, bodies that could not be traced. Many of them were about the right age—between twenty-five and forty years old—and many, even though they were tortured, had no external wounds. Like any good competitive business, the supply was geographically diversified between Dalian (von Hagens and Sui), Jinzhou (Wang Lijun) and Shenyang (Bo Xilai). Uyghurs, certain House Christian sects, such as Eastern Lightning, and Tibetans may also have been targeted through the occasional prison transfer, but there is little question that Falun Gong provided the lion's share and sadly, this was often a young person's game.

Second, international sales. With the growth of the organ-harvesting industry, Liaoning developed a culture and discreet procedures for medical trade with foreigners—on one hand, extensive organ tourism from Europe, Japan, and North America; on the other, a system for promoting foreign investment in the medical field with Chinese bodies as an export product. That continues today as Taobao, an online Chinese retail platform, is, as I write this, reported to be selling plastinated bodies to medical schools at $21,000 per specimen.[27]

Third, a sympathetic provincial Public Security Bureau. There is little question, based on phone calls by Falun Gong investigators directly to Sui Hongjin, that even if von Hagens was not fully aware of the sources, Sui

FIGURE 10.2
LIAONING PROVINCE 1999 TO 2006[28]

THE LIAONING TRIANGLE

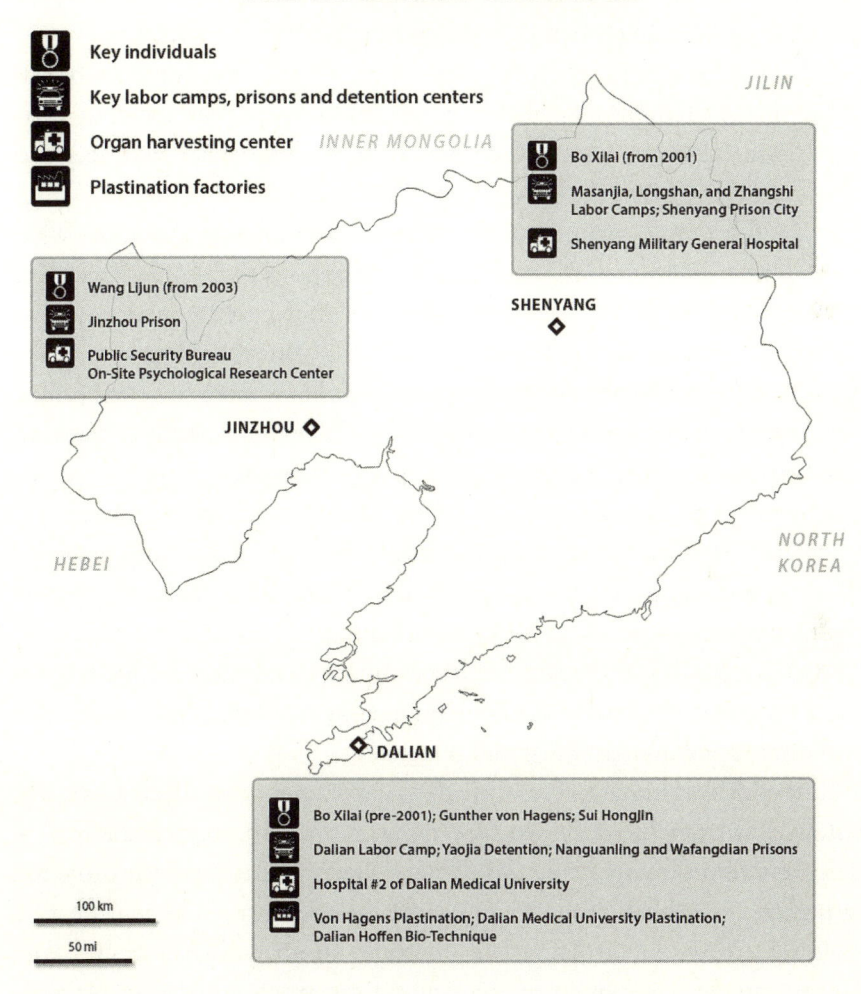

- Key individuals
- Key labor camps, prisons and detention centers
- Organ harvesting center
- Plastination factories

Bo Xilai (from 2001)
Masanjia, Longshan, and Zhangshi Labor Camps; Shenyang Prison City
Shenyang Military General Hospital

Wang Lijun (from 2003)
Jinzhou Prison
Public Security Bureau On-Site Psychological Research Center

Bo Xilai (pre-2001); Gunther von Hagens; Sui Hongjin
Dalian Labor Camp; Yaojia Detention; Nanguanling and Wafangdian Prisons
Hospital #2 of Dalian Medical University
Von Hagens Plastination; Dalian Medical University Plastination; Dalian Hoffen Bio-Technique

was—and he acknowledged that most of the bodies were coming directly from the PSB.[29] Wang Lijun was not only the head of the PSB in Jinzhou; hitched to the rising star of Bo Xilai he had clout far beyond that position. Li Feng, Liaoning's PSB head and PLAC Secretary in 2001, had control on paper, but he seems to have been part of the same clique that Bo represented: Jiang Zemin loyalists who were building their careers on one part discretion, two parts persecution.[30] The Falun Gong campaign was in full swing and those who wanted to get ahead had to show how tough they were. No province had better performance reviews.

Fourth, and put in corporate speak: *synergy*. Harvesting centers like Wang Lijun's required a stable of prisoners (to get tissue matches with wealthy foreigners), and so did the plastination factories (to meet the demands of medical schools and ambitious global exhibitions). Yet Wang Lijun and others like him were not necessarily competing for bodies with von Hagens and Sui—judging by the Vienna show, they could have even been sharing them. *Der Spiegel* reported an intercepted e-mail from Sui to von Hagens dating from the end of 2001: "This morning, two fresh, top quality corpses arrived at the factory. The livers were removed only a few hours ago."[31] Now there are two ways to take that statement, but one very obvious reading is that the bodies were harvested at another location—Jinzhou, Shenyang, or, given the short time frame, Hospital #2 of Dalian Medical University—just before they arrived for plastination. Given the extraordinary profit involved in both harvesting and plastination—approximately two hundred thousand dollars on both procedures if exploited fully—there was little reason not to cut deep in Jinzhou or Shenyang and then make the four hour drive to Dalian. As long as the cadaver arrived quickly, Sui could plastinate.

The fifth and final essential element: a collapse of medical ethics. We know that from July 1999 to December 2005 Liaoning led the rest of China in terms of reported cases of Falun Gong torture, and the province was third in terms of reported deaths through torture.[32] But the effect of collusion in the secret harvest of essentially innocent prisoners of conscience on the Liaoning medical community simply can't be quantified, filed, or rationalized. We smell the rot in Vienna, New York, Las Vegas—anywhere the "bodies" exhibitions go, but China will be dealing with the decomposing landfill for years to come.

There's a postscript for Doctor Professor Sui Hongjin. After von Hagens found out about Sui's mirror plastination factory, Sui opened his own "bodies" show on January 1, 2004, at Beijing's Natural History Museum. The "Plastinated Human Body" exhibition featured six full-body exhibits. It was met with a hushed silence, then murmurs of disapproval, even in the state-run press—unscripted rumblings that spoke volumes about the fault lines of Chinese culture. It was commonly whispered that it was a "corpse show," but to no avail. On April 8, 2004, the "Body Worlds" exhibition—Sui even stole the name this time—opened at the Beijing Exhibition Hall of China Architectural Culture Center, with the approval of the Health Ministry, the Chinese Society for Anatomy, and the China Science and Technology Association. The show of twenty bodies—von Hagens complained that Sui had stolen some of the postures, too—was backed by the Beijing Zhonghai Shangda Advertising Company, a favorite of the party's Shanghai clique. The show was promoted throughout Beijing with an image of a human cadaver proudly holding his own skin. This time, when the murmurs began in the press, the central propaganda department simply squelched them. The show went on to tour throughout China with apparent, if somewhat force-fed success. On August 8, 2005, it landed in the United States.[33]

Sui went on to expand plastination production and to build a bigger and greater show than the wizard himself. In 2007, von Hagens ended all production in Dalian. But he had made a permanent contribution to building the New China. Whether the bodies in the Beijing exhibition were Falun Gong or not, the cadavers proved that even the mystery of life must obey those who hold power, not those who hold their own skin.

But are the bodies Falun Gong? Or were the corpses of prisoners of conscience used exclusively for organ harvesting and not for plastination? It is certainly possible that von Hagens is telling the truth when he insists he burned all his plastinated Chinese bodies and that Sui, though he received corpses from the PSB, has good reasons for his apparent confidence that they included no prisoners of conscience—okay, that's a stretch. But if the question deserves an answer, there is actually a long shot way of finding one: test the DNA.

According to medical specialists I've consulted, mitochondrial DNA can be extracted from fixed anatomical specimens and used to prove relationships out to third-degree relatives.[34] In other words, one could give Doctors against Forced Organ Harvesting, or some other responsible entity, DNA samples from both shows, test the samples from von Hagens's figures to see if all the bodies are Caucasian, then attempt to match the DNA from any that turn out to be Chinese. The same procedure could be used to test DNA from Sui's displays against DNA from Chinese families who lost a loved one through an "enforced disappearance"—a PSB arrest for religious or political beliefs—during the years of high plastination.

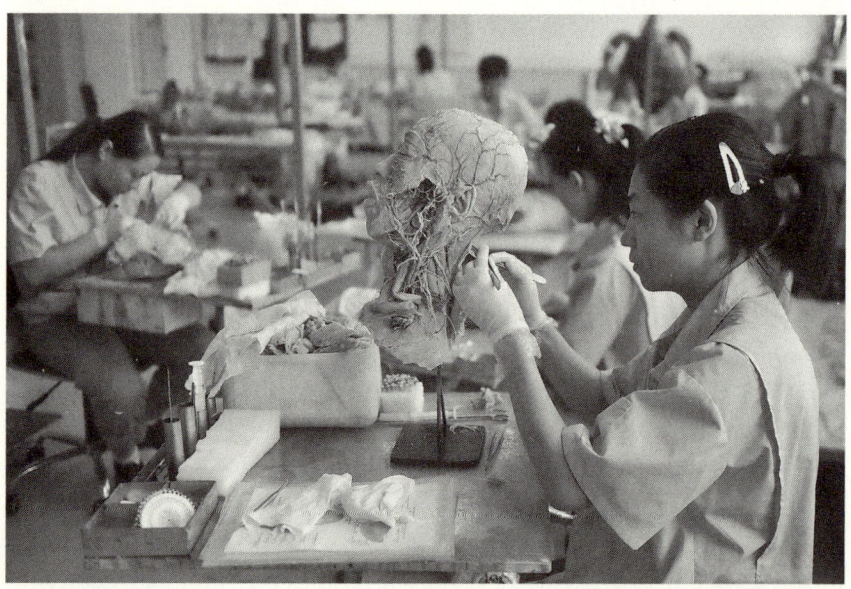

Sui Hongjin's "corpse factory" in Dalian. Photo from Reuters/Sheng Li.

Could matches be found? Initially, it would be harder than finding a needle in a haystack—although Minghui has compiled a formidable list of Falun Gong members missing from Liaoning Province alone. The families could be contacted. If enough families became aware of this effort and provided samples—a little saliva is best—then the chances would increase dramatically.

Families, not institutions, are the repository of memory. But there could be a role for institutions, too. We must learn from history, and

European parliament vice president Edward McMillan-Scott has suggested an impunity index—a central database, similar to efforts during the Cold War, in which dissidents can record exactly who ratted on them, who sentenced them, and who tortured them so that when reform or revolution occurs, justice is possible.[35]

From Dalian with love? The cadaver on the billboard appears to adopt a classic Falun Gong pose: the first stretching motion of the first exercise. Photo courtesy of Levi Browde.

But for now, DNA testing would require cooperation. I thought perhaps von Hagens would agree in an effort to clear his name of any lingering doubts. I thought that if he realized that DNA samples could be taken from his figures without damaging them—any more than a van Gogh is damaged when a tiny sample of paint is taken to prove its authenticity—he might cooperate. I thought he would do this because if he were exonerated, Dr. Death could rightfully jeer at my dark fantasies of a night at the museum, and I would gladly laugh along with him. So far, von Hagen's representatives have rejected the idea, although I still sense that public pressure could change that.[36] Dr. Sui's case is a little different. Given the money involved in Sui's operation—and the old adage that every criminal makes one mistake—like, um, shipping possible murder victims carrying DNA around the globe—the show could ultimately be considered an accessory to a crime against humanity. If Sui were to cooperate, he could mitigate his past involvement in the eyes of the world and, most important, in the eyes of the Chinese people.

But let us be realistic about the Chinese, too. They have been through a lot. This will not last forever, and this will be forgotten. What's more, the most advanced Chinese laboratories may be growing livers within ten to fifteen years. So the sourcing of organs, organ transplants, organ surrogates, kidneys for sale—these are not the burning ethical quandaries of our age. It's the same old quandary it's ever been: not the inevitability of death, as Gunther von Hagens would have it, but the inevitability of human descent into mass murder.

AFTERWORD

Back in the first chapter I gave the brief testimony of a Uyghur guard—Nijat—working with the Chinese PSB. Among the many incidents he related that day was the story of a young Chinese male incarcerated in an Urumqi Prison who was slated for execution after committing some horrible crime. Nijat said: "It is not nice to say this about anyone, but you could tell by looking at this man's face that he was simple." The PSB cleverly put some plainclothes officers in the cell with the simple man to persuade him to sign papers donating his organs to the state. After a couple days the simple man banged on the bars of the cell, and Nijat responded.

"I want to sign the form that donates my organs to the state."

Nijat, knowing that the organ harvesting would be done while the man was still alive, cautiously replied: "You know this might be quite painful."

"My mother is very poor. It will cost her too much money to come to Xinjiang to collect my body. I want to repay my debt to the state."

Nijat got the form. The simple man signed it with an "X."

As Nijat related the story he began weeping silently. Okay, in truth, there wasn't a dry eye in the room. But we did not shed tears because the simple man had been manipulated into donating his organs. Yes, it was depressing. Yes, harvesting prisoners' organs creates a financial incentive for a higher rate of executions. Yet the sorrow we all shared in that room was clearly about something greater than prisoners' rights. The sorrow was rooted in something involving universal human waste, isolation, and tragedy.

As Westerners, we gravitate toward technical fixes. We think in legal categories. We have a tendency to mix all our compassionate causes together, like my grandmother's Jell-O mold. Thus, the Indian man who sells one of his kidneys and the murderer in a Chinese jail who is coerced into donating his organs before his execution and the Uyghur activist who is dragged into an operating room are all just subsets of the greater tragedy of human exploitation and transplant abuse. Perhaps we blur the edges further: the state of Texas and Liaoning Province are equally sinister because they both employ the death penalty. And further still: a hardened killer or a rapist has the same rights as a young mother who refuses to lie about her beliefs.

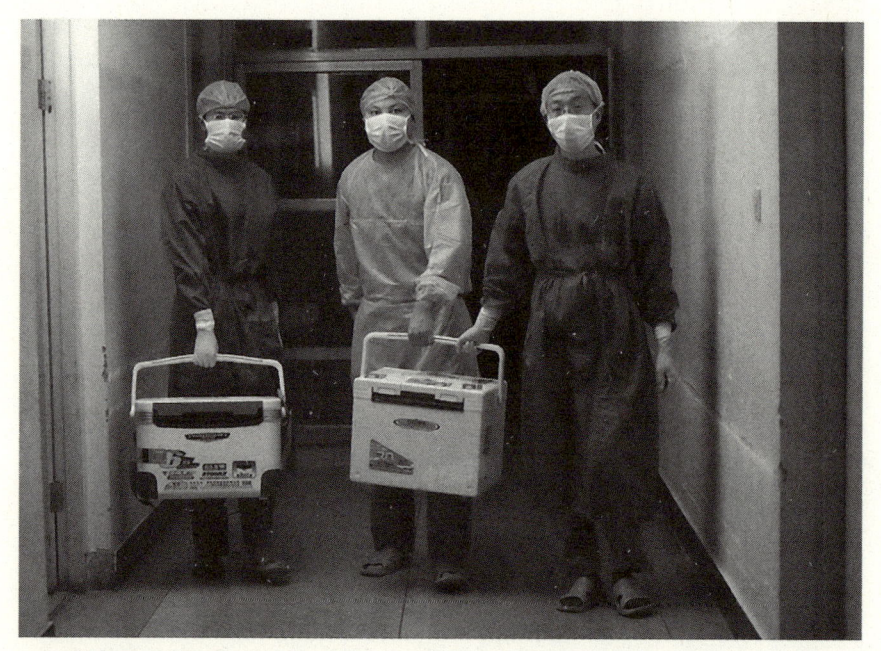

Chinese surgeons carry freshly extracted organs for transplant. From Xinhua.

This ethical shorthand, this unyielding logic of perfectionism, dishonors not only the television hijackers of Changchun, but also the simple man and his concern for his mother's wretched circumstances. It may complicate the picture, but Huang Jiefu isn't altogether wrong: just as Chinese citizens occasionally donate their organs (that's why the photograph above was published), prisoners convicted of capital crimes also occasionally choose to donate their organs without duress. Yet do you believe that any prisoner of conscience, Falun Gong, Uyghur activist,

Tibetan monk, or House Christian, *ever, even one time*, freely consented "to repay their debt to the state" in such a manner?

Regardless of one's opinion of the death penalty—even a fully democratic China might well continue the practice—it is a bureaucratic fantasy that prisoners of conscience are just a subset of a wider problem of prisoner's rights. Thus, what has been done to prisoners of conscience, indeed what is being done to them right now, is not a breach of protocol or a manipulation of free will or penal corruption or against Chinese tradition. No signatures are required of prisoners of conscience—not even an "X." They are harvested like animals, and that is why this book is not titled "Malpractice" but *The Slaughter*.

* * *

I wrote this book to present evidence, not to construct a platform for political and social action. There are others who are more experienced in law and the politics of human rights, and I leave that to them. I prefer presenting evidence rather than telling the reader what to think. And yet I am a product and a part of Western society so a few parting observations about own culture may be of some value to Chinese and Westerners alike.

Having filed stories from China myself, I refuse to whine about press coverage. I understand the Beijing waterfront; you can study Falun Gong from a distance, as long as your writing reflects that distance along with a high degree of disengagement. Perhaps, like Ian Johnson, you can go beyond that a bit by using a third-person narrative. Or like Phillip Pan, you can even do a quick hit that punctures a propaganda campaign like the Tiananmen self-immolation. But if you openly testify on the full scale of the atrocities—atrocities that all serious China journalists instinctively understand are occurring—you're dead on this waterfront and every waterfront from Dalian to Behai. You don't get your accreditation, you don't interview a party official, you don't write for anyone. You're dead.

Yet I do wish that a China-based reporter would proactively write his or her own China burn notice by digging deep into this issue. Are you out there? You can't stay in Beijing forever you know. What a way to go.

Outside of the China beat, I've sensed that many journalists would like to report on the organ harvesting of prisoners of conscience, but they don't have the confidence to go to their editors with a story that goes beyond a routine binary—the *Bloody Harvest* report alleges terrible atrocities; the Chinese government denies them. Back in 2006, the harvesting story was still manageable for a daily reporter. But if one wants to dive in now, days of research, retrieving references, sifting through imperfectly translated reports and tape recordings filled with barely intelligible conversations is required—and that's just to fact check one of my chapters.

Fine. Check our work. It's good for the field. Yet what about some primary research?

Follow the leads. Look at what Arne Schwarz came up with simply using a computer and a suspicion about Western pharmaceutical companies performing medical testing on transplant patients in China. Or look at the Uyghurs and Tibetans—when it comes to recent harvesting, Jaya Gibson and I have barely scratched the surface. Look at the demand side of organ harvesting: the gaping hole in our knowledge of the shape and composition of Western organ tourism. Want to fill that hole? Want a searing human-interest story? Instead of reinventing the harvesting wheel, an enterprising reporter could track antirejection medications and elicit a few discreet interviews with those who have received transplants in China. It's an important issue—in my experience it comes up in practically every government hearing, from Washington to Brussels to Geneva. But the critical point is that journalists stop merely kibitzing over what has already been done and begin building on it.

In the last two years the evidence surrounding organ harvesting has been getting far more of a hearing with Western governments than it has with the press. I suspect it's because political staffers actually have the responsibility—and critically, the time—to read the published material closely. I also suspect that the US State Department knows everything that Wang Lijun (Bo Xilai's protégé) knows about harvesting. Yet the State Department needs Chinese cooperation—on al Qaeda, North Korea, and Iran. And if the United States government openly accuses

China of an ongoing crime against humanity, what should the State Department do? Hand the Chinese ambassador a list of hospitals?

Perhaps they should. Yet at the very least, *follow your values*. What can the United States tolerate? A Jewish state, forged in the Holocaust, could not tolerate its citizens traveling to China to receive organs from slaughtered religious dissidents. So they banned Israeli HMOs from paying for organ tourism to China. And when Gunther von Hagens's "bodies" show came to town, they banned that, too. In April 2014, the Tazpit News Agency reported that a prominent Israeli Rabbi, Shlomo Aviner, called for protests on behalf of Falun Gong. His message was a simple one: "Do not forget the Chinese. They are human beings created in the image of God."[1]

European states may have a neurotic aversion to following Israel's example, but the United States does not. And the US dollar—even from the occasional wealthy organ tourist—speaks to China quite loudly indeed.

I am afraid that my advice to the Western medical world comes too late: *Follow your oath. First do no harm.*

I understand that the Transplantation Society had good intentions. The Chinese Communist Party has brought Chinese surgeons to a new low, lower even than the forced abortions and sterilization of previous years. So it was up to the most venerated and respected members of the Western medical societies to do something about it, and the transplant surgeons wanted to save lives.

Well, we all want to save lives. But in China's current configuration, that may be a mirage. When *Epoch Times* came out with the story on Sujiatun in March 2006 they did not know they would be consigning thousands of Falun Gong to a clearance sale in May. When I published my suspicions that fifty thousand Uyghurs, hardcore criminals, and Falun Gong were being held in the Tarim Desert, I imagined the grateful expressions of the living would flash before me on my death bed. It is far more likely that I inadvertently assisted in their liquidation. When Francis Delmonico lends the reputation of the Transplantation Society to Chinese civilian hospitals that claim they will no longer harvest death-row criminals, he may simply be providing the public appearances that will allow military hospitals to continue making up the organ shortfall with Falun Gong. The Chinese leadership is a black box. It does not respond to "best practices" or "ethical training."

So may I ask the international medical community, particularly the Transplantation Society: What was your "engagement" with Chinese doctors such as Huang Jiefu really based on? Was it about saving lives? Or was it about saving China's medical community, and your own profession, from further embarrassment? Are you sure they are the same thing? You never publicly mentioned prisoners of conscience. Why? Because you really don't believe there is any evidence that they have been harvested? Or because you were told not to offend your Chinese hosts? In exchange you received a fig leaf of cooperation from the Chinese medical establishment. In the end, was that all you thought you could really get?

Did you have trouble reading those sentences? Did you find yourself skipping through them and tightening your lips? If you did, perhaps it's because your first responsibility is not to save the lives of those who many of you deny are being killed anyway. Your first responsibility is to establish the full medical history, to establish the condition of the patient—yes, that would be China—before you operate. Tread softly here. Do no harm.

You dismiss much of the information you are given. You prefer to talk to medical professionals rather than to patients. But your job is to listen to the patients—those who are still alive—very carefully, no matter how irritating, emotional, or unschooled they may be. Do you have a problem with my survivor interviews? Perhaps you have a point. Perhaps, given your medical expertise, you should be doing these interviews, not me.

You gave the Chinese medical establishment an extra two years to clean up the mess, an extra two years for the military hospitals of China to make up for any minor shortfalls by butchering Uyghurs, Tibetans, and Falun Gong. Why would the party waste two years of your time and then begin again? Because the party cannot stop organ harvesting. Like a game of musical chairs, when the music stops one faction will not be seated. And then the digging into the past begins.

So the music plays on, because the party fears history. And I have spoken harshly to the Transplantation Society because it made a contract to help the party bury history. I'm glad that contract fell apart. No Western entity possesses the moral authority to allow the party to impede the excavation of a crime against humanity in exchange for promises of medical reform. As a survival mechanism of our species, we must contextualize, evaluate, and ultimately learn from *every* human descent into mass murder. Ultimately it doesn't matter if historians reach a consensus that Chinese organ harvesting has an echo of the medical corruption of Unit 731, or the systemic brutality of the Gulag Archipelago, or the conversion methods of the Spanish Inquisition. The critical thing is that there is a history. And only the victims' families can absolve the party from its weight.

APPENDIX

A SURVEY-BASED ESTIMATE OF FALUN GONG HARVESTED FROM 2000 TO 2008

For a more detailed version of this appendix see my chapter "How Many Harvested," in David Matas and Torsten Trey, eds., State Organs *(Woodstock, ON: Seraphim, 2013), pp. 49–67.*

Over several years I interviewed more than one hundred subjects, some interviews lasting several days. Just over fifty of my subjects were Falun Gong refugees from labor camps, prisons, and long-term detention facilities. Of these, sixteen had been subjected to suspicious medical testing.

Fifty subjects would be a statistical trifle in most consumer studies, but wartime studies and intelligence operations often have to make do with far less. It's not a perfectly random sample—I spent an evening in Bangkok actively seeking out a practitioner who had experienced unusual medical examinations—but there was no attempt to load the dice. My research interests are wide, so Bangkok was balanced by interviews in Hong Kong, Taipei, North America, Europe, and Australia, where my selection process favored practitioners who had direct experience of Falun Gong's rise in the nineties or of the early days of the crackdown. Most of these practitioners served relatively short sentences by current standards, and they were released before organ harvesting became common. In acknowledgment of the sample size, I try to avoid trying to fix a single number of fatalities from organ harvesting, which skeptics might justifiably seize on as an example of false precision, in favor of establishing a plausible range of fatalities and constructing a "best guess" or a middle number from that range.

APPENDIX

To begin, we must have some basic agreement about the overall numbers of prisoners in China. The only rational count is one that includes the entire network of prisons, jails, labor camps (*Laogai*), detention centers, black jails, and psychiatric institutions that the Laogai Research Foundation refers to as the *Laogai System*—a definition that captures the real-life experiences of Falun Gong practitioners in China. The Laogai Research Foundation is the only institution or NGO in the world actually making such estimates from primary evidence. Taking into account the Laogai Research Foundation's caveat that "it is impossible to know with certainty how many inmates are imprisoned in the Laogai or how many camps exist," and even without including detention or psychiatric centers, the Laogai Research Foundation counts well over a thousand nodes—prison and labor camp facilities—throughout the mainland. Its staffers researched each location for any indications of its economic output, and then used these figures and other clues to estimate how many prisoners might be contained within it. I used similar calculations and methods at the Brookings Institution to come up with the true lifecycle expense of combat units and weaponry. In short, I believe the building-blocks approach is a legitimate and defensible method. The Laogai Research Foundation currently estimates the number of prisoners in the Laogai System as between three and five million.

In terms of establishing a base Falun Gong population in 1999, the problem is significantly easier because we know that the 6-10 Office's internal, working estimate of Falun Gong's pre-crackdown population was seventy million.

Baseline estimates	Low estimate	High estimate
Total prisoners in Laogai System at any given time	3,000,000	5,000,000
Falun Gong base population in 1999	70,000,000	70,000,000

How many of the Laogai System prisoners were Falun Gong? Practitioners on the ground in China assumed that over one million Falun Gong were incarcerated in the first years of the crackdown. Based on clues from my interviews, these claims have a bearing in reality, yet they come from people who had no previous experience in analyzing the Chinese penal system. Under the skeptical eye of the Western press, in 2002 the overseas Falun Gong persecution-tracking sites established the ultra-cautious number one hundred thousand as a lowball, and presumably defensible, estimate of practitioners in custody. United Nations Special Rapporteur on Torture Manfred Nowak made a statement in 2009 indicating that Falun Gong comprised fully 50 percent of the population of China's prison camps; Nowak relied on refugee testimony, and his statement was consistent with an earlier report in which he asserted that Falun Gong constituted 66 percent of the alleged torture cases in China. Nowak's torture percentage feels intuitively accurate to me, but the one hundred thousand estimate and the 50 percent estimate cannot both be correct unless the Laogai population was two hundred thousand or less. I commend Nowak for having the courage to treat practitioner claims seriously, but the fact is that in the atomized world of the Laogai, no practitioners are in a position to make plausible system-wide estimates.

In any given interview with a refugee from the Laogai System, I don't ask the subjects about the overall system, but I do ask them for an accurate breakdown of the number of practitioners within their own cellblocks. Based on fifty interviews in which each practitioner gave me a personal snapshot of his or her particular situation, I estimate that the practitioner representation in China's Laogai System averages out to about 30 percent of women and 10–15 percent of men. Given the overrepresentation of men in the Laogai System, I further estimate that, on the low end, male and female practitioners collectively represent around 15 percent of the prisoners in the Laogai System at any given time. On the high end, 20 percent. While the high estimate may have been operative in 2001 and the low estimate is more likely to have been operative in 2008, we can say that the average number of practitioners in the Laogai System at any given time ranges between 450,000 (15 percent of three million) and 1,000,000 (20 percent of five million).

If these numbers seem high, consider our starting point of seventy million. If you use the lower estimate, less than 1 percent of the Falun Gong base population is actually in the Laogai System at any given time. In the high estimate, it's approximately 1.5 percent.

Falun Gong in Laogai System at any given time	Low estimate	High estimate
Percentage of total prisoners in Laogai System at any given time	15%	20%
Average number of Falun Gong in Laogai System at any given time	450,000	1,000,000

The next step is to determine how many practitioners have been in the Laogai System at some point over the survey period. Again, based on my interviews with fifty refugees, I came up with answers across the board: in the early years, a year or two in detention was common. By 2008, five-year sentences were routine. A not quite three-year term (or to be precise, a 2.66 multiplier) on average captures the variability with reasonable accuracy.

Total Falun Gong in Laogai System 2000 to 2008	Low estimate	High estimate
Average amount of time a practitioner is in the Laogai System	3 years	3 years
Total Falun Gong in Laogai System at some point, 2000 to 2008	1,200,000	2,666,667

Of my fifty practitioner subjects, sixteen, or approximately 30 percent, received physical examinations that were in some aspect inexplicable and incongruous other than as an assessment of organ transplant viability. Those sixteen, in turn, can be divided into two groups.

In the first group I have placed eight practitioners, or 15 percent of my sample, who seem to have been examined "for show"—that is, they were obviously too old, too sick, or too weakened by hunger strike to be plausible candidates for harvesting. My theory, borne out by the signs of anxiety with which the authorities viewed these tests (in an extreme example, an armed guard was matched up with every female practitioner), is that the "for-show" practitioners were given the same examinations as every other practitioner out of bureaucratic inertia, or to make the procedure seem normal and to keep the prisoners from panicking.

A SURVEY-BASED ESTIMATE OF FALUN GONG HARVESTED FROM 2000 TO 2008

In the second group, I have placed eight practitioners, or 15 percent of my sample, who were younger, relatively healthy, and were not on hunger strike. Their exams differed from location to location, but they invariably included these central components: blood tests, a urine test, an EKG, and X-rays of the abdomen (examination of the cornea was standard practice in 2002, but it had been dropped by 2006). Crucially, they were then given a series of follow-up medical tests usually corresponding with tissue matching. Members of this group were candidates for harvesting.

Falun Gong examined in Laogai System	Low estimate	High estimate
Percentage of Falun Gong examined in custody	30%	30%
Falun Gong examined in custody	360,000	800,000
Percentage of Falun Gong examined "for show"	50%	50%
Falun Gong examined as candidates for harvesting	180,000	400,000
Percentage of Falun Gong selected for harvesting	5%	30%

What percentage of the practitioners examined for harvesting were actually selected for surgery? On the low estimate, I premise that in spite of all the testing, and the profits to be made, only one out of every twenty practitioners was actually selected, and a selection rate lower than that strains credulity, and wouldn't have even been worth the trouble. But what drives the high estimate of 30 percent? Most practitioners in the Laogai System had only an amorphous awareness of the organ-harvesting issue during their detention, yet their recollections establish that following a series of medical tests in labor camp one out of every three or four of the practitioners who had received the follow-up exams might be "relocated." It is exceedingly difficult for most practitioners to say definitively if this was an actual selection for organ harvesting. However, they were better positioned to make such an estimate than any outsider that I am aware of, so I accept their percentage as the top range.

As you can see in the chart below, those selection percentages, plus the accumulation of previous assumptions regarding high and low estimates, leads to a wide differential. Fair enough. Given the uncertainties in the process, I have consciously tried to avoid precision where the evidence does not justify it. Yet both the low estimate and the high estimate are genuine outliers, and I don't really believe in either extreme. The truth is found somewhere in the middle and that's why I provide a best estimate of 64,500, which I have rounded up to 65,000.

Best estimate of Falun Gong harvested 2000 to 2008	Low estimate	High estimate
Total Falun Gong harvested 2000 to 2008	9,000	120,000
"Best estimate"	**65,000**	

Thus the figure of 65,000 is my ball-park estimate for the period. This figure happens to be in rough accordance with the organ-harvesting rate that was premised by David Kilgour and David Matas in *Bloody Harvest* (which relies on numerical gaps in the official Chinese count) and the more recent estimates of practitioners harvested in David Matas's chapter in *State Organs* (which relies on a wide range of evidentiary points, for example the extremely high rate of hepatitis infection among regular prisoners in China).

An estimate of how many Uyghurs, Tibetans, or House Christians were harvested during the same period (clearly it would be a fraction of the Falun Gong numbers, collectively, say 5 percent, or in the range of two to four thousand) would be nothing more than a guess at this time. Nor do I have the accumulation of witness testimony to make a legitimate estimate of the harvesting of prisoners of conscience from 2009 to the present, although I do speculate that as practitioners in custody age, the percentage of Falun Gong harvested might fall while the number of Tibetans and Uyghurs—who have injected new blood into the system following their respective rebellions—might be expected to rise.

Finally, I sincerely hope that Dr. Ko's willingness to speak on the record will spark other medical personnel to come forward and shed much needed light on the composition and scale of organ harvesting in China.

ACKNOWLEDGMENTS

Field research takes money. Without the ability to buy airline tickets and pay for expenses on the ground, including translation and research assistance, my investigation would have been confined to whatever was available on the web—worthy of an op-ed or a long-form essay at best. Yet for all the sound and noise and hashtags, human rights research funding is scarce. Whatever is in the kitty tends to be funneled into activism. When it comes to investigating a long-running, slow-motion crime against humanity, the old saying rings true: the first dollar really *is* the hardest. So I reserve a very special sense of gratitude for the Earhart Foundation of Michigan, particularly program officer Montgomery Brown. After awarding me a respectable grant for my first book, Earhart chose to gamble on my second book, awarding me its maximum research grant (on what was admittedly a rather speculative research plan). In short, Earhart paid for my North American interviews.

Because the Chinese diaspora is distributed throughout the Pacific Rim, the Asia research component was just as financially challenging. The Peder Wallenberg family of Sweden filled the gap by supplying two research grants. The first paid for the interviews in Thailand, Hong Kong, Taiwan, and Australia. Following Leeshai's aborted expedition to Dharamsala (he was stopped in Hong Kong, interrogated, and ultimately sent back to Taipei because, as an active Falun Gong practitioner, he had been placed on the Chinese "terrorist list"), I passed on the majority of the second grant to Jaya Gibson. Jaya is an investigative bulldog, and he single-handedly launched an extended investigation into the organ harvesting of Tibetans using Dharamsala as his field office. I appreciate the opportunity to present Jaya's seminal contribution in this book, yet, as always, it comes down to the funding. Speaking for Jaya, Leeshai, and myself, we wish to express our gratitude for the Wallenberg's support of our work.

ACKNOWLEDGMENTS

You may get a new laptop out of a grant, but you can't make a living by traveling around the world interviewing refugees. When the research funds were gone, my household's funds were equally depleted. A donor stepped in and bridged that financial gap, no strings attached, at exactly the right time. He prefers to remain in the background. I respect that, but he should know that his support made it possible for Leeshai and I to begin the process of sifting through what we had collected, and I thank him for his generosity.

Finally, the National Endowment for Democracy (NED) furnished me with a modest travel budget to undertake what must have seemed like a fairly speculative investigation into Uyghur organ harvesting. I had a start on the Uyghur investigation—and it should be mentioned that Jaya Gibson played a significant role in the Nijat Abdureyimu interview in Italy, and he also conducted the taped interview of Enver Tohti in London—yet the critical "missing link" of the organ-harvesting story was hidden in Central Europe. I'm grateful, not only to Louisa Coan Greve of NED, but also to various individuals, particularly Omer Kanat, Alim Seytoff, and Dolkun Isa, who actually oversaw the bureaucratic grunt work of administering the travel grant, and also persuaded confidential witnesses to talk to me.

Money came from several other sources, but this is the category where I also had to earn my keep. The most important was the *Weekly Standard*, where Richard Starr and Bill Kristol had the guts to run just about every long-form essay on China that I proposed. *World Affairs Journal*, with the help of my old editor Peter Collier, also published several of my essays, as did Rich Lowry of *National Review*.

I make no apologies for prepublishing portions of this book. At a difficult time for the publishing world, this was a reasonable financial strategy, and it also allowed me to assuage some of the guilt that builds up when you feel you are sitting on important material (although, as I pointed out in the afterword, trying to actually take credit for saving lives in China is a fool's game).

In addition, New Tang Dynasty Television hired me as consultant for a couple months back in 2006 in an effort to get a film project started with the BBC. That project never received mainstream backing, but I'm grateful to NTDTV, particularly Shiyu Zhou and Zenon Dolnyckyj, for rustling up the seed money that facilitated my first interviews with Hao Fengjun, Chen Yonglin, and Jennifer Zhang in Australia. A few years later, some Canadian Falun Gong practitioners defrayed the expenses for a trip to speak to the Canadian parliament. I took that opportunity to complete the Uyghur interviews and paint an accurate portrait of the Ghulja Incident.

In the interests of full disclosure I should also mention that I often stayed on practitioner and Uyghur couches throughout the world as a way to save money on the road, and I appreciate the individuals who offered me such hospitality on short notice (Sound of Hope Radio Network in Taipei, I'm particularly thinking of you here). Yet before anyone accuses me of going native, let me be clear on this point: neither a consultancy nor a couch has ever influenced my research or what I report. I would have accepted funding from the PSB—or the devil himself—to complete this book.

Yet there was one person whose influence I could not ignore, someone who I had to listen to very closely. However, she did not dictate anything other than the directive that I should write. It's traditional to speak about one's wife in the last paragraph of the acknowledgments. I did that in the last book, and those feelings have only intensified over a decade. So this time, let me put it in financial terms instead: this book would not exist without my wife's support. Beyond the institutions and the patrons I have mentioned, my wife made this book possible simply by getting up early and going to work. Her love was her loyalty. And anyone who really appreciates the publication of this book should be aware that my wife's love was the hidden force behind it.

There were several individuals who can also take credit for bringing this book to print. One is no longer with us. Theron Raines, my literary agent, passed away in Medusa, New York, in November 2012. Theron had a great heart, and his confidence in my work was infectious. I am sorry that we were not able to make the journey to publication together.

Following Theron's death, Cliff May, the president of the Foundation for Defense of Democracies (FDD), persuaded me to reframe the book with a more intense focus on organ harvesting—in other words, to paint the target around the hole I shot in the barn. Jonathan Schanzer, vice-president for research at FDD, introduced me to the woman who would become my new literary agent, Maryann Karinch. She not only found a great publisher in record time, Maryann made it look easy. She is the answer to a prayer.

Maryann chose wisely in Prometheus Books, whose editor-in-chief Steven L. Mitchell treated my book both as a special project and a shared vision from day one. He showed great flexibility not only following the death of my father last year, but all the way through the final editing. During the difficult process of arranging over seventy photos, Melissa Raé Shofner from the editorial department was unflaggingly cheerful, practical, and incredibly patient. Finally, there is the guy I was actually in the trenches with—Brian McMahon, my editor, who quietly matched my pace when I was advancing, whispered to me when I lost my sense of direction, and covered my back while I regrouped. I apologize to the whole staff for the blitzkrieg at the end, but I thank you for making this a better product.

Several individuals read the early drafts with a critical eye: Caylan Ford, Matthew Robertson and Leeshai Lemish. Their comments, corrections, and late-night phone calls were extremely helpful. Olli Törmä of Finland volunteered to produce graphics throughout the book (thanks also to Luba Pishchik and Jared Pearman for the Fuyou Street graphic), such as the brilliantly simple map of the Liaoning Triangle, and he tirelessly responded to last-minute requests as well. Finally, several people were asked to read the book and respond with blurbs. Among those were William Kristol, Jasper Becker, Congressman Chris Smith, and Chen Guangcheng. Every person I have mentioned in this paragraph is a writer and had better things to do; every one of them responded with intelligence and care.

The actual investigation is where the heart of a book is won or lost. I have already spoken of Jaya Gibson's contribution to the battle. I would also like to mention several translators: Dongxue Dai and Turki Rudush, among many others. I have learned much from my close contact with David Kilgour and David Matas, and I thank them for incorporating my research, however late in the day it appeared, into their findings.

There were two other critical sources for my work, and I mention them for the benefit of future researchers.

Minghui is a spiritual resource for practitioners, not a pure research operation. Yet any researcher who avoids the Minghui archives because there is spiritual content present is simply being a prig. Minghui is *the* essential location to study the formation of Falun Gong and its repression, and I expect that it will remain so.

The World Organization to Investigate the Persecution of Falun Gong (WOIPFG) is not widely read by reporters. That's a big mistake. The organization's reports have an idiosyncratic Chinese quality to them—conclusions are often overstated and the English isn't perfect—but there is cutting-edge research in there. If you don't believe me, just follow my endnotes.

I also have a few words for the witnesses themselves—the defectors, the medical personnel who stepped forward, but particularly the refugees from the labor camps. I could not give up on the idea of a book because I could not bear the thought of your testimony never reaching the wider world. That was our unspoken contract, and I have kept faith with it. But I also failed to bring the majority of your stories into this book. A writing project takes on a life of its own at some point, and personal narratives begin to predominate. Plans for entire chapters, particularly those that captured the global battle between Falun Gong and the Chinese state, had to be left on the cutting-room floor. But I'll pick them up now. So I will eschew the laundry list of thanks in favor of a different idea. I believe that your interviews have value to future researchers. A comprehensive history remains to be written. I hope that I have assisted in preparing the ground for it.

Finally, I want to close with a few words about my researcher.

Leeshai Lemish is, simply put, the most professional person I have ever worked with. On our very first interview for the book, the back window of my car—alone among all the vehicles in a vast, supposedly "safe," central Montreal parking lot—was shattered. Our bags, including electronic equipment and my medications, were gone in the night. Standing among the shards of broken glass, with our passports, laptops, and the clothes on our backs, I mournfully asked Leeshai what we should do now. "Walmart," he replied.

Such are the benefits of working with an Israeli Falun Gong practitioner. I highly recommend that combination to future researchers. Beyond being a fixer, translator, and researcher, Leeshai was an integral part of every aspect of this entire investigation. He was my constant intellectual companion, and a friend in the truest sense of the word. His practitioner status was never an issue, but a resource—and an increasingly essential one as we moved closer to the mainland. I asked Leeshai to put aside a full two years of his life. When you add it all up, it was probably double that.

I am profoundly grateful.

NOTES

CHAPTER 1. THE XINJIANG PROCEDURE

1. For an earlier version of this chapter see Ethan Gutmann, "The Xinjiang Procedure," *Weekly Standard*, December 5, 2011, vol. 17, no. 12, pp. 19–24.

2. Uyghur Surgeon (name and location withheld for witness protection), interview by author, 2010.

3. In 1978, a dissident, Ms. Zhong Haiyuan, was shot in a semi-lethal fashion and then harvested for her kidneys on behalf of a high-ranking military officer's son. The operation was ultimately a failure; the officer's son did not live out the year. Given the semi-public, state-sanctioned nature of the execution, I strongly suspect the organ removal was staged for Maoist vindictive drama and was not used as a precedent for harvesting prisoners of conscience in the coming decades. On the Zhong case see Philip F. Williams and Yenna Wu, *The Great Wall of Confinement* (Berkley: University of California Press, 2004), pp. 145–48.

4. Human Rights Watch, "China Organ Procurement and Judicial Execution in China," vol. 6, no. 9 (August 1994), http://www.hrw.org/reports/1994/china1/china_948.htm, (accessed September 23, 2013). On harvesting during the 1970s, see Emily Lenning, "Execution for Body Parts: A Case of State Crime," *Contemporary Justice Review: Issues in Criminal, Social, and Restorative Justice* 10, no. 2 (2007): 173–91, published online June 18, 2007 10:2, DOI: 10.1080/10282580701372053.

5. Huang Jiefu, China's Vice-Minister of Health since 2001, under pressure from an ABC Australia television reporter, admitted in 2013 that he had previously harvested organs from death-row prisoners. See chapter 9.

6. In what is clearly a tiny compensation to the Uyghurs who assisted me in this investigation—leads, references, translation, and even the occasional couch to sleep on when the research funding was running out—I am following their spelling preference (i.e., Uyghur, not Uighur).

7. See James A. Millward, *Eurasian Crossroads: A History of Xinjiang* (New York: Columbia University Press and Hurst Press, 2007), chapters 6–7.

8. Nijat Abdureyimu, interview by author and Jaya Gibson, Centro Enea Refugee Camp (Rome), June 2009.

9. Hearing before the Subcommittee on International Organizations, Human Rights and Oversight of the Committee on Foreign Affairs, House of Representatives, "Chinese Interrogation vs. Congressional Oversight: The Uighurs at Guantanamo," One Hundred Eleventh Congress, First Session, July 16, 2009, serial no. 111-53.

10. Millward, *Eurasian Crossroads*, pp. 336–38.

11. Richard Hering and Stuart Tanner, producers, "Death on the Silk Road," *Dispatches* (Channel Four, UK), 1999.

12. Enver Tohti, interview by author, London, April 2013.

13. The presence of a large camp in Xinjiang containing massive numbers of Falun Gong practitioners was a recurring allegation among Falun Gong refugees that I interviewed. It was ultimately confirmed by Rebiya Kadeer and Alim Seytoff, interview by author, Washington, DC, June 2009.

14. Abdureyimu interview.

15. Enver Tohti, on-camera interview by Jaya Gibson and Simon Gross, London, 2010.

16. See NTDTV, "Organ Harvesting in China—Scottish Parliament—Enver Tohti—Donor was Alive," published May 2, 2013, http://www.youtube.com/watch?v=NTIbdXQ36FE (accessed September 24, 2013).

17. Bahtiyar Shemshidin, interview by author, Montreal, October 2010.

18. Uyghur Nurse (name and location withheld for witness protection), interview by author, 2010.

19. Throughout her interview, the nurse never speculated on the larger picture in Xinjiang. For example, the witness made no claim that the infanticide went beyond her specific hospital (during a period of intense anti-Uyghur propaganda, when Chinese animosity ran deepest) and indeed the twenty-one-year-old could have been an outlier—just a military hospital making a quick profit from a crisis. The nurse has agreed to testify before the US Congress upon request.

20. "Murat" (name and location withheld for witness protection), interview by author, 2010. "Murat" has agreed to testify before the US Congress upon request.

21. Ethan Gutmann, "China's Gruesome Organ Harvest," *Weekly Standard* 14, no, 10 (November 24, 2008): 21–22.

22. Actually we didn't need the party's confession; for those who paid

attention to obscure Congressional hearings on human rights, harvesting of criminals was established by Wang Guoqi's testimony back in 2001.

23. David Kilgour and David Matas, "Report into Allegations of Organ Harvesting of Falun Gong Practitioners in China," July 6, 2006, http://organharvestinvestigation.net/report0607/report060706-eng.pdf (accessed January 27, 2014).

24. David Matas and Torsten Trey, eds., *State Organs: Transplant Abuse in China* (Seraphim Editions: Toronto, 2012); World Organization to Investigate the Persecution of Falun Gong, http://www.upholdjustice.org/ (accessed January 27, 2014).

25. "Auntie C" (name and location withheld for witness protection), interview by author, Toronto, September 2007.

CHAPTER 2. THE PEACEABLE KINGDOM

1. Changchun practitioners, interviews by author, Bangkok, July 2008.

2. This chapter was informed by my interviews and the following books: David A. Palmer, *Qigong Fever: Body, Science, and Utopia in China* (London: Hurst and Company, 2007); David Ownby, *Falun Gong and the Future of China* (New York: Oxford University Press, 2008); Benjamin Penny, *The Religion of Falun Gong* (Chicago: University of Chicago Press, 2012); James W. Tong, *Revenge of the Forbidden City: The Suppression of Falun Gong in China, 1999–2005* (New York: Oxford University Press, 2009); Danny Schechter, *Falun Gong's Challenge to China: Spiritual Practice or Evil Cult?* (New York: Akashic Books, 2000).

3. Li Youfu, interview by Leeshai Lemish, San Francisco, June 2007. On the development of qigong from 1949, see Palmer, *Qigong Fever*, chapters 1–3.

4. See Palmer, *Qigong Fever*, chapter 2.

5. Zhu Jie, interview by Leeshai Lemish, Los Angeles, 2007. For other practitioner accounts, see "Personal Accounts of Early Days," Minghui.org, http://en.minghui.org/cc/62/ (accessed August 29, 2013).

6. "A Chronicle of Major Events of Falun Dafa (3rd Edition)," Pureinsight.org, March 2, 2004, http://www.pureinsight.org/node/2097 (accessed September 2, 2013).

7. Liu Xinyu, "Remembering Master's Hardships and Righteous Purity in the Process of Teaching the Fa," March 2, 2003, Minghui.org, http://en

.minghui.org/html/articles/2003/3/2/32698.html (accessed September 1, 2013).

8. Li Youfu interview.
9. Zhao Ming, interview by author, Dublin, September 2007.
10. Zhao Ming interview. See also Tsinghua University practitioner, "Stories about Zhao Ming," Minghui.org, April 2, 2002 [sic] http://en.minghui.org/emh/articles/2002/4/8/20749p.html (accessed December 9, 2013).
11. Ding Jing, interview by author, Toronto, October 2007.
12. A practitioner in Dalian City, "Remembering Master's Lectures in Dalian City," Minghui.org, August 14, 2010, http://en.minghui.org/html/articles/2010/8/14/119243.html (accessed May 15, 2014).
13. Caylan Ford, letter to author, January 2014. See also FDIC (Falun Dafa Information Center), "Falun Gong: Timeline," May 17, 2008, http://faluninfo.net/topic/24/ (accessed September 7, 2013).
14. Palmer, *Qigong Fever*, pp. 246–47.
15. Tong, *Revenge of the Forbidden City*, pp. 10–11. Party estimates of Falun Gong finances make no allowance for the counterfeiting, free web downloads, and photocopying that is ubiquitous throughout the mainland. Falun Gong still relies on these methods to distribute materials throughout China.
16. Palmer, *Qigong Fever*, pp. 246–47.
17. CCTV raw footage, NTDTV television archives, New York, January 2006.
18. "Chinese Embassy woman" (name and location withheld for witness protection), interview by author, 2007.
19. FDIC, Timeline.
20. "Minister X" (name and location withheld for witness protection), interview by author, 2007.
21. Palmer, *Qigong Fever*, pp. 249–51; Ownby, *Falun Gong and the Future of China*, p. 168.
22. Chu Tianxing, "A Reporter's Notes from Secret Documents: The Plot Hatched in April and May, 1999 (Part 1)," Minghui.org, May 29, 2004, http://en.minghui.org/emh/articles/2004/5/29/48668.html (accessed September 26, 2013).
23. Palmer, *Qigong Fever*, p. 267.
24. Palmer, *Qigong Fever*, p. 257.
25. Amy Lee, interview by author, New York City, November 2007.
26. Palmer, *Qigong Fever*, p. 252.

27. It's interesting to take a step back at this point and observe that what was considered to be an outrageously negative report by Chinese Falun Gong practitioners might strongly resemble a balanced report in the West (and to this day, the Chinese practitioner effect on Falun Gong media suffers from their mainland media imprinting). Practitioner hair-trigger reaction may account for the annoyance some objective Western historians experience when examining Falun Gong history. The catch, of course, is that it is China, and balanced reports in China are so rare that literally every Chinese person reads a balanced report as a thinly disguised kill signal. Scholars of Falun Gong history are free to criticize Falun Gong's methods, yet they might also acknowledge the choices available. They are also free to adopt a faint echo of the tone of party indignation at the disruption practitioners caused to various media outlets as long as they are aware that roughly the same conversation—carried out in more spiritual terms—was taking place among practitioners at the time.

28. Xie Weiguo, interview by Leeshai Lemish, London, August 2007.

29. Hao Fengjun, interview by author, Melbourne, August 2007.

30. Ethan Gutmann, *Losing the New China* (San Francisco: Encounter Books, 2004), pp. 40–41.

31. For examples of these sorts of *Zhuan Falun* critiques see Maria Hsia Chang, *Falun Gong: The End of Days* (New Haven, CT: Yale University Press, 2004) and Ian Adams, Riley Adams, and Rocco Galati, *Power of the Wheel: The Falun Gong Revolution* (Toronto: Stoddart Publishing, 2001).

32. The current Falun Gong self-definition is "an advanced self-cultivation practice of the Buddha School." See English Falun Dafa home page, "Brief Introduction to Falun Dafa," http://en.falundafa.org/ (accessed September 23, 2013).

33. In 2004, I (rather ignorantly) defined Falun Gong as a "religion with Chinese cult characteristics." See Gutmann, *Losing the New China*, p. 40.

34. Arthur Waldron, "The Falun Gong Factor," *Compassion*, no. 6 (2007): 5.

35. The Chinese authorities claimed that fourteen hundred practitioners died prematurely because of Falun Gong. Even if one were to accept that figure as accurate, it represents .002 percent—that is, an insignificant fraction of 1 percent—of the seventy million practitioners in China, a death rate that is a tiny fraction of the national average. Of course when organ harvesting of Falun Gong became routine, practitioner organs were particularly prized because of the absence of hepatitis and the healthy practitioner lifestyle.

36. I've never actually met a former practitioner who was deeply angry over

his or her time practicing Falun Gong. So if mad-as-hell-post-practitioner.com suddenly emerges in the year 2014, verify the dates closely; I would strongly suspect it to be state-sponsored AstroTurf created in response to an early draft of this chapter.

37. All these spiritual movements have made efforts to reform in recent years, the Unification Church being the most prominent example, yet those reforms cannot negate the experiences of those who devoted their lives to a cause that they now see as essentially empty or exploitative. See for example: Ex-Premie.org (Divine Light Mission), http://www.ex-premie.org/index.html; Ex Scientologist, http://www.exscn.net/; "Done with Moon: Stories from one of the World's Most Manipulative Cults," http://donewithmoon.tumblr.com/; and Moving On (Children of God), http://archive.xfamily.org/www.movingon.org/default.asp%3FsID=5.html (all sites accessed September 30, 2013).

38. The number of Falun Gong has been estimated to be as high as one hundred million and, improbably, as low as two million. As a leading cadre in the 6-10 office—the agency specifically set up by the party to eliminate Falun Gong—Hao Fengjun told me that the 6-10 Office's working number was seventy million Falun Gong in China in July 1999.

CHAPTER 3. AN OCCURRENCE ON FUYOU STREET

1. "The Truth about the April 25 Appeal," Minghui.org, April 24, 2012 http://en.minghui.org/html/articles/2012/4/10/132642.html (accessed October 20, 2013). For an earlier version of portions of this chapter see Ethan Gutmann, "An Occurrence on Fuyou Street," *National Review* 61, no. 13 (July 20, 2009): 37–40.

2. David A. Palmer, *Qigong Fever: Body, Science, and Utopia in China* (London: Hurst and Company, 2007), p. 269.

3. "The Truth about the April 25 Appeal."

4. Beijing Falun Gong practitioner, "Recalling 'April 25,'" Minghui.org, April 22, 2010, http://en.minghui.org/html/articles/2010/4/22/116249.html (accessed October 1, 2013).

5. Ibid.

6. Palmer, *Qigong Fever*, p. 269.

7. Archives, NTDTV New York, November 2006.

8. Jiang Xinxia, interview by author, London, August 2007.

9. Hao Fengjun, interview by author, Melbourne, December 2006. I conducted four interviews with Hao over a three-year period.

10. Tianjin Falun Gong practitioner, "A Witness to the Event That Triggered the April 25, 1999 Appeal," Minghui.org, April 25, 2011, http://en.minghui.org/html/articles/2011/4/25/124635.html (accessed October 1, 2013).

11. Li Hongzhi, "Lunyu" from *Zhuan Falun* (English), Internet Version, third translation edition (updated in March, 2000), falundafa.org, http://www.falundafa.org/book/eng/lecture0.html (accessed October 1, 2013).

12. Jennifer Zeng, interview by author, Sydney, December 2006. Other practitioners concur that they heard a similar message from the police. See also Palmer, *Qigong Fever*, p. 269.

13. See Zhou Zheng, "Inciting Anger as a Tool to Instigate Societal Persecution of 'Outsiders,'" PureInsight.org, http://www.pureinsight.org/node/2263 (accessed October 6, 2013). Zhou places it on Xi'anmen Street, but the location of Tiananmen Square is mislabeled (possibly through a translation error).

14. Zeng interview. See also "The Truth about the April 25 Appeal."

15. "Practitioner couple," interview by author (names and location withheld for witness protection), 2008.

16. Luo Hongwei, interview by author, Los Angeles, February 2007.

17. "Auntie Dee," interview by author (name and location withheld for witness protection), 2007.

18. Xie Weiguo, interview by Leeshai Lemish, London, August 2007.

19. Luo interview.

20. Xie interview.

21. "Recalling 'April 25.'"

22. James W. Tong, *Revenge of the Forbidden City: The Suppression of Falun Gong in China, 1999–2005* (New York: Oxford University Press, 2009), p. 33.

23. World Organization to Investigate the Persecution of Falun Gong (WOIPFG), "An Investigation Report on Jiang Zemin's Crime of Genocide in the Persecution of Falun Gong—Part One," upholdjustice.org, January 27, 2004, http://www.upholdjustice.org/sites/upholdjustice.org/files/record/2004/08/89-en_89.pdf (accessed October 4, 2013).

24. Palmer, *Qigong Fever*, p. 274.

25. Wei Jingsheng, interview by author, Washington, DC, October 2007. Wei believes that the party's anti–Falun Gong prejudice was not just the result of Jiang Zemin's obsessions but was almost tribal in nature.

26. Jiang Zemin on April 25 is reported by an insider source to have asked the question, "What is the Falun Gong?" Perhaps Jiang was playing along, for the record, with the "surprised" charade. Or perhaps Jiang was asking the question to test his staff, much the way that George W. Bush is said to have asked the joint chiefs why America needed a military. Or perhaps Jiang was genuinely surprised by the high party rank of the Falun Gong practitioners who had been in Zhongnanhai for discussions that day, and he wanted to flush out any more of them that happened to be in the room. Or perhaps Jiang never said this at all. Jiang had direct control over various committees that were directly in charge of handling the Falun Gong problem, and he had a close relationship with the Public Security Bureau (which meant that Jiang would have seen the very same red-headed document that Minister X was privileged to read through in 2006). The statement is also thrown into question by Zhu Rongji's statement that he had written a circular about the Beijing TV incident—which, whether he actually wrote something or just thought about writing something, or it was just a throwaway politician line—was at least plausible because the Beijing TV incident was of relatively high visibility. At any rate, it is not clear why anyone should take Jiang's quote at face value.

27. Palmer, *Qigong Fever*, p. 271.

28. Ibid., p. 272.

29. Ibid., p. 269. Li Hongzhi did add some ballast to the idea that he hadn't played much of a role in April 25 by retroactively posing a question: If he was giving the orders, then why didn't a much greater number than ten thousand show up in Beijing on April 25? Ultimately I think the point is that Li did not stress that practitioners *had* to go.

30. Ibid., p. 269.

31. Ibid., p. 270

32. Jiang Xinxia interview.

33. Tong, *Revenge of the Forbidden City*, p. 51.

34. "Auntie Sha," interview by author (name and location withheld for witness protection), 2007.

35. Zeng interview.

36. Tong, *Revenge of the Forbidden City*, p. 41.

37. Ibid., p. 46.

38. Ibid., p. 43.

39. Zhang Yijie, interview by Leeshai Lemish, Flushing, NY, October 2008. Although it is nearly impossible to come up with some sort of number

here, it appears that women such as Zhang were the exception. Most practitioners in the party's upper echelons appeared to have simply drifted away from the practice (although there are a handful of Falun Gong fellow travelers still in place to this day in several top-ranking political, media, and military institutions, and they have been an invaluable source of information).

40. Tong, *Revenge of the Forbidden City*, p. 39.
41. Hao interview.
42. Caylan Ford, letter to author, January 2014.
43. "Auntie Jun," interview by author (name and location withheld for witness protection), 2007.
44. On Shenyang intelligence, see Tong, *Revenge of the Forbidden City*, p. 40.
45. For detailed explanation and documentation of how several well-known Western corporations helped to create China's "Big Brother Internet," see Ethan Gutmann, *Losing the New China* (San Francisco: Encounter Books, 2004), pp. 127–72.
46. Tong, *Revenge of the Forbidden City*, pp. 32–43, 48–49.
47. Ibid., pp. 52–53.
48. Luo interview.
49. See Tong, *Revenge of the Forbidden City*, pp. 53–54.
50. Wang Yuzhi, interview by author, Vancouver, July 2007.
51. Gutmann, *Losing the New China*, pp. 42–43.
52. Wang Huilian (Lotus), interview by author, Bangkok, July 2008.
53. Tong, *Revenge of the Forbidden City*, pp. 43–45.
54. On Jinzhou registration, see Tong, *Revenge of the Forbidden City*, p. 61.
55. CCTV reels, NTDTV archives, New York, November 2006.
56. See Tong, *Revenge of the Forbidden City*, pp. 62–64.
57. Zhang Erping, interview by author, London, February 2009.
58. I have been informed that the majority of the practitioners were envisioning a series of one-on-one rescue missions and that any empty rooms were quickly inhabited by Falun Gong workers (and ultimately by Shen Yun performers in training). Nonetheless, I include this story because even if only a minority believed in the idea, it captures the full pain of exile.
59. "A Mother Exposes the Truth behind the Death of Her Daughter," Minghui.org, January 9, 2001, http://en.minghui.org/emh/articles/2001/1/9/5327.html (accessed October 19, 2013).
60. "Dong Buyun: Falun Gong Practitioners Killed in Persecution,"

Minghui.org, http://en.minghui.org/emh/special_column/death_cases/31/v3189.html (accessed October 20, 2013).

61. "Zhao Dong: Falun Gong Practitioners Killed in Persecution," Minghui.org, http://en.minghui.org/emh/special_column/death_cases/31/v3191.html (accessed October 20, 2013).

62. "Zhu Shaolan: Falun Gong Practitioners Killed in Persecution," Minghui.org, http://en.minghui.org/emh/special_column/death_cases/31/v3187.html (accessed October 20, 2013).

63. "Zhao Jinhua: Falun Gong Practitioners Killed in Persecution," Minghui.org, http://en.minghui.org/emh/special_column/death_cases/31/v3188.html (accessed October 20, 2013).

64. "Wang Guoping: Falun Gong Practitioners Killed in Persecution," Minghui.org, http://en.minghui.org/emh/special_column/death_cases/31/v3190.html (accessed October 20, 2013).

65. John Pomfret and Michael Laris, "China Confronts a Silent Threat," *Washington Post*, October 30, 1999, http://www.washingtonpost.com/wp-srv/inatl/longterm/china/stories/falun103099.htm (accessed October 20, 2013).

66. Reuters, "China Says Treat Falun Gong Members Compassionately," November 11, 1999, archived at Center for Studies on New Religions, http://www.cesnur.org/testi/falun_012.htm (accessed October 20, 2013).

67. Zeng interview.

CHAPTER 4. SNOW

1. This chapter is based on three interviews: Ma Lijuan, interview by author, New York, October 2007; "Angel" (name and location withheld for witness protection), interview by author, 2007; and Zhao Ming, interview by author, Dublin, September 2007. Some Tiananmen Square details are based on surreptitious footage taken by practitioners in winter 2000, NTDTV archives, November 2006.

CHAPTER 5. THE EVENTS ON DRAGON MOUNTAIN

1. Zhao Ming, interview by author, Dublin, September 2007.
2. See appendix.

3. Han Guangsheng, interview by author, Toronto, October 2007.

4. See Gabriel Quintin, "Chinese Defector to Canada Fears Deportation," *Epoch Times*, June 30, 2005, http://www.theepochtimes.com/news/5-6-30/29943.html (accessed December 14, 2013). Apparently Han is currently stuck in limbo: no asylum but no deportation either.

5. Han interview.

6. Ibid.

7. Han interview; see also Yan Zhen and Ya Mei, "A '610' Office Insider Exposes What Goes on in China's Labor Camps," *Epoch Times*, July 13, 2005, http://www.theepochtimes.com/news/5-7-13/30289.html (accessed December 14, 2013).

8. Shenyang practitioner, "A Record of the Crimes Committed by Authorities at Longshan Forced Labor Camp—Part 1," Minghui.org, November 5, 2004, http://en.minghui.org/html/articles/2004/11/5/54195p.html (accessed January 29, 2014); see also part 2.

9. Australian Falun Dafa Information Center, "Falun Gong Urges Australia to Deny Chinese Minister of Commerce Entry for APEC on Torture Claims," September 3, 2007, http://www.falunau.org/newsArticle.jsp?itemID=2041&cat=newsAus (accessed January 29, 2014). I do not accept the party convention of counting Taiwan as a province.

10. In 2013, the party renamed the labor camps "Legal Re-Education Centers" or "Drug Detox Centers."

11. "The Longshan Reformatory Exerts Tremendous Efforts to Persecute Falun Gong Practitioners for the Sake of Advancement," Minghui.org, August 15, 2004, http://en.minghui.org/html/articles/2004/8/15/51391.html (accessed January 29, 2014).

12. Shenyang practitioner, "A Record of the Crimes Committed by Authorities at Longshan Forced Labor Camp—Part 1; Australian Falun Dafa Information Center, "Falun Gong Urges Australia to Deny Chinese Minister of Commerce Entry"; see also "Atrocities Committed at the Longshan Forced Labor Camp: Repeated Shocking of Open Wounds with Electric Batons," Minghui.org, April 12, 2003, http://en.minghui.org/html/articles/2003/4/12/34410.html (accessed January 30, 2014).

13. Li Jing, "Thoughts on the Dining Conditions in Longshan Labor Camp," Minghui.org, February 24, 2003, http://en.minghui.org/emh/articles/2003/2/24/32510.html (accessed November 20, 2013).

14. Yin Liping, "I Still Tremble When I Think about It—I Was Locked

up in a Men's Cell at Masanjia Forced Labor Camp," Minghui.org, October 13, 2013, http://en.minghui.org/html/articles/2013/10/13/142691.html (accessed January 30, 2014).

15. "Details of the Torture and Abuse of Ms. Ren Shujie, Who Died from the Persecution," Minghui.org, October 8, 2005, http://en.minghui.org/emh/articles/2005/10/8/65666p.html (accessed January 30, 2014).

16. "Police Use Electric Baton to Shock Innocent Young Girl, Little Practitioner Remains Unyielding under Torture," Minghui.org, December 24, 2001, http://en.minghui.org/emh/articles/2001/12/24/17088.html (accessed January 30, 2014).

17. "Ms. Tong Chunshi, 57, from Shenyang City, Liaoning Province, Dies following Torture at the Longshan Forced Labor Camp," Minghui.org, December 20, 2006, http://en.minghui.org/html/articles/2006/12/20/81016.html (accessed January 30, 2014).

18. Practitioner from China, "Falun Dafa Practitioner Wang Hong Tortured to Death in Shenyang City's Longshan Labor Camp," Minghui.org, September 6, 2001, http://en.minghui.org/html/articles/2001/9/6/13614.html (accessed January 30, 2014).

19. "The Longshan Reformatory Exerts Tremendous Efforts to Persecute Falun Gong Practitioners for the Sake of Advancement," Minghui.org, August 15, 2004, http://en.minghui.org/html/articles/2004/8/15/51391.html (accessed January 30, 2014).

20. Hao Fengjun, interview(s) with author, Melbourne, 2006–2009. Hao would ultimately defect in 2005. While this is not the venue to make the full argument, Hao persuaded me that the struggle with Falun Gong was the primary impetus to the Chinese hacking movement and the advanced techniques that the United States government is so concerned with today. See Ethan Gutmann, "Hacker Nation," *World Affairs Journal* (May/June 2010): 70–79.

21. See Gutmann, "Hacker Nation." See also Ethan Gutmann, "China's Big Brother Internet: Ten Essential Publications," eastofethan.com, http://wp.me/psRnQ-4q (accessed May 12, 2014).

22. Hao thought the violent policeman's name might have been Mu Ruili.

CHAPTER 6. ALIVE IN THE BITTER SEA

1. Wang Yuzhi, interview by author, Vancouver, November 2007.

2. Hao Fengjun, interview(s) with author, Melbourne, 2006–2009. Hao and the rest of the 6-10 Office believed that the Fu Yubin story was fabricated.

3. Li Hongzhi, "Eliminate Your Last Attachment(s)," Minghui.org, August 12, 2000, http://en.minghui.org/html/articles/2000/8/14/9117.html (accessed May 12, 2014).

4. Simone Gao, interview by author, Los Angeles, November 2007.

5. Stephen Gregory, "Impresario of Hatred Taken down in China," *Epoch Times*, December 25, 2013, http://www.theepochtimes.com/n3/416288-impresario-of-immolations-gets-comeuppance-in-china/ (accessed January 30, 2014).

6. Rebecca Mackinnon, interview by author, Hong Kong, July 2008.

7. Phillip Pan, "Human Fire Ignites Chinese Mystery—Motive for Public Burning Intensifies Fight over Falun Gong," *Washington Post*, February 4, 2001, p. 1.

8. Wang Yuzhi interview.

9. Hao Fengjun interview(s).

10. The "Nine Commentaries," a series of editorials published in 2004 by the *Epoch Times*, has been translated and published in book form under the title *Nine Commentaries on the Communist Part Party* (Mountain View, CA: Broad Press, 2005).

11. Michael S. Chase and James C. Mulvenon, *You've Got Dissent! Chinese Dissident Use of the Internet and Beijing's Counter-Strategies* (Washington DC: Rand Corporation, 2002).

12. Hao Fengjun interview(s). Hao's point on "refugee-bots" was confirmed by several background interviews with practitioners who work within NTDTV and *Epoch Times*; they tended to be embarrassed about the spy problem, but they were equally proud of the vetting procedures that they had put into place over time. I also met several supposed Falun Gong practitioners who I strongly suspected of working for Chinese intelligence based on their interest in my witnesses (most practitioners had no reason to ask about this) or their stories (flamboyant) or their insistence that they were quite close with Master Li (a very un-practitioner thing to say).

13. Chen Yonglin, interview by author, Sydney, December 2006.

14. Zhao Ming, interview by author, Dublin, September 2007.

15. Zhao Ming also briefly considered the possibility that the Wild Room boys wanted to preserve the organs for the camp officials. But at the time, he rejected this thought: "Transformation, signing, renouncing is not an end in itself. They want to break our will, our determination. Totally. If they could, they would rather kill us. But they cannot kill us because this is not a secret camp but an open camp. They can't harvest all our organs. They would have to say something to the outside. Our family members know we are here. So they kill our spirits instead."

16. Jennifer Zeng, interview by author, Sydney, December 2006.

17. Practitioner in Mainland China, "The Radiance of an Enlightened Being—The Story of Zhao Ming," Minghui.org, April 5, 2002, http://en.minghui.org/html/articles/2002/4/5/20618.html, (accessed January 30, 2014).

18. Jennifer Zeng, *Witnessing History* (Crows Nest, Australia: Allen and Unwin, 2005).

19. Wang Huilian ("Lotus"), interview by author, Bangkok, July 2008.

20. Wang Yuzhi interview.

21. Wang would go on to buy the first printing presses for the *Epoch Times*, the first Falun Gong–run newspaper, located in key publishing locations such as Hong Kong and the US West Coast.

22. Male practitioners were initially held in Wanjia, but because of overcrowding they were transferred to Changlinzi Forced Labor Camp.

23. "Lotus" interview.

24. A personal note: When I asked Lotus if there were leftover candy wrappers and automobile exhaust traces in the melting snow—my Midwestern, institutional memory of the first warm days in March—she said, "No. It was perfect. Like the world was a garden."

25. Heizuizi Female Prison was notorious for severe torture. See Refugee Review Tribunal, February 22, 2008, http://www.refworld.org/pdfid/4b6fe1a00.pdf (accessed January 30, 2014).

CHAPTER 7. INTO THIN AIRWAVES

1. Ethan Gutmann, "Who Lost China's Internet?" *Weekly Standard* 7, no. 23 (February 25, 2002): 24–29. See also John Markoff, "Suit Claims Cisco Helped China Pursue Falun Gong," *New York Times*, May 22, 2011, http://www.nytimes.com/2011/05/23/technology/23cisco.html?_r=0 (accessed January 30, 2014).

2. Hillary Clinton, "Remarks on Internet Freedom," Newseum, Washington, DC, January 21, 2010. See http://www.realclearworld.com/articles/2010/01/21/hillary_clinton_remarks_on_internet_freedom_97494.html (accessed January 30, 2014).

3. John Markoff, "Iranians and Others Outwit Net Censors," *New York Times*, April 30, 2009, http://www.nytimes.com/2009/05/01/technology/01filter.html?pagewanted=all&_r=0 (accessed May 10, 2014).

4. A correspondent from Jilin, "Additional Information Regarding the Death of Mr. Liang Zhenxing," Minghui.org, May 31, 2010, http://en.minghui.org/html/articles/2010/5/31/117520p.html (accessed May 10, 2014).

5. The portraits of the hijackers, the events, and the dialogue emerged from the extended interviews with seven Falun Gong refugees from Changchun that Leeshai Lemish and I conducted over ten days in Bangkok in June and July 2008. All of the witnesses were intimately familiar with a particular hijacker or in several cases were accessories in the hijacking and its aftermath. With the exception of Tang Feng and Siyi Fang, all of these practitioners preferred confidentiality to avoid further harassment of their families. For an earlier version of this chapter see Ethan Gutmann, "Into Thin Airwaves" *Weekly Standard* 16, no. 12 (December 6, 2010): 16–22. The timing of Liu Chengun's initial escape from prison has been revised for accuracy. The backstory to Liu's ultimate capture has also been expanded to reflect new information that I kindly received from Lucia Dunn. I have preserved the minimalist style of the hijackers' deaths out of respect for the surviving spouses and children of the hijackers.

6. Big Truck claimed he had walked through security without the guards seeing him, but there are equally superhuman accounts running both ways.

7. Bill Xia, interview(s) with author, Washington, DC, North Carolina, 2005–2008.

8. David Liang, interview by author, Sydney, July 2008.

9. *Epoch Times* employees, group interview by author, Hong Kong, July 2008.

10. According to Hao Fengjun, the plan to kill Li Hongzhi was a 6-10 operation ("stop the blood") based on the model of Zhang Hongbao, the founder of Zhong Gong, who died in a "car accident" in July 2006. Hao Fengjun, interview(s) with author, Melbourne, 2006–2009.

CHAPTER 8. THE NAMELESS

1. An early version of this chapter was published as Ethan Gutmann, "China's Gruesome Organ Harvest: Why Isn't the Whole World Watching?" *Weekly Standard* 14, no. 10 (November 24, 2008): 18–25.

2. Wang Xiaohua, interview by author, Montreal, October 2007.

3. David Matas and David Kilgour, "Report into Allegations of Organ Harvesting of Falun Gong Practitioners in China,"organharvestinvestigation.net, July 6, 2006, http://www.david-kilgour.com/2006/Kilgour-Matas-organ-harvesting-rpt-July6-eng.pdf (accessed January 3, 2014).

4. See appendix.

5. Hao Fengjun, interview(s) with author, Melbourne, 2006–2009.

6. "Crystal," interview by author (name and location withheld for witness protection), 2007.

7. Ibid.

8. In 2013, the verified number of practitioners killed in custody would finally go below one hundred. See Leeshai Lemish, "Media and New Religious Movements: The Case of Falun Gong," 2009 CESNUR Conference, June 11–13, 2009, http://www.cesnur.org/2009/slc_lemish.htm (accessed January 4, 2014).

9. See chapter 6.

10. Ethan Gutmann, "Why Wang Wenyi Was Shouting," *Weekly Standard* 11, no. 32 (May 8, 2006): 33–35.

11. Harry Wu raised this objection with me in a private conversation in April 2006.

12. Gutmann, "Why Wang Wenyi Was Shouting," p. 34.

13. "Annie," interview by author, Washington, DC, April 2006.

14. To get a general sense of how cyclical and destructive these sorts of dissident conflicts can be, see Ian Baruma, *Bad Elements* (New York: Random House, 2001). Here are the basic outlines of the conflict: Harry Wu claimed that he had sent an investigator over to Sujiatun who had determined that it was an ordinary hospital (potentially interesting evidence, but because Wu never released any specifics on that investigation, it is difficult to judge the value of the findings). Wu also claimed that a practitioner had made an offensive post on the Internet charging that Wu was a spy for the Chinese Communist Party. Wu had spent years as a prisoner in China's Laogai System, so it's easy to understand why he would be offended. Yet it is still unclear why a single practitioner— Falun Gong is a vast, not terribly hierarchical organization, if it can be called

an organization at all—should have precipitated such a severe conflict that, over time, became increasingly divorced from substance and more about saving face. I've spoken in depth to both parties and I still don't know quite what happened. However, I do genuinely wonder whether both Falun Gong and Harry Wu's inner circle were subtly influenced by party spies during this period. The inability to resolve a few missteps on both sides bears an uncanny resemblance to what Hao Fengjun of the 6-10 Office described as the goal of his office's professional infiltrators, or "refugee-bots": "For example, you two might be good friends. But then I come and tell you that he said bad things about you. Tell him that you said bad things about him. ... The party is terrified that democracy activists, Falun Gong, Taiwan, Tibet, and Xinjiang will work together. So right now they are focusing on not letting Falun Gong and democracy activists work together." Hao Fengjun, interview by author, Melbourne, 2006.

15. See Laogai Research Foundation, *Laogai: The Machinery of Repression in China* (Brooklyn, NY: Umbrage, 2009), p. 110

16. The hospitals (other than the ones presented in the text) are Tianjin No.1 Central Hospital, the Qianfoshan Hospital Liver Transplant Center, Jiaotong University Affiliated Hospital, and the No. 2 Affiliated Hospital of Hubei Province Medical University. In general, the military hospitals were more guarded on the phone, yet among the many transplant centers that Crystal called, the Urumqi Air Force Hospital (now the 474 Hospital of the PLA) closely fits the harvesting profile that "Murat" described in chapter 1.

17. See Mary Silver, "Good Organs for Sale, but You Have to Hurry," *Epoch Times*, April 20, 2006, http://www.theepochtimes.com/news/6-4-20/40617.html (accessed January 3, 2014).

18. It helps that brain death was not legally recognized in China; only when the heart stops beating was the patient actually considered dead. That means policemen could shoot a prisoner, surgically as it were, then the doctor could remove the organs before the heart stops beating. Or the doctor could administer a light or modified anesthesia, remove the organs, and when the operation is nearing completion introduce a lethal injection—a more recent method.

19. "Witness to China's Organ Harvesting," NTDTV, November 21, 2008, http://www.youtube.com/watch?v=68pOislukB4 (accessed January 14, 2014).

20. Wei Jingsheng, interview by author, Washington, DC, October 2007.

21. "Nine Commentaries on the Communist Party," *Epoch Times*, January 12, 2005, http://www.epochtimes.com/9pingdownload/English/9ping_en.pdf (accessed January 30, 2014).

22. David Kilgour and David Matas, *Bloody Harvest: the Killing of Falun Gong for their Organs* (Woodstock, ON: Seraphim Editions, 2009), pp.11–13.

23. Kilgour and Matas, *Bloody Harvest*, pp. 94–108.

24. Robin Munro, interview by author, Hong Kong, July 2008.

25. See "European Parliament Addresses Forced Organ Harvesting in China," NTDTV, December 7, 2012, http://goo.gl/V8hRMI (accessed May 26, 2014).

26. Dr. Huang Shiwei, interview by author, Taiwan, July 2008.

27. Qu Yangyao, interview by author, Sydney, July 2008.

28. Hao Fengjun interview.

29. Dai Ying, interview by Leeshai Lemish, Sweden, April 2008.

30. Lin Jie, interview by author, Sydney, July 2008.

31. Jing Tian (En Mu), interview by author, Bangkok, July 2008.

32. Chen Jiansheng, interview by author, Hong Kong, July 2008.

33. "Crystal" interview.

34. Huang Shiwei interview.

35. Dai Ying interview.

36. Fang Siyi, interview by author, July 2008.

37. At the end of the 2000s, Jaya Gibson and the author worked together on several investigations into organ harvesting outside of the Falun Gong community. The goal was to create a documentary titled "Shalu (The Slaughter), Part 1." Although funding for a comprehensive documentary was scarce, there was enough financial support from the Peder Wallenberg family to allow Gibson to conduct field research in the Dharamsala region of India along with an excursion to Nepal in the summer and fall of 2009. The author's account of Gibson's results is partially based on Leeshai Lemish's comprehensive phone interview with Gibson in December 2013.

38. This may be Meyang Prison, said to be near Chengdu.

39. See "Tibetan Monks Still Held in Qinghai," Radio Free Asia, August 28, 2008, http://www.rfa.org/english/news/monks-08282008164711.html (accessed January 17, 2014).

40. "Masanjia Confidential," interview by author, Bangkok, July 2008.

41. Yu Xinhui, interview by author, Bangkok, July 2008.

42. Liu Guifu, interview by author, Bangkok, July 2008.

43. "Crystal" interview.

CHAPTER 9. ORGANS OF THE STATE

1. Dr. Ko Wen-je, interview by author, Taipei, July 2008.

2. My impressions of the beginning of the interview—the discomfort, the harsh language—are simply my best recall. It is not "authorized" by Dr. Ko, and any errors in tone or recollection of phrases used are my own.

3. I seldom run my writing by an interview subject before publication, but I consider Dr. Ko's testimony to be extremely important. Because we did not record our interview, in the interests of accuracy I gave Dr. Ko an advance draft of the following section, and he signed off on it. I made a few minor edits.

4. The "Chinese price" for a kidney could go as low as two thousand dollars. Dr. Huang Shiwei, interview by author, Taiwan, July 2008.

5. Possibly Dr. Ko was banned from the mainland for other reasons. This could be one of them.

6. See Charlotte Cuthbertson and Louise Nightingale, "Organ Harvesting in China: Professor Frustrated by Silence," *Epoch Times*, December 11, 2009, http://www.theepochtimes.com/n2/world/organ-harvesting-in-china-26322.html (accessed January 18, 2014).

7. "Capitol Hill Forum Exposes China's Forced Organ Harvesting," Minghui.org, July 23, 2013, http://en.minghui.org/html/articles/2013/7/23/141192p.html (accessed January 30, 2014).

8. To date, the Israeli Knesset is the only national legislature that has openly acknowledged that there is no way to determine if a Chinese organ is sourced from a prisoner of conscience, and Israel is the only country in the world to have banned medical insurance corporations from facilitating organ tourism to China. Attention to the issue in Israel began after *Yediot Aharonot*, its largest paper, exposed an Israeli organ tourism broker. The November 17, 2006 article by Oron Meiri and three other journalists, can be found here: http://atruechineserenaissance.blogspot.cz/2007/09/falun-gong-organ-traders-evade-tax-in.html (accessed May 10, 2014). See also Jacob Lavee's chapter, "The Impact of the Use of Organs from Executed Prisoners," in David Matas and Torsten Trey, eds., *State Organs* (Woodstock, ON: Seraphim, 2013), pp. 108–13.

9. These are facts that I learned while searching for a photograph of Dr. Ko, who was not particularly well-known when I interviewed him. By mutual consent, our conversation back in 2008 was off the record. Last year I asked him if he would allow me to publish my account of what he experienced in China. As the deadline for the book draft approached, Leeshai asked Dr. Ko if we could

reveal his name. He consented with one caveat: he is not interested in repeating this account for reporters, but he would consider testifying under oath in the US Congress or an equivalent political body.

10. For an earlier version of portions of this chapter see Ethan Gutmann, "Bitter Harvest," *World Affairs Journal* 174, no. 2 (July/August 2012): 49–56.

11. Jonathan Ansfield and Ian Johnson, "Ousted Chinese Leader Is Said to Have Spied on Other Top Officials," *New York Times*, April 25, 2012, http://www.nytimes.com/2012/04/26/world/asia/bo-xilai-said-to-have-spied-on-top-china-officials.html?pagewanted=all&_r=0 (accessed January 30, 2014).

12. As I write this (April 2014), Bo Xilai and Gu Kailai are in prison and Zhou Yongkang is under investigation; others appear to be targets of a slow-motion purge.

13. Bill Gertz, "Defection Denied," *Washington Free Beacon*, March 26, 2012, http://freebeacon.com/national-security/defection-denied/ (accessed April 9, 2012).

14. "Crackdown in China after Coup Rumours," *Statesman*, March 31, 2012, http://202.144.14.20/index.php?option=com_content&view=article&id=405043&catid=35&show=archive&year=2012&month=4&day=1 (accessed January 30, 2014).

15. Matthew Robertson, "Chinese Internet Allows Searches for 'Live (Organ) Harvest,'" *Epoch Times*, March 26, 2012, http://www.theepochtimes.com/n2/china-news/chinese-internet-allows-searches-for-live-organ-harvest-210507.html (accessed April 9, 2012).

16. See Keith Bradsher, "China Moves to Stop Transplants of Organs after Executions," *New York Times*, March 23, 2012, http://www.nytimes.com/2012/03/24/world/asia/china-moves-to-stop-transplants-of-organs-after-executions.html?pagewanted=all (accessed January 30, 2014); "China to End Organ Donations from Executed Prisoners" *BBC*, March 23, 2012, http://www.bbc.co.uk/news/world-asia-china-17485103 (accessed January 30, 2014); Laurie Burkitt, "China to Stop Harvesting Inmate Organs," *Wall Street Journal*, March 23, 2012, http://online.wsj.com/news/articles/SB10001424052702304724404577298661625345898 (accessed January 30, 2014).

17. Didi Kirsten Tatlow, "Inside China's Greatest Mystery," *New York Times*, February 12, 2012, http://rendezvous.blogs.nytimes.com/2012/02/12/inside-chinas-greatest-mystery/?_r=0, (accessed August 8, 2013); "Wang Lijun," China Vitae, http://www.chinavitae.com/biography/Wang_Lijun/career (accessed August 8, 2013).

18. World Organization to Investigate the Persecution of Falun Gong (WOIPFG), "Investigative Report: China's Public Security Bureau's On-Site Psychology Research Center Implicated in Live Organ Harvesting on Falun Gong Practitioners," February 15, 2012, http://www.zhuichaguoji.org/en/node/214 (accessed August 8, 2013).

19. James W. Tong, *Revenge of the Forbidden City: The Suppression of Falun Gong in China, 1999–2005* (New York: Oxford University Press, 2009), pp. 61–66.

20. "Investigative Report"; Lisa Lee, telephone interview by author, July 2013.

21. Dr. Huige Li, "Unethical Organ Harvesting in China," PPT presentation, Welsh National Assembly, November 2013.

22. Matthew Robertson, "Phone Logs Reveal Top Chinese Officials' Knowledge of Organ Harvesting," *Epoch Times*, May 1, 2012, http://www.theepochtimes.com/n2/china-news/phone-logs-reveal-top-chinese-officials-knowledge-of-organ-harvesting-230616-all.html (accessed January 22, 2014).

23. "Letter to Hillary Rodham Clinton," from members of the United States Congress, October 3, 2012, http://media.faluninfo.net/media/doc/2012/10/U.S._Congress_Dear_Colleague_Letter_Organ_Harvesting_10.4.2012.pdf (accessed January 22, 2014).

24. This section on Huang Jiefu is partially based on Arne Schwarz, "The Dark Side of Huang Jiefu: Facts and Sources," e-mail to author, May 2013, and WOIPFG, "Investigative Report on How the Chinese Regime Uses the Former Vice Minister of Health, Huang Jiefu, to Conceal Its Unethical Organ Procurement Practices," World Organization to Investigate the Persecution of Falun Gong, April 30, 2014, http://www.upholdjustice.org/node/247 (accessed May 16, 2014). The author also wishes to thank Matthew Robertson for his insights.

25. See Zhuang Pinghui, "Minister Wants Humane Stance on Organ Cases," *South China Morning Post*, March 25, 2012, http://www.scmp.com/article/996480/minister-wants-humane-stance-organ-cases (accessed May 17, 2014); Stephen McDonell, "Australian-Trained Doctor Huang Jiefu Hits Back at Critics over Ties to China Organ Harvesting," ABC News, May 21 2013, http://www.abc.net.au/news/2013-05-20/chinese-doctor-hits-back-at-critics-over-organ-donation-program/4701436 (accessed May 17, 2014); "Huang Jiefu: Salute to Donors" dayoo.com (source: *Guangzhou Daily*), March 13, 2013, http://news.dayoo.com/guangzhou/201303/13/73437_29475945.htm (accessed May 17, 2014); see also WOIPFG, p. 10.

26. Author's personal correspondence with DAFOH associates, 2013–2014.

27. "China Promises Prisoner Organ Donation Phasing Out," ABC News (Australia), YouTube, May 20, 2013, https://www.youtube.com/watch?v=0L1SV1m6PEc (accessed May 17, 2014).

28. Matthew Robertson, "Chinese Officials' Denials on Organ Harvesting Suggest Culpability," *Epoch Times*, June 10, 2013, http://www.theepochtimes.com/n3/99667-chinese-officialss-denials-on-organ-harvest-suggest-culpability/ (accessed May 17, 2014).

29. This view is self-reinforcing—it presumes a sophisticated understanding of the difficulties of transforming China and a belief in inevitable eventual reform. Anyone of good will who has entered China—including me, actually—has indulged a very similar fantasy of working within the system to rescue China at some point. From the mainland perspective, any Western critique or mistrust of attempts to reform within the existing system is unfair; the party cannot be asked to break the self-created taboos, and we must accept this, and men like Huang Jiefu, as a precondition for negotiations. It is ironic that the one thing that Western skeptics always asked for, the smoking gun of organ harvesting, has always been a doctor who did terrible things with his own hands.

30. Daniel Asa Rose, *Larry's Kidney* (New York: Harper, 2009).

31. Ibid., p. 98.

32. Ibid., pp. 190–91.

33. Ibid., p. 198.

34. Ibid., pp. 197–98.

35. Rose's account, in addition to confirming that the Chinese ban on foreign organ tourism is a sham, also contains little nuggets of useful information that can help us build a crude picture of the overall scale of organ tourism to China. Rose met the families of organ tourists while he was in China—from Pakistan, Yemen, Saudi Arabia, Egypt, and Morocco. So we should think beyond the usual bases of organ tourism—Hong Kong, Japan, Russia, the United States, and the wealthier countries of the European Union—and include the Middle East as well. His account also hints that India is no longer a competitive kidney provider.

36. David Kilgour and David Matas, *Bloody Harvest: the Killing of Falun Gong for their Organs* (Woodstock, ON: Seraphim Editions, 2009), pp. 59–70.

37. Ibid., pp. 94–108.

38. David Matas, "Numbers," in David Matas and Torsten Trey, eds., *State Organs* (Woodstock, ON: Seraphim, 2013), p. 91.

39. But then consider his following sentence "The darkness cast by data cover-up makes organ transplant abuse easier to perpetrate." Matas is referring to the firewall that has been erected in China across all sensitive sites, such as the liver transplant registry, since 2007. Ibid., p. 80.

40. The party's move to spruce up the image of the labor camps has garnered mild praise from the international community, but, thankfully, far less than the equally empty "village elections" of years past. The initiative appears to be a reaction to the recent embarrassment when a practitioner note describing the conditions in Masanjia was discovered in an American Halloween decoration box, and the subsequent exposé of Masanjia in *Focus Magazine* by a Chinese *New York Times* freelancer. The comprehensive history of Masanjia has yet to be told.

41. Matas, "Numbers," p. 84.

42. Simone Gao, "Recent Case Studies," letter to author, November 2013.

43. Jaya Gibson, conversation with author, January 2014.

44. Rebiyah Kadeer and Alim Seytoff, interviews with author, Washington, DC, and Paris, 2009.

45. Lisa Zhang, telephone interview by author, March 2014; Zhang Fengying, interview by Leeshai Lemish, April 2014.

46. Matthew Robertson, "China Transplant Official Backtracks on Prisoner Organs," *Epoch Times*, March 12, 2014, http://www.theepochtimes.com/n3/558858-china-transplant-official-backtracks-on-prisoner-organs/ (accessed May 16, 2014).

47. Matthew Robertson, "Top Chinese Transplant Official Says There's No Plan to Stop Using Prisoner Organs," *Epoch Times*, April 11, 2014, http://m.theepochtimes.com/n3/614808-top-chinese-transplant-official-says-theres-no-plan-to-stop-using-prisoner-organs/ (accessed May 16, 2014).

CHAPTER 10. A NIGHT AT THE MUSEUM

1. For an abbreviated version of this chapter see Ethan Gutmann "Bodies at an Exhibition," *Weekly Standard* 18, no. 43 (July 29, 2013): 22–26.

2. There are many odd features to this mini-opera. The confidential informant, eventually revealed to be one Sun Deqiang, exposed, once again, the hazards of relying excessively on mainland witnesses: the tendency to please the interviewer and the equally strong tendency to change the story under pressure. It is possible that Mr. Sun may be the same confidential witness who described a

corpse processing factory in Dalian—run by von Hagens—that dumps formaldehyde into the sea, pays a one million yuan annual bribe to party officials, and receives its bodies from Dalian Medical University. See Minghui.org, "Reference Material: Eyewitness Describes the 'Corpse Processing Factory' in Dalian," 4 August 2006, http://en.minghui.org/html/articles/2006/8/4/76338.html (accessed August 8, 2013).

3. See "Bodies . . . The Exhibition Disclaimer," Premier Exhibitions, 2012, http://www.prxi.com/disclaimer.html (accessed August 8, 2013).

4. Von Hagens's website claims that a normal plastination exhibit takes approximately one year to prepare. See "The Method of Plastination," Bodyworlds.com, http://www.bodyworlds.com/en/plastination/method_plastination.html (accessed August 8, 2013).

5. Rather than cremating the Chinese bodies, von Hagens might have chosen to sell them to a medical school or institution instead, so DNA testing of the specimens may still be a possibility.

6. "A Life in Science," Bodyworlds.com, http://www.bodyworlds.com/en/gunther_von_hagens/life_in_science.html (accessed August 8, 2013).

7. Von Hagens has been legally charged with exaggerating his academic credentials and misrepresenting himself as an anatomy professor at Heidelberg. See Annette Tuffs, "Von Hagens Faces Investigation over Use of Bodies without Consent," *British Medical Journal*, November 8, 2003, http://www.ncbi.nlm.nih.gov/pmc/articles/PMC1126850/ (accessed August 8, 2013). See also "Titel-Streit Gunther von Hagens: Landgericht revidiert Urteil der ersten Instanz," Koerperwelten, http://www.koerperwelten.newmedia-net.de/de/presse/pressemeldungen_statements/pressemeldungen_statements_2006.html?edit#280906 (accessed August 8, 2013). For von Hagens's depiction of his life history see also "Gunther von Hagens—Milestones, Pathways, and Goals," Plastinarium, http://www.plastinarium.de/en/gunther_von_hagens/etappen_wege_ziele_copy.html (accessed August 8, 2013). In Sui's case, he identifies himself as "Sui Hongjin Dr. Prof" on the Dalian Hoffen Bio-Technique Co. Ltd. webpage. See http://www.hoffen.com.cn/english/leadership.asp (accessed August 8, 2013). It's not clear that either title is fully accurate.

8. World Organization to Investigate the Persecution of Falun Gong (WOIPFG), "An Investigative Report on the Source of Human Cadavers Used in the Plastination Industry in China," November 13, 2012, updated on July 23, 2013, http://www.zhuichaguoji.org/en/node/236 (accessed August 8, 2013). Referred to hereafter as WOIPFG Investigative Report.

9. Von Hagens's website gives the date as 2001, yet according to a report on New Tang Dynasty Television, which actually shows the document in question, the date is 1999. See Matt Gnaizda, "China Focus: Gu Kailai, Bo Xilai, and Plastination Exhibits Using Executed Prisoners," http://www.youtube.com/watch?v=0jZM4wDODB0 (accessed August 8, 2013). See also WOIPFG Investigative report.

10. It is interesting to speculate that von Hagens's plastination was thought of as part of the "scientific" initiative against Falun Gong. For a comprehensive portrait of that structure see James W. Tong, *Revenge of the Forbidden City* (New York: Oxford University Press, 2009), pp. 107–109.

11. WOIPFG Investigative Report.

12. WOIPFG Investigative Report.

13. WOIPFG Investigative Report.

14. There's little evidence of such a comprehensive effort in Liaoning during the same period, aside from Dalian Public Security's arrest of a practitioner for printing and distributing Li Hongzhi's book on June 4 (which I surmise could well be a byproduct of the intense security surrounding the ten-year anniversary of Tiananmen and the imperative for local law enforcement to produce at least one scapegoat). See Tong, *Revenge of the Forbidden City*, pp. 39, 41.

15. "Bo Xilai," China Vitae, http://www.chinavitae.com/biography/Bo_Xilai/career (accessed August 8, 2013).

16. WOIPFG Investigative Report.

17. Zhong Yan, "Falun Gong Practitioners Are Primary Victims of Labor Camp Torture in China," Minghui.org, April 22, 2013, http://en.minghui.org/html/articles/2013/4/22/139015p.html (accessed August 8, 2013).

18. Lisa Lee, correspondence with author, July 2013; Yiyang Xia correspondence with author, July 2013.

19. WOIPFG Investigative Report.

20. WOIPFG Investigative Report.

21. "Investigation Leads: Jinzhou City Number 205 Hospital in Liaoning Province Harvests Organs from Living People for Huge Profit, and Other Information (Photo)," Minghui.org, August 29, 2006, http://en.minghui.org/html/articles/2006/8/29/77447.html (accessed August 8, 2013).

22. Sometimes this same threat was brandished about the "Northwest," referring to the Tarim Prison Camp. See chapter 1.

23. See WOIPFG, "WOIPFG Case Report: Witness to a Killing during Live Organ Harvesting of Falun Gong Practitioner," December 12, 2009, http://www.zhuichaguoji.org/en/node/192 (accessed August 8, 2013); "Investigation

Leads: Shenyang Military General Hospital Has a Large Supply of Organs," Clearharmony.net, February 18, 2007, http://h2074909.stratoserver.net/articles/Investigation_Leads_Shenyang_Military_General_Hospital_Has_a_Large_Supply_of_Organs-a38081.html#.UgQonZKTino (accessed August 8, 2013); WOIPFG, "Investigative Report on the Role of Chinese Military and Armed Police Hospitals in Live Organ Harvesting from Falun Gong Practitioners," June 24, 2012, http://www.zhuichaguoji.org/en/node/218 (accessed August 8, 2013).

24. Transcript of Sound Of Hope Radio Network broadcast, April 13, 2006, "Chinese Hospital Admit Harvesting Organs—Falun Gong Practitioners Targeted," http://concentrationcamp.blogspot.co.uk/2006/04/chinese-hospital-admit-harvesting.html (accessed August 8, 2013). See also "Investigation Leads: Possible Organ Harvesting Link Between the Huanbao Hotel in Dalian City and the No. 2 Hospital Affiliated with Dalian Medical University," Minghui.org, August 26, 2006, http://en.minghui.org/html/articles/2006/8/26/77343.html (accessed August 8, 2013); "Investigation Lead: The Second Hospital of Dalian Medical University Provides Liver Donor Within Three to Ten Days," Minghui.org, July 12, 2006, http://en.minghui.org/emh/articles/2006/7/12/75392p.html (accessed August 10, 2013).

25. A Falun Gong practitioner, Wang Hongjun, in Fushun Municipality was charged with industrial sabotage for allegedly planning to derail a train, but the practitioner received life imprisonment rather than execution. See Tong, *Revenge of the Forbidden City*, p. 72. Given that the case took place in 2001, when the Chinese authorities were attempting to build a violent profile for Falun Gong (in part to justify the stories of violence that were leaking out of the Laogai System to the general public), it's difficult to assess the truth of the charges.

26. WOIPFG Investigative Report.

27. "Dead but Not Buried," *Economist*, December 18, 2013, http://www.economist.com/news/china/21591890-there-little-you-cannot-buy-chinese-internet-dead-not-buried (accessed January 31, 2014).

28. Note to figure. Graphics by Olli Törmä. Special thanks to Yiyang Xia and Lisa Lee for the Shenyang Prison City reference.

29. WOIPFG Investigative Report.

30. Lisa Lee, interview by author, July 2013.

31. WOIPFG Investigative Report.

32. Tong, *Revenge of the Forbidden City*, pp.122–23.

33. WOIPFG Investigative Report.

34. Dr. Maria Fiatarone Singh, correspondence with author, June 2013.

35. Edward McMillan-Scott, "We Need New Powers to Rein in China," *Independent*, January 3, 2010, http://www.independent.co.uk/voices/commentators/edward-mcmillanscott-we-need-new-powers-to-rein-in-china-1855920.html (accessed August 9, 2013).

36. Thus far, von Hagens's legal and public relations department has only repeated that all the bodies in the show are from North American or European donors without explaining—to take an example—where the fetuses in advanced stages of development came from. See Gail Hamburg's comment (Ms. Hamburg is the media and public liaison for BODY WORLDS North America) in Wesley J. Smith, "Murdered Falun Gong as 'Art?'" *National Review* Online, July 27, 2013, http://www.nationalreview.com/human-exceptionalism/354588/murdered-falun-gong-art-wesley-j-smith#comments (accessed February 1, 2014). See also : "Famous German Anatomist Destroys Falun Gong's Organ Harvesting Lie," *China Daily*, August 5, 2013, http://www.chinadaily.com.cn/hqzx/2013-08/05/content_16872126.htm; permanent link, and http://www.peeep.us/67a9d19f; (both accessed August 9, 2013). The article was published during the media ramp-up for Bo Xilai's sentencing, so it may have been intended to subliminally remind Chinese readers of some of the wilder rumors (there are many) about Bo Xilai and Gu Kailai's personal involvement in organ harvesting.

AFTERWORD

1. See Aryeh Savir, "Rabbi Calls for Protests in Behalf of Falun Gong," *San Diego Jewish World*, April 9, 2014, http://www.sdjewishworld.com/2014/04/09/rabbi-calls-protests-behalf-falun-gong/ (accessed May 15, 2014).

INDEX

ABC News Australia, 273
ABC News, 291
Abdureyimu, Nijat, 15–17, 20, 309
abortion, forced, 23, 313
acupuncture, 33
Agence France-Presse, 87
airport, Beijing, 88, 100, 109
airport, Johannesburg, 214
algorithms, evolutionary, 213
al Qaeda, 12, 312
Amazon.com, 64
American Chamber of Commerce Beijing, 164
Amnesty International, 230–31, 251, 266, 279
"Angel," 113–18, 177
Anhui Province, 111, 122
"Annie," 223–25, 227, 230
Anshan, 146, 203–204
Appeals Office,
    Andingmen location, 121–30,
    Fuyou street appeal, 73, 79–83, 87–88
    Han Tianzi, 150
    Liang Zhenxing, 195
    mystery surrounding location, 79, 80
April 25 Incident. *See* Zhongnanhai
Assange, Julian, 191, 215
Associated Press, 87, 105, 106
"Auntie Dee," 82–83, 97
"Auntie Jun," 97
"Auntie Sha," 83, 92
Australia, 52, 88, 108, 173–74, 273, 317
Aviner, Rabbi Shlomo, 313

Bai Suxia, 150
Baidu.com, 263, 269
Bangkok witnesses, 180, 217, 235, 236, 239, 240, 241, 246–49, 317

Beijing Zhonghai Shangda Advertising Company, 305
Beijing Olympics
    damage control, 231–32, 277
    medical testing through, 246, 249, 273–74, 281–82
    temporary hiatus in harvesting, 257
Beijing practitioners, 79, 105–106, 114–15, 135
"Big Truck" (Liu Chengjun), 196–97, 199–200, 202–203, 210–11
Bloody Harvest, 28, 230–32, 277, 312, 322
"Body worlds"
    author's reaction to von Hagens's exhibition, 287–89
    and Chinese public reaction to Sui Hongjin's "Body Worlds," 305
    DNA testing, 305–308
    necrophilia, 289
    plastination, 287–89, 291–97, 301–302, 304–306
    See also Vienna "Body Worlds" Exhibition
Bo Xilai
    attempted prisoner lawsuit on, 144
    and Gunther von Hagens, 293, 297–99, 302–304
    key dates, 297
    in "Liaoning Triangle," 303
    and Wang Lijun's aborted defection, 260–64, 268–69, 312
    and Xinghai Friendship Award Ceremony, 296
British Broadcasting Corporation (BBC), 28
Broadcasting Board of Governors (BBG), 215
Browde, Levi, 307
Brooklyn, 102
Brussels, 312

357

INDEX

Burma, 180, 217
Bush, George W., 231

Canada, 20, 151–52, 173, 229
Central Intelligence Agency, 12, 97
Chang'an Avenue, 73, 79, 82, 87
Changchun
    birthplace of Falun Gong, 31–32, 38
    birthplace of Zhao Ming, 43, 128
    corpse landfill, 250
    Daguang Detention Center, 175
    Falun Gong splinter group, 50
    labor camp, 184
    local police, Beijing, 130–32
    and "Lotus," 180
    PLA interview, 51
    television hijackers, 136, 193–95, 197, 199–200, 203–204, 206, 208–209, 211, 310
Cheney, Dick, 191
"Chen Jiansheng," 235–38
Chen Rongshan, 266, 268
Chengdu University, 258
Chengdu, US consulate, 260, 262, 264, 268
Chen Ying, 106–108
Chen Yonglin, 173
Chicago, 104
China Central Television (CCTV), 46, 48, 52, 62, 72, 99–101, 106, 166–67
China Falun Gong, 37
Chinese leadership crisis, apex of, 263
Chongqing, 38, 260–61, 263, 265
Chuncheng Hospital, radiology, 197
Chu Tong, 45–46
Clearwisdom.net, 172
CNN, footage of "self-immolation" incident, 166–167, 199
Communist Party of China (selected issues)
    and battle for the Chinese diaspora, 173
        anti-Falun-Gong-campaign planning, 92–97
        cleansing party leadership, 93
        cold sweat over Falun Gong growth rate, 54
        culture, 54, 60, 89, 228
        harvesting and suppression strategy, 269
        nationalism, 55
        physical attacks, 214
Congress, United States, 215, 224, 263, 268
Congress, World Uyghur, 13
Congress, World Qigong, 36
Congressional Research Service, 231
consent forms for organ donation, 232, 257, 275, 278, 310–11
Court of Justice, 138
"Crystal," 220–21, 225–28, 230, 237–39, 243, 250, 275, 301

Dai Ying, 234, 239
Dalai Lama, 104, 173, 241, 245
Dalian
    crackdown, 132, 143, 146
    Li Hongzhi lectures, 43, 48
    and Masanjia, 281
    mayor, Bo Xilai, 263
    plastination, 291, 294–99, 301–302, 304–307
Dalian Hoffen Bio-Technique Co., 297
Dalian Medical University Plastination Co. Ltd., 297, 302
Daoism, 33, 102–103
Dargyay, Tenpa, 244–45
David Kilgour and David Matas, 219, 229–31, 272, 280, 322
Dawkins, Richard, 65
Daxing Satellite District, 113–18
Delmonico, Francis 271–72, 313
Deng Xiaoping, 35–36, 54, 238
Department of Defense (US), 173
Dharamsala, 240, 242, 245
Ding Guan'gen, 48, 59
Ding Jing, 46–48, 52, 54, 56, 59, 62–63, 71, 72
Ding Yan, 105
DNA, 305–308
Doctors against Forced Organ Harvesting (DAFOH), 259, 272–73, 280, 306
Dong Buyun, 107
Dublin, 44, 128, 131–32, 179

INDEX   **359**

Eastern Lightning, 239–40, 280, 302
East Turkestan, 11. *See also* Xinjiang
Edinburgh, Royal College of Surgeons, 273
electroencephalography (EEG), 36
Epoch Times, 28, 166, 212, 214, 222–25, 227–28, 231, 263, 280, 313
espionage
    Bo Xilai private surveillance, 261
    inside Falun Gong, 56, 59, 63, 96, 115–16, 134
    and refugee-bots, 173, 214, 341, 344–45
    and spies, 139, 166, 172, 261, 265, 298
    using electronic means, 75, 86, 90–94, 97, 119, 154–55, 166, 191
European Parliament, 307
executions
    anticoagulant, 17, 20
    as a plastination resource, 291
    ethics, 254, 309–10
    and harvesting, 9–11, 24
    and harvesting of dissidents, 25–27, 222, 266
    and live harvesting, 16–20, 23, 263–64
    and new methods, 238, 265
    numerical shortfall for transplants, 230–232, 278–80
    optics of, 256, 258–59, 269–72
    structure of, 138, 237–38
    to order, 226–28
    use of bullets, 18,19, 26, 298
Expo, Oriental Health, 37
extraordinary powers
    politics of, 49–50
    reading techniques, 35
    ridicule of, 100
    supernormal powers, 32–35, 42–43
    teleportation, 33, 42
    "Three No's," 35–37, 51, 58, 75, 84–85, 93, 103
    UFOs, 32
    See also Li Youfu

Falundafa.org, 64
Falun Gong, reasons for party repression
    author's explanation, 53–56
    belief that Falun Gong will weaken China, 56
    Jiang Zemin jealousy theory, 90
    "Minister X" explanation, 57–58
    party leadership attitudes, 89–92
    unchecked growth concern, 54
    worship of Chinese power, 55
Falun Gong, selected pre-1999
    birthplace of, 31, 194
    Falun Gong's guanxi, 51
    "Falun Gong surrounded Zhongnanhai," summary, 80, 87–88
    "false peace," 60
    indigenous to China, 66
    "nice, sloppy, definition," 66
    party exercise site: CCTV, 48
    party exercise site: Science Academies, 52
    party exercise site: Xinhua News Agency, 48
    rapid growth, 60
    relation to Buddhism, 31, 40, 56, 66–67, 103, 105, 113
    splinter group accusations, 50–51
Falun Gong, selected post-1999
    anthem, 187–89
    attitude toward homosexuality, 67
    author's embedded experiences, 67–69
    author's suggested test for readers, 69–70
    belief in altering prison guard behavior, 237
    deaths in custody, early years, 106–108, 221
    Falun Gong definitional dilemmas, 104, 106
    "Falun Gong is rehabilitated!" 207
    "Go to the people," 135
    hunger strikes, 107, 127, 149–51, 170–71, 175, 186, 196, 233–34, 320–21
    in the American wilderness, 103–105, 171–72

360 INDEX

July 1999 crackdown, 66, 97–102, 161, 132, 195, 219, 296, 304
   mature harvest era, 247
   nameless ones, 221, 250–51, 302
   party definition, 57, 62–63, 93, 102, 124, 143, 164
   percentage of Laogai System, 319–20
   percentage of torture cases, 319
   Pudu miracle, 114, 118
   "Quit the CCP," 214
   splinter group accusations recycled by party, 100
   state religious leaders denounce, 102
   Taiwanese perspective, 260
   toxic new phase, 108
   young protester, 113, 117–18
Faluns, 239
Fang Siyi, 239–40
Farsi, 214
Fragrant Hill, 92–93
Freegate, 214–15
France, 52, 258
Fudan University, 227
Fuxing Street, 83
Fu Yubin, 164, 341
Fuyou Street, 73–74, 79–84, 87, 98, 121, 178

Gao Qiuju, 132
Gao, Simone, 166
Gao Rongrong, 152, 153
Gansu Province, 244
"General Wu," 52
Germany, 285, 287, 293, 295
"Ghostnet," 173
Ghulja, 12, 20–23, 25–27, 283
Gibson, Jaya, 240–45, 246, 312
Global Internet Freedom Consortium, 192, 213–15
Golden Shield, 154, 191
Google, 248, 263, 299
GPS, 97
Great Firewall, 191–92, 213
"Great Sea" (Liu Haibo), 197–209
Green Army, 171

Gregory, Stephen, 166
Guangdong, 94, 163
Guanghua Science and Technology Foundation, 265, 297
Guangming Ribao, 58–59, 93
Guangzhou, 9, 38, 111, 122, 180, 295
Guantánamo, 12
guanxi, 49, 51
Gu Kailai, 261, 262, 264, 296
Gulag, 315
Guo Lin, 33
Guru Maharaji, 69

hacking, Chinese
   and US response, 191–92, 215
   from the 6-10 Office, 97, 172–74, 213–14
Han Guangsheng
   background, 136–42
   "learn from Masanjia," 146–47
   Longshan director, 145–54, 219
Hangzhou Resolution, 272, 285
Han Tianzi, 149–52
Hao Fengjun, 76–77, 96, 154–55, 171–74, 220, 233
Harbin, 79, 98, 159, 161–63, 168–69
Harry Wu, 104, 224–25, 344–45
Harvard University, 273
Heilongjiang Province, 107, 161
Heywood, Neil, 261–62, 296
He Zuoxiu, 58, 62, 75, 84, 91
Hollywood, 104
Hong Kong, 97, 108, 166, 214, 229, 235, 237, 317
House Christians, 27, 239, 240, 279–80, 285, 322
hospitals
   Dalian Medical University Hospital No. 2, 266, 294–300, 301–302, 304
   First Affiliated Hospital of Qinghai University, 227–28
   Gongzhuling Central Hospital, 194
   Jiaotong University Affiliated Hospital, 345

No. 2 Affiliated Hospital, Hubei Province Medical University, 345
Qianfoshan Hospital Liver Transplant Center, 345
Shanghai Zhongshan Hospital (Fudan University), 227
Shenyang Military General Hospital, 300–301
Sun Yat-sen Medical University, 9, 269–70
Tianjin No.1 Central Hospital, 345
Tongji Hospital (Wuhan), 226–27
Urumqi Air Force Hospital (now 474 PLA Hospital), 345
Urumqi Central Railway Hospital, 17
Wanjia Labor Camp Hospital, 185–87
Zheng Ye military hospital, 242
See also Jinzhou City PSB On-Site Psychological Research Center; Western Mountain Execution Grounds; Zhenjiang City Cremation Center
Huang Jiefu
  awards and honorary titles, 273
  background, 269–70
  broken promises, 285,
  ethical dilemma, 310
  inoculation strategy, 273
  photograph, 272
  role in leadership struggle, 263, 266, 269
  western approval, 270–73, 280, 314
Huang Shiwei, 278
Hubei Province, 105, 111, 122
Hu Jintao, 223, 226, 261
Huo Mingkai. See "Monkey"

Immer, Franz, 258
immunosuppressive drugs, 10
India, 11, 240, 259, 309
Indonesia, 171
Internet
  censorship of Western reporting, 106
  freedom efforts, 192–93
  getting around the blockade, 161
  "It's just like that here," 191–92
  searches for "live harvesting," 263, 269
  surveillance, 97, 154–55, 191–92, 213–15
  threat from Falun Gong, 221
  websites for former cult members, 69–70, 333–34
  Xinjiang shutdown, 14, 282
Internews, 215
Iran, 192, 312
Ireland, 44, 128, 131–32, 179
Islam, 12, 14, 22, 67, 102
Israel, 217, 254, 258–59, 313

Japan, 171, 293, 294–95, 302
Jiangsu Province, 250
Jiang Xinxia, 60, 75, 89
Jiang Zemin
  "call it suicide," veracity of, 147
  "kill without mercy," veracity of, 208
  "Make June 4th go away," 58
  "What is the Falun Gong?," veracity of, 336
  6-10 Office, creation of, 96
  and 2012 leadership struggle, 261–62,
  approval of Falun Gong repression, 140, 304
  April 25th, Zhongnanhai Incident, 85–87, 89–92,
  as a sentient being, 112
  as harvesting fall guy, 269
  failure to convict, 104
  practitioner media attacks on, 161, 206, 211
  spiritual aspirations, 55, 90
Jiaotong University, Shanghai, 60
Jia Yahui, 280–82
Jia Xiarong, 235
Jilin City, 200, 208, 211
Jilin Province, 75, 95, 101, 108, 197, 298
Jinan City, 40
Jing Tian, 235, 236, 239
Jinzhou City, 102, 107
Jinzhou City PSB On-Site Psychological Research Center
  organ harvesting, 265–66, 268

and plastination, 297, 299, 301–304
    Wang Lijun directing, 267
Jixi City, 107
Johannes Gutenberg University, 266
Johnson, Ian, 106, 311
journalism, Western
    apathy over time, 14, 212–13
    blindsided by Zhongnanhai Incident, 87
    blocked from interviews, 14, 167, 282
    lack of primary research, 312
    October 1999 secret press conference, 105–106, 115
    and "self-immolation," 166–67
Judicature Bureau, 138
June 4 (1989), 37, 58, 93

Kadeer, Rebiya, 12–13
Kaifeng, 167
Kamm, John, 251
Kang Xiaoguang, 88
Karamay, 12
Kashgar, 12
Kazakhstan, 11–12
Kilgour, David. *See* David Kilgour and David Matas
Koppel, Ted, 104
Körperwelten, 290
Ko Wen-je, 253–60, 322
Kunming train-station incident, 14
Kyap, Lhamo, 244–45
Kyrgyzstan, 11

labor camps
    Changlinzi Labor Camp, 185
    Dalian Labor Camp, 299, 303
    Masanjia Labor Camp, 143–47, 149, 152, 246–47, 265, 281–82, 298, 302, 303
    Sanshui Labor Camp, 239
    Tarim desert labor camp, 14, 313
    Tiantanghe Women's Labor Camp, 282, 284
    Tuanhe Labor Camp, 175–76, 179
    Xin'an Women's Labor Camp, 177–79
    Yunnan Forced Labor Camp No. 2, 218–19
    Zhangshi Reformatory (labor camp), 143, 145, 299
    See also Longshan Labor Camp
Lanzhou, 132
Laogai, definition of, 143
Laogai System, definition of, 143
Laogai Research Foundation, 224, 318
Larry's Kidney, 273–74
Las Vegas, 304
Lavee, Jacob, 258–59
Lee, Amy, 61, 94–95
Lee, Lisa, 264–65
Lei Ming. *See* "Little Brother" (Lei Ming)
Lemish, Leeshai, 172, 234, 236, 240, 247, 278
Liang Zhenxing (the leader), 193–200, 202–204, 206, 215
Liaoning Province
    Anshan, 203
    crackdown, 93, 102, 142–44, 146–47, 149
    Falun Gong, 50, 95, 139
    "Liaoning Triangle," 303
    organ harvesting, 236, 263–66, 268, 280, 310
    plastination, 291–92, 294, 296–99, 301–304, 306
    PSB, 137
Lhasa, 242, 282
Liaosheng Evening News, 280
Li Chang, 85
Li Changchun, 268
Li Dongsheng, 166
Li Hongzhi
    at the Health Expo, 37–42
    birth date, Sakyamuni Buddha, 50, 100
    bowing to, 41
    dissenters, 50–51
    first teaching sessions, 31
    first US lecture, 53
    and "last attachments," 165

leaving China, 48–49
Li Hongzhi: The Man and His Deeds, 95
Paris lecture, 52
practitioner perception of humility of, 38–40
Li Huige, 266
Li Lanqing, 96
Lin Bizi, 146
Lin Jie, 234
Li Peng, 55, 90–91
Li, Peter, 214
"Little Brother" (Lei Ming), 200–203, 207–208
Liu Chengjun. *See* "Big Truck" (Liu Chengjun)
Liu Chunling
as mother of Siying, 167
as prostitute, 167, 199
"self-immolation" incident, 164–68
Liu Guifu, 249
Liu Haibo. *See* "Great Sea" (Liu Haibo)
Liu Jing, 214
Liu Tianchun, 197, 208, 209
Li Youfu, 32–37, 42–43
Lop Nur, 14
Longshan Labor Camp
Han Guangsheng's direction of, 140–54
sexual abuse, 144–45
Western exports, 141, 148–49, 151
Los Angeles, 37, 42–43, 53, 153
"Lotus" (Wang Huilian), 101, 180–84, 187–88, 221, 236
"Lu," 53–54
Luo Gan, 58–60, 84, 87, 90–92, 96, 147, 221, 270
Luo Hongwei, 82, 98

Mackinnon, Rebecca, 166
Ma Lijuan, 109–12, 118–30
Manhattan, 94
Maoism, 12, 27, 35, 43, 54, 79, 110, 256
Massachusetts Institute of Technology (MIT), 273

Matas, David. *See* David Kilgour and David Matas
Mcleodganj, 241
McMillan-Scott, Edward, 307
Melbourne, 173
Meshrep, 22
military hospitals, 25–26, 237–38, 242, 250, 258, 268, 272, 275, 300–301, 314. *See also* hospitals
military surgeons, 24, 231, 236, 237–39, 242, 248
Minghui
and bad publicity, 185, 220
and Han Guangsheng, 152
and Lotus, 181–83
as paper of record for Changchun hijackers, 194, 199, 204, 215
as resource for DNA matching, 306
role in early accounts of repression, 108, 117
and Zhao Ming, 132, 135, 179
mitochondrial DNA, 305–306
Mongolian, 11, 95, 264
"Monkey" (Huo Mingkai), 202–11, 12
Montreal, 217
"Mr. Chen," 228
"Mr. Hua," 177–78
"Murat," 25–27

National Aeronautics and Space Administration (NASA), 173
National Security Agency (NSA), 191
National Security Bureau, 138
New Tang Dynasty Television (NTDTV), 149, 166, 213
New Zealand, 144
Nightline, 104
Nijat. *See* Abdureyimu, Nijat
Nong'an, 197, 210
nontransformable, 144, 150–51, 177–79, 235, 239, 249, 251, 302
nonviolent, 12, 61, 75, 139, 195, 210, 221, 235
Northeast, "we will send you to the," 301
North Korea, 312

Norway, 239
Nowak, Manfred, 319

organ harvesting, death-row prisoners
    abandonment of party declaration, 285, 313–15
    continuing from prisoners, 285
    corneas, extraction, 9, 222
    ethics of, 310–15
    live organ, 9–11, 15–20, 265–66
    morality of, 9–10, 15–20, 258–59, 269–73, 309–11
    party declaration to end, 263, 269–73
    sourced from a criminal, 9–10, 28
    and Wang Lijun, 265–74
    Western medical awareness of, 28, 258–59, 269–73, 330–31
organ harvesting, prisoners of conscience
    abdominal examinations, 217, 218, 233, 244, 321
    anesthesia, 17–19, 222, 238, 293
    blood tests, Falun Gong, 186, 217–18, 236, 233–37, 246–50, 260–64, 281–82, 321
    blood tests, Falun Gong and Christians, 239, 240
    blood tests, Falun Gong and ordinary criminals, 283
    blood tests, Tibetans, 240–46
    blood tests, Uyghurs, 25–27
    cornea examination, 233, 239, 266, 321
    Doctor Ko Wen-je "smoking gun interview," 253–58, 259–60
    electrocardiogram (EKG), 186, 218, 239, 240, 282–83, 321
    ethics of, 310–15
    Falun Gong witness credibility, 30, 88, 224, 229, 231, 234
    Kilgour and Matas investigation into transplant sources, 229–32
    limitations of findings, 27
    numbers, 275–80, 317–22
    organs-only physical examinations, 233, 239, 244, 248, 251, 283

    "Party Central," 269
    and plastination, 297–308
    Sujiatun allegations, 222–25
    urine test, 186, 217–18, 239, 249, 283, 321
    and Wang Lijun, 265–74
    WOIPFG investigation into transplant sources, 226–28, 237–39, 250
    X-ray, 217–18, 233–34, 239, 240, 283, 321
organ tourism, Western
    advertising, 253, 255
    average waiting times, 230
    Chinese official ban, 270, 273, 285
    from Taiwan, 253–60
    in Liaoning Province, 302
    Israeli ban, 254, 258–59, 313, 347
    Larry's Kidney, 273–75, 350
    numbers, 275, 279
    Omar Healthcare Service, 275, 276
    price, liver, 239, 266
    research landscape, 275–76, 312
    "wait is only one or two days," 226
Operation Aurora, 174
Owen, Richard, 251

Pakistan, 11–12
Pan, Phillip, 144, 167, 311
Patriot Act, 191
Paris, 52, 132
People's Daily, 93, 97, 264
"Peter," 223–24
politburo, 55, 85, 91, 96, 260–61, 268, 296–97
Political and Legal Affairs Committee (PLAC), 92, 261–62, 303–304
"Politics and Law Committee," 138
Pomfret, John, 106
Premier Exhibitions, 289, 291, 297, 305, 308
Pretoria, 214
"princeling," 263
prisons and detention centers
    Chaoyang Guo Prison, 199
    Chengde City Prison, 105

INDEX

Chongqing Yongchuan Women's Jail (Prison), 234
Chushul Prison, 244
Dabei Jail, 143
Daguang Detention Center, 175
Drapchi Prison, 242–43
Golmud "Military Detention Center," 246
Guangdong Prison, 248–49
Gutsa Detention Center, 242
Haidian District Detention Center, 175
Harbin City No. 2 Detention Center, 169
Heizuizi Female Prison, 184, 187
Jilin City No. 2 Prison, 211
Jilin Detention Center, 239
Jinzhou Prison, 299
Nanguanling Prison, 299
Shenyang Prison City, 299, 303
Wafangdian Prison, 299
Procuratorate, 138
Public Security Bureau (PSB)
    appeals office, 126–29
    April to July 1999, 92–94
    crackdown plan, 70, 72
    emergence of 6-10 Office, 95–97
    "false peace," 60–64
    Falun Gong crackdown, 98–103, 106–108
    and Han Guangsheng, 137–54
    and harvesting, 270
    live organ harvesting, 16–20
    "Minister X," 57–59
    and plastination, 296–99, 302–303, 305–306, 309
    television-hijacker crackdown, 208, 211
    and Tiananmen, 134
    Tianjin to Beijing, 74, 76, 79, 84–86, 88, 90
    and torture 159, 161, 166, 168, 172, 180, 182–84
    and Wang Lijun case, 260, 264–65, 267
    use of Western corporate technologies, 191
    Uyghur police, 15, 20–23

Qian Xuesen, 36
Qigong boom, 32–33, 35–36, 42–43, 100
Qinghai Province, 243
Qingming Police Station, 211
Qu Yangyao, 233

Ramadan, 22
Rawat, Prem, 69
Red Hacker Alliance, 171
"red-headed" document, 57
Ren Jinyang, 265
Ren Shujie, 149
Reuters, 87, 105, 306
Reverend Moon, 69
Rome, 16
Royal College of Surgeons of Edinburgh, 273
Rose, Daniel, 273–75

SARS, 223, 234
Scientology, 69–70
Schwarz, Arne, 312
Scotland, 275
Seraphim, 317
Seytoff, Alim, 13
"self-immolation" incident
    background, 164–67
    centerpiece of the tableau, 168
    "False Fire," 206
    hijacking effect on, 211
    individuals, 166
    Phillip Pan, 167, 311
sexual abuse in Laogai System
    male-to-male sodomy, 176, 209
    rape, 16, 145, 298–99
    using humiliation, 144, 236
Shandong Province, 61, 107, 154
Shanghai, 91–92, 227, 295, 305
Shanghai Jiaotong University, 60
Shanxi University, 33
Shanxi Province, 42, 122–23, 127–28, 130, 238–39
Sheba Medical Center, 258
Shemshidin, Bahtiyar, 20–23

Shenyang
  detention facilities, 235, 264–65, 298–99, 302–304
  hospitals, 222, 226, 300–303
  practitioner activity, 50, 79, 97
  PSB, 137–42, 146
Shen Yun Performing Arts, 213
Shenzhen, 111, 172, 295
Shi Bingyi, 273
Sichuan Province, 243–44
Singapore, 241
Siping, 75, 89
6-10 Office
  creation, 95–96
  global operations, 172–74
  initial success of blitzkrieg strategy, 97–102, 108
  internal numerical estimates, 219–20, 318
  plan to kill Li Hongzhi, 214
  reaction to Changchun television hijacking, 208
  role in organ harvesting, 187, 233–34, 237–39, 268
  and the "self-immolation" incident, 164–66
  and 6-11 Office, 138
  Tianjin, 154–55
Snowden, Edward, 191, 215
Stanford University, 273
State Department, US, 173, 192–93, 215, 222, 262, 268, 312–13
Stockholm Syndrome, 177
Sui Hongjin, 289, 291–98, 301–302, 304–306, 308
Sujiatun, 222–26, 235, 247, 266, 270, 301, 313
Sunnyvale, 53
"Sun Shufen," 188
Sun Ti, 155–57
supernormal powers. *See* extraordinary powers
Sweden, 234
Swiss National Foundation for Organ Donation and Transplantation, 258
Sydney, 173, 233–34
Sydney University, 273

tai chi, 33, 36, 42
Taiwan
  attitudes about Falun Gong, 259–60
  and Chinese hackers, 171, 173
  Chinese tensions with, 97
  differences in practitioner culture, 69
  flight to, 108
  Li Hongzhi lectures, 52
  and organ tourism, 253–56, 278
  Taipei, 214, 317
Tajikistan, 11
Taliban, 12
Tang Feng, 204–208
Taobao, 302
Tarim. *See* labor camps
Tashkent, 11
Tazpit News Agency, 313
Tehran, 193
"The Cook" (Zhou Runjun), 202–203, 206, 211
Thailand, 52, 101, 148, 180
"Three Represents," 90
Tiananmen Square, battle of, 115–21, 128, 133–34, 167, 199, 204, 219, 338. *See also* "self-immolation" incident
Tianjin, 43
  local "6-10 Office," 96, 154, 172
  silent demonstration, 75–79, 87–89
  "Tianjin 45," 84–85
Tieling, 264, 297
Titan Rain, 173
Tohti, Enver, 17, 19, 265
Tong Chunshi, 151
Tong, James, 45, 92
Tongzhou district, 115
Top-floor Daxing, 118
Toronto, 71, 137
torture
  by beating, 129–30, 131, 133, 139, 155–57, 169
  by hanging, 180–84

by horse clamp, 170
Changchun hijackers' deaths, 194, 207–11
"clever fakes," 155
electric shocks, 142–44, 146–47, 149–52, 153, 175, 176, 179, 188, 194, 237
estimated numbers, 219–21, 319
and first casualties, 106–108, 111
force-feeding, 144, 151, 159, 170–71, 184–86, 194
and harvesting, 235–38, 239, 248
illicit press conference on, 105, 115
justification for, 153–54
"Learn from Masanjia," 146–47, 149
long-term, 194
of a minor, 149–52
of Uyghurs, 16, 22–23
and plastination, 304
pregnant woman, 169
proposed impunity index, 306–307
resistance to, 174–79, 180–86, 195–97, 202, 206
soft methods, 140–41, 177–78
tableaux, 228
transformation, 131, 170, 175–79, 183–85, 220, 298–99
transformation and harvesting, 233, 235–37
transformation case study, 141–54
and trauma, 127
See also sexual abuse in Laogai System
Transplantation Society (TTS)
"prisoners of conscience" problem, 10, 313–15
reaction to Huang Jiefu's reversal, 285
support of Huang Jiefu's reforms, 271–73
Tsinghua University, 43–45, 63, 128

Ultrareach, 214–15
Unification Church, 69–70, 334
United Kingdom, 28, 152, 229, 231, 245, 261

United States, 151, 171, 209, 220, 229, 305
Urumqi, 14–15, 17, 19, 25–26, 282, 309
Uyghurs
and Afghanistan, 11–12
energy resources, 12
enforced disappearances since 2009, 282, 283
and estimated casualties, 280, 322
ethics of Uyghur harvesting, 309–14
ethnicity, 11
five poisons, 173
harvesting numbers, 279–80, 322
heroin addiction, 20–22
and infanticide, 23
party charges of an al-Qaeda connection, 12
political future, 12
terrorists, 12–14

Vienna "Body Worlds" Exhibition, 287, 290–92, 304
von Hagens, Gunther, 287–89, 291–98, 301–302, 304–308, 313
Von Hagens Plastination (Dalian) Co. Ltd., 295–96, 297

Waldron, Arthur, 66
Wang Baogang, 183–84, 221
Wang Chunying, 281–82
Wang Guoping, 108
Wang Haibo, 285
Wang Hong, 151–52
Wang Huachen, 111
Wang Lijun
"cold-faced Yama," 264
directing organ harvesting, 267
general, 260–69, 271, 293, 296–99, 301–304, 312
"Wang Lijun live harvest," 263, 269
See also Jinzhou City PSB On-Site Psychological Research Center
Wang Wenyi, 226
Wang Xiaohua, 217–19
Wang Yuzhi, 159–63, 168–71, 180, 183–87

368 INDEX

Wang Zhiyuan, 97
Wei Jingsheng, 228–29
Weizigou Drug Rehabilitation Center, 175
Wen Jiabao, 269, 271
Wenjin Street, 79–80, 83, 87
Western Mountain Execution Grounds, 17
World Health Organization, 10
World Organization to Investigate the Persecution of Falun Gong (WOIPFG)
    Chinese access to, 263
    Phone calls to officials, 266, 268
    political impact, 280
    Wang Lijun investigation, 263–64, 267
    as a web resource, 28
Wuhan, 38, 95, 226
Wu, Harry, 224–25, 344–45. *See also* Laogai Research Foundation

Xia, Bill, 213
Xi'anmen Street, 79–80
Xi Jinping, 261, 285
Xinhua News Agency, 48, 52, 63, 93, 310
Xinjiang (East Turkestan),
    as China's laboratory, 15, 19, 25, 27, 228, 270, 309–11
    competing names 11–12
    energy resources, 12
    increasing violence, 14, 283
"Xinjiang Procedure," 13, 15–20, 23, 25–27, 29, 70, 251, 309

Yaojia Detention Center, 299
Ye Jianying, Marshal, 36
Yida, 235, 266, 301
Yuan Jiang, 132
Yu Pan, 144
Yu Xinhui, 247–49
"Yuyuantan Region," 46–47, 62, 71–72

Zeng, Jennifer, 81, 83–84, 92–93, 108, 178–79
Zhang Baosheng, 36
Zhang Erping, 104
Zhang Fengying, 282–83, 284
Zhang Xiansheng, 146
Zhang Yijie, 93–94
"Zhao and Ren," 147
Zhao Dong, 107
Zhao Jian, 111
Zhao Jinhua, 107
Zhao Ming
    appeals office, 124, 126–27, 128–30
    "go to the people" strategy, 131–36
    resistance in Laogai, 174–79
    Tsinghua years, 43–46, 56, 63
    "Wild Room," 175–76
Zhao Ziyang, 36, 52
Zhenjiang City Cremation Center, 250
Zhong Gong, 42, 72, 343
Zhongnanhai, 36, 74, 79–89, 92, 97–98, 100, 102
Zhongnanhai Incident
    "hour by hour" description, 81–85
    Li Hongzhi's role, 88–89, 102
    practitioner afterglow, 87–88, 92
    practitioner motivations, 89
    presence of armed PLA, 82
    surveillance, 83, 97
Zhou Runjun. *See* "The Cook" (Zhou Runjun)
Zhou Yongkang, 92, 96, 261, 262, 268–69
Zhu Jie, 37–38, 41
Zhu Jin, 139–40
Zhu Rongji, 84, 90–92
Zhu Shaolan, 107
Zhuan Falun
    banning of, 57–60
    burning of, 102–103
    conversion after reading, 42–43
    police usage, 79
    publication, 48–49
    public reciting, 78
    as theology, 64–65, 111
    and Zhao Ming, 130
    and Zhongnanhai Incident, 84

Relevant Sites and Locations

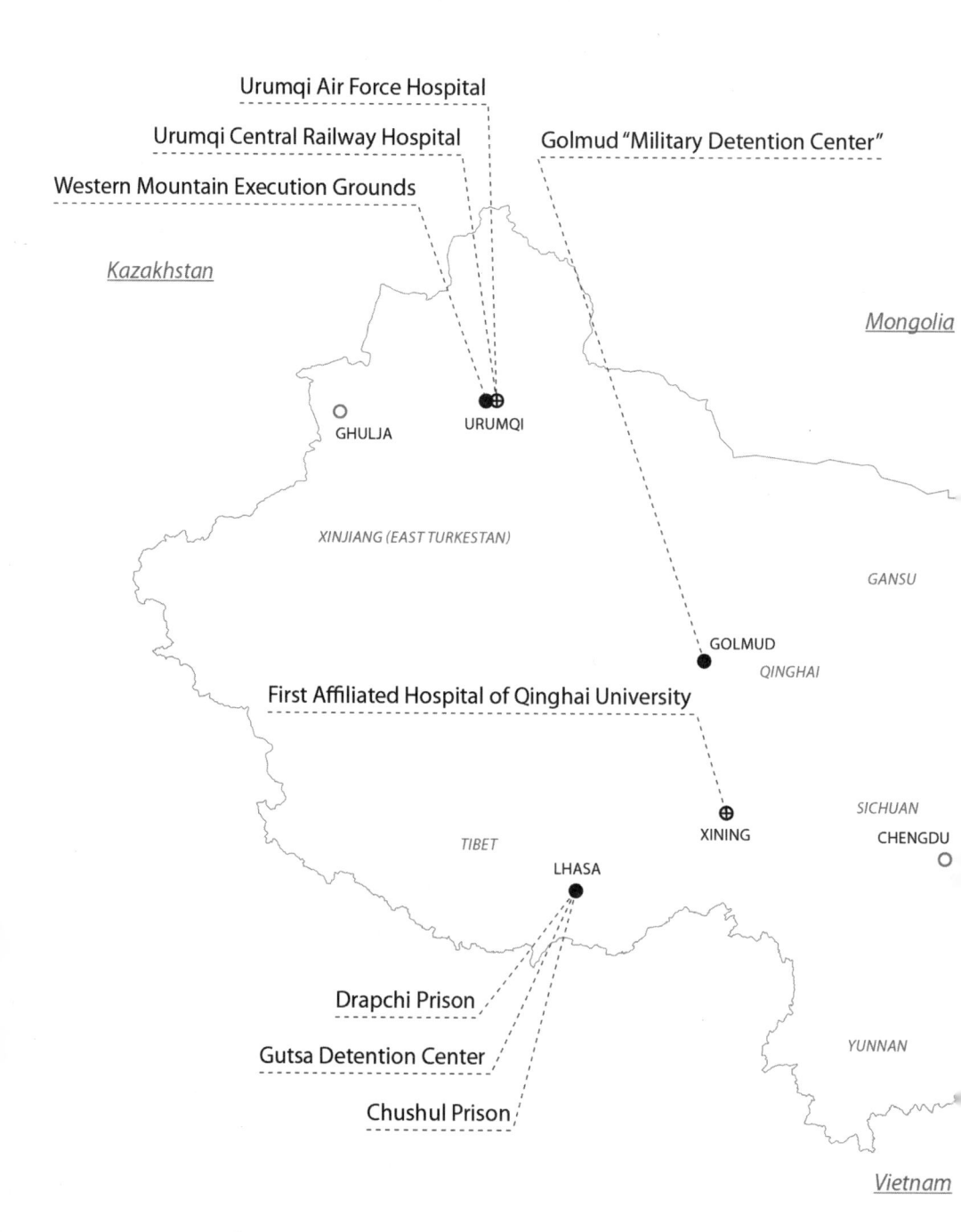

- Urumqi Air Force Hospital
- Urumqi Central Railway Hospital
- Western Mountain Execution Grounds
- Golmud "Military Detention Center"
- First Affiliated Hospital of Qinghai University
- Drapchi Prison
- Gutsa Detention Center
- Chushul Prison

Kazakhstan

Mongolia

GHULJA

URUMQI

XINJIANG (EAST TURKESTAN)

GANSU

GOLMUD

QINGHAI

TIBET

XINING

SICHUAN

CHENGDU

LHASA

YUNNAN

Vietnam